Social Trends

2002 edition

Editors: Jil Matheson
Penny Babb

London: The Stationery Office

A National Statistics publication

National Statistics are produced to high professional
standards set out in the National Statistics Code of
Practice. They undergo regular quality assurance
reviews to ensure that they meet customer needs.
They are produced free from any political interference.

Contact points
For enquiries about this publication, contact
the Editor, Penny Babb:
Tel: 020 7533 5168
E-mail: **social.trends@ons.gov.uk**

To order this publication, call The Stationery Office
on **0870 600 5522**. See also back cover.

For general enquiries, contact the National Statistics
Public Enquiry Service on **0845 601 3034**
(minicom: 01633 812399)
E-mail: **info@statistics.gov.uk**
Fax: 01633 652747
Letters: Room DG/18, 1 Drummond Gate,
           London SW1V 2QQ

You can also find National Statistics on the internet –
go to **www.statistics.gov.uk**.

About the Office for National Statistics
The Office for National Statistics (ONS) is the
government agency responsible for compiling,
analysing and disseminating many of the United
Kingdom's economic, social and demographic
statistics, including the retail prices index, trade
figures and labour market data, as well as the
periodic census of the population and health
statistics. The Director of ONS is also the National
Statistician and the Registrar General for England
and Wales, and the agency that administers the
registration of births, marriages and deaths there.

Fonts: Frutiger
        Frutiger Condensed
Paper: Stock
  Inks: Cover: Pantone 280 and Pantone 573
          Inside pages: Pantone 280 and Pantone 032

Contents

Page

Page

National Income and expenditure

6: Expenditure

Household and personal expenditure

Transactions and credit

Prices

7: Health

The nation's health

Trends in deaths

9: Crime and Justice

Offences

Offenders

Police and courts action

Probation and prisons

Civil justice

10: Housing

Housing stock and housebuilding

Page

List of Contributors

Authors: Ben Bradford

                            Victoria Busuttil

                            Jenny Church

                            Vicki Eftichiadou

                            Steve Howell

                            Nigel King

                            Christine Lillistone

                            Hannah McConnell

                            Conor Shipsey

                            Mike Short

                            Anna Upson

Production Managers: Kate Myers/Shaun Flanagan

Production Team: Sunita Dedi

                            Nigel Physick

                            Shiva Satkunam

                            Steve Whyman

Picture Research: Frances Riddelle

Acknowledgements

The Editors wish to thank all their colleagues in the contributing Departments and other organisations for their generous support and helpful comments, without whom this publication would not be possible. Our thanks also go to the following for their help in the production of this volume:

Design and Artwork: Michelle Franco

Charts: ONS Desktop Publishing Services

Tables: Spire Origination, Norwich

Maps: Alistair Dent, ONS Geography

Data: SARD Data Collection Team

Picture Credits: Chapter 1:   Photography by Bonneys Newsagency, Image courtesy of Gateshead Council

Chapter 2:   Photography by www.JohnBirdsall.co.uk

Chapter 3:   International Press Section, Foreign and Commonwealth Office

Chapter 4:   International Press Section, Foreign and Commonwealth Office

Chapter 5:   Newcastle Document Services, The City of Newcastle upon Tyne

Chapter 6:   International Press Section, Foreign and Commonwealth Office

Chapter 8:   Photography by www.JohnBirdsall.co.uk

Chapter 9:   © Crown Copyright.NMR

Chapter 10: © English Heritage

Chapter 11: © English Heritage

Chapter 12: © English Heritage

Chapter 13: Flora London Marathon

Introduction

This is the 32nd edition of *Social Trends* – one of the flagship publications from the Office for National Statistics. It draws together statistics from a wide range of government departments and other organisations to paint a broad picture of British society today, and how it has been changing. Each of the 13 chapters focuses on a different social policy area, described in tables, charts and explanatory text. This year *Social Trends* features an article, 'Children', which presents an overview of social trends since the early 1980s that have impacted on children in the United Kingdom.

Social Trends is aimed at a very wide audience: policy makers in the public and private sectors; service providers; people in local government; journalists and other commentators; academics and students; schools; and the general public.

The editorial team always welcomes readers' views on how *Social Trends* could be improved. Please write to the Editors at the address shown below with any comments or suggestions you have.

New material and sources

To preserve topicality, half of the 311 tables, charts and maps in the chapters of *Social Trends 32* are new compared with the previous edition, and draw on the most up-to-date available data.

In all chapters the source of the data is given below each table and chart, and where this is a major survey the name of the survey is also included. At the end of each chapter a list of contact telephone numbers is given, including the contact number for the chapter author, as well as a list of useful website addresses. A list of further reading, directing readers to other relevant publications, can be found towards the back of the book, beginning on page 222. Regional and other sub-national breakdowns of much of the information in *Social Trends* can be found in the ONS's publication *Regional Trends*, published by The Stationery Office.

Appendix

The Appendix gives definitions and general background information, particularly on administrative and legal structures and frameworks. Anyone seeking to understand the tables and charts in detail will find it helpful to read the corresponding entries in the Appendix, as well as the footnotes on the tables and charts. A full index to this edition starts on page 254.

Availability on electronic media

Social Trends 32 is available electronically as an interactive PDF via the National Statistics website, www.statistics.gov.uk/socialtrends.

Jil Matheson
Penny Babb
Social Analysis and Reporting Division
Office for National Statistics
B5/10
1 Drummond Gate
London
SW1V 2QQ
Email: social.trends@ons.gov.uk

Overview

Children

Beverley Botting

Background

There is a growing awareness of children as individuals in their own right with needs equal to but different from those of adults. Norway was the first European country to appoint an advocate for children, in 1981, and the UK ratified the United Nations Convention on the Rights of the Child in 1991. This Convention is the most universally accepted human rights instrument in history – every country in the world except two has ratified it. It guarantees children's rights in the following basic areas: to survival; to develop to the fullest; protection from harmful influences, abuse and exploitation, and to participate fully in family, cultural and social life. The Convention protects children's rights by setting standards in health care, education and legal, civil and social services.

More recently in the UK there has been legislation and guidance with children as the focus. In England and Wales, The Children Act[1] was passed in 1989. The Northern Ireland equivalent of this Act is the Children (Northern Ireland) Order 1995.[2] Both had as their purpose to protect and promote children's welfare. It integrated the private law relating to bringing up children, which involves the rights of both child and parents, with the public law covering the duties of local authorities towards children and families. The Children's Commissioner for Wales Bill[3], which became law in May 2001, resulted in the first Children's Commissioner in the United Kingdom starting work in Wales in March 2001. The Northern Ireland Assembly plans to introduce legislation to establish a Commissioner for Children for Northern Ireland early in 2002, with the view of having a Commissioner in post by June 2002.[4] Their broad remit is to be an advocate for children's rights, to be a champion for all children, and to make children's views heard. In addition, they will have a role to assess legislation from a child's viewpoint, to bring forward recommendations and to make proposals for change. In England and Wales, The Special Educational Needs and Disability Act 2001[5], strengthens the rights of children with special educational needs or with a disability. Children's opinions are to be taken into account by the Department of Health when drawing up the Children's National Service Framework.

This overview focuses on the main trends over the past 20 years in the social position and demographic characteristics of the child population and how their changing needs are being met. Further details can be found in other chapters throughout this volume.

The child population

In 2000 there were 12.1 million children aged under 16 in the United Kingdom, with more boys than girls. This represents 3 per cent more than the 11.7 million children in 1991, but less than the 12.5 million children in the United Kingdom in 1981. The age distribution of the child population has changed a little. In 1981, 28 per cent of the child population were aged 0 to 4 years, 29 per cent aged 5 to 9 years, and 43 per cent aged 10 to 15. In 2000, there were proportionately fewer children aged 10 to 15 (38 per cent), while the proportion aged 0 to 4 and 5 to 9 had risen slightly to 30 and 32 per cent respectively reflecting changes in the birth rate over the period.[6] In 2000, 10 per cent of the population of children were from a minority ethnic group.[7] This varied in different parts of the UK. In London, for example, one in three children aged under 18 was from a minority ethnic group.[8]

Changing family framework

Although the size of the child population has changed little in the past two decades, there have been considerable changes to the family environment in which many of these children live.

The majority of children grow up in a family with two parents. In 2000–01, 74 per cent of families with dependent children in Great Britain were of this family type (Chart A.1).[9] However, this proportion has fallen since 1971 when 92 per cent of children lived in a couple family. Children are living in an increasing variety of different family structures, and these are not static. Due to changes in cohabitation, marriage and divorce patterns, children may experience a range of different family structures during their life. Parents separating can result in one-parent families, and new relationships can create stepfamilies.

In 2000–01, 26 per cent of families with dependent children in Great Britain were headed by a lone parent, three times higher than in 1971.[9] A large part of the increase up to the mid-1980s was due to divorce, compared with the increase in more recent years which has been due to a rise in single lone mothers. There is a similar proportion of lone parent families in Northern Ireland – in 1999–00 a lone parent headed one quarter of all families. Seven per cent of the lone parents were men.[10] It has been estimated that in England and Wales 28 per cent of children living in married couple families will experience divorce in their family before reaching age 16.[11]

In 1991 just over 1 million dependent children in Great Britain lived in stepfamilies.[12] Stepfamilies (with married or cohabiting couples) accounted for 6 per cent of all families with dependent children in Great Britain. Ten per cent of children live with one birth parent and a step-parent. Over 90 per cent of stepfamilies consisted of a couple with at least one child from a previous relationship of the woman. This is mainly because children are more likely to remain with their mother rather than their father following divorce or separation.

Less than 1 per cent of all children in 1991 were living with adoptive parents, one-third of these children having been adopted by a step-parent.[13] In 2000, there were 4,942 adoption orders, compared with 7,170 in 1991 and 9,284 in 1981.[14] This reflects fewer babies being put up for adoption rather than a fall in demand.

There are different patterns of family structure in different minority ethnic groups. Among families with dependent children, in Autumn 2000, 79 per cent of children from white families were living in couple families. This proportion was higher for those of Indian (92 per cent) or Pakistani/Bangladeshi (81 per cent) origin, but in contrast, just under one half of families with dependent children headed by a black person were lone-parent families (see the Family relationships section of Chapter 2: Households and families).[7]

Chart **A.1**

Families with dependent children by family type

Great Britain

Percentages

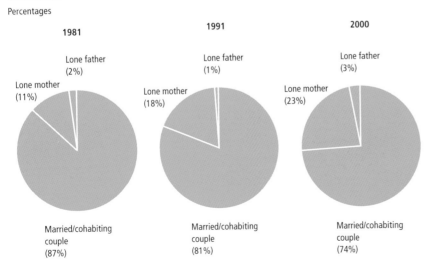

1981

Lone father (2%)

Lone mother (11%)

Married/cohabiting couple (87%)

1991

Lone father (1%)

Lone mother (18%)

Married/cohabiting couple (81%)

2000

Lone father (3%)

Lone mother (23%)

Married/cohabiting couple (74%)

Source: General Household Survey, Office for National Statistics

Some children are looked after by local authorities. One of the main aims of the Children Act 1989 (England and Wales) is for authorities to work together with families to provide help to keep the family together. Parents retain parental responsibility for their children even when they are being looked after. At 31 March 2000, just over 61 thousand children were being looked after by local authorities in England and Wales and almost two-thirds of these were with foster placements (see Chart 8.19 of Chapter 8: Social protection).[15,16] This represents 5.1 per thousand children. The proportion being fostered has been increasing gradually as fewer children are being placed in community homes. In 1985 only half of all children in local authority care were being looked after in foster placements.

Scotland has different legislation on the care of children that means that data on children being looked after in Scotland are not comparable with those from the rest of the United Kingdom. The number of children being looked after in Scotland increases with age until age 15. At 31 March 2000, 10 children in every thousand were being looked after.[17] The difference is explained by the differences in legislation from that for England and Wales.

In 2000, there were 32.7 thousand children on Child Protection Registers in England and Wales,[17,18] slightly fewer than in 1993. The most common reason for being on the register was neglect, but several thousand of these children were reported as the victim of sexual or physical abuse (see Chart 8.20 in Chapter 8: Social protection). There were more boys than girls on the register, 51 per cent compared with 49 per cent respectively. Girls were more likely to be on the register than boys because of sexual abuse. Girls are also more likely to use the services of Childline. Childline is a charity which was launched in October 1986 and more recently was introduced in Northern Ireland.[19] It is a free national helpline for children in trouble or danger, and over 1 million children have been counselled through its services. In 1999/00, 127 thousand calls and letters were received, 19 per cent of these were for physical and/or sexual abuse, 18 per cent for bullying and 15 per cent for family problems, many of which concerned stepfamilies.

Socio-economic characteristics

Housing tenure has traditionally reflected the economic status, social class and age of the occupiers, and therefore tenure varies considerably for different types of family. In general, couples with dependent children are more likely than lone parents to own their own home, either outright or with a mortgage. In 2000–01, 80 per cent of couples with dependent children owned their homes outright or with a mortgage, in contrast to lone parents of which two-thirds were renting, the majority from a local authority or housing association.[20] In Great Britain in 2000–01 combined, 9 per cent of lone parent families lived in overcrowded accommodation (based on the bedroom standard) compared with 4 per cent of other families with dependent children.[9]

Families with children tend to be disproportionately concentrated in the lower part of the income distribution (see Low income section of Chapter 5: Income and wealth). After adjustment for housing costs, one-third of all children lived in a household with an income below half the mean for Great Britain.[21] In Spring 2001, over 2.1 million children were living in families receiving housing benefit.[22] Fifty three per cent of these children lived in families that also received income support. Working Families' Tax Credit (WFTC) is a tax credit available to working families who are responsible for at least one child under 16 (or under 19 if in full-time education up to A-level or equivalent standard). It is payable to two-parent and one-parent families. The applicant or the partner (if they have one) must be working 16 hours or more per week. In May 2001, 2.5 million children were in families receiving WFTC awards. Of these families, 51 per cent were headed by a lone parent.

There have been increases in the proportion of children whose mothers work. One in four mothers in the UK with a child aged under 18 were working full time in Spring 2001, and a further 40 per cent were working part time.[7] This is slightly higher than in 1996, when 61 per cent of mothers with dependent children worked at least part time.[9] These proportions varied according to the age of their youngest child. Three-quarters of mothers whose youngest child was aged 10 or over were working at least part-time compared with around half of those whose youngest child was aged under 5 (see the Economic activity section of Chapter 4: Labour market for further detail). Employment rates are much lower for lone mothers than for mothers who are married or cohabiting. However, employment growth in the last three years has been higher among lone mothers.[23]

Services for Children

Education

With the growing recognition of the different needs of children, the services available for them have also been evolving. The Early Learning Goals announced by the Qualifications and Curriculum Authority (QCA) in October 1999 set goals for three to six-year olds that every child will be expected to meet through "structured and focused" play.[24]

Pre-school activities are seen as the route to building firm foundations for future learning in schools and as a result there has been a growth in the availability and range of pre-school provision. The proportion of three and four year olds enrolled in schools in the UK has trebled since 1970/71 (see Chart 3.2 in Chapter 3: Education and training). In addition there are other forms of pre-school provision. Since 1998 all four year olds have been entitled to a free part-time early education place. In January 2000 97 per cent of children aged 4 in England had such a place with 16 per cent enrolled in non-state provision from the private and voluntary sector, such as local playgroups. As a result of the increase in the number of pre-school age children being enrolled in schools, the total number of playgroups and pre-schools reported in 2001 fell to 14 thousand. This was a decrease of 300 from the previous year. The number of places had also fallen, by 23 thousand to 330 thousand in 2001, a fall of 6 per cent.[25]

School children in England and Wales are formally assessed at three key stages, at ages 7, 11 and 14. In 2001, the proportion of boys in England reaching the required standard for English was lower than for girls at all key stages, particularly at ages 11 and 14; however, similar proportions of boys and girls reached the expected level in mathematics and science. From age 14 onwards, young people study for public examinations. In 1999/00 girls performed better than boys in English with 64 per cent achieving grade A* to C at GCSE or equivalent compared with 46 per cent of boys. Girls were also more likely than boys to have obtained grades A* to C in modern languages and science. Attainment at GCSE varies according to the family background of young people. Large differences in attainment exist between the different socio-economic groups. Two-thirds of young people with parents in non-manual occupations achieved five or more GCSEs at grades A* to C in year 11 in 2000, compared with one-third of those with parents in skilled manual occupations (Chart A.2).

Although there have been improvements in achievement at GCSE in all ethnic groups, differences still remain. In 2000, using data from the Youth Cohort Study (YCS), 50 per cent of White young people in England and Wales gained five or more GCSEs at grades A* to C, compared with 39 per cent of Black young people in England and Wales, 60 per cent of Indian young people, 29 per cent for both Pakistani and Bangladeshi and 72 per cent of 'other Asian' young people (see Table 3.16 in Chapter 3: Education and training for further details).

At age 16, young people are faced with the choice of whether to remain in education, go into training or seek employment. Over the last decade young people have become more likely to continue their education. In Great Britain in 1998/99, 78 per cent of young people aged 16–17 were in education compared to 75 per cent in 1995/96. Increasing numbers of young people are continuing their education at university. Between 1990/91 and 2000/01 the numbers of young women attending university almost doubled to 922 thousand undergraduates; the corresponding figure for young men was 739 thousand.

There has been growing concern over the number of children excluded from schools or playing truant. The total number of children permanently excluded decreased from 12,700 in 1996/97 to 8,300 in 1999/00. The rate of exclusion has fallen from 17 children in every 10,000 of the school population in 1996/97 to 11 per 10,000 in 1999/00. The majority were boys, 84 per cent in 1999/00. The number of children excluded increased with age reaching a maximum at age 14. There is a positive association between the proportion

Chart **A.2**

Attainment of 5 or more GCSE grades A*-C in year 11[1]: by parents occupation[2]

England & Wales

Percentages

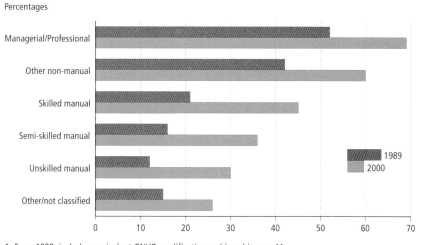

Legend: 1989, 2000

1 From 1998, includes equivalent GNVQ qualifications achieved in year 11.

2 Includes a high percentage of respondents who had neither parent in a full-time job.

Source: Youth Cohort Study, Department for Education and Skills.

of children permanently excluded and the percentage of pupils eligible for free school meals. Black Caribbean boys are almost 4 times more likely to be excluded than White pupils, compared with a lower proportion of Indian, Pakistani, and Chinese pupils. Looked after children are 10 times more likely to be excluded from school than their peers. The YCS also found that the proportion of 16 year olds in England and Wales reporting that they played truant at sometime during year 11 fell from 50 per cent in 1989 to 35 per cent in 2000.

Out of school care is becoming a part of the lives of an increasing number of children. In 2001, there were 4,900 Out of School clubs in England, providing 152,800 places for children aged 5 to 7, compared with 4,400 clubs in 2000 and 350 in 1992. The number of places available was 12 times higher than in 1992.

Health

Health services for children have been recognised in the appointment of a 'National Clinical Director for Children' in England. In addition, the Children's National Service Framework is being developed, which will be addressing a broad range of aspects of child health. There are a number of health targets designed to reduce inequalities. One health inequality target announced in February 2001 relates to infant mortality: starting with children under one year, by 2010 to reduce by at least 10 per cent the gap in mortality between manual groups and the population as a whole.[26] There has been an overall reduction in infant mortality, and especially a fall in cot deaths. The United Kingdom infant mortality rate has been cut by more than half between 1981 and 2000, from 11.2 per 1,000 live births in 1981 to 5.6 in 2000.[27] The proportional fall in England and Wales cot death rates over the same period has been even higher falling from 1.99 per 1,000 live births in 1981 to 0.40 in 2000[27], the majority of this fall occurring in the second decade.

In the United Kingdom, accidental death rates are higher for boys than girls. In 1999, the rate for boys aged 15–19 was 340 per million boys of that age, three times that for girls.[28,29] Childhood injury death rates in England and Wales by social class have been compared for the years around the 1981 and 1991 Censuses.[30] Death rates from injury and poisoning fell between the two periods for children in each social class, although the differential between the social classes increased. The decline in rates for children in Social Classes IV and V (21 per cent and 2 per cent respectively), was smaller than those for children in Social Classes I and II (32 per cent and 37 per cent). Motor vehicle accidents accounted for half of all childhood injury deaths and showed a similar social class gradient to that of all accidental deaths in childhood.

A previous analysis of social class specific mortality in England and Wales for children noted that death rates from fire and flames showed one of the steepest socio-economic gradients.[31] Between 1981 and 1991, the death rate due to fire and flames decreased for children in Social Classes I and II but increased for children in Social Classes IV and V. Most of the deaths in this category were from residential fires.

In England, current immunisation targets are for 95 per cent of all children to be immunised by age 2 against diphtheria, tetanus, polio, pertussis (whooping cough), Haemophilus influenza b, measles, mumps and rubella (MMR). In 2000–01, these targets had been met for all but the MMR immunisation. Only 87 per cent of children in England had received MMR by the age of two years.[32]

In 2000–01, 4 per cent of children aged under five in Great Britain were reported to have a limiting long-standing illness (unchanged since 1991) compared with 8 per cent aged 5 to 15 (unchanged since 1995).[9] There were only small differences between the figures for boys and girls. Asthma is far more prevalent amongst children of school age than among any other age group. In 1998, 132 boys in every 1,000 aged 5 to 15 were treated for asthma, compared with 104 girls.[33]

The 1999 survey of the mental health of children and adolescents[34] showed that the proportion of children and young people with any mental disorder was greater among boys than girls; 11 per cent compared with 8 per cent. Among children aged 5 to 10 years, 10 per cent of boys and 6 per cent of girls had a mental disorder. At ages 11–15, 13 per cent of boys and 10 per cent of girls had a mental disorder. Children of lone parents were twice as likely to have mental health problems than those from couple families (16 per cent compared to 8 per cent). Mental health problems were more prevalent amongst children from reconstituted families (stepfamilies with at least one stepchild) than those without stepchildren (15 per cent compared with 9 per cent). There were marked differences by social class, with mental health problems affecting three times as many children in Social Class V (14 per cent) as those in Social Class I (5 per cent).

According to data collected from parents in 1999, 2 per cent of 11–15 year-olds had tried to harm, hurt or kill themselves. The highest rate, 3 per cent was found among 13–15 year old girls. These figures represent all forms of self-harm and are not the numbers of children and young people who had suicide as their intent. The prevalence of self-harm among those aged 5–15 was greater for children in lone parent families compared with two-parent families, and greater for families living in rented accommodation compared with owner-occupiers.[35]

There has been concern because the United Kingdom has the highest teenage pregnancy rate in Europe.[36] The proportion of teenage girls in England and Wales becoming pregnant rose in the 1980s reaching 47.7 conceptions per thousand girls aged 15–17 in 1990. A report by the Social Exclusion Unit[36] in 1999 included a target to halve the rate of conceptions to girls aged under 18 by 2010: in 1999 the conception rate was 45 per thousand girls aged 15-17.[37]

Good nutrition is important from birth, and studies have shown that breastfeeding gives health benefits to both mother and child. Compared to bottle-fed babies, those who are breast-fed are only half as likely to be admitted to hospital with a respiratory infection and 20 per cent less likely to become obese in childhood. Between 1995 and 2000 all countries in the UK showed a statistically significant increase in the incidence of breastfeeding, as had been the case also between 1990 and 1995. In all countries, mothers in Social Classes I and II had the highest breastfeeding rates. However, the greatest changes between 1995 and 2000 were in other social classes, with a significant increase in the incidence of breastfeeding in England and Wales in Social Class V from 50 per cent in 1995 to 62 per cent in 2000 (Chart A.3).[38]

There are a number of other general measures that can be used to monitor children's health. These include height, weight, diet and dental health. The Health Survey for England[39] and its predecessors showed that the average height and weight of children varied little between 1992 and 1997, although children were taller and heavier than the children studied in 1982–83 in the Survey of the Diets of British School Children.[40] The average height of an 8-year-old boy in 1995–97 was 1 metre 31 centimetres, the same as in 1992. Average weight has also remained static over the same period.

There are, however, concerns about obesity and dietary intake. Good nutrition is important to ensure optimum growth and development and to maximise the benefits for good health. The prevalence of obesity increases with age throughout childhood. From 1989 to 1998 there was a highly significant increasing trend in the proportion of overweight children and obese children aged 0–4.[41] In 1996, around 13 per cent of 8-year-olds and 17 per cent of 15-year-olds in England were obese. These levels of childhood obesity are likely to exacerbate the trend towards increased overweight and obesity in the adult population: compared to thin children, obese children have a two-fold increase in the risk of becoming overweight adults.[42] Research into the eating habits of 11 to 16 year olds in 2001 in England and Wales found that 6 per cent had either eaten no fruit or no vegetables in the previous week. On average, children had consumed less than 13 portions of fruit or vegetables compared to Government guidelines that 35 portions should be consumed each week to protect against heart disease, cancer and obesity.[43]

The National Diet and Nutrition Survey[44] showed differences in the consumption of different foods between children from different social classes. Children from non-manual backgrounds were more likely to have eaten rice, wholemeal bread, wholegrain and high-fibre breakfast cereals than were children from manual backgrounds. These latter children were more likely to have eaten white bread than those from non-manual backgrounds. Only 47 per cent of boys and 59 per cent of girls ate raw and salad vegetables, 40 per cent of children ate cooked leafy green vegetables and 60 per cent ate other cooked vegetables. There were no differences in mean daily intake of energy for boys or girls associated with social class. The World Health Organisation Health Behaviour in School-Aged Children Study 1997–98[45] found that more than 20 per cent of the students in 13 countries surveyed reported eating potato crisps every day. The highest figures were from the four countries of the United Kingdom, ranging from 45 per cent to 78 per cent. A study covering a period from 1988 to

Chart A.3

Breastfeeding by social class[1]

United Kingdom[2]

Percentages

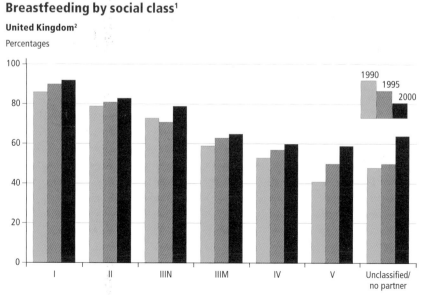

1 Incidence of breastfeeding by social class as defined by current or last occupation of husband/partner.
2 Data for 1990 are for Great Britain.
Source: Infant Feeding Survey, Office for National Statistics; Infant Feeding Survey, Department of Health

1994, using the General Practice Research Database shows that those most at risk of developing anorexia are between 10–19 years of age, with GPs detecting a rate of 34 per 100,000 in this age group. The rate for those with bulimia in the 10–19 age group is also high, at 41 per 100,000.[46]

Children's dental health has improved in recent years. Five year olds in Great Britain in 1999/00 had an average of 1.57 teeth that were decayed, missing or filled. The average in 1989 was 1.80 teeth. Sixty per cent of 5 year olds had no decayed, missing or filled teeth in 1999/00, compared to 56 per cent in 1989.[47]

Previous health targets in England, as well as the health strategies of Wales, Scotland and Northern Ireland have been to reduce smoking amongst children. The target in England, established in 1998,[48] is to reduce the rate of teenage smoking from a baseline of 13 per cent in 1996 to 11 per cent by 2005 and to 9 per cent by 2010.[49] This target was met in 1999 when overall, 9 per cent of 11 to 15 year old children in England were regular smokers. However, in 2000 the percentage of children in this age group who were regular smokers rose to 10 per cent. In this age group girls were more likely to smoke than boys, with 12 per cent of girls and 9 per cent of boys having at least one cigarette a week. Children were more likely to smoke if their parents or siblings smoked.

The proportion of children in England aged 11 to 15 who had had an alcoholic drink in the previous week rose steadily from 20 per cent in 1988 to 27 per cent in 1996.[49] It then fell for the first time to 21 per cent in 1998 and 1999, but rose again to 24 per cent in 2000. Boys were slightly more likely to drink than girls. As children become older they are more likely to have had an alcoholic drink (see Chart 7.16 in Chapter 7: Health). In 2000 only 5 per cent of children aged 11 had had an alcoholic drink in the last week, but by age 15, 49 per cent had done so. The mean alcohol consumption for boys who had drunk in the last week had risen from 5.7 units in 1990 to 11.7 units in 2000. For girls the mean alcohol consumption over the same period increased from 4.7 units to 9.1 units. The WHO Health Behaviour in School-Aged Children Study[45] found that in 1997–98 weekly beer drinking among 15-year-olds in Wales was 50 per cent, the highest of all the participating countries. England was the fourth highest with 40 per cent.

In 2000, 14 per cent of children aged 11–15 had used drugs in the last year compared to 11 per cent in 1998 (see Table 7.19 in Chapter 7: Health for further detail). Drug usage varied by age; 3 per cent of 11-year-olds used illegal substances in 2000, compared with 29 per cent of 15-year-olds. Cannabis was the most likely to be used, with 12 per cent of pupils surveyed admitting to taking the drug in the previous year.[49]

Leisure and health related activities

Children are filling their spare time with a range of different activities. There is a reduction in physical exercise, plus an increase in computer games. While the majority of children walk to school, fewer children do so than 15 years ago (see Table 12.19 in Chapter 12: Transport for further detail). The 'Are you doing your bit?' survey commissioned by the Department of the Environment, Transport and the Regions (DETR)[50] showed that 38 per cent of children who are driven to school said that they would rather walk or cycle. They regarded the opportunity to interact with their friends when travelling to and from school as important. They also showed some awareness of the benefits of exercise and fresh air.

There are variations in access and take up of sport and leisure opportunities. Information on the extra-curricular participation of 11 to 16 year olds in sport in Wales in 1999–00[51] showed that football and rugby were the most popular sports for boys, with about half of all boys playing either or both outside school. Netball was the most popular sport for girls. Girls' activity levels tend to drop sharply between school year 7 (age 11–12) when three-quarters of girls participated in extra-curricular sporting activities, to year 11 (age 15–16), when just over one half of all girls participated in some form of extra-curricular sporting activity. Activity levels among boys remained at between 71 and 78 per cent between the ages of 11 and 16. For younger children[52], football was again the most popular extra-curricular sport for boys, with 62 per cent of boys aged 7 to 11 having participated. For girls of the same age the most popular extra-curricular sport was netball, with 40 per cent having participated. The Health Survey for England[39] found that one-third of boys aged 2 to 7 and 38 per cent of girls of the same age were not meeting the Government's recommended activity guidelines. In 1999 the Culture, Media and Sport select committee accepted research findings that exercise and participation in sport can help to combat social exclusion. It improves both physical and mental well being, and is associated with measurable increases in self esteem in children.[53]

Most expenditure on children is by the parents, but most children receive pocket money or earn an income that they can spend how they choose (see Table 6.6 in Chapter 6: Expenditure for further detail). The average amount of weekly pocket money for children in the UK in 2001 was £3.19.[54] The amount of pocket money increases with age. For children aged between 8 and 10 the average pocket money was £2.29 per week. Those aged 14–16 had, on average, £12.64 total income, almost twice that of 11–13 year olds whose average weekly income was £7.16. These included some money from paid work such as Saturday jobs, paper rounds and other part-time jobs. In addition, children received some income as cash gifts from other relatives.

Crime

Children can be either perpetrators or victims of crime. In 1999 there were 120 thousand known child offenders aged 10 to 17 in England and Wales who were found guilty or who had been cautioned for indictable offences. This was a fall compared to 1991, when the equivalent figure was 137.5 thousand, and to 1981 when it was 212 thousand. Boys were three times more likely to offend than girls but this ratio reduced from almost 5 to1 in 1981. One-third of all indictable offences in 1999 of 10–17 year olds were for theft and handling stolen goods. Just over 9.5 thousand children aged 10–17 were found guilty of or cautioned for drug offences in 1999, over four times the number in 1992 and over 30 times the number in 1981. The peak age for those aged 10 to 17 offending in England and Wales was 17 for boys in 1999 and 1991 (15 in 1981) and 15 for girls.[55]

Children are also victims of crime. It is only possible to identify those offences that come to the attention of the criminal justice system. In 2000, lone parent households were the most at risk of burglary and these are the family types most likely to be living in council estates and low-income areas.[56]

Tackling inequalities

The various aspects of children's lives discussed in previous sections have indicated that children in certain minority ethnic groups, children with lone parents or in stepfamilies, and in social rented housing tend to have experienced educational, health and other disadvantages compared to other children. Recently there has been a trend towards greater attention being given to the well being of children and of tackling child poverty and its associated conditions. There have been a number of initiatives in the UK to tackle inequalities. Some of these initiatives aim to increase family income through, for example, working families tax credit, whilst others bring together different services to work together to help those families in most need.

The Children and Young People's Unit (CYPU) was created in 2000 to drive forward the Government's agenda for children and young people. As part of its remit, the CYPU is drawing up a cross government strategy for children, seeking to articulate outcome related objectives for all children with associated outcome indicators. It will manage the new £450 million Children's Fund, part of the Government's strategy to tackle child poverty and social exclusion. The Fund is aimed at children aged 5–13, and will support services to identify children and young people who are showing signs of disturbance and provide them and their families with the support they need to

get back on track. Its aim is to prevent children falling into drug abuse, truancy, exclusion, unemployment and crime. Linked to this, the On Track Programme (originally launched as part of the Government's Crime Reduction Programme, now integrated into the Children Fund) aims to improve the life opportunities of children and young people in deprived areas and to reduce the likelihood of their becoming involved in antisocial or criminal behaviour.

Other initiatives include a Quality Protects programme for transforming children's social services to ensure the delivery of the Children Act 1989. The Sure Start initiative works on the inter-relationship of individual, family, peer group and neighbourhood and is aimed specifically at pre-school age range. Finally, the Connexions service has been set up for children and young people over the age of thirteen, to provide guidance, advice and support to enable young people to make the right decisions about life, education and career choices.

The need for long term follow up of these initiatives has been recognised in both specific evaluation studies for Sure Start and other initiatives, and in the UK-wide Millennium Cohort Study which has a special focus on children from disadvantaged areas.

Conclusion

The size of the child population has been stable recently, but children are experiencing a greater variety of family structures during childhood. Fewer children are dying in childhood. More children are being breast-fed, which helps protect against a number of diseases and infections in childhood. However, children's diets are not meeting guidelines to protect them against disease and premature death in adulthood and an increasing proportion of children are obese. Their levels of exercise are lower than recommended, but there have been falls in smoking levels and improvements in dental health. Nevertheless, more young people are continuing in education beyond the minimum school leaving age, and achieving more qualifications.

In all areas of children's lives inequalities still exist. Disadvantaged children experience more mental health problems, more self harm, are more likely to live in rented accommodation in families with lowest income, and are more likely to be victims of burglary. It will be some years before it is possible to measure the impact of some government initiatives aimed at reducing these inequalities; regular monitoring and reporting will help us understand their nature and extent, and changes in the lives of children in the UK.

References

1. *The Children Act 1989, England and Wales.* HMSO.

2. *The Children (Northern Ireland) Order* 1995.

3. *The Children's Commissioner for Wales Bill, Wales.* 2001

4. Northern Ireland Assembly – Committee of the Centre: *Report into the proposal to appoint a Commissioner for Children for Northern Ireland,* June 2001.

5. *Special Educational Needs and Disability Act 2001,* HMSO.

6. Population Estimates Unit, Office for National Statistics.

7. Labour Force Survey, Office for National Statistics

8. *The State of London's Children.* Office of Children's Rights Commissioner for London, October 2001.

9. General Household Survey, Office for National Statistics

10. 'Gingerbread' NI: based on 1999–2000 information from Northern Ireland Social Security Agency

11. Children who experience divorce in their family. J. Haskey. *Population Trends* 87. TSO 1997

12. Stepfamilies and stepchildren in Great Britain. J. Haskey. *Population Trends* 76. HMSO 1994

13. *Report – children in Britain.* Family Policy Studies Centre 1995

14. *Marriage, Divorce and Adoption Statistics 2000,* Series FM2 no.27

15. *Children and Young People on Child Protection Registers,* England, 31 March 2000, Department of Health

16. *Social Services Statistics* Wales 2001, The National Assembly for Wales

17. *Children looked after in the Year to 31 March 2000,* Scotland, Scottish Executive

18. *Local Authority Child Protection Registers,* Wales, 31 March 2000, The National Assembly for Wales

19. Childline Internet website (www.childline.co.uk)

20. *2000/01 Survey of English Housing: Preliminary results.* Department of Transport, Local Government and Regions

21. *Households Below Average Income 1999/00,* Department for Pensions and Work

22. *Working Families' Tax Credit Quarterly Enquiry – May 2001.* Inland Revenue

23. *Trends in Female Employment.* Bower C. 2001

24. Qualifications and Curriculum Authority

25. *Statistics of Education: Children's Day Care Facilities at 31 March 2001.* England, Department for Education and Skills

26. *The National Health Inequalities Targets.* Department of Health 2001

27. *Health Statistics Quarterly* no.12, Office for National Statistics 2001

28. General Registrar Office for Scotland

29. Northern Ireland Statistics and Research Agency

30. Does the decline in child injury mortality vary by social class? A comparison of class specific mortality in 1981 and 1991, Roberts I and Power C. *British Medical Journal* 1996.

31. *Occupational mortality – childhood supplement 1979–80, 1982–83,* Series DS no.8, HMSO 1988

32. *NHS Immunisation Statistics. England 2000–01,* Department of Health 2001

33. *Key Health Statistics from General Practice 1998.* Series MB6 no.2, Office for National Statistics 2000

34. *Mental health of children and adolescents in Great Britain 1999.* Office for National Statistics 2000

35. *Children and adolescents who try to harm, hurt or kill themselves, Great Britain 1999.* Office for National Statistics 2001

36. *Teenage Pregnancy.* Report by the Social Exclusion Unit, 1999

37. Report: Conceptions in England and Wales 1999. *Population Trends* 103, Office for National Statistics 2001

38. *Infant Feeding Survey 2000.* Department of Health, 2001

39. *Health Survey for England – the health of young people 95–97.* Department of Health 1998

40. *The Diets of British Schoolchildren 1982/83.* Department of Health 1989

41. Prevalence of overweight and obese children between 1989 and 1998: population based series of cross sectional studies. Bundred P, Kitchiner D and Buchan I. *British Medical Journal* 2001, 322:326

42. British Heart Foundation Statistics Database 2000

43. *The MORI Annual Schools Omnibus Survey* 2001

44. *National Diet and Nutrition Survey – young people aged 4 to 18 years.* Volume 1 report of the diet and nutrition survey MAFF 2000

45. *The WHO Health Behaviour in School-Aged Children Study 1997/98,* WHO 2000

46. The demand for eating disorder care: An epidemiological study using the General Practice Research Database. Turner S et al. *British Journal of Psychiatry* 169, 705-712, 1996

47. The dental caries experience of 5-year-old children in Great Britain. Surveys co-ordinated by the British Association for the Study of Community Dentistry in 1999/2000. Pitts NB, Evans DJ and Nugent ZJ. *Community Dental Health*, Vol 18, 49-55.

48. *Smoking kills – A white paper on tobacco.* Department of Health. The Stationery Office 1998

49. *Smoking, Drinking and Drug Use among Young People in England 2000.* Department of Health. 2001

50. *Are you doing your bit?* DETR Survey of schoolchildren 2001

51. *Widening the Net?* Young People's Participation in Sport 1999/2000. The Sports Council for Wales March 2001

52. *Swings and Roundabouts?* Primary School Children's Participation in Sport 2000. The Sports Council for Wales September 2001

53. *The Value of Sport: Executive Summary.* Sport England. June 1999

54. BirdsEye Walls *Children's Pocket Money 2001*

55. *Crime statistics England and Wales.* Home Office

56. *British Crime Survey 2001.* Home Office

57. The ESRC Millennium Cohort Study: Child of the New Century. (www.cls.ioe.ac.uk)

Chapter 1

Population

Population profile

■ At mid-2000 the population of the United Kingdom was estimated to be 59.8 million, the 20th largest in the world. (Table 1.1)

■ The population is projected to increase gradually to reach nearly 65 million by 2025. Longer term projections suggest the population will peak around 2040 at nearly 66 million and then gradually start to fall. (Page 28)

■ Projections for the United Kingdom show that by 2014 it is expected the number of people aged 65 and over will exceed those aged under 16. (Page 29)

■ In 2000–01, about one person in 14 in Great Britain was from a minority ethnic group. (Table 1.4)

Population change

■ Between 1991 and 2000, net natural change in the UK was exceeded by net migration and other changes. Projections suggest that this trend will continue with net migration accounting for 70 per cent of the overall change in population between 2001 and 2011. (Table 1.6)

■ The number of deaths is projected to start increasing in the 2020s, overtaking the number of births in the late 2020s. (Chart 1.7)

Migration

■ At a regional level, the greatest fall in population occurred in London where 69 thousand more people moved to other regions of the United Kingdom than moved into London. (Table 1.12)

International perspective

■ In 2001 the world's population exceeded 6 billion people, an increase of over three and a half billion over the previous 50 years. (Table 1.18)

Table **1.1**

Population[1] of the United Kingdom

Thousands

	1901	1951	1991	2000	2011	2021	2025
England	30,515	41,159	48,208	49,997	52,151	54,262	55,013
Wales	2,013	2,599	2,891	2,946	3,000	3,067	3,085
Scotland	4,472	5,096	5,107	5,115	5,047	4,973	4,926
Northern Ireland	1,237	1,371	1,607	1,698	1,759	1,803	1,813
United Kingdom	38,237	50,225	57,814	59,756	61,956	64,105	64,836

1 Data are census enumerated for 1901 to 1951; mid-year estimates for 1991 and 2000;
  2000-based projections for 2011 to 2025. See Appendix, Part 1: Population estimates and
  projections.
*Source: Office for National Statistics; Government Actuary's Department; General Register
Office for Scotland; Northern Ireland Statistics and Research Agency*

Chart **1.2**

Population: by gender and age, 1971 and 2000

United Kingdom

Thousands

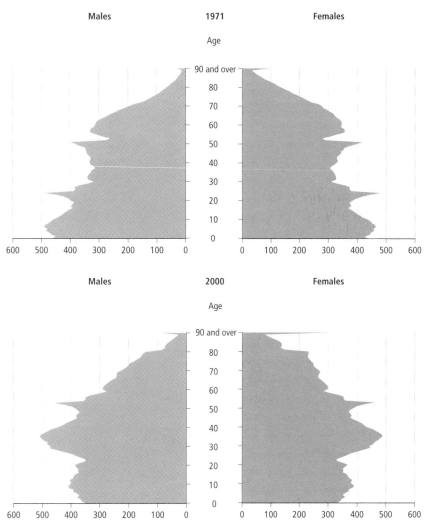

*Source: Office for National Statistics; General Register Office for Scotland; Northern Ireland Statistics and
Research Agency*

Reliable information on the size and structure of the population is essential for understanding many aspects of society such as the labour market and household composition. Changes in demographic patterns not only affect social structures but they also have implications for public policy decisions, including those on housing and the provision of health, education and social services.

Population profile

There are now more people living in the United Kingdom than at any time in the past. As at mid-2000 the population was estimated to be 59.8 million (Table 1.1), the 20th largest in the world. The population of the United Kingdom increased by almost 22 million between 1901 and 2000, although there are variations in the rate of increase between the constituent countries. The population of England increased by 64 per cent, while Scotland experienced the smallest population increase of 14 per cent.

The United Kingdom population is projected to increase gradually to reach nearly 65 million by 2025. Longer term projections suggest the population will peak around 2040 at nearly 66 million and then gradually start to fall. Different rates of growth are expected in the four constituent countries. A small decline in the population of Scotland is projected from 2000, while the populations of Wales and Northern Ireland are projected to peak in around 30 years' time and then start to fall. The population of England is still projected to be rising at 2040, but at a low rate of growth.

The number of people in any age group within the population is dependent on how many are born in a particular period, and how long they survive. It is also dependent on the numbers and ages of migrants moving into and out of the country, which is examined in greater detail in the migration section on page 33. Further information on factors affecting population change can be found in the Population Change section of this chapter on page 31.

Chart 1.2 shows the age distribution of the population for the years 1971 and 2000. The age structure of the population reflects the different levels of births, deaths and migration over time. There were 48 million people aged over 15 in the United Kingdom in 2000, of whom 23 per cent were over state pension age (females aged 60 and over and males aged 65 and over). This represented an increase in the number of people over state pension age of 18 per cent by 2000 compared with 1971. There were over three times as many people over the age of 90 in 2000 than in 1971. Women accounted for 78 per cent of this age group.

Table **1.3**

Population[1]: by gender and age

United Kingdom   Percentages

	Under 16	16–24	25–34	35–44	45–54	55–64	65–74	75 and over	All ages (=100%) (millions)
Males									
1901[2]	34	20	16	12	9	6	3	1	18.5
1931[2]	26	18	16	13	12	9	5	2	22.1
1961[2]	25	14	13	14	14	11	6	3	25.5
1991	21	14	16	14	12	10	8	5	28.2
2000	21	11	16	16	13	10	8	5	29.5
2011	18	12	13	15	15	12	9	6	30.8
2025	18	10	13	13	13	14	10	9	32.3
Females									
1901[2]	31	20	16	12	9	6	4	2	19.7
1931[2]	23	17	16	14	12	9	6	2	24.0
1961[2]	22	13	12	13	14	12	9	5	27.3
1991	19	12	15	13	11	10	9	9	29.6
2000	19	10	14	15	13	10	9	9	30.3
2011	17	11	12	14	14	12	9	9	31.1
2025	17	10	13	13	12	14	11	11	32.5

1 Data for 1901 and 1931 are Census enumerated; data for 1961 to 2000 are mid-year estimates. Figures for Northern Ireland for 1931 relate to the 1937 Census. 2000-based projections.

2 Data for 1901, 1931 and 1961 for under 16 and 16 to 24 relate to age bands under 15 and 15 to 24 respectively.

Source: Office for National Statistics; General Register Office for Scotland; Governments Actuary's Department; Northern Ireland Statistics and Research Agency

Chart 1.2 shows that there were three peaks in the age distribution of the population in 1971. There were peaks for people in their early fifties, mid-twenties and those under the age of 10, and reflect increases in the birth rate following the First and Second World Wars, and as a consequence of the high fertility rates of the 'baby boom' during the 1960s. Men and women born during these periods moved up the population pyramid to correspond with two peaks in 2000 of those in their early fifties and those aged in their mid to late thirties. There were 72 per cent more people in their eighties in 2000 compared with 1971, and this corresponds to the peak of those in their early fifties seen in 1971. During the 1970s fertility declined, resulting in fewer people in their late teens and twenties in 2000 than in 1971.

Historically, the ageing of the population structure was largely a result of the fall in fertility that began towards the end of the 19th century. Early in the 20th century lower mortality helped to increase the number of people surviving into old age, but the effects of improved survival were greater among younger people which operated as a counterbalance to the trend towards population ageing. More recently, there have been lower fertility rates and improvements in mortality rates for older people, both of which have

contributed to the ageing of the population. The percentage of the population of both males and females for age groups over 55 are projected to continue to increase (Table 1.3). The assumptions underlying the projections for the United Kingdom mean that these trends will continue so that by 2014 it is expected the number of people aged 65 and over will exceed those aged under 16. The average age of the population is expected to rise from 38.8 years in 2000 to 42.6 years in 2025.

An ageing population is a characteristic the United Kingdom shares with the other countries in the European Union (EU). In the year 2000 the proportion of the total population that was aged 65 and over in the United Kingdom was 15.6 per cent, slightly lower than the EU average of 16.2 per cent. The percentage of the EU population aged 65 and over has increased by over half since 1960. The largest increases were in Finland and Spain, where the proportions doubled. Conversely, the proportion in the Irish Republic, the country with the lowest percentage of people aged 65 and over in the year 2000, has remained steady since 1960. Globally the number of people aged 60 years or over is expected to triple by 2050, increasing from 606 million currently to 2 billion. The increase in the number of people aged 80 and over is expected to be

Table **1.4**

Population: by ethnic group and age, 2000–01[1]

Great Britain Percentages

	Under 16	16–34	35–64	65 and over	All ages (=100%) (millions)
White	20	25	39	16	53.0
Black					
Black Caribbean	23	27	40	10	0.5
Black African	33	35	30	2	0.4
Other Black groups	52	29	17	..	0.3
All Black groups	34	30	31	5	1.3
Indian	23	31	38	7	1.0
Pakistani/Bangladeshi					
Pakistani	36	36	24	4	0.7
Bangladeshi	39	36	21	4	0.3
All Pakistani/Bangladeshi	37	36	23	4	0.9
Other groups					
Chinese	19	38	38	4	0.1
None of the above	32	33	32	3	0.7
All other groups[2]	30	34	33	3	0.8
All ethnic groups[3]	20	26	39	15	57.1

1 Population living in private households. Combined quarters: Spring 2000 to Winter 2000–2001.
2 Includes those of mixed origin.
3 Includes those who did not state their ethnic group.
Source: Labour Force Survey, Office for National Statistics

Chart **1.5**

Population of working age[1]: by gender and social class, Spring 2001

United Kingdom

Percentages

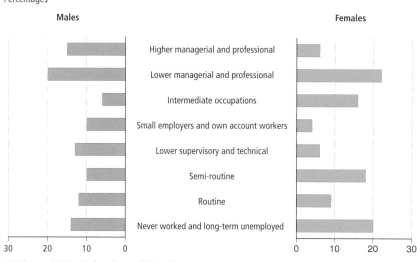

1 Males aged 16 to 64, females aged 16 to 59.
Source: Labour Force Survey, Office for National Statistics

even more marked, rising from 69 million in 2000 to 379 million in 2050, more than a five-fold increase.

The age profile of the population varies between ethnic groups. Members of minority ethnic groups were present in the United Kingdom in small numbers throughout the period of the British Empire. However, their numbers increased significantly after the Second World War. This growth was initiated by large scale immigration from the countries of the New Commonwealth following the passing of the *1948 British Nationality Act*. This trend was subsequently curtailed by legislation passed in the 1960s and 1970s.

In 2000–01, about one person in 14 in Great Britain was from an minority ethnic group (Table 1.4). In general, minority ethnic groups have a younger age structure than the White population, reflecting past immigration and fertility patterns. The 'Other Black' group has the youngest age structure with 52 per cent aged under 16. The Bangladeshi group also has a young age structure, with 39 per cent aged under 16. This was almost double the proportion of the White group. In contrast, the White group had the highest proportion of people aged 65 and over at 16 per cent, compared with 4 per cent of the Pakistani, Bangladeshi and Chinese groups. Progressive ageing of the ethnic minority population is anticipated in the future, but changes will be dependent upon fertility levels, mortality rates and future net migration.

The occupational composition of the population has also changed during the 20th century. Among men of working age, there has been a strong upward trend in the share of professional, managerial and supervisory grades. There have also been increases in the numbers of women in higher socio-economic occupations, albeit more slowly than for men, along with rises in clerical and unskilled manual groups. In Spring 2001 men were two and a half times more likely than women to be in higher managerial and professional occupations (Chart 1.5). Conversely, women were nearly twice as likely as men to be in the semi-routine group. This reflects the predominance of women in certain occupations such as clerical and secretarial jobs. These trends are accompanied by other factors such as the increasing participation of women in the workforce. Further information on economic activity rates is presented in Chart 4.6 of the Labour Market chapter.

Population change

The rate of population change depends upon the net natural change – the difference between the numbers of births and deaths – and the net effect of people migrating to and from a country. Most of the overall population growth of the United Kingdom during the 20th century can be attributed to net natural change (Table 1.6). However, in recent years net inward migration has become an increasingly important determinant of population growth. Between 1991 and 2000 net natural change in the United Kingdom as a whole was exceeded by net migration and other change. Projections suggest that this trend will continue with net migration accounting for 70 per cent of overall change in population between 2001 and 2011.

The fastest population growth of the 20th century occurred in the first decade, when the population increased by an average of 385 thousand each year. This rapid growth at the start of the century, and again during the 1960s, was due to the high number of births during these decades. The considerable fall in the number of births following the 1960s' 'baby boom' helps to explain the slower population growth of the 1970s.

The two World Wars had a major impact on the number of births in the United Kingdom (Chart 1.7). There was a noticeable fall in births during the First World War, followed by a post-war 'baby boom' when the number of births peaked at more than 1.1 million in 1920 – the highest number in any year of the 20th century. The number of births then decreased and remained low during the 1930s' depression and the Second World War. This was followed by a 'baby boom' shortly after the Second World War and another in the 1960s. The number of births are projected to remain fairly constant over the next 40 years. However, deaths are projected to start increasing in the 2020s when the larger numbers of people born after the Second World War start to reach advanced ages. As a result, deaths are then projected to overtake births, something that occurred only once during the 20th century.

One factor influencing trends in the number of births is the number of women of reproductive age. For example, the number of births rose during the 1980s as the increasing numbers of women born between the mid-1950s and the mid-1960s, entered their peak reproductive years. The peak in births in 1990 has been followed by a decrease in the number of births over the 1990s, in part as a result of smaller cohorts of women born in the 1970s, but also lower fertility rates, particularly amongst women aged under 30. More information about fertility is contained in the Family Formation section of Chapter 2: Households and Families (page 45).

Table **1.6**

Population change[1]

United Kingdom   Thousands

	Annual averages					
	Population at start of period	Live births	Deaths	Net natural change	Net migration and other[2]	Overall change
Census enumerated						
1901–1911	38,237	1,091	624	467	–82	385
1911–1921	42,082	975	689	286	–92	194
1921–1931	44,027	824	555	268	–67	201
1931–1951	46,038	785	598	188	25	213
Mid-year estimates						
1951–1961	50,287	839	593	246	6	252
1961–1971	52,807	962	638	324	–12	312
1971–1981	55,928	736	666	69	–27	42
1981–1991	56,357	757	655	103	43	146
1991–2000	57,814	738	636	102	114	216
Mid-year projections[3]						
2000–2001	59,756	674	602	72	160	232
2001–2011	59,987	677	617	60	137	197
2011–2021	61,956	700	621	80	135	215

1 See Appendix, Part 1: Population estimates and projections.
2 Other changes apply to estimates only and refer to changes in the numbers of armed forces stationed in the UK. This includes foreign armed forces and their dependents stationed in the UK and British military personnel and their dependents stationed overseas.
3 2000-based projections.
Source: Office for National Statistics; Government Actuary's Department; General Register Office for Scotland; Northern Ireland Statistics and Research Agency

Chart **1.7**

Births[1,2] and deaths[1]

United Kingdom

Millions

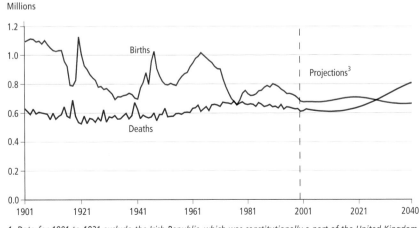

1 Data for 1901 to 1921 exclude the Irish Republic, which was constitutionally a part of the United Kingdom during this period.
2 Data from 1981 exclude the non-residents of Northern Ireland.
3 2000-based.
Source: Office for National Statistics; Government Actuary's Department; General Register Office for Scotland; Northern Ireland Statistics and Research Agency

Table **1.8**

Deaths: by gender and age

United Kingdom
Death rates per 1,000 in each age group

	Under 1[1]	1–15	16–34	35–54	55–64	65–74	75 and over	All ages	All deaths (thousands)
Males									
1961	26.3	0.6	1.1	5.0	22.4	54.8	142.5	12.6	322
1971	20.2	0.5	1.0	4.8	20.4	51.1	131.4	12.1	329
1981	12.7	0.4	0.0	4.0	18.1	46.4	122.2	12.0	329
1991	8.3	0.3	0.9	3.1	14.2	38.7	110.6	11.1	314
2000	6.1	0.2	0.9	2.7	10.8	30.5	98.3	9.9	291
2011[2]	4.2	0.2	0.8	2.6	10.0	24.3	86.6	9.7	298
2021[2]	3.6	0.1	0.8	2.4	8.6	22.9	79.2	10.3	329
Females									
1961	18.2	0.4	0.6	3.2	11.0	31.6	110.4	11.4	310
1971	15.5	0.4	0.5	3.1	10.3	26.6	96.6	11.0	317
1981	9.5	0.3	0.4	2.5	9.8	24.7	90.2	11.4	329
1991	6.3	0.2	0.4	1.9	8.4	22.3	83.9	11.2	332
2000	5.1	0.1	0.4	1.8	6.6	18.7	81.5	10.5	319
2011[2]	3.7	0.1	0.3	1.7	6.0	15.8	79.1	10.0	312
2021[2]	3.1	0.1	0.3	1.6	5.0	14.6	69.5	9.7	312

1 *Rate per 1,000 live births.*
2 *2000-based projections.*
Source: Office for National Statistics; Government Actuary's Department; General Register Office for Scotland; Northern Ireland Statistics and Research Agency

Along with population change, babies' names are constantly changing. Jack and Chloe were the most common names given to boys and girls born in Great Britain in 2000. However, neither of these names featured in the top 50 most popular names in 1984, and they were not even in the top 100 names ten years before that. By contrast, John was a very popular boy's name in the first half of the 20th century, but was in fifth place in 1964 and by 2000 was outside the top 50. Similarly, Margaret was a popular girl's name in the earlier years of the 20th century, but by 1964 it was the 39th most popular name and was also outside the top 50 in 2000.

Despite the considerable population growth since 1901, the annual number of deaths in the UK remained relatively constant over the century. This is because of large declines in mortality rates. For example, between 1961 and 2000 alone, infant mortality rates fells by over 70 per cent, while death rates for men aged between 55 and 64 fell by more than 50 per cent (Table 1.8). Rising standards of living, the changing occupational structure and new developments in medical technology and practice help to explain these declines in mortality rates.

Death rates are higher for males than for females in all age groups, resulting in the life expectancy of females being higher than that for males (see Table 7.1 in the Health chapter). The fact that the overall crude death rate has been higher for females than for males since 1991 can be explained by the older age structure of the female population compared with that for males. At most ages for both males and females, death rates in 2000 were higher in Scotland than in any other constituent country of the United Kingdom – this was most noticeable for age groups over 55.

Geographical distribution

In 2000 the majority of the population of the United Kingdom (about 84 per cent) lived in England, with Northern Ireland having the smallest population of the four constituent countries at 1.7 million (3 per cent) (See Table 1.1 on page 28).

Population change between mid-1981 and 2000 in the United Kingdom has produced significant changes in geographical distribution (Map 1.9), with the largest population increases being in Milton Keynes Unitary Authority (UA), with a population rise of 67 per cent and Bracknell Forest UA which grew by 31 per cent. These contrast with Inverclyde and Dundee City, which have both experienced a decline in population of 16 per cent between mid-1981 and 2000.

In 2000 the area with the highest proportion of people of state pension age or over was Conwy in Wales and Torbay UA in England, where over one in four people was over state pension age (Map 1.10). This compares to an average of less than one person in five for the United Kingdom as a whole. In England there are also high proportions of older people in some areas along the south coast, including the Isle of Wight, East Sussex and Dorset. Of the four constituent countries of the United Kingdom, Northern Ireland has the lowest proportion of older people.

Migration

Migration flows influence the size, growth and profile of the population. Regional populations are affected by people relocating within the UK, supplemented by international migration flows. During much of the 20th century there has been a movement of population out of the old coal, shipbuilding and steel industry areas in the north of England, Scotland and Wales and into the light industries and services of the south of England and the Midlands. Population gains and losses due to internal migration have important implications for local land use and the planning of housing, as well as for the provision of welfare services.

During 2000 Wales gained 7 thousand people due to moves within the UK (internal migration), while England, Scotland and Northern Ireland experienced net losses of population of 2, 4 and 1 thousand respectively. At a regional level within England, the greatest fall in population occurred in London where 69 thousand more people moved to other regions of the United Kingdom than moved into London (Table 1.11). However, this was more than offset by the net inflow of international migrants settling in the capital. Two-fifths of people leaving London for elsewhere in the United Kingdom moved into the neighbouring South East region. The South West experienced the highest net gain of all the regions due to internal migration, of almost 29 thousand people.

Map **1.9**

Population change, mid 1981-2000[1]

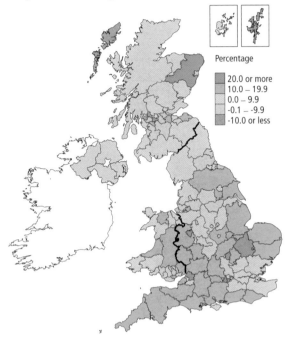

1 See Appendix, Part 1: Population estimates and projections, and Boundaries.
Source: Office for National Statistics; General Register Office for Scotland; Northern Ireland Statistics and Research Agency

Map **1.10**

Population of state pension age[1] : by area[2], 2000

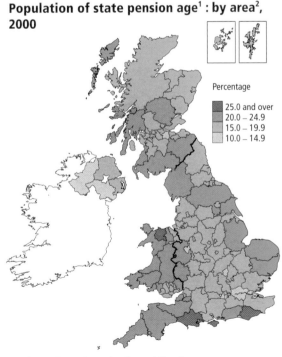

1 Males aged 65 and over, females aged 60 and over.
2 Counties and Unitary Authorities for England, Unitary Authorities for Wales, Council Areas for Scotland, boards for Northern Ireland. See Appendix, Part 1: Boundaries.
Source: Office for National Statistics; General Register Office for Scotland; Northern Ireland Statistics and Research Agency

Table **1.11**

Inter-regional movements[1] within the United Kingdom, 2000

United Kingdom   Thousands

						Origin							
	North East	North West	York-shire and the Humber	East Mid-lands	West Mid-lands	East	London	South East	South West	England	Wales	Scot-land	Nor-thern Ireland	United Kingdom
Destination													
North East	.	6	8	3	3	3	4	5	2	34	1	4	1	39
North West	7	.	18	9	13	8	12	13	8	87	9	8	2	106
Yorkshire and the Humber	9	19	.	16	8	8	9	12	6	88	3	5	1	97
East Midlands	3	10	18	.	16	18	12	19	8	105	3	4	1	112
West Midlands	3	13	7	13	.	8	11	15	13	82	8	3	1	94
East	3	8	8	13	7	.	59	28	10	137	3	5	1	146
London	5	13	11	10	12	29	.	53	16	149	5	8	1	163
South East	5	13	11	14	14	28	88	.	33	207	8	8	1	224
South West	2	10	6	8	16	13	22	47	.	125	10	5	1	140
England	38	91	87	88	88	115	218	192	96	.	50	49	9	109
Wales	1	11	3	3	10	4	5	10	10	57	.	2	0	59
Scotland	4	7	5	3	3	4	7	8	4	45	2	.	2	49
Northern Ireland	0	1	1	1	1	1	2	1	1	8	0	2	.	11
United Kingdom	43	111	96	95	101	125	232	210	111	111	52	53	12	.

1 Based on patients re-registering with NHS doctors in other parts of the United Kingdom. Moves where the origin and destination lie within the same region do not appear in the table.

Source: Office for National Statistics; General Register Office for Scotland; Northern Ireland Statistics and Research Agency

Young adults are the most mobile age group, reflecting in part the move most young people make from their parental home either to study, seek employment or set up their own home. In 2000 London experienced the largest net increase of people aged 16 to 24 due to migration within the United Kingdom, of 18.6 thousand, while the West Midlands experienced the biggest net loss of people in this age group, of over 4 thousand. However, London also experienced the largest net losses among all other age groups, particularly those aged 35 to 44. The regions with the highest net gains in this age group were the South West, East and South East. Further information about some of the reasons why people move home can be found in Table 10.22 in the Housing chapter.

The pattern of people entering and leaving the United Kingdom changed over the 20th century. There was a net loss due to international migration during the first three decades of the 20th century and again during the 1960s and 1970s. However, since 1983 there has been net migration into the United Kingdom.

Over the period 1996 to 2000, net international migration to the United Kingdom averaged 89 thousand a year (Table 1.12). This was nearly three and half times the annual average of the preceding five years. Between 1991–1995 and 1996–2000 the largest increase in migration to the United Kingdom was from the Old Commonwealth, an annual average of 30 thousand, followed by other EU member states with an annual increase of 19 thousand. Of those migrating from the United Kingdom to other countries between 1996 and 2000, most were leaving for other parts of the EU or Old Commonwealth countries, such as Canada, Australia and New Zealand. Migration from the United Kingdom to the United States saw the largest fall as an average of 3 thousand fewer people a year moved to the United States in the period between 1996 and 2000 than in the preceding 5 years.

Between 1990 and 2000 the numbers of UK nationals living outside the United Kingdom but still within the EU increased overall. This percentage increase was greatest in Finland, where the number of resident UK nationals has increased by nearly 80 per cent. In absolute terms the largest increase was seen in Germany where the number of UK nationals increased by nearly 28 thousand to reach 113 thousand, a rise of 32 per cent. International migration is projected to remain high during the 21st century, with the more developed regions expected to continue to be net receivers, with an average gain of about 2 million migrants per year over the next 50 years. Because of low fertility, international migration has a significant impact upon population growth in many developed countries. Data from the United Nations suggest that without migration, the population of the more developed regions of the world as a whole would start declining in 2003 rather than 2025.

There are various reasons why people choose to move into or out of a country. The most common reason given by immigrants in the period 1991 to 1995 was to accompany or join a partner already in the country while the most common reason for emigrants was work-related. Recent figures for the period 1996 to 2000 show that the most common reason given for migration, by both immigrants and emigrants, was work-related (Table 1.13).

Nationals of the European Economic Area (EU plus Norway, Iceland and Liechtenstein) have the right to reside in the United Kingdom provided they are working or able to support themselves financially. Nearly all other overseas nationals wishing to live permanently in the United Kingdom require Home Office acceptance for settlement. The number of people accepted for settlement in the United Kingdom increased by 28 thousand to 124 thousand between

Table **1.12**

Average international migration[1]: by region of next or last residence, 1991–1995 and 1996–2000

United Kingdom   Thousands

	1991–1995			1996–2000		
	Inflow	Outflow	Balance	Inflow	Outflow	Balance
New Commonwealth	46.5	24.4	22.1	58.5	22.4	36.1
European Union	70.7	61.8	8.9	89.2	72.9	16.3
Old Commonwealth	45.2	50.0	−4.8	75.5	62.3	13.1
United States of America	24.6	30.6	−6.0	29.6	27.6	2.0
Middle East	8.8	10.9	−2.1	11.7	9.5	2.3
Rest of Europe	14.7	11.4	3.3	15.0	13.7	1.3
Rest of America	2.5	4.1	−1.6	4.4	3.3	1.0
Other	25.9	19.7	6.3	37.6	20.7	16.9
All countries	238.9	212.8	26.1	321.5	232.5	89.0

1 Derived from International Passenger Survey migration estimates only. Excludes migration between the United Kingdom and the Irish Republic. Excludes asylum seekers. See also Appendix, Part 1: International migration estimates.

Source: International Passenger Survey, Office for National Statistics

Table **1.13**

Average annual international migration[1]: by main reason for migration, 1991–1995 and 1996–2000

United Kingdom   Thousands

	1991–1995			1996–2000		
	Inflow	Outflow	Balance	Inflow	Outflow	Balance
Work-related	45	64	−19	81	77	4
Accompany/join partner	74	58	16	71	50	20
Formal study	49	11	38	77	11	66
Other[2]	47	45	2	72	64	8
No reason stated	24	35	−11	22	30	−9
All reasons	239	213	26	322	233	89

1 Derived from International Passenger Survey migration estimates only. Excludes migration between the United Kingdom and the Irish Republic. See also Appendix, Part 1: International migration estimates.

2 Includes those looking for work.

Source: Office for National Statistics

Chart **1.14**

Acceptances for settlement: by selected region of origin

United Kingdom

Thousands

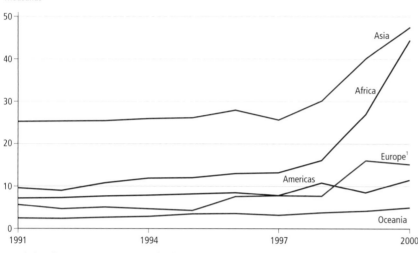

1 Includes all European Economic Area (EEA) countries throughout the period covered. EEA nationals are not obliged to seek settlement and the figures relate only to those who chose to do so.

Source: Home Office

Chart **1.15**

Asylum applications[1]: by region of origin, 1991-2000

United Kingdom

Thousands

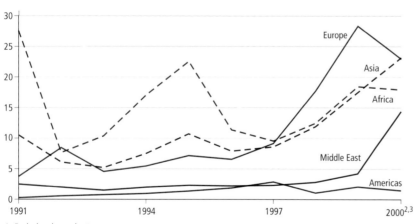

1 Excludes dependents.

2 Provisional.

3 Applications where the nationality of the applicant was not known have been excluded. These accounted for 0.6 per cent in 2000.

Source: Home Office

1999 and 2000, the highest annual number since July 1962 when Commonwealth citizens became subject to immigration control, and equivalent to 0.2 per cent of the UK population (Chart 1.14). The number of people accepted for settlement from European countries outside the UK declined by around 5 per cent between 1999 and 2000; this figure had doubled between 1998 and 1999, mainly due to asylum-related settlement from the Former Yugoslavia and to a lesser extent Turkey.

The proportion of acceptances increased from all world regions in 2000, except Europe, with the largest increase of 65 per cent occurring from Africa. The high percentages of acceptances from Asia and Africa in the late 1990s are mainly asylum-related, but also reflect the increase in acceptances in spouses of those already accepted for settlement, after the abolition of the primary purpose rule in June 1997 (see Appendix, Part 1: Asylum).

The number of people seeking asylum varies considerably from year to year (Chart 1.15), although there has been an overall increase from about 4 thousand a year during 1985 to 1988 to around 80 thousand in 2000. The countries from which people arrive to claim asylum vary with world events. In 2000, most asylum seekers came from Iraq, Sri Lanka, the Former Yugoslavia, Iran and Afghanistan, areas that have seen escalations of internal conflict. In 2000 an estimated 10 thousand applications were recognised as refugees and granted asylum. An additional 11.5 thousand were not recognised as refugees but granted exceptional leave.

International perspective

The Commonwealth had a membership of 54 countries in 2001 and a collective population of 1.7 billion people. It includes a number of diverse countries; for example, the world's second largest in terms of territory (Canada); some of the world's smallest and remote countries (Nauru), and poorest in terms of capita GNP (Mozambique and Tanzania), as well as varying in population size and demographic structure. Less than half of the people in Bangladesh, the Gambia, India, Namibia and Sierra Leone lived in urban areas in 1990–99 compared with 90 per cent in the United Kingdom and 100 per cent in Singapore (Table 1.16). Nearly one in five babies born in Sierra Leone die before their first birthday, compared with less than one in 100 born in the United Kingdom. Those babies from Sierra Leone that do survive childhood can expect to live to only about half the age of their contemporaries born in the United Kingdom.

Table **1.16**

Demographic indicators of selected countries in the Commonwealth

	Population (Millions) 2000	Average annual growth rate 1995–2000[1] (percentage)	Percentage in urban areas 1990–99	Infant mortality rate[2]	Life expectancy at birth (years)	
					Males	Females
Australia	18.9	1.0	85	6	76	81
Bangladesh	129.2	1.7	25	79	58	58
Canada	31.1	1.0	77	6	76	82
The Gambia	1.3	3.2	33	122	45	49
India	1,013.7	1.6	28	72	62	63
Nambia	1.7	2.2	31	65	52	53
New Zealand	3.9	1.0	86	7	74	80
Sierra Leone	4.9	3.0	37	170	36	39
Singapore	3.6	1.4	100	5	75	79
United Kingdom[3]	59.8	0.2	90	7	75	80

1 Medium variant.

2 Per 1,000 live births.

3 Population figure for 2000 provided by Office for National Statistics; General Register Office for Scotland; Northern Ireland Statistics and Research Agency.

Source: Department of Economic and Social Affairs, United Nations

Population growth in Europe has been considerably slower than the average growth rate for the world in recent years. The world's population is now more than six times larger than in 1800 (Table 1.17). Much of this increase occurred in the 20th century: in 2001 the population was more than three and a half times the size it was in 1900. In October 2001 the world's population exceeded 6.1 billion people, an increase of over three and a half billion in the previous 50 years. The world population is currently growing at a rate of 1.2 per cent, or 77 million people per year, with six countries accounting for half of this annual growth: India for 21 per cent; China for 12 per cent; Pakistan for 5 per cent; Nigeria for 4 per cent; Bangladesh for 4 per cent, and Indonesia for 3 per cent. By 2050, world population is expected to be between 7.9 and 10.9 billion. China, with a population of 1.3 billion in 2000 is currently the country with the largest population, although India is expected to have overtaken it by 2050.

Table **1.17**

World population

Millions

	1800	1850	1900	1950	2001
Asia	635	809	947	1,402	3,721
Africa	107	111	133	224	813
Europe	203	276	408	547	726
Latin America and Caribbean	24	38	74	166	527
North America	7	26	82	172	317
Oceania	2	2	6	13	31
World	978	1,262	1,650	2,524	6,134

Source: United Nations

Websites

National Statistics	www.statistics.gov.uk
Eurostat	http://europa.eu.int./comm/eurostat
General Register Office for Scotland	www.gro-scotland.gov.uk
Government Actuary's Department	www.gad.gov.uk
Home Office Immigration and Asylum Statistics	www.homeoffice.gov.uk/rds
National Assembly for Wales	www.wales.gov.uk/keypub
Northern Ireland Statistics Research Agency	www.nisra.gov.uk
Scottish Executive	www.scotland.gov.uk
United Nations Population Information Network	www.un.org/popin
The Commonwealth	www.thecommonwealth.org
Labour Market Trends	www.statistics.gov.uk/products/p550.asp

Contacts

Office for National Statistics

Chapter author	020 7533 5283
Internal migration	01329 813 889
International migration	01329 813 255
Labour market enquiries helpline	020 7533 6094
Population estimates general enquiries	01329 813 255
General Register Office for Scotland	0131 314 4254
Government Actuary's Department	020 7211 2622
Home Office	020 8760 8280
National Assembly for Wales	029 2082 5085

Northern Ireland Statistics and Research Agency

Population enquiries	028 9034 8132
Eurostat	00 352 4301 35487
United Nations	020 7630 2709

Chapter 2

Households and Families

Households and families

- The proportion of households comprising a couple with dependent children fell from 35% of all households in 1971 to 23% in 2001. (Table 2.1)

- The proportion of people living alone doubled from 6 per cent in 1971 to 12 per cent in 2001. (Table 2.3)

Partnership

- Around three-fifths of men and women who were aged 35 to 39 when they married for the first time had cohabited with their future partner. (Chart 2.6)

- The number of divorces in the United Kingdom peaked in 1993 at 180 thousand, but has since fallen by 12 per cent to reach 159 thousand in 1999. (Chart 2.8)

Family formation

- Around nine out of ten conceptions within marriage in England and Wales in 1999 resulted in a maternity compared with three-fifths of conceptions outside marriage. (Table 2.10)

- The abortion rate for women aged 20–24 in 2000 in England and Wales was 31 abortions per 1,000 women, higher than for any other age group. (Chart 2.11)

Family relationship

- In 2000 seven in ten children affected by divorce were aged ten or under and around one in four children were under five years. (Chart 2.19)

Table **2.1**

Households[1]: by size

Great Britain   Percentages

	1961	1971	1981	1991	2001[2]
One person	14	18	22	27	29
Two people	30	32	32	34	35
Three people	23	19	17	16	16
Four people	18	17	18	16	14
Five people	9	8	7	5	5
Six or more people	7	6	4	2	2
All households					
(=100%)(millions)	16.3	18.6	20.2	22.4	24.1
Average household					
size (number of people)	3.1	2.9	2.7	2.5	2.4

1 See Appendix, Part 2: Households.
2 At Spring 2001.
Source: Census: Labour Force Survey, Office for National Statistics

Table **2.2**

Households[1]: by type of household and family

Great Britain   Percentages

	1961	1971	1981	1991	2001[2]
One person					
Under state pension age	4	6	8	11	14
Over state pension age	7	12	14	16	15
Two or more unrelated adults	5	4	5	3	3
One family households					
Couple[3]					
No children	26	27	26	28	29
1-2 dependent children[4]	30	26	25	20	19
3 or more dependent children[4]	8	9	6	5	4
Non-dependent children only	10	8	8	8	6
Lone parent[3]					
Dependent children[4]	2	3	5	6	6
Non-dependent children only	4	4	4	4	3
Multi-family households	3	1	1	1	1
All households[5]					
(=100%)(millions)	16.3	18.6	20.2	22.4	24.1

1 See Appendix, Part 2: Households and Families.
2 At Spring 2001.
3 Other individuals who were not family members may also be included.
4 May also include non-dependent children.
5 Includes couples of the same gender in 2001, but percentages are based on totals
  excluding this group.
Source: Census; Labour Force Survey, Office for National Statistics

The types of household people live in during their lives are now more varied than in the past. Where once people lived with their parents until marriage, increasingly people spend time living on their own, whether before or instead of marriage/cohabitation or as a result of divorce or the breakdown of a relationship. Some may then start new relationships and second families, leading to new households and families.

Households and families

The average household size in Great Britain was around 4.6 people for many years before falling to 3.1 in 1961. Since then it has reduced further to 2.4 people per household in 2000–01, as the number of households has grown at a faster rate than the population (Table 2.1). The population of Great Britain increased by a half over the 20th century, while the number of households tripled. Trends towards smaller families, and more people living alone, contribute to this increase in the number of households. The Continuous Household Survey estimated that at Spring 2001, the average household size in Northern Ireland was 2.7, slightly higher than in Great Britain.

Household composition has become more varied in recent decades, and increasing numbers of people are living alone. In Spring 2001 almost three in ten households in Great Britain comprised one person living alone, more than twice the proportion in 1961 (Table 2.2). The proportion of households consisting of a couple with dependent children fell from 38 per cent in 1961 to 23 per cent in Spring 2001, while the proportion of lone parent households with dependent children tripled, accounting for 6 per cent of all households in both 1991 and 2001. Multi-family households formed 3 per cent of all households in 1961, but have since declined to around 1 per cent. From the 1960s there was emphasis on the provision of first public, and then private, housing which encouraged the acquisition of separate accommodation. There is also evidence that lone parents, who historically were more likely than other families to live in multi-family households, increasingly became one-family households throughout the period.

Table 2.2 shows that about three-fifths (58 per cent) of households in Great Britain comprised couples with or without children in Spring 2001. Table 2.3 is based on people within households and it shows that almost three-quarters of people living in private households were in couple family households. The 'traditional' family household of a couple with dependent children was the single most common type of family in which people lived in Spring 2001. However, since 1971, the proportion living in such households fell by a quarter (from 52 per cent to 39 per cent) and the proportion of people living in couple family households with no children increased from less than a fifth of all households to nearly a quarter. One in ten people in Great Britain in Spring 2001 and almost one in six people in Northern Ireland in 2000–01 lived in a lone parent household.

The increase in the proportion of one-person households is one of the most notable changes in household composition during the past 40 years in Great Britain. The number of such households increased from under 2 million in 1961 to around 7 million in Spring 2001. Twelve per cent of people in Great Britain now live alone. The rate of change has not been uniform across all categories of those living alone. In recent years, the largest rate of increase in the proportion of one person households was among men aged under 65: 10 per cent in 1999, which was almost three times the proportion in 1971 and formed the largest proportion of households living alone in England (Chart 2.4). The proportion of households consisting of women aged 65 and over living alone was also around 10 per cent – this proportion has remained fairly stable since the beginning of the 1970s. At the same time, the proportion of women aged under 65 and living alone has almost doubled. These increases in part reflect the decline in marriage and the rise in separation and divorce, as well as people first marrying at an older age these days.

Table **2.3**

People in households[1]: by type of household and family in which they live

Great Britain Percentages

	1961	1971	1981	1991	2001[2]
One family households					
Living alone	4	6	8	11	12
Couple					
No children	18	19	20	23	24
Dependent children[3]	52	52	47	41	39
Non-dependent children only	12	10	10	11	9
Lone parent	3	4	6	10	10
Other households	12	9	9	4	5
All people in private households					
(=100%)(millions)	..	53.4	53.9	55.4	..
People not in private					
households (millions)	..	0.9	0.8	0.8	..
Total population (millions)	51.4	54.4	54.8	56.2	57.2

1 See Appendix, Part 2: Households and Families.
2 At Spring 2001.
3 May also include non-dependent children.
Source: Census, Labour Force Survey, Office for National Statistics

Chart **2.4**

Percentage of all households where heads of household were living alone[1]: by age and gender

England

Percentages

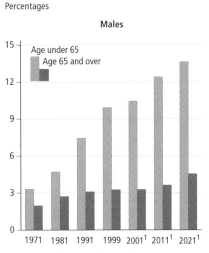

Males

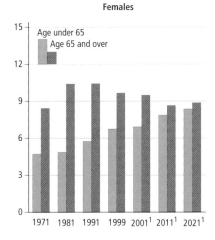

Females

1 1996-based household projections.
Source: Department for Transport Local Government and the Regions

Table **2.5**

Proportion of the population by marital status[1] and gender[2]

Great Britain | | | | Percentages

	1971	1981	1991	2000
Males				
Single	24	27	31	34
Married	71	66	60	53
Divorced	4	4	4	4
Widowed	1	3	6	8
All males[2]	100	100	100	100
Females				
Single	19	21	23	26
Married	65	61	56	52
Divorced	15	15	14	12
Widowed	1	4	7	9
All females[2]	100	100	100	100

1 Population estimates by marital status for 1971 are based on the 1971 Census and those for 1981 are based on the 1981 Census and have not been rebased using the 1991 Census.
2 Adults aged 16 and over.
Source: Office for National Statistics; General Register Office for Scotland

Chart **2.6**

Cohabitation prior to first marriage[1]: by age at first marriage and gender, 1996-1999[2]

Great Britain

Percentages

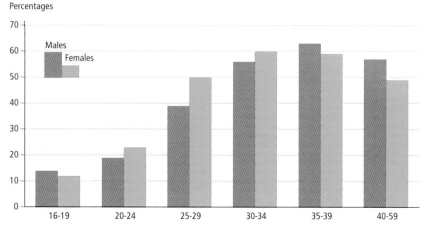

1 Those who cohabited with their future partner prior to their first marriage as a proportion of all ever married men and women.
2 Combined years: 1996–97 and 1998–99.
Source: General Household Survey, Office for National Statistics

Partnerships

The pattern of partnership formation has changed since the mid-1970s, and although the majority of men and women still get married, the proportion of the population that are married is not as large as it once was (Table 2.5). While the proportion of men and women who are married has been declining, the proportions who are cohabiting have been increasing, and the proportion living outside a partnership has also increased. In a combined estimation and projections exercise, undertaken by the Government Actuary's Department and the Office for National Statistics, it was estimated that there were just over one and a half million cohabiting couples in England and Wales in 1996 – representing about one in six of the adult non-married population. If current trends continue, the proportion of the population cohabiting would almost double from 12 per cent in 1996 to 22 per cent in 2021. The number of cohabiting men and women who are single is projected to increase by 130 per cent between 1996 and 2021.

For non-married women aged under 60, the proportion cohabiting in Great Britain almost doubled from 13 per cent to 25 per cent between 1986 and 1998–99 and for men, more than doubled from 11 per cent to 26 per cent over the same time period. The longest time series on cohabitation exists for women aged 18 to 49. Between 1979 and 1998 the proportion of non-married women in this age group in Great Britain who were cohabiting almost tripled, from 11 per cent to 29 per cent. In Northern Ireland, although the proportion of non-married people aged under 60 who were cohabiting has also increased since the mid-1980s, this proportion has remained below that of Great Britain. Data from the 1986 Continuous Household Survey show that in Northern Ireland 2 per cent of non-married men and women aged between 16 and 59 were cohabiting. Combined data for 1996–97 and 1998-99 suggest that this had increased to around ten per cent non-married people aged 16 to 59.

For some couples cohabitation may precede marriage, in the same way as a long engagement before marriage may have been customary in the past. Among couples about to marry, living together before marriage has become the norm rather than the exception and all but a few couples cohabit premaritally. Combined data from the 1996–97 and 1998–99 General Household Surveys show that for adults of all ages three in ten men and over a quarter of women in Great Britain who had ever been married had cohabited before their first marriage. The proportion who had cohabited with their future partner before their wedding increased with age at marriage. Around three-fifths of people who were aged 30 to 39 when they married for the first time had cohabited with their future partner (Chart 2.6).

An analysis undertaken using data from the British Household Panel Survey (BHPS) demonstrated that for women whose first partnership was a cohabitation which dissolved, almost all of those who repartnered cohabited in their second partnership. It was estimated that after a cohabiting first partnership had dissolved, the median duration to the next partnership was around five years.

Results from the 1998 BHPS indicate that nearly three-quarters of never married childless people aged under 35 who were cohabiting expected to marry each other (Table 2.7). Thus, for most people, cohabitation is part of the process of getting married and is not a substitute for marriage. About two-fifths of the cohabiting adults perceived advantages to just living together rather than marrying. Of the male cohabitants who did perceive there to be advantages, over half mentioned the idea of a trial marriage, compared with just over two-fifths of women. Around three in ten of both men and women mentioned the advantage of no legal ties. Only a small proportion (4 per cent of men and 8 per cent of women) reported the benefit of personal independence. Over half of the men and just over two-fifths of the women who perceived a disadvantage to cohabiting, cited financial insecurity as the reason. Almost a fifth of the women cited no legal ties as a perceived disadvantage of cohabiting, compared with less than a tenth of men. The social stigma of cohabiting was mentioned by less than 15 per cent of cohabiting men and women as a disadvantage.

Cohabitation does not always result in marriage. In 1998–99 15 per cent of men and 13 per cent of women reported at least one cohabitation not leading to marriage. Cohabitation is not restricted to periods before first marriage. Combined data from the 1996–97 and 1998–99 General Household Survey and Continuous Household Survey showed that 12 per cent of separated women and 36 per cent of divorced women aged 25 to 34 were cohabiting.

At the beginning of the 1960s there were around 340 thousand first marriages a year in the United Kingdom (Chart 2.8). Marriage was 'fashionable' in the 1960s, despite it being the so-called 'permissive age'. The growth in the number of marriages in the mid- to late-1960s was largely as result of three factors: babies born in the post-war boom were passing through the marriageable ages; people were marrying younger; and a higher proportion of people were getting married. The number of first marriages peaked in 1970 at almost 390 thousand, and since has decreased to less than half this number – 179 thousand in 1999. Remarriages increased by about a third between 1971 and 1972 following the introduction of the Divorce Reform Act 1969 and the number of remarriages has remained fairly constant

Table 2.7

Marriage expectations of never married childless males and females aged under 35 in a cohabiting union, 1998

Great Britain   Percentages

	Males	Females
Planning to marry	30	25
Probably get married at some point	46	46
Probably just keep living together without marrying	14	18
Have not really thought about the future	8	8
Other[1]	3	4
All	100	100

1 Includes 'don't know' and refusals.

Source: British Household Panel Survey, Institute for Social and Economic Research

Chart 2.8

Marriages and divorces

United Kingdom

Thousands

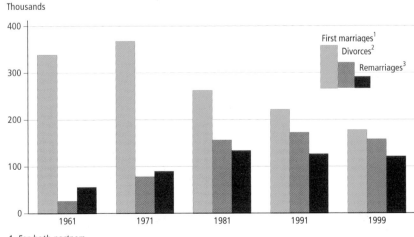

1 For both partners.
2 Includes annulments.
3 For one or both partners.

Source: Office for National Statistics; General Register Office for Scotland; Northern Ireland Statistics and Research Agency

over the last quarter century. In 1999 there were 122 thousand remarriages for one or both partners, accounting for two-fifths of all marriages.

Over the last few decades here has been a tendency for first marriages to take place later in life than previously. In 1961 the average age at first marriage in England and Wales was 26 for men and 23 for women; by 1999 this had risen to 29 and 27 respectively. Rises in pre-marital cohabitation help to explain the recent trend towards later marriage, but other factors such as the increased and longer participation in further and higher education, particularly among women, have also contributed.

The average age at first marriage in the EU as a whole in 1998 was around three years higher than in 1961: 30 for men and 27 for women in 1998, compared with 27 and 24 in 1961. Differences exist between the countries of the European Union (EU) in the ages at which people marry for the first time. In 1998 the country with the youngest newly-weds was Portugal while Denmark had the oldest (Table 2.9). Traditionally, women marry men older than themselves. The greatest difference in the average ages of men and women marrying for the first time was just under four years in Greece while the Irish Republic had the least difference in age between partners, at under 2 years.

In the United Kingdom, along with the trend for people getting married later in life, there has been an increase in the proportion of people getting divorced. The number of divorces doubled between 1961 and 1969 in the United Kingdom, and had doubled again by 1972 (Chart 2.8). This latter increase was partly a 'one-off' effect of the *Divorce Reform Act 1969* in England and Wales, which came into effect in 1971. The Act introduced a single ground for divorce – irretrievable breakdown – which could be established by proving one or more of certain facts: adultery; desertion; separation either with or without consent; or unreasonable behaviour. Although there was a drop in the number of divorces in 1973 in the United Kingdom, the number increased again in 1974 and peaked in 1993 at 180 thousand. The annual number of divorces then fell by 12 per cent to reach 159 thousand in 1999. Average divorce rates across the EU have more than trebled since 1961, from 0.5 divorces per 1,000 population to 1.8 per thousand in 1996.

The rate of divorce in England and Wales rose from 2.1 per 1,000 married people in 1961 to around 13.5 per 1,000 in 1991. The divorce rate then fell in males by 5 per cent and by 6 per cent in females by 2000. Since the 1970s this rate was highest for those aged between 25 and 29. However, in 1999 the divorce rate for both males and females aged between 16 and 24 was almost as high as that for those aged 25 to 29. Among those who were married in the latter half of the 1980s, around one in eight men and one in six women had separated within the first five years. This was double the proportion for those who first married 20 years earlier. Teenage marriages were also more likely to break down than those which occurred later in life. Among those married in the late 1980s, 24 per cent of women who were under 20 when they first married had separated within five years compared with 8 per cent of women married between the ages of 25 and 29. The earlier a partnership is formed, the more likely it is to break down. Other demographic factors that have been implicated in marital breakdown include having a pre-marital birth, cohabiting prior to marriage and having a spouse who has previously been married. In 1999 the most common reason for women to be granted divorces in England and Wales was the unreasonable behaviour of the husbands, while for men it was separation for two years with consent. Results from the BHPS showed that in 1998 around four in ten adults in Great Britain either strongly agreed or agreed that 'divorce is better than an unhappy marriage'.

Table **2.9**

Average age at first marriage: by gender, EU comparison, 1961 and 1998

	1961		1998	
	Males	Females	Males	Females
Denmark	25.7	22.8	31.7	29.4
Sweden	26.6	23.8	31.7	29.3
Greece	29.2	25.2	30.3	26.5
Italy	28.5	24.7	30.0	27.1
Irish Republic	30.8	27.6	30.0	28.2
Netherlands	26.4	24.1	30.0	27.6
Germany	25.4	23.4	29.5	26.9
Finland	25.8	23.6	29.5	27.5
France	25.6	23.0	29.6	27.6
Spain	28.8	26.1	29.4	27.4
Luxembourg[1]	26.9	25.4	29.6	27.2
Austria	26.5	23.8	29.2	26.7
England & Wales	25.6	23.1	29.1	27.0
Belgium	25.0	22.8	27.8	25.7
Portugal	26.9	24.8	27.1	25.1
EU average	26.7	24.1	29.6	27.3

1 Data are for 1990, not 1998.
Source: Eurostat

Family formation

Changes in fertility patterns influence the size of households and families, and also affect the age structure of the population. At the start of the 20th century there were about 115 live births per 1,000 women aged 15 to 44 in the United Kingdom. The fertility rate has fluctuated since then, falling until the 1930s, rising up to the 1960s and then falling again. Since the early 1980s the fertility rate has been relatively stable, though it has decreased gradually since 1996. In 2000 there were 55 births per 1,000 women of childbearing age in the United Kingdom.

Of all women born in England and Wales since the 1920s, those born around the mid-1930s had the largest families, with an average of 2.4 children per woman. Subsequent cohorts have had smaller families: those born in the early 1950s had a completed family size of just under 2.1 children. In the early 1970s fertility fell below the level needed for natural population change, to keep the population at a stable size, and has remained below that level since.

There were 774 thousand conceptions in England and Wales in 1999, a fall of nearly 3 per cent from 797 thousand on the previous year (Table 2.10). For women of all ages just over three-quarters of conceptions led to a maternity. This proportion has remained relatively stable at between 75 and 85 per cent over the past decade. Around nine out of ten conceptions within marriage resulted in a maternity compared with three-fifths of conceptions outside marriage. In 1999, just over half of conceptions were outside marriage compared with just under two-fifths of conceptions in 1987.

Around one-third of conceptions outside marriage are terminated in an abortion. The *1967 Abortion Act* permitted termination of pregnancy by a registered practitioner subject to certain conditions and was introduced in 1968. Following its introduction the number of abortions for women of all ages resident in England and Wales rose rapidly to 111 thousand in 1973. This fell to 102 thousand in 1976 but was followed by an upward trend through to 1990, after which numbers fell again each year to 1995.

Trends in abortion rates vary by age of the woman. Since 1969, abortion rates have risen particularly rapidly for young women (aged 16 to 24) (Chart 2.11). For women in these age groups, the rates were about four times higher in 2000 than in 1969, increasing from 6.1 abortions per thousand women aged 16 to 19 to 26.7 per thousand, and from 7.0 to 30.9 abortions per thousand women aged 20 to 24.

Table **2.10**

Conceptions[1]: by marital status and outcome

England & Wales   Percentages

	1987	1991	1995	1998	1999
Conceptions inside marriage leading to					
Maternities	56	52	49	44	44
Legal abortions[2]	5	4	4	4	4
Conceptions outside marriage leading to					
Maternities inside marriage	5	4	3	3	3
Maternities outside marriage	20	25	28	30	31
Legal abortions[2]	14	15	16	18	18
All conceptions (=100%) (thousands)	850	854	790	797	774

1 See Appendix, Part 2: Conceptions.
2 Legal terminations under the 1967 Abortion Act.
Source: Office for National Statistics

Chart **2.11**

Abortion rates[1]: by age

England & Wales

Rates per 1,000 women

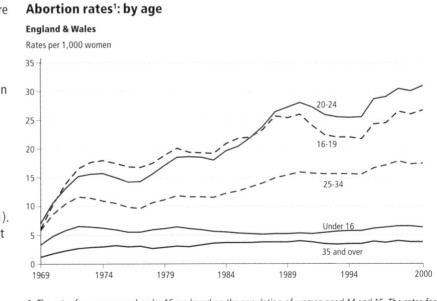

1 The rates for women aged under 16 are based on the population of women aged 14 and 15. The rates for women aged 35 and over are based on the population of women aged 35 to 49.
Source: Office for National Statistics

Table **2.12**

Fertility rates: by age of mother at childbirth

United Kingdom   Live births per 1,000 women

	1961	1971	1981	1991	2000
Under 20[1]	37	50	28	33	29
20–24	173	154	107	89	69
25–29	178	155	130	120	95
30–34	106	79	70	87	88
35–39	51	34	22	32	40
40 and over[2]	16	9	5	5	8
All ages[3]	91	84	62	64	55

1 Live births to women aged under 20 per 1,000 women aged 15 to 19.

2 Live births to women aged 40 and over per 1,000 women aged 40 to 44.

3 Total live births per 1,000 women aged 15 to 44.

Source: Office for National Statistics; General Register Office for Scotland; Northern Ireland Statistics and Research Agency

Fertility patterns have also varied by age. In general, fertility rates for older women have increased since the early 1980s while those for younger women have declined. The fertility rate for women aged 35 to 39 has risen fastest, nearly doubling between 1981 and 2000, although it still remains lower than in 1961 (Table 2.12). Women aged 25 to 29 are still the most likely to give birth, but since 1992 those in the 30 to 34 age group have been more likely to give birth than those aged 20 to 24. Increased female participation in higher education and the labour market, and the greater choice and effectiveness of contraception have encouraged the trend towards later childbearing and lower fertility.

Despite the overall trend towards later childbearing, the proportion of teenage girls becoming pregnant rose in the 1980s, after fluctuating during the 1970s. By 1990 there were 68 conceptions per 1,000 women aged 15 to 19 in England and Wales; in 1999 the rate was slightly lower at 63 (Table 2.13). In June 1999 the Social Exclusion Unit produced a report on teenage pregnancy and parenthood. One of the action points in the report was to halve the rate of conceptions of women aged under 18 in England by the year 2010. In 1999 the rate of conceptions to teenagers under 18 was 45 conceptions per 1,000 women aged 15 to 17 years. This rate has remained within the range of 42 to 48 conceptions for the last ten years. Three-fifths of conceptions to women aged under 20 in England and Wales in 1999 led to a maternity.

Table **2.13**

Teenage conception rates: by age at conception and outcome

England & Wales   Rates per 1,000 conceptions

	Leading to maternities						Leading to abortion				
	1971	1981	1991	1996	1999		1971	1981	1991	1996	1999
Age at conception											
Under 14[1]	0.5	0.4	0.5	0.6	0.5		0.5	0.7	0.7	0.8	0.7
14	2.8	1.7	2.6	2.7	2.4		2.4	2.9	3.5	3.6	3.3
15	13.5	7.1	9.8	11.0	9.0		6.9	8.7	9.3	9.4	9.2
All aged under 16[1]	5.5	3.1	4.3	4.8	3.9		3.2	4.1	4.6	4.7	4.4
16	41.0	21.5	25.0	27.1	24.0		13.0	16.2	17.1	17.9	18.8
17	68.5	36.7	41.5	42.5	40.8		15.2	20.1	22.7	24.1	25.9
18	95.0	54.6	57.0	56.5	53.5		16.7	21.6	26.6	29.2	30.3
19	114.5	73.0	66.2	66.5	61.6		16.4	21.0	28.6	31.4	32.4
All aged under 20[1]	67.3	38.9	42.0	40.4	38.6		14.3	18.2	22.1	23.0	24.3

1 Rates for girls aged under 14, under 16 and under 20 are based on the population of girls aged 13, 13 to 15 and 15 to 19, respectively.

Source: Office for National Statistics

Births to teenage mothers are particularly likely to take place outside marriage. In 2000 almost nine in ten live births to women aged under 20 in England and Wales occurred outside marriage. Mothers in this age group are also the most likely to have a birth outside marriage registered without the father's details: just over a quarter (27 per cent) of births to teenage mothers were registered solely by the mother. The teenage fertility rate in Scotland peaked in 1991 at 33.3 per 1,000 women aged 13 to 19 before falling by 13 per cent to reach 29.1 per 1,000 in 2000. In that year, 96 per cent of births to teenage girls occurred outside marriage, compared with 80 per cent in 1990.

With the exception of the periods immediately after the world wars, few births occurred outside marriage during the first 60 years of the 20th century. During the 1960s and 1970s this proportion rose and the increase became more rapid from the late 1970s onwards (Chart 2.14). Almost two-fifths of live births in Great Britain in 2000 occurred outside marriage, more than four times the proportion in 1975. Most of the increase in the number of births outside marriage since the late 1980s has been to cohabiting couples, that is parents living at the same address. In 2000 about four-fifths of births outside marriage were jointly registered by both parents; three-quarters of these births were to parents living at the same address.

In most European states there have been significant increases in recent decades in the proportions of births occurring outside of legal marriage, but there continue to be marked differences in the extent of non-marital childbearing between countries (Chart 2.15). The highest proportion of births outside marriage (over 40 per cent) occurred in northern European countries in 1999, compared with 10 per cent or fewer in the southern European countries of Italy (9 per cent) and Greece (4 per cent), and in Switzerland (10 per cent). Between these two extremes two broad groupings are distinguishable with proportions between 10 and 20 per cent and a set with 30 to 40 per cent which includes Ireland, Finland and the United Kingdom.

Chart **2.14**

Births outside marriage as a percentage of all live births

Great Britain

Percentages

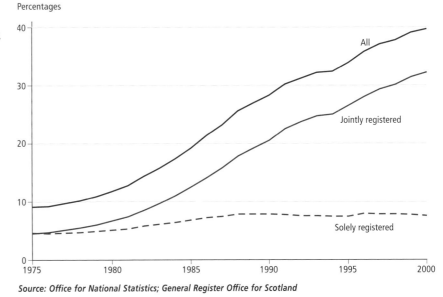

Source: Office for National Statistics; General Register Office for Scotland

Chart **2.15**

Percentage of births outside marriage: EU comparison 1980, 1990 and 1999

Births outside marriage per 100 births

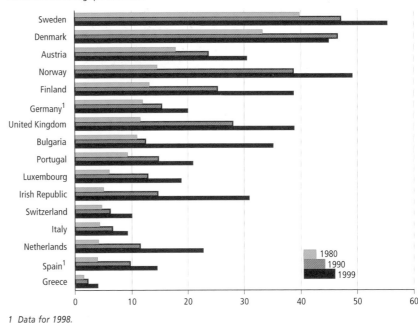

1 Data for 1998.

Source: Council of Europe

Table 2.16

Percentage of dependent children[1] living in different family types

Great Britain   Percentages

	1972	1981	1991–92	2001[2]
Couple families				
1 child	16	18	17	18
2 children	35	41	37	37
3 or more children	41	29	28	24
Lone mother families				
1 child	2	3	5	6
2 children	2	4	7	7
3 or more children	2	3	6	5
Lone father families				
1 child	–	1	–	1
2 or more children	1	1	1	1
All dependent children[3]	100	100	100	100

1 See Appendix, Part 2: Families.
2 At Spring 2001.
3 In Spring 2001, includes cases where the dependent child is a family unit, for example a foster child.
Source: General Household Survey and Labour Force Survey, Office for National Statistics

Table 2.17

Families with dependent children headed by lone parents[1]

Great Britain   Percentages

	1971	1981	1991	1999	2001[2]
Lone Mothers					
Single	1	2	6	8	9
Widowed	2	2	1	1	1
Divorced	2	4	6	6	6
Separated	2	2	4	4	4
All lone mothers	7	11	18	20	20
Lone fathers	1	2	1	2	2
All lone parents	8	13	19	22	22

1 Lone mothers (by their marital status) and lone fathers.
2 At Spring 2001.
Source: General Household Survey and Labour Force Survey, Office for National Statistics

Family relationships

Families and especially those with children are the focus for many policy issues. However, the type of family in which a child grows up has changed over the past 30 or so years, with an overall decrease in the percentages of dependent children living in couple families and an increase in those living in lone-parent families (Table 2.16). The traditional couple family remains the most common type of family in which dependent children live in Great Britain – 79 per cent lived in such a family in Spring 2001. The substantial rate of growth in lone parent families over the last 25 years appears to have stabilised in recent years. Lone parents headed around 22 per cent of all families with dependent children in Great Britain in Spring 2001, which was around three times the proportion in 1971 (Table 2.17). There was an increase in the number of lone parent families up to the mid-1980s after which there was a more rapid rise. However since 1999 the proportion of loan parent families has remained constant at 22 per cent. A large part of the increase up to the mid-1980s was due to divorce, whilst after 1986 the number of single lone mothers grew at a faster rate with the growth in the proportion of live births outside marriage. A loan mother heads the majority of loan parent families; a loan father heads around 10 per cent of lone parent families.

Different demographic structures, cultural traditions and economic characteristics of the various ethnic groups in Great Britain underlie distinctive patterns of family and household size and composition. In autumn 2000, of families with dependent children in Great Britain, nearly half of those headed by a Black person were lone parent families compared with one in 13 Indian families (Chart 2.18). Indian and Pakistani/Bangladeshi households tended to be larger than those from other ethnic groups, at 3.6 and 4.5 persons per household respectively. Such households may contain three generations with grandparents living with a married couple and their children.

As was seen earlier in the chapter, from the early 1970s there was an increase in the number of divorces following the implementation of the *Divorce Reform Act 1969*. The percentage of children experiencing divorce consequently increased (Chart 2.19). The number of children aged under 16 in England and Wales who experienced the divorce of their parents in England and Wales peaked at almost 176 thousand in 1993. Since then the number has fallen to 143 thousand in 2000 when around one in four children affected by divorce were under five years old and seven in ten were aged ten or under.

There is some evidence that experiencing divorce has an impact upon children's relationship formation later in life. Analyses of the National Child Development Study suggest that people who experience parental divorce during childhood are more likely to form partnerships at a younger age than those whose parents did not divorce. For example, 48 per cent of women born in 1958 who had experienced parental divorce during childhood had entered their first cohabiting partnership as a teenager, compared with 29 per cent of women brought up with both parents. Furthermore, by the age of 33, men and women born in 1958 who had experienced parental divorce were also more likely to have experienced partnership and marriage dissolution themselves.

Stepfamilies are one reflection of the diversity of family life that young people experience. Such family types may be formed when lone parents, whether single, separated or widowed, form new partnerships. According to the General Household Survey, in 1998–99 stepfamilies (married and cohabiting) where the head of the family was aged under 60 accounted for about 6 per cent of all families with dependent children in Great Britain. There is a tendency for children to remain with their mother after a partnership breaks up. Almost nine in ten stepfamilies consisted of a couple with at least one child from a previous relationship of the female partner.

Chart 2.18

Families with dependent children[1]: by ethnic group, Autumn 2000

Great Britain

Percentages

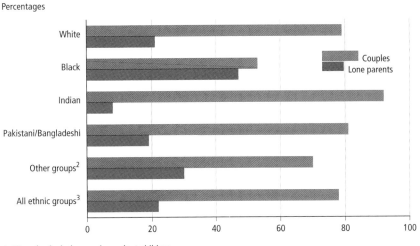

1 May also include non-dependent children.
2 Includes those of mixed origin.
3 Includes those who did not state their ethnic group.
Source: Labour Force Survey, Office for National Statistics

Chart 2.19

Children of couples divorced: by age of child

England and Wales

Thousands

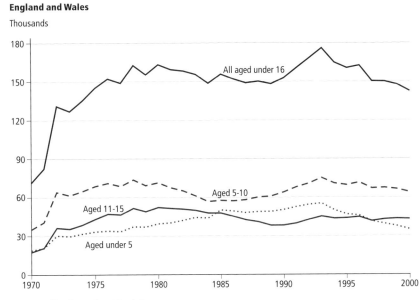

Source: Office for National Statistics

Chart **2.20**

Adoption orders

England and Wales

Thousands

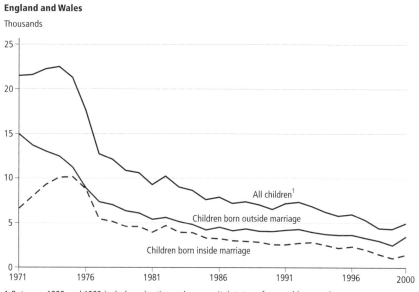

1 Between 1985 and 1989 includes adoptions where marital status of parent(s) was unknown.

Source: Office for National Statistics

Table **2.21**

Adoptions: by age of child

Great Britain

Percentages

	1981	1991	1995	1996	2000
Under 1	26	12	6	5	5
1–4	20	29	26	26	40
5–9	30	34	38	39	31
10–14	20	19	25	24	19
15–17	4	6	6	6	4
All ages (=100%)					
(thousands)	10.4	8.0	6.4	6.5	5.3

Source: Office for National Statistics; General Register Office for Scotland

Families may be formed or extended by the adoption of children. Since the early 1970s the number of adoptions each year has fallen in England and Wales so that the total of almost 5 thousand in 2000 was a quarter of the number at the peak 30 years earlier (Chart 2.20). In particular, the number of children available for adoption has fallen since the introduction of legal abortion. Other factors include the use of contraception and changes in attitudes towards lone parents. Children born outside marriage have always formed the majority of children adopted since 1971. There were also large falls in adoption in 1976 and 1977, following the implementation of the *1975 Children Act*. The percentage of all children adopted in Great Britain who were below the age of one decreased from 26 per cent in 1981 to 5 per cent in 2000: 275 babies below the age of one were adopted in 2000 (Table 2.21). The proportion of adopted children who were between the ages of 1 and 4 increased during the same time period from 20 per cent to 40 per cent; in 2000, 2,158 1 to 4 year olds were adopted.

This chapter has illustrated that families are constantly evolving as a result of life events such as childbirth or marital breakdown. Results from the BHPS show the different experiences of life course events in a one-year period by age group in 1998–99 (Table 2.22). While 96 per cent of people aged 65 and over had experienced no change in their family in the previous year, almost a third of 16-24 year olds had seen some change. The younger age groups are more likely to experience changes such as birth of a child, separation from a partner or joining a new partner, while people at older ages were more likely to experience the departure of a child or death of partner.

Analyses of the BHPS by Evandrou, Falkingham, Rake and Scott further examined the changes in living arrangements resulting from the experience of different life events for older people aged 60 and over. Bereavements were important at all ages over 60, but occurred more frequently to women than to men, reflecting women's longer life expectancy (Chart 2.23). For the most elderly people (aged 80 and over), more than half of all changes were a move into an institution. This was also more common for women than for men, partly due to their longevity and the previous experience of other major changes, such as bereavement.

In contrast, older men were twice as likely as older women to have younger people move out of their household. Men tend to marry women younger than themselves, and so were consequently less likely to experience bereavement in early old age, but more likely to have relatively young adult children. It might be expected that moving in with younger relatives would increase with age as the need for family care increases; however, this was not found in these analyses, with only 3 per cent of all changes involving such a move.

Table **2.22**

Adults'[1] experience of family change: by age group, 1998 to 1999

Great Britain | | | | | | Percentages

Age	16–24	25–34	35–44	45–54	55–64	65 and over
No change	69	78	89	83	91	96
Change						
Birth of child	5	9	3	0	0	0
Departure of child	0	1	3	12	5	0
Separation from partner	3	3	2	1	0	0
Death of partner	0	0	0	0	1	2
Join new partner	4	4	1	1	0	0
Other changes	19	6	3	2	2	2
All changes	31	22	11	17	9	4
All adults	100	100	100	100	100	100

1 Aged 16 and over.
Source: British Household Panel Survey, Institute for Social and Economic Research

Chart **2.23**

Changes in living arrangements in later life: by gender

Great Britain
Percentage of all changes

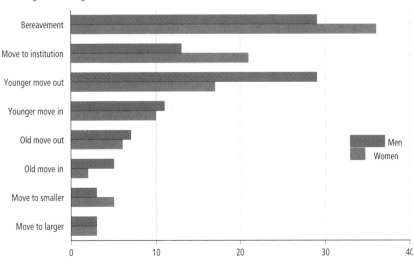

Source: London School of Economics and Kings College, London, from British Household Panel Survey

Websites

National Statistics	www.statistics.gov.uk
Labour Market Trends	www.statistics.gov.uk/products/p550.asp
Department for Transport, Local Government and the Regions	www.dtlr.gov.uk
ESRC Research Centre for Analysis of Social Exclusion, London School of Economics	www.sticerd.lse.ac.uk/case.htm
General Register Office for Scotland	www.gro-scotland.gov.uk
Institute for Social and Economic Research	www.iser.essex.ac.uk
National Assembly for Wales	www.wales.gov.uk
National Centre for Social Research	www.natcen.ac.uk
Northern Ireland Statistics Research Agency	www.nisra.gov.uk
Scottish Executive	www.scotland.gov.uk
Teenage Pregnancy Unit	www.teenagepregnancyunit.gov.uk
Eurostat	www.europa.eu.int/comm/eurostat

Contacts

Office for National Statistics	
Chapter author	020 7533 5798
Fertility	01329 813339
General Household Survey	020 7533 5444
Labour Market Enquiry Helpline	020 7500 6094
Marriages and Divorces	01329 813465
Department for Transport, Local Government And the Regions	0207 944 3303
Home Office Family Policy Unit	020 7217 8545
National Assembly of Wales	0209 2082 5055
Northern Ireland Statistics and Research Agency	0208 9034 8243
Institute for Social and Economic Research	01206 872957
ESRC Research Centre for Analysis of Social Exclusion, London School of Economics	0207 7955 6679
London School of Hygiene and Tropical Medicine	020 7299 4614
National centre for Social Research	020 7250 1866

Chapter 3

Education and training

Schools, pupils & staffing

- In 1970/71, 21 per cent of three and four year olds in the United Kingdom attended schools; by 2000/01 this had risen to 63 per cent. (Chart 3.2)

- In 2001, 96 per cent of primary and 99 per cent of secondary schools in England were connected to the Internet compared with 17 and 83 per cent respectively in 1998. (Chart 3.6)

Post-compulsory education

- In the United Kingdom there were nearly five times as many women enrolled on undergraduate courses in 2000/01 as in the early 1970s. The number of male undergraduates doubled over the period. (Table 3.13)

- In Spring 2001, of the 6.3 million people of working age in the United Kingdom who were studying towards a qualification, over half were aged between 16 and 24 while a quarter were aged 35 and over. (Table 3.14)

Educational attainment

- The proportion of young women in the United Kingdom achieving two or more A levels (or equivalent) has increased by around a fifth since 1995/96, to 39 per cent in 1999/00. For men the increase has been more modest, with a rise of 14 per cent over this period to 31 per cent. (Chart 3.18)

Lifelong learning & training

- In 2000, almost half of employers in the Yorkshire and Humber region had provided off the job training in the last 12 months, the highest proportion among the English regions, followed by 46 per cent of employers in the North West and East Midlands regions. The lowest proportions were in the West Midlands and East regions where 37 per cent of employers had provided such training. (Table 3.25)

- In November 2000, 1.1 million adults in England and Wales were enrolled on adult education courses (Table 3.27)

Table 3.1

School pupils[1]: by type of school[2]

United Kingdom   Thousands

	1970/71	1980/81	1990/91	1994/95	1998/99	1999/00	2000/01
Public sector schools[3]							
Nursery[4,5]	50	89	105	111	109	144	152
Primary[4]	5,902	5,171	4,955	5,230	5,374	5,337	5,298
Secondary							
Comprehensive[6]	1,313	3,730	2,843	3,093	3,207	3,266	3,340
Grammar	673	149	156	184	203	204	205
Modern	1,164	233	94	90	92	108	112
Other	403	434	300	289	291	282	260
All public sector schools	9,507	9,806	8,453	8,996	9,276	9,341	9,367
Non-maintained schools[3]	621	619	613	600	617	618	626
Special schools[7]	103	148	114	117	116	114	113
Pupil referral units	.	.	.	.	9	9	10
All schools	10,230	10,572	9,180	9,714	10,018	10,082	10,116

1 Headcounts

2 See Appendix, Part 3: Main categories of educational establishments and stages of education.

3 Excludes special schools.

4 Nursery classes within primary schools are included in primary schools except for Scotland
from 1990/91 when they are included in nursery schools.

5 Nursery schools figures for Scotland prior to 1998/99 only include data for Local Authority
pre-schools. Data thereafter include partnership pre-schools.

6 Excludes sixth form colleges from 1980/81.

7 Includes maintained and non-maintained sectors.

*Source: Department for Education and Skills; National Assembly for Wales; Scottish
Executive; Northern Ireland Department of Education*

Chart 3.2

Children under five[1] in schools as a percentage of all children ages three and four

United Kingdom

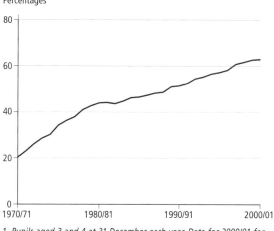

Percentages

1 Pupils aged 3 and 4 at 31 December each year. Data for 2000/01 for
Wales and Scotland relate to 1999/00.

*Source: Department for Education and Skills; National Assembly for
Wales; Scottish Executive; Northern Ireland Department of Education*

For increasing numbers of people, their experience of formal education is no longer confined to their years of school. Early learning and participation in pre-school education is seen as being vital in building important foundations for future learning in schools. More people continue in education beyond school, and many return to education later in their lives.

Qualifications attained at school are increasingly supplemented by further education and training to equip people with the ever-changing skills required by modern employment.

Schools, pupils and staffing

The number of children of school age in the United Kingdom has fluctuated due to factors such as the raising of the school-leaving age and changes in the birth rate. The declining birth rates during the late 1970s led to a fall in pupil numbers in the 1980s and early 1990s. Since then, pupil numbers have continued to increase but they are still below the peak level of the 1970s.

There have also been changes in the structure of secondary education. Prior to the introduction of comprehensive schools in England and Wales, children were required to take the '11 plus' which determined whether they would attend a grammar or secondary modern school. In England and Wales the '11 plus' had largely been abolished by the late 1960s when comprehensive schools replaced grammar and secondary modern schools. Comprehensive schools were introduced with the aim of providing equality of opportunity for children of all abilities. In 2000/01, 85 per cent of pupils attending secondary schools in the United Kingdom attended comprehensives while only 5 per cent went to grammar schools and 3 per cent attended secondary modern schools; this compares with 37 per cent, 19 per cent and 33 per cent respectively in 1970/71 (Table 3.1). All secondary schools in Scotland and Wales are comprehensive in nature.

In recent years there has been a major expansion of pre-school education with an increased emphasis on children beginning school with a basic foundation in literacy and numeracy. In 1970/71, 21 per cent of three and four year olds in the United Kingdom attended schools; by 2000/01 this had risen to 63 per cent (Chart 3.2). In addition, there are other forms of pre-school education which children attend. In January 2001, 28 per cent of three and four year olds in the United Kingdom were enrolled in non-school education settings in the private and voluntary sector, such as local playgroups.

A survey on the use of nursery education and childcare by children aged three and four in England conducted between Summer 1999 and Spring 2000 found that there were many reasons parents chose a particular pre-school provider. Table 3.3 shows that about half of parents chose their main or sole provider because it was local and around a third said it was easy to get to. On the educational side, around two-fifths of parents reported they had chosen the provider because it had a good reputation, while 13 per cent mentioned that the provider was attached to their chosen school and so would provide a continuity of education for their child.

Class sizes in primary schools have for some years been seen as an issue in the drive to improve standards and reductions have been made, although regional differences do exist. In 2000/01, the average class size for key stage 1 pupils (5 to 7 year olds) in Great Britain was 25 pupils and 28 pupils for key stage 2 pupils (8 to 11 year olds) (Table 3.4). Overall key stage 2 pupils were more likely to be in classes of more than 31 pupils than key stage 1 pupils, 28 per cent and 4 per cent respectively. Regional differences exist: around 65 per cent of key stage 2 classes in the South West, North West and the East Midlands had 30 or fewer pupils in 2000/01 compared with 90 per cent in Northern Ireland and 85 per cent in Scotland.

Table **3.3**

Parents reasons[1] for choosing main or sole nursery education provider[2], used in Spring term 2000

England	Percentages
Social & Environmental	
Local	49
Easy to get to	30
Offered suitable hours	4
To get to know other local children	8
Only one available	8
Provides care for the whole day	3
Educational	
Good reputation	41
Recommended to me	18
Attached to school of choice/ continuity of primary education	13
Well qualified staff	10
Children learn a lot there	12
Good facilities	12
Most appropriate for my child's age	6
High staff:child ratio	6
Personal	
Siblings went there	30
Know other children there	13

1 Parents could state more than one reason, thus, percentages do not add to 100 per cent.

2 Nursery education providers covered are nursery schools, nursery classes, reception classes, special day schools and nurseries, day nurseries, playgroups and pre-schools, and combined centres.

Source: National Centre for Social Research, for Department for Education and Skills

Table **3.4**

Class sizes in primary schools[1]: by region, 2000/01

	Key stage 1[2]		Key stage 2[2]		All primary schools	
	Average number in class	Percentage of classes with 31 or more pupils	Average number in class	Percentage of classes with 31 or more pupils	Average number in class	Percentage of classes with 31 or more pupils
Great Britain	25.2	3.7	27.7	28.1	26.5	17.3
North East	24.5	1.8	27.2	25.6	25.9	15.2
North West	25.0	3.4	28.3	36.7	26.8	21.8
Yorkshire and the Humber	25.1	3.9	28.0	30.4	26.8	19.5
East Midlands	24.8	2.8	28.3	34.3	26.8	20.7
West Midlands	25.1	3.6	27.8	29.0	26.6	17.7
East	25.2	3.3	27.8	28.5	26.5	16.6
London	26.8	3.8	27.7	18.2	27.2	12.2
South East	25.8	4.0	28.2	30.8	27.1	18.8
South West	25.4	3.0	28.3	35.8	26.8	20.4
England	25.4	3.4	28.0	29.9	26.8	18.2
Wales	24.1	4.7	26.7	23.6	25.4	14.9
Scotland[2,3]	23.9	5.1	25.2	14.8	24.4	11.1
Northern Ireland[3]	23.1	2.6	24.6	10.4	23.7	5.8

1 Maintained schools only. Figures relate to all classes - not just those taught by one teacher. In Northern Ireland a class is defined as a group of pupils normally under the control of one teacher.

2 In Scotland primary P1-P3 is interpreted to be key stage 1 and P4-P7, key stage 2.

3 Pupils in composite classes which overlap key stage 1 and key stage 2 are included in the 'All primary schools' total, but are excluded from all other categories.

Source: Department for Education and Skills; National Assembly for Wales; Scottish Executive; Northern Ireland Department of Education

In an annual survey conducted by the National Foundation for Educational Research, head teachers were asked what their views were on optimum class sizes for single-age and mixed-age classes at reception, key stage 1 and key stage 2 with responses ranging from 20 to 25 pupils per class.

There has been an increase in the number of non-teaching staff who provide additional learning support within the classroom. In England, between 1996 and 2001 there was a 56 per cent increase in the number of non-teaching staff (Table 3.5).

Between 1989 and 1996 the National Curriculum was introduced in England and Wales with the aim of ensuring that children receive a comparable and balanced programme of study throughout their compulsory schooling. The subjects taught to children between the ages of 5 and 16 in state schools are to a large extent determined by the National Curriculum, which has four key stages. The core subjects of the National Curriculum, compulsory at each of the four stages, are English (and Welsh in Wales), mathematics, science and physical education (in England). The second level of curriculum comprises the so-called 'foundation' subjects, such as history, geography, art, music, technology and physical education (in Wales).

A modern foreign language is added to the curriculum at key stage 3. At key stage 4, the study of many of the 'foundation' subjects becomes optional. Northern Ireland has its own common curriculum, which is similar but not identical to the National Curriculum in England and Wales.

Unlike England and Wales, there is no statutory national curriculum in Scotland. Pupils aged 5 to 14 study a broad curriculum based on national guidelines which set out the aims of study, the ground to be covered and the way the pupils' learning should be assessed and reported. Progress is measured by attainment of six levels based on the expectation of the performance of the majority of pupils on completion of certain stages between the ages of 5 and 14: Primary 3 (age 7/8), Primary 4 (age 8/9), Primary 7 (age 11/12) and Secondary 2 (age 13/14). It is recognised that pupils learn at different rates and some will reach the various levels before others. The curriculum areas are language; mathematics; environmental studies; expressive arts; and religious and moral education with personal and social development and health education. Achievement at these stages is discussed in the section on educational attainment on page 60.

Table 3.5

Number of Non-Teaching Staff[1,2]: by type of school

England   Thousands

	1996	1997	1998	1999	2000	2001
Nursery	2.1	2.2	2.1	2.2	2.3	2.4
Primary[3]	50.6	54.1	58.1	61.7	68.7	83.1
Secondary[3]	23.1	24.9	26.5	28.8	31.8	37.3
Special[4]	15.2	15.7	16.6	17.1	18.1	19.2
Pupil Referral Units	0.3	0.4	0.4	0.5	0.7	0.7
Total Non-Teaching Staff	91.4	97.3	103.8	110.3	121.5	142.7

1 Includes both full-time and the full-time equivalent of part-time non-teaching staff.
2 Includes teaching assistants, technicians and other non-administrative staff.
3 Includes middle schools as deemed.
4 Includes non-maintained special schools, special and general hospital schools.
Source: Department for Education and Skills

Society is becoming increasingly dependent on technological knowledge and skills, as is the labour market. Students with little or no exposure to Information Communications Technology (ICT) in schools may face difficulties in making the transition to the modern labour market. Computers have been widespread as resources for learning in schools since the 1980s, and ICT has been part of the National Curriculum since 1990. Chart 3.6 shows results from the 1998 to 2001 ICT surveys of schools in England. Over this period there has been a considerable increase in the percentage of schools connected to the Internet. In 2001, 96 per cent of primary and 99 per cent of secondary schools in England were connected compared with 17 and 83 per cent respectively in 1998.

For a child to succeed and progress through the education system, learning needs to continue outside of lesson time and homework is seen by many as an important aspect of this. In a study conducted in 1997 by the Office for Standards in Education (OfSTED) pupils in England were asked who helped them with their homework (Table 3.7). Overwhelmingly, parents were the most frequent source of help, for pupils of all ages. Pupils were more likely to look for help from friends as they got older, with over half of key stage 3 pupils doing so. It should be noted that these data were collected prior to the introduction in November 1998 of the Department's homework guidelines for primary and secondary schools. These guidelines are intended to help schools work in partnership with parents to develop good practice in planning and managing homework.

In order for parents to be able to support and help children with their schoolwork they have to have adequate literacy and numeracy skills themselves. Family learning programmes have been devised in which adults and children come together, to work and learn collaboratively. The most common examples of family learning are family literacy and numeracy schemes, although there is also a small number of programmes which cover wider subjects such as: arts and crafts, ICT, music, cookery, and language teaching. OfSTED carried out a survey of family learning in a number of local authorities in England and found that adult participants experienced increased confidence in contact with schools, and their children's teachers, and had a readiness to take a more active role with schools in their children's learning.

Chart **3.6**

Access to the Internet: by type of school[1]

England

Percentages

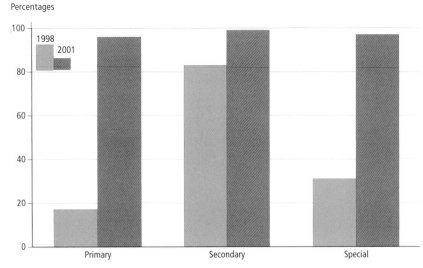

1 See Appendix, Part 3: Main categories of educational establishments and stages of education.

Source: Department for Education and Skills

Table **3.7**

Sources of help with homework, Autumn 1997

England   Percentages

	Key stage 2 pupils	Key stage 3 pupils
Mother and/or father	92	88
Brothers and/or sisters	33	41
Teachers	41	39
Friends	35	54
Grandparents or other relations	37	24
No response	2	2

Source: KS2/KS3 Pupil Survey, OFSTED

Table **3.8**

Permanent exclusions from schools: by gender

England   Thousands

	Males	Females	All as a percentage of school population[1]
1995/96	10.4	2.1	0.17
1996/97	10.5	2.1	0.17
1997/98	10.3	2.0	0.16
1998/99	8.6	1.8	0.14
1999/00	7.0	1.3	0.11

1 *The number of permanent exclusions expressed as a percentage of the number (headcount) of full and part-time pupils of all ages (excluding dually registered pupils in special schools) in January each year.*
Source: Department for Education and Skills

Chart **3.9**

Percentage of exclusions[1]: by reason, 1999/00

Scotland

Percentages

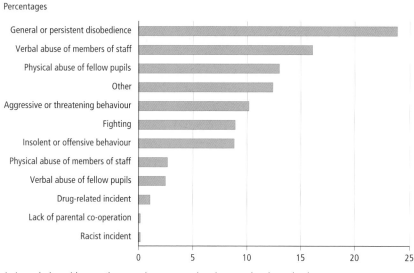

1 *An exclusion with more than one circumstance given is counted under each relevant category.*
Source: Scottish Executive Education Department

There has been growing awareness and concern over the number of children outside the education system. Some have been excluded from schools, while others truant. In 1999/00, over 8 thousand children in England were permanently excluded from schools (Table 3.8). The number of boys excluded outnumbered girls by over five to one. Between 1997/98 and 1999/00 the number of pupils permanently excluded from schools in England declined by four thousand. The highest exclusion rates in England in 1999/00 were among Black Caribbean pupils, with 46 in every 10 thousand pupils of compulsory school age being excluded compared with only 1 in every 10 thousand Chinese pupils.

The Youth Cohort Study (YCS) found that only 17 per cent of those who had been excluded in years 10 or 11 in England and Wales attained five or more GCSE grades A* to C in comparison with 53 per cent of those who had not been excluded. Persistent truants and those excluded from school were also found to be much more likely to achieve no GCSEs A* to G than young people who had not truanted or been excluded.

The Scottish Executive Education Department produces an annual survey on exclusion from schools, including the reasons for it. Chart 3.9 shows that in 1999/00, 24 per cent of all exclusions in Scotland were due to general or persistent disobedience, followed by verbal abuse of members of staff and physical abuse of fellow pupils, 16 per cent and 13 per cent respectively.

In the last decade or so, there have been changes in the number of nursery and primary, and secondary school teachers in the United Kingdom. Between 1984/85 and 1999/00 the number of full-time female nursery primary teachers in the United Kingdom increased from 159 thousand to 179 thousand while the number of male teachers declined from 42 thousand to 33 thousand over the same period (Chart 3.10). In nursery and primary schools females represented the majority of all full-time primary school teachers, while in secondary schools, the gender split between full-time teachers is more balanced. However, the number of male full-time secondary school teachers has fallen more than for female teachers, with most of the decline occurring in the 1980s.

There have also been changes in the age structure of the teaching profession. For example, the proportion of women secondary school teachers aged under 40 declined from three-fifths in 1986 to around two-fifths in 2000. These changes in the age structure reflect a large cohort of teachers recruited in the 1970s, with smaller numbers of teachers recruited since then.

Post-compulsory education

At age 16 young people are faced with the choice of whether to remain in education, go into training or seek employment. Over the last decade young people have become more likely to continue with their education. In 1998/99, around 78 per cent of young people aged 16 to 17 in Great Britain were in education or training compared with 75 per cent in 1995/96.

There are many factors which contribute to the decision taken by young people to continue with their education beyond school leaving age. Analyses undertaken by the YCS show that young people with at least one parent holding a degree are much more likely to be studying for A/AS levels than those with parents holding A levels as their highest qualification, 63 per cent and 44 per cent respectively (Table 3.11). These young people in turn are more likely to be studying A/AS levels than those with parents not having A levels (29 per cent). The study also found that young people with parents in unskilled manual occupations are less likely than those from managerial/professional occupations to be studying for A/AS levels.

However, the YCS also found that young people whose parents were in unskilled manual occupations achieved the largest rise in attainment between 1989 and 2000, with 30 per cent of this group achieving 5 or more GCSEs A* to C in 2000 compared with 12 per cent in 1989. There were also marked increases for the skilled manual and semi-skilled manual groups (from 21 per cent in 1989 to 45 per cent in 2000 and from 16 per cent in 1989 to 36 per cent in 2000 respectively).

Chart **3.10**

Full-time nursery & primary and secondary school teachers[1]: by gender

United Kingdom

Thousands

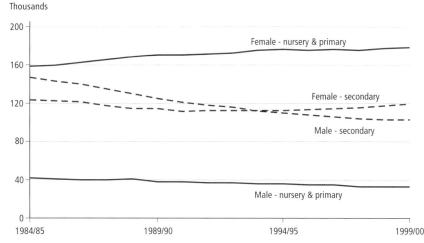

1 Qualified teachers only. As at 31 March of each year.

Source: Department for Education and Skills, National Assembly for Wales; Scottish Executive; Northern Ireland Department of Education

Table **3.11**

Main study aim of 16 year olds: by parents' qualifications, 2000

England & Wales   Percentages

	At least one parent with		Neither parent with
	Degree	A level	A Level
GCE A/AS level	63	44	29
Advanced GNVQ	6	9	8
NVQ 3 and other equivalent	3	5	5
GCSE	2	2	3
Intermediate/Foundation GNVQ	7	9	13
NVQ 1/2 and other equivalent	6	10	12
Level unclear/not stated	2	3	5
Any qualification	89	82	75

Source: Youth Cohort Study, Department for Education and Skills

Chart **3.12**

GCE A level or equivalent entries[1]: by selected subject and gender 1999/00

United Kingdom
Percentages

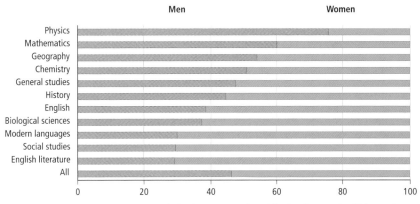

1 SCE H grade in Scotland. For 1999/00 includes the new Scottish qualification framework which contains different subject categories to those previously used. The new Intermediate 1 and 2 qualifications (which overlap with Standard Grades and Highers) are not included in the table.

Source: Department for Education and Skills; National Assembly for Wales; Scottish Executive; Northern Ireland Department of Education

Table **3.13**

Students[1] in higher education[2]: by type of course and gender

United Kingdom Thousands

	Undergraduate		Postgraduate		All higher education
	Full time	Part time	Full time	Part time	
Males					
1970/71	241	127	33	15	416
1980/81	277	176	41	32	526
1990/91	345	193	50	50	638
2000/01	511	228	82	118	940
Females					
1970/71	173	19	10	3	205
1980/81	196	71	21	13	301
1990/91	319	148	34	36	537
2000/01	602	320	81	124	1,128

1 Home and overseas students.

2 At December each year. Includes Open University.

Source: Department for Education and Skills; National Assembly for Wales; Scottish Executive; Northern Ireland Department for Employment and Learning

There is a wide variety of choice of subjects to study for those who continue with their education although gender differences in subject choice do exist, with fewer young women than men taking A level courses in mathematics or physics (Chart 3.12). In 1999/00, 76 per cent of 16 to 18 year olds entered for A level physics and 60 per cent for mathematics in the United Kingdom were men. In comparison, 71 per cent of those entered for social studies or English Literature were women.

Alongside the increases in the proportions of young people staying on in education after the age of 16 there have also been substantial increases in the number of students going onto higher education in the United Kingdom. The number of enrolments by men on all undergraduate courses more than doubled between 1970/71 and 2000/01 (Table 3.13). For women the increase was even more dramatic, with nearly five times as many enrolments on undergraduate courses in 2000/01 as in the early 1970s. In 2000/01 there were 2.1 million students in higher education, 55 per cent of whom were women.

Not everyone working towards a qualification beyond the age of 16 will have worked their way continuously through the various levels of education. Table 3.14 shows that of the 6.4 million people of working age who were studying towards a qualification in the United Kingdom in Spring 2001, over half were aged between 16 and 24 while a quarter were aged 35 and over.

Age composition differs widely from qualification to qualification. For example, in Spring 2001, while the majority of those studying towards an A level or equivalent were in the 16 to 24 age group, almost a fifth were aged 25 and over. Among those taking higher education qualifications below degree level, around three-fifths were aged 25 and over, while among those studying for degrees or equivalent, over two-fifths were aged 25 and over.

Educational attainment

School pupils in England and Wales are formally assessed at three key stages before GCSE level – at the ages of 7, 11 and 14. The assessment at all three key stages covers the core subjects of English (and Welsh in Wales), mathematics and science. The purpose of these tests is to help inform teachers and parents about the progress of individual pupils and to give a measure of the performance of schools. There are two forms of assessment: tests and teacher assessment. Pupils' attainment is shown as a level on the national curriculum scale. A typical 7 year old is

Table **3.14**

People working towards a qualification[1]: by age, Spring 2001

United Kingdom   Percentages[2]

	Degree or higher and equivalent	Higher education[3]	GCE A level/ NVQ3 or equivalent	GCSE/ NVQ2 or equivalent	Other qualification[4]	Total working towards any qualification
16–24	58	39	79	72	22	52
25–34	21	26	9	11	30	20
35–44	14	23	7	10	26	16
45–54	6	11	4	6	18	9
55–59/64	1	2	1	..	4	2
All aged 16–59/64 (=100%)(thousands)[5]	1,777	564	1,272	889	1,827	6,373

1 For those working towards more than one qualification the highest is recorded.
2 Percentages are based on the total studying towards each qualification group.
3 Below degree level but including NVQ4.
4 Includes those who did not state which qualifications.
5 Working age is defined as males aged 16–64 and females aged 16–59.
Source: Department for Education and Skills from the Labour Force Survey

expected to achieve level two, a typical 11 year old level four, and a typical 14 year old between levels five and six. A similar system of key stage assessment exists in Northern Ireland. However, in Northern Ireland key stage one is assessed at age 8, and at key stages one and two there is only teacher assessment.

In 2001, the proportion of boys in England reaching the required standard for English, at all key stages was lower than for girls, particularly at key stages 2 and 3 (Table 3.15). However, similar proportions of boys and girls reached the expected level in tests for mathematics and science at all key stages. The proportion of pupils achieving the expected level generally reduced with age for both genders (the same was also true of Wales). At key stage 1, for example, over 80 per cent of both boys and girls achieved the expected level in English. By key stage 3, this had fallen to 74 per cent of girls and 57 per cent of boys. In science, almost 9 out of 10 of key stage 1 pupils reached the expected level, compared with two-thirds of those at key stage 3. In Northern Ireland, in 2000, there were smaller differences between boys and girls in key stage 1 teacher assessments, 92 per cent and 97 per cent respectively achieving the expected levels in English and 94 and 96 per cent in mathematics. In contrast, a greater gender difference was seen between boys and girls in key stage 2 and key stage 3 teacher assessments in English.

Table **3.15**

Pupils reaching or exceeding expected standards[1]: by key stage and gender, 2001

England   Percentages

	Teacher assessment		Tests	
	Males	Females	Males	Females
Key stage 1[2]				
English	81	89	.	.
Reading	80	88	80	88
Writing	79	88	82	90
Mathematics	87	90	90	92
Science	88	90	.	.
Key stage 2[3]				
English	67	78	70	80
Mathematics	73	74	71	70
Science	81	83	87	88
Key stage 3[4]				
English	57	74	56	73
Mathematics	67	70	65	67
Science	63	66	66	66

1 See Appendix, Part 3: The National Curriculum: assessments and tests.
2 Percentage of pupils achieving level 2 or above at key stage 1.
3 Percentage of pupils achieving level 4 or above at key stage 2.
4 Percentage of pupils achieving level 5 or above at key stage 3.
Source: Department for Education and Skills

Table **3.16**

Examination achievements[1] of pupils[2] in schools: by gender and ethnic origin, 2000

England & Wales   Percentages

	5 or more GCSEs grades A* to C	1–4 GCSEs grades A* to C	No graded GCSEs
Males			
White	45	26	5
Black	31	31	6
Indian	54	25	0
Pakistani/Bangladeshi	22	34	4
Other groups[3]	40	24	15
All males	44	26	5
Females			
White	55	25	3
Black	46	29	5
Indian	66	21	2
Pakistani/Bangladeshi	37	35	4
Other groups[3]	44	22	14
All females	54	25	4

1 See Appendix, Part 3: Qualifications.
2 Pupils aged 16.
3 Includes those who did not state their ethnic group.
Source: Youth Cohort Study, Department for Education and Skills

From the age of 14 onwards young people study for public examinations, which, for some, mark the end of their compulsory education. In England, Wales and Northern Ireland young people aged 15 and 16 sit GCSEs and Standard Grades are taken in Scotland.

In 2000, 44 per cent of boys and 54 per cent of girls achieved 5 or more GCSEs graded A* to C in England and Wales. Girls do as well as, or outperform, boys in all ethnic groups (Table 3.16). A greater proportion of Indian boys and girls achieved five or more GCSE grades A* to C than those in any other group. The greatest difference in performance between boys and girls is for pupils from the Black and Bangladeshi/ Pakistani groups.

These differences between ethnic groups follow a similar pattern when the highest qualification is looked at. In 2000/01, 14 per cent of men from the White group in Great Britain held no qualification compared with 20 per cent from the Indian/Pakistani/ Bangladeshi group (Table 3.17). The gap between corresponding figures for women was bigger, at 18 per cent and 29 per cent respectively.

Table **3.17**

Highest qualification held[1]: by gender and ethnic group, 2000–01[2]

Great Britain   Percentages

	Degree or equivalent	Higher education[3]	GCE A-level or equivalent	GCSE grades A* to C or equivalent	Other qualification	No qualifications	All
Males							
White	17	8	31	18	13	14	100
Black	16	9	20	17	22	16	100
Indian/Pakistani/Bangladeshi	20	4	16	15	24	20	100
Other groups[4]	23	5	18	12	30	12	100
All	17	7	30	18	13	15	100
Females							
White	13	10	17	28	14	18	100
Black	14	11	18	22	21	15	100
Indian/Pakistani/Bangladeshi	13	5	14	16	23	29	100
Other groups[4]	18	10	14	13	30	15	100
All	14	9	17	27	14	18	100

1 Males aged 16 to 64, females aged 16 to 59.
2 Combined quarters: Spring 2000 to Winter 2000–01.
3 Below degree level.
4 Includes those who did not state their ethnic group.
Source: Department for Education and Skills from the Labour Force Survey

There has been an increase in the proportion of young men and women in the United Kingdom achieving two or more A levels (or equivalent) (Chart 3.18). The proportion of young women who achieved this has increased by around a fifth since 1995/96, to 39 per cent in 1999/00. The increase in the proportion of young men achieving this has been more modest, with a rise of 14 per cent over this period to 31 per cent.

Graduation rates vary across the European Union. In 1999, the United Kingdom had the highest graduation rate from first degrees in the European Union at 37 per cent, followed by Finland and the Netherlands, whose rates were both around 34 per cent (Chart 3.19). The graduation rate in Austria was 12 per cent, lower than in any other country in the EU. A possible explanation for the varying graduation levels in different countries is the variation in the provision of vocational education and apprenticeships which may reduce the perceived need of some students to enrol in formal university-level studies as preparation for work.

As Table 3.17 shows the highest qualification held by individuals is related to a number of factors such as ethnic group and Table 3.20 shows highest qualification in relation to gender and age. In Spring 2001, males in the United Kingdom were nearly twice as likely as females to be qualified to GCE A level (or equivalent) standard, the greatest difference between the genders. In respect to age, both males and females aged 55 to 59/64 were the most likely to hold no qualifications, the difference being more pronounced for females.

While many people have enjoyed the benefits of education, there are some who have problems with basic literacy and numeracy. Basic skills are essential to functioning in most areas of modern life. Those whose basic skills are poor suffer from a wide range of disadvantage. Men tend to enter into unskilled casual jobs and unemployment; women leave the labour market early.

In 1996, Great Britain participated in the International Adult Literacy Survey, which examined the levels of literacy of people aged 16 to 65. Literacy was measured on three scales: prose, document and quantitative. Prose literacy is the ability to understand such things as newspaper articles and passages of fiction; document literacy involves the ability to locate and use information in graphs, timetables and charts, and quantitative literacy is the ability to apply arithmetic operations, such as calculating the interest on your bank account. Performance was grouped into five literacy levels with level 1 being the lowest and level 5 being the highest. The Organisation for Economic Co-operation and Development considers level 3 to be the minimum level required to cope with modern life and work (see also Appendix Part 3: Literacy levels).

Chart **3.18**

Achievement at GCE A level[1] or equivalent: by gender[2]

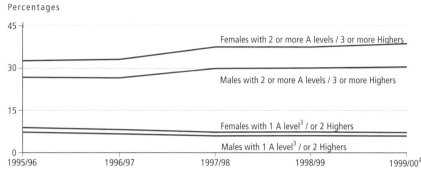

United Kingdom

Percentages

Females with 2 or more A levels / 3 or more Highers

Males with 2 or more A levels / 3 or more Highers

Females with 1 A level[3] / or 2 Highers

Males with 1 A level[3] / or 2 Highers

1 2 AS levels count as 1 A level pass.

2 Pupils in schools and students in further education institutions aged 16-18 at the start of the academic year in England, Wales and Northern Ireland as a percentage of the 17 year old population. Pupils in Scotland generally sit Highers one year earlier and the figures tend to relate to the results of pupils in Year S5/S6.

3 Includes those with 1.5 A level passes.

4 From 1999/00 National Qualifications (NQ) were introduced in Scotland. NQs include Standard Grades, Intermediate 1 & 2 and Higher Grades. The figures for Higher Grades combine the new NQ Higher and the old SCE Higher.

Source: Department for Education and Skills; National Assembly for Wales; Scottish Executive; Northern Ireland Department of Education

Chart **3.19**

Graduation rates from first university degrees: EU comparison, 1999

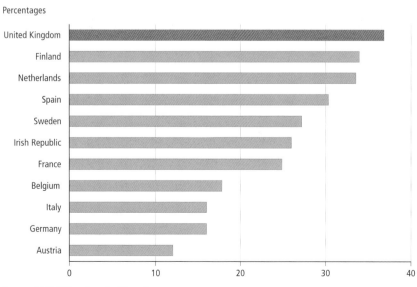

Percentages

Source: OECD "Education at a Glance"

Table **3.20**

Highest qualification[1]: by gender and age, Spring 2001

United Kingdom   Percentages

	Degree or equivalent	Higher education[2]	GCE A-level or equivalent	GCSE Grades A* to C or equivalent	Other qualifi- cation	No qualifi- cations	All
Males							
16–24	8	4	30	34	10	15	100
25–34	22	8	26	20	15	9	100
35–44	19	8	30	16	14	12	100
45–54	19	9	33	11	13	16	100
55–64	13	7	31	8	14	25	100
All males	17	7	30	18	13	15	100
Females							
16–24	8	4	30	37	8	13	100
25–34	20	9	18	29	13	10	100
35–44	15	11	15	29	14	15	100
45–54	12	11	12	20	17	26	100
55–59	7	10	10	17	20	37	100
All females	14	9	17	27	14	18	100

1 Males aged 16 to 64, females aged 16 to 59.
2 Below degree level.
Source: Department for Education and Skills from the Labour Force Survey

Table **3.21**

Document literacy level of adults[1]: by gender and age, 1996

Great Britain   Percentages

	Males			Females		
	16–49	50–65	All aged 16–65	16–49	50–65	All aged 16–65
Level 1	15	31	20	22	40	27
Level 2	24	29	25	30	30	29
Level 3	33	28	31	31	24	30
Level 4/5	28	12	24	17	6	15
All	100	100	100	100	100	100

1 Level 1 is the lowest level of literacy; level 4/5 is the highest. See Appendix, Part 3: Literacy levels.
Source: Adult Literacy Survey, Office for National Statistics

In general, a greater proportion of women than men in Great Britain had lower levels of both document and quantitative literacy, although there was little difference on the prose scale. In addition, a greater proportion of those aged 50 to 65 than those aged under 50 had lower levels on all three types of literacy scales. On the document scale a higher proportion of both older women and men scored at the lower levels of 1 and 2 (Table 3.21).

Lifelong learning & training

In recent years there has been a focus on the concept of 'lifelong learning'. National Learning targets for England have been set which state that by 2002, 85 per cent of 19 year olds should be qualified to NVQ level 2 or its equivalent and that 60 per cent of 21 year olds should be qualified to NVQ level 3 or its equivalent. Some progress has been made towards the targets. In 2001, more female 19 year olds than males of the same age had met the targets for 19 year olds, 78 per cent and 74 per cent respectively (Chart 3.22), whereas for 21 year old males and females there was only a 1 percentage point difference between those who met the target, 54 per cent and 55 per cent respectively.

In addition to these targets for young people, a set of targets also exist for economically active adults of working age. The first states that by the year 2002, 50 per cent of the workforce should be qualified to NVQ level 3 or its equivalent, while the second states that 28 per cent of the workforce should have a professional, vocational, management or academic qualification at NVQ level 4 or above by the same year. In 2001, a greater proportion of economically active adult males than females held NVQ level 3 qualifications, 51 per cent and 42 per cent respectively. However, similar proportions of adult economically active males and females held NVQ level 4 qualifications.

Wales also has National Lifelong Learning targets, although it should be noted that the targets and the way in which they are monitored are different to England. In particular, a four quarter average of data is used from the Labour Force Survey and the adult targets relate to the whole adult population (aged 18–59/64) and not to those economically active. Also the targets only relate to persons and not to men and women seperately.

One of the Lifelong learning targets for Wales is that the number of 16 to 18 year olds without qualifications is to reduce from some 1 in 5 in 1996 to 1 in 10 by 2002 and 1 in 20 by 2004. In 2000, the percentage of 16 to 18 year olds in Wales with no qualifications was estimated as 10 per cent (approximately 8.6 thousand persons), 3 percentage points lower than in the previous year and 7 percentage points lower than in 1996. For adults the target for the proportion of adults of working age without qualifications is to reduce from some 1 in 4 in 1996 to 1 in 7 by 2001 and to fewer than 1 in 8 by 2004. In 2000 the percentage of adults who have no qualifications was estimated at 19 per cent, about 1 in 5, 1 percentage point lower than the previous year and 4 percentage points lower than in 1996. This represents almost a third of a million adults of working age.

There are various options available to young people who decide not to continue in full-time education, including a number of government-supported training initiatives. In England and Wales, Work-based Training for Young People (WBTYP) was introduced in 1998 (replacing Youth Training) with the aim of ensuring that all young people have access to post-compulsory education or training. Included within this initiative are Advanced Modern Apprenticeships (AMAs) and Foundation Modern Apprenticeships (it should be noted that AMAs and FMAs are called Modern Apprenticeships and National Traineeships in Wales). AMAs are aimed at developing technical, supervisory and craft-level skills among 16 to 24 year olds. In March 2001 there were 266 thousand young people on Work-based Training Schemes in England.

Some apprenticeship sectors are highly gender specific. By June 2001, almost all apprenticeship participants in England in the areas of construction, electrical installation engineering and motor industry were men (Chart 3.23). In contrast, men were greatly outnumbered by women in hairdressing, health and social care.

Chart **3.22**

National Learning Targets[1]: by gender

England

Percentages

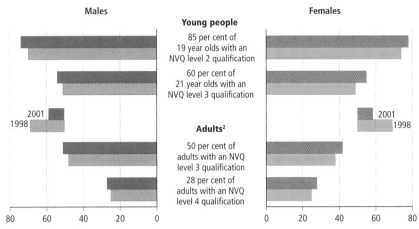

1 At Spring each year. Targets relate to objectives for the year 2002. See Appendix, Part 3: National Learning Targets.

2 Males aged 18 to 64 and females aged 18 to 59, who are in employment or actively seeking employment.

Source: Department for Education and Skills from the Labour Force Survey

Chart **3.23**

Advanced Modern Apprenticeships: by selected subject and gender, in training on 24th June 2001

England

Percentages

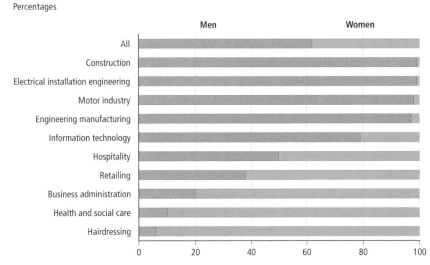

Source: Department for Education and Skills

Table **3.24**

Destination of leavers from Work-based Training[1,2], 1999–00

Percentages

	Work-based Learning for Adults	Work-based Training for Young People[3]
England		
In employment	40	70
Unemployed	48	12
In a positive outcome[4]	46	84
Percentage who gained full qualification	40	51
Northern Ireland[1]		
In employment	60	63
Unemployed	25	19
In further education or training	7	9
Other	8	9
Percentage who gained full qualification	91	88

1 Schemes in Northern Ireland differ from those in England and Wales.
2 Status six months after leaving.
3 Includes Foundation Modern Apprenticeships.
4 A positive outcome represents those leavers in a job, full-time education or other government supported training.
Source: Department for Education and Skills; Northern Ireland Department for Employment and Learning

Chart **3.25**

Employees[1] receiving job-related training: by gender and age, Spring 2001

United Kingdom

Percentages

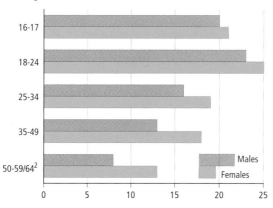

1 Percentage who received job-related training in the four weeks before interview.
2 Males aged 50 to 64 and females aged 50 to 59.
Source: Department for Education and Skills from the Labour Force Survey

In 1999–00, 84 per cent of young people in England and Wales were classified as in a 'positive outcome' six months after leaving Work-based Training for Young People, that is, they were either in a job, in full-time education, or in other government supported training (Table 3.24). Another government-supported scheme is Work-based Learning for Adults. This is designed to help unemployed and disadvantaged adults find jobs through training and work experience, and is open to those aged over 25 who have been unemployed for six months or longer. The proportion of adult leavers who were in a job six months after leaving the scheme in 1999–00 was 40 per cent compared with 33 per cent in 1990–91. Forty six per cent were in a positive outcome of some kind. In Northern Ireland, 91 per cent of adult leavers and 88 per cent of young people leavers gained the full qualification.

Training is not just for school leavers or the unemployed; it is also an increasingly important aspect of working life for employees. In Spring 2001, 14 per cent of male and 19 per cent of female employees of working age had received some job-related training in the previous four weeks (Chart 3.25). Young people aged between 18 and 24 were the most likely to have received training while men aged 50 to 64 were the least likely.

Most employers now invest in their workforce by providing training opportunities and many have training plans and budgets. Regional differences exist (Table 3.26). In 2000, almost half of employers in the Yorkshire and Humber region had provided off the job training in the last 12 months, the highest proportion among the English regions, followed by 46 per cent of employers in the North West and East Midlands regions. Employers in Yorkshire and Humber were also more likely to have reported an increase in skill needs in the previous 12 months while employers in the North East were least likely.

Many adults continue their education, either for enjoyment or to develop new skills, and among the many general courses that are available are subjects as diverse as languages, physical education/sport/ fitness and practical crafts/skills such as embroidery and woodwork. In November 2001, 1.1 million adults in England and Wales were enrolled on adult education courses (Table 3.27). Enrolment rates are generally higher for women than men.

Table 3.26

Changes in skill needs and employers' commitment to training[1]: by region, 2000

Percentages

	Reporting an increase in skills needed in an average employee	With a training plan	With a training budget	Providing off-the-job training in the last 12 months
England	61	39	27	41
North East	54	45	31	42
North West	63	36	27	46
Yorkshire and the Humber	68	50	32	48
East Midlands	62	50	32	46
West Midlands	56	30	19	37
East	61	38	29	37
London	64	42	23	38
South East	55	32	23	39
South West	59	36	32	39

1 Fieldwork was carried out in July and October 2000 and asked if any training provision had been made 12 months prior to the interview. See Appendix, Part 3: Learning and Training at Work.

Source: Learning and Training at Work, IFF Research Limited for the Department for Education and Skills

Table 3.27

Enrolments on adult education courses: by age, type of course and gender, November 2000

England & Wales

Thousands

	Academic		Vocational		Other[1]		All enrolments[2]
	Males	Females	Males	Females	Males	Females	
16–18	5.5	7.6	8.6	11.6	9.7	16.6	59.6
19 and over	11.5	31.8	73.5	183.2	182.0	550.4	1,032.5
All aged 16 and over	17.0	39.4	82.2	194.8	191.7	567.0	1,131.4

1 Includes those on basic education and general courses (that is, languages, physical education/sport/fitness, practical craft/skills, other adult education).

2 The all aged 16 and over figure for Wales includes contracted out and assisted numbers, which are not available by age or qualification.

Source: Department for Education and Skills; National Assembly for Wales

Websites

National Statistics	www.statistics.gov.uk
Department for Education and Skills	www.dfes.gov.uk
Scottish Executive	www.scotland.gov.uk
Northern Ireland Department of Education	www.deni.gov.uk
Northern Ireland Department for Employment and Learning	www.delni.gov.uk
National Assembly for Wales	www.wales.gov.uk
National Foundation for Education Research	www.nfer.ac.uk
Office for Standards in Education	www.ofsted.gov.uk
Organisation for Economic Co-operation and Development	www.oecd.org

Contacts

Office for National Statistics	
Chapter author	020 7533 6174
Department for Education and Skills	01325 392658
National Assembly for Wales	029 2082 3507
Northern Ireland Department of Education	028 9127 9279
Scottish Executive	0131 244 0442
Office for Standards in Education	020 7421 6617

Chapter 4

Labour Market

Overview

■ In Spring 2001, there were 27.3 million people of working age in employment in the United Kingdom, the highest number since current records began in 1959. (Table 4.3)

Economic activity

■ The number of women in the labour force has risen from 10.0 million in 1971 to 13.2 million in 2001. (Table 4.5)

■ In Spring 2001, there were 6.8 million people of working age with long-term or work-limiting disabilities, of whom just over half were economically active. (Table 4.8)

Patterns of employment

■ Just over one in five male employee jobs in 2001 were in manufacturing, compared with one in three in 1981. (Table 4.13)

■ Around one-fifth of Pakistani/Bangladeshi people in employment were self employed in Spring 2000 to Winter 2000–01, compared to one in ten White people and less than one in ten Black people. (Chart 4.15)

■ Around 20 per cent of employees working full-time and 23 per cent of those working part-time had adopted some type of flexible working arrangement in Spring 2001. (Table 4.17)

Labour market dynamics

■ Of those young people in Great Britain leaving the New Deal between January 1998 and August 2001, 59 per cent went into unsubsidised and sustained jobs. (Table 4.29)

Working lives

■ The number of employees with temporary work increased during the early 1990s and has since stabilised at around 1.7 million people. (Chart 4.31)

Chart **4.1**

Employment rates[1]: by gender

United Kingdom

Percentages

1 At Summer each year. In 1959 to 1971, males aged 15 to 64 and females aged 15 to 59; from 1972 onwards males aged 16 to 64 and females aged 16 to 59.

Source: Department for Work and Pensions

Map **4.2**

Employment rates[1], by area[2], Spring 2001

Percentages

- 80.0 and over
- 75.0 – 79.9
- 70.0 – 74.9
- 69.9 and under
- Not available

1 Total employed as a percentage of all people of working age.
2 Counties and Unitary Authorities, except for Northern Ireland.
Source: Labour Force Survey, Office for National Statistics

Most people spend a large part of their lives in the labour force, and so their experience of the world of work has an important impact on their lives and attitudes. The proportion of time spent in the labour force has been falling as the increase in longevity means more years spent in retirement. At the beginning of the 21st century, more women than ever before are entering paid employment, and employment in service industries is increasing whilst employment in manufacturing has been falling.

Overview

The proportion of the total working age population in employment has varied between 70 and 75 per cent for most of the period from 1959 (when current records began) to 2000, peaking at 76 per cent in 1974. There are business cycle effects in evidence – for example the dip in employment rates between 1980 and 1983, and recovery from 1984 to 1989 – but over the period as a whole there is no sign of a long-run change in employment rates.

However, trends in the overall rate mask large differences for men and women (Chart 4.1). Since the mid-1960s, the trend in employment rates for men has been gradually downwards. Each time a dip in the economic cycle has resulted in a faster fall, the following recovery has not been sufficient to restore rates to their pre-recession levels, and these cyclical effects have been more marked since 1979. Taken over the 40 year period, the effect has been to reduce the male employment rate from 94 per cent to 79 per cent, a fall of 15 percentage points. There is some evidence that the downward trend has now stabilised with a gradual rise between 1993 and 2000 which appears not simply to be an economic cycle effect.

The picture for women is very different. Employment rates among women have risen from 47 per cent to 70 per cent between 1959 and 2000. As with men, the proportion of women in employment has followed the economic cycle, but for them such effects have generally been less marked. For example between 1980 and 1983 the female employment rate fell less sharply than the male rate and recovered more quickly thereafter. However, since 1993 it has risen at virtually the same rate as the male employment rate.

The data in Chart 4.1 are provisional. The estimates for 1959 to 1983 have been calculated by the Department for Work and Pensions to be consistent with Labour Force Survey (LFS) estimates available from 1984, but the whole series is currently being refined (see Appendix, Part 4: Estimates of employment rates). ONS estimates of employment rates for all aged 16 and over are expected to be published in 2002.

Employment rates are not uniform across the country. Many inner city areas and former industrial areas had the lowest rates in Spring 2001 – for example, 53 per cent in Blaenau Gwent and 61 per cent in Glasgow City (Map 4.2). Conversely, some of the highest employment rates are in Scotland and the South of England. The highest rates of all are in the Western Isles and the Shetland Isles (both 86 per cent), with Oxfordshire (85 per cent), Leicestershire, Northamptonshire and Surrey (all 82 per cent) being the highest in England. Angus, Perth and Kinross, Aberdeenshire and Midlothian all have employment rates between 82 and 85 per cent. However, there can also be substantial differences in employment rates within regions as well as between regions, and most regions have areas with high rates and areas with low rates.

In March 2000, the Lisbon European Council agreed an aim to achieve an overall EU employment rate as close as possible to 70 per cent by 2010 and, for women, an employment rate of more than 60 per cent by 2010. In 2000, the overall employment rate in the EU was 63.1 per cent and the United Kingdom was one of only four out of the fifteen member states having employment rates above the 2010 target.

In Spring 2001, there were 36.6 million people of working age in the United Kingdom, of whom 27.3 million were in employment (Table 4.3). This is the highest number of people in employment since the series began in 1959 – although the highest employment rate was recorded in 1974, it only represented 24.4 million people. Over a fifth of those in employment in Spring 2001 were working part-time, and just under half were women. Comparing the structure of the labour market in Spring 2001 with that in Spring 1986, we can see that the number of people working part-time has increased at a faster rate than the number working full-time, among both men and women. The number of self-employed people has also risen, whereas the number of people unemployed (on the ILO measure – see Glossary of terms on page 86) has more than halved. However, the number of men who are economically inactive has risen and the number of economically inactive women has fallen. The changes in economic inactivity result from increased early retirement and long-term sickness and disability among men, and the decreased likelihood of women staying at home for long periods looking after children.

The age at which young people first enter the labour market depends to a large extent on the length of time they remain in full-time education. Overall, in 2000 just under half the young people aged 15–24 in the European Union (EU) were either in employment or unemployed (Table 4.4) – in other words, were part of the labour market. However, this proportion differs considerably between EU countries. The highest levels of employment were to be found in the Netherlands,

Table **4.3**

Population of working age[1]: by employment status and gender, 1986 and 2001

United Kingdom   Millions

	1986			2001		
	Males	Females	All	Males	Females	All
Economically active						
In employment						
Full-time employees	11.3	5.3	16.6	11.8	6.4	18.3
Part-time employees	0.3	3.9	4.2	1.0	4.8	5.8
Self-employed	2.0	0.6	2.7	2.2	0.7	3.0
Others in employment[2]	0.3	0.1	0.4	0.1	0.1	0.2
All in employment	13.9	10.0	23.9	15.2	12.1	27.3
Unemployed[3]	1.8	1.2	3.1	0.9	0.5	1.4
All economically active	15.8	11.2	26.9	16.0	12.6	28.6
Economically inactive	2.2	5.3	7.5	3.1	4.8	7.9
Population of working age	18.0	16.4	34.4	19.2	17.4	36.6

1 At Spring each year. Males aged 16 to 64, females aged 16 to 59.
2 Those on government employment and training schemes and unpaid family workers.
3 Based on the ILO definition. See Appendix, Part 4: ILO unemployment.
Source: Labour Force Survev. Office for National Statistics

Table **4.4**

Young people[1]: by employment status, EU comparison, 2000

Percentages

	In employment	Unemployed	Economically inactive	All (=100%) (millions)
Austria	52.5	3.5	43.9	0.9
Portugal	42.0	3.8	54.2	1.5
Irish Republic	47.7	3.3	48.9	0.7
United Kingdom	55.9	7.7	36.4	6.9
Germany	46.1	4.3	49.6	8.9
Sweden	36.9	3.8	59.2	1.0
Denmark	67.0	4.9	28.1	0.6
Luxembourg	30.6	2.0	65.3	0.0
Netherlands	68.4	3.8	27.8	1.9
Italy	26.1	12.0	61.9	6.7
Finland	45.4	17.9	36.7	0.6
Belgium	30.3	5.5	64.2	1.2
Spain	31.8	10.8	57.4	5.8
France	28.3	7.4	64.4	7.2
Greece	26.9	11.2	61.8	1.4
EU average	39.9	7.6	52.5	45.5

1 Aged 15–24.
Source: Labour Force Surveys, Eurostat

Table **4.5**

Labour force[1]: by gender and age

United Kingdom   Millions

	16–24	25–44	45–54	55–59	60–64	65 and over	All aged 16 and over
Males							
1971	3.0	6.5	3.2	1.5	1.3	0.6	16.0
1981	3.2	7.1	3.0	1.4	1.0	0.3	16.0
1991	3.1	8.1	3.0	1.1	0.8	0.3	16.4
2001[2]	2.4	8.3	3.4	1.2	0.7	0.3	16.3
Females							
1971	2.3	3.5	2.1	0.9	0.5	0.3	10.0
1981	2.7	4.6	2.1	0.9	0.4	0.2	10.9
1991	2.6	6.1	2.4	0.8	0.3	0.2	12.4
2001[2]	2.0	6.6	3.0	1.0	0.4	0.2	13.2

1 The former civilian labour force definition of unemployment has been used to produce the estimates for 1971 and 1981; in later years the ILO definition has been used and members of the armed forces excluded. See also Appendix, Part 4: Labour Force.

2 At Spring.

Source: Census; Labour Force Survey, Office for National Statistics

Chart **4.6**

Economic activity rates[1]: by gender

United Kingdom

Percentages

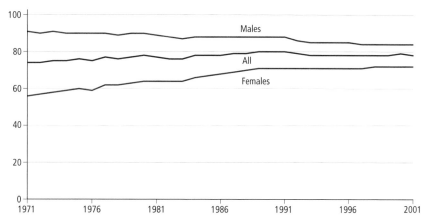

1 Males aged 16 to 64, females aged 16 to 59. The percentage of the population that is in the labour force. The definition of the labour force changed in 1984 when the former Great Britain civilian labour force definition was replaced by the ILO definition which includes members of the armed forces.

Source: Labour Force Survey, Office for National Statistics and Department of Enterprise, Trade and Investment for Northern Ireland

Denmark, United Kingdom and Austria, all at over 50 per cent, whilst the lowest employment rates were in Greece, France, and Italy, all at less than 30 per cent. Note that a student in full-time education or training is regarded as economically active if they have a part-time job.

Economic activity

This section concentrates on those people who are economically active – those who are aged 16 and over and are considered to be in the labour force because they are either in work or actively looking for work.

Table 4.5 shows the rise in the number of women in the labour force over the last 30 years from 10 million in 1971 to 13.2 million in 2001. The rise over the last thirty years has been greatest among those in the 25 to 44 age bracket, followed by those aged 45 to 54. However, the number of young women aged 16 to 24 in the labour force has fallen, particularly between 1991 and 2001, as their participation in post-compulsory full-time education has risen.

The number of men in the labour force has risen much more slowly from 16.0 million in 1971 to 16.3 million in Spring 2001. Men aged over 55 formed only 13 per cent of the male labour force in Spring 2001, compared with 21 per cent in 1971. Note that this table does not include projections of the labour force as it has in previous editions of Social Trends since new projections are in the course of preparation. They will be published around Spring 2000.

Economic activity rates for the population as a whole as well as for men and women separately, as shown in Chart 4.6, show broadly similar trends over the last 30 years as the employment rates illustrated in Chart 4.1. However, because the economically active population includes those who are unemployed as well as those who are employed, economic activity rates are less liable to be affected by economic cycle effects. Thus the trend in the male economic activity rate shows less marked peaks and troughs around a generally downward trend, falling from 91 per cent in 1971 to 84 per cent in 1997, the level at which it has remained over the succeeding four years. The female economic activity rate on the other hand has risen steadily, from 56 per cent in 1971 to 72 per cent from 1998 onwards. In 2001 therefore the gap between male and female economic activity rates was only 12 percentage points, compared with 35 percentage points 30 years earlier. Projections to 2011 indicate a further increase in female economic activity rates to reach 75 per cent and a fall in male rates to 82 per cent, narrowing the gap between the two even further, to only 7 percentage points.

The average economic activity rate among people aged 15 to 64 in the European Union in 2000 was 78 per cent for men and 60 per cent for women (Table 4.7). However, these averages mask a wide range of rates between countries, especially for women. In some of the southern European countries around 50 per cent or fewer of women were active in the labour market – for example, 46 per cent in Italy and 50 per cent in Greece. In contrast, the Scandinavian countries showed the highest rates of economic activity among women – 76 per cent in Denmark, 74 per cent in Finland and 73 per cent in Sweden. In all countries for which data are available, economic activity rates amongst women rose between 1992 and 2000, the most dramatic rise of 12 percentage points having taken place in the Irish Republic. Among men the rates in 2000 varied within a rather narrower band, ranging from 74 per cent in Belgium and Italy to 84 per cent in Denmark, Austria and Netherlands. The United Kingdom has economic activity rates above the EU average for both men and women: the rate for men is one of the highest in the EU, but that for women is some way behind Denmark, Finland and Sweden.

Note that there is a wide range of factors underlying these comparisons: as well as economic cycle effects which will vary across countries for a given year, they will also be affected by population structures and differing retirement ages and participation in post-compulsory full-time education across countries.

Disability has a considerable impact on an individual's labour market participation. In Spring 2001 there were 6.8 million people of working age with long-term or work limiting disabilities in the United Kingdom, of whom just over half were economically active (Table 4.8). This compares with an economic activity rate for the whole working age population of 78 per cent. Disabled men are more likely than disabled women to be in employment, though the gap between the rates is smaller than for the population as a whole – over 4 percentage points compared with 9 percentage points.

The rates of ILO unemployment among disabled people were much higher than those for the non-disabled (8 per cent compared with 4 per cent), and unemployed disabled people were more likely than the non-disabled to have been unemployed for at least a year (35 per cent compared with 26 per cent). Disabled people were also much more likely to be economically inactive than non-disabled people (49 per cent overall compare with 15 per cent). Among the economically inactive, disabled people were more likely than non-disabled to want a job.

Table **4.7**

Economic activity rates[1]: by gender, EU comparison, 1992 and 2000

Percentages

	1992			2000		
	Males	Females	All	Males	Females	All
Denmark	..	..	..	84.0	75.9	80.0
Finland	..	..	..	79.4	74.1	76.8
Sweden	..	..	..	77.2	73.4	75.3
United Kingdom	86.3	66.8	76.6	83.0	67.8	75.5
Netherlands	79.4	55.3	67.4	83.9	65.7	74.9
Austria	..	..	..	83.9	65.7	74.9
Germany	80.9	61.1	71.1	78.8	63.0	71.0
Portugal	80.0	58.6	68.7	78.8	63.6	71.0
France	75.5	58.9	67.0	75.3	62.5	68.8
Irish Republic	76.4	43.4	60.0	79.1	55.7	67.5
Belgium	71.8	49.3	60.6	73.8	56.6	65.2
Luxembourg	77.6	47.5	62.8	76.4	51.7	64.2
Greece	76.2	41.7	58.3	77.1	49.7	63.0
Spain	76.0	41.8	58.7	77.1	50.7	63.7
Italy	74.0	42.0	57.8	73.8	46.2	59.9
EU average	..	..	..	78.1	59.8	68.9

1 People aged 15 to 64, except for United Kingdom where data refer to those aged 16 to 64.
Source: Labour Force Surveys, Eurostat

Table **4.8**

Economic activity status of disabled[1] people: by gender, Spring 2001

United Kingdom

Percentages

	Males	Females	All
In employment			
Working full time	43.5	22.9	33.8
Working part time	5.6	21.6	13.1
All in employment	49.1	44.6	46.9
Unemployed[2]	5.1	3.2	4.2
Less than one year	3.1	2.3	2.7
One year or more	2.0	0.9	1.5
Economically inactive	45.8	52.2	48.8
All disabled (=100%)(millions)	3.6	3.2	6.8

1 Males aged 16 to 64 and females 16 to 59 with current long-term or work limiting disability.
2 Based on the ILO definition. See Appendix, Part 4: ILO Unemployment.
Source: Labour Force Survey, Office for National Statistics

Table **4.9**

Employment rates[1]: by ethnic group, gender, age and highest qualification, 2000–01[2]

United Kingdom

Percentages

	Males				Females			
	Higher qualification	Other qualification	No qualification	All aged 16–64[5]	Higher qualification	Other qualification	No qualification	All aged 16–59[5]
White	89.9	81.7	58.4	80.4	85.1	72.5	47.7	70.9
Black	83.5	62.3	48.6	64.8	77.4	56.3	32.6	57.6
Indian	92.1	72.1	52.7	75.5	80.4	59.9	36.4	60.1
Pakistani/Bangladeshi	82.9	57.7	49.5	59.7	68.6	30.2	7.2	24.7
Other ethnic groups[3]	85.4	56.9	50.9	64.4	68.2	42.5	28.1	47.7
All ethnic groups[4]	89.7	80.5	57.7	79.5	84.3	71.0	45.5	69.3

1 The percentage of the working age population in employment.
2 Combined quarters: Spring 2000 to Winter 2000–01
3 Includes those of mixed origin.
4 Includes those who did not state their ethnic group.
5 Includes those who did not state their qualifications.
Source: Labour Force Survey, Office for National Statistics

Table **4.10**

Economic activity status of women[1]: by age of youngest dependent child, 1991 and 2001

United Kingdom

Percentages

	Age of youngest dependent child				No dependent children	All
	Under 5	5–10	11–15	16–18[2]		
1991						
Working full time	14	21	31	38	50	38
Working part time	28	44	42	37	20	27
Unemployed[3]	6	6	4	3	5	5
Looking after family/home	47	22	15	13	6	17
Students[2]	1	1	..	..	6	4
Other inactive	4	5	7	8	11	9
All (=100%)(millions)	3.1	2.1	1.4	0.5	9.7	16.8
2001						
Working full time	18	26	37	44	49	39
Working part time	36	44	38	37	23	30
Unemployed[3]	3	3	4	2	3	3
Looking after family/home	38	18	12	7	4	13
Students[2]	1	2	1	..	8	5
Other inactive	3	6	8	10	13	10
All (=100%)(millions)	3.0	2.4	1.6	0.6	9.9	17.4

1 Aged 16–59. At Spring each year.
2 Those in full-time education.
3 Based on the ILO definition. See Appendix, Part 4: ILO Unemployment.
Source: Labour Force Survey, Office for National Statistics

For a variety of cultural reasons, as well as because of differing age structures, employment rates vary between people of different ethnic groups in the United Kingdom. Table 4.9 explores the degree to which the presence of qualifications accounts for differences in employment rates between the various ethnic groups. Having qualifications, and the level of those qualifications, has an important influence on employment rates. In each ethnic group, and for both men and women, employment rates are much higher among those with qualifications than among those with none, and are higher according to the level of qualifications attained. However, the contrast in employment rates between qualification levels is greater for minority ethnic groups than it is for the White population. For example, employment rates amongst men with higher qualifications were 90 per cent for the White population and 92 per cent for the Indian population, but fell to 58 per cent for White men with no qualifications compared with 53 per cent for Indian men. Overall, the lowest employment rates for women of working age are among the Pakistani/ Bangladeshi communities, averaging only 25 per cent in 2000–01. However, among these women the presence of qualifications makes an even greater difference to whether or not they are in employment than it does for men: 69 per cent of those with a higher qualification were in employment, compared with only 7 per cent of those with no qualification. Table 3.17 in the Education chapter gives more information on educational attainment by gender and ethnic group.

One of the main themes already to emerge in this chapter is the increased labour market participation of women over the last decades. However, the presence of a dependent child in the family still has a major effect on the economic activity of women. About 44 per cent of women of working age had dependent children in Spring 2001 (Table 4.10). Only 18 per cent of women whose youngest child was under 5 worked full-time, but this proportion rose with the age of the youngest child so that for those whose youngest dependent child was aged 16–18 it reached 44 per cent, only five percentage points lower than for women with no dependent children. Among women with pre-school children, most were either working part-time (36 per cent) or were economically inactive and looking after family and home (38 per cent).

Between 1991 and 2001, the economic activity rate for women with pre-school children increased from 48 per cent to 57 per cent. Women on maternity leave are classified as in employment, so this rise reflects a greater number of women returning to the labour market sooner after the birth of their children than previously, and also an increase in the number who may not leave the labour market at all while having their children. For women without dependent children the economic activity rate in 2001, at 75 per cent, was the same as in 1991. Therefore the main driver behind the increase in female economic activity rates during the 1990s has been the increased economic activity of women with dependent children.

Overall, about 7.9 million people in the United Kingdom were classified as economically inactive in Spring 2001, about the same number as in 1996 (Table 4.11). These people are of working age, but for a variety of reasons either are not looking for paid work or not available to start work. The majority (72 per cent) do not want a job. We have already seen that looking after a family is a major factor in women's labour market participation and in fact this was the reason for not wanting a job for about half the women. For men, long-term sickness or disability was the major reason for not wanting a job, followed by being a student.

There are now more people in the United Kingdom in employment than at any other time in the post-war period, and most working age households are work-rich – that is, households including at least one person of working age where all persons in the household of working age are in employment. There were 10.8 million work-rich households in Spring 2001, an increase of more than a million since Spring 1996. Work-rich households as a proportion of all working age households fell from 53 per cent in 1990 to 50 per cent in 1992, but has since risen to 57 per cent in 2000 and 2001 (Chart 4.12). In Spring 2001, around 16 per cent of working age households were workless – that is, households where at least one person is of working

Table **4.11**

Reasons for economic inactivity[1]: by gender, 1996 and 2001

United Kingdom   Percentages

	1996			2001		
	Males	Females	All	Males	Females	All
Does not want a job						
Looking after family or home	3	36	24	3	33	22
Long-term sick or disabled	28	13	19	26	14	19
Student	21	12	15	21	15	17
Other	16	9	12	19	11	14
All	68	71	70	69	73	72
Wants a job but not seeking in						
last four weeks						
Looking after family or home	2	14	10	2	12	8
Long-term sick or disabled	12	4	7	14	6	9
Student	5	3	4	5	3	3
Discouraged worker[2]	2	1	1	1	-	-
Other	6	4	5	5	4	4
All	28	27	27	27	24	25
Wants a job and seeking work						
but not available to start[3]	4	2	3	4	2	3
All reasons (=100%)(millions)	2.9	4.9	7.8	3.1	4.8	7.9

1 At Spring each year. Males aged 16 to 64, females aged 16 to 59.
2 People who believed no jobs were available.
3 Not available for work in the next two weeks. Includes those who did not state whether or not they were available.
Source: Labour Force Survey, Office for National Statistics

Chart **4.12**

Working age households[1,2,3]: by household economic status and household type

United Kingdom

Percentages

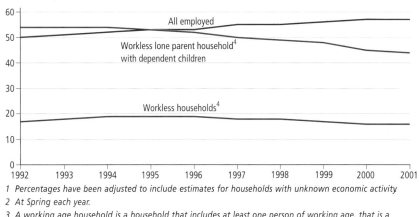

1 Percentages have been adjusted to include estimates for households with unknown economic activity
2 At Spring each year.
3 A working age household is a household that includes at least one person of working age, that is a woman aged between 16 and 59 or a man aged between 16 and 64.
4 A workless household is a household that includes at least one person of working age where no-one is in employment.
Source: Labour Force Survey, Office for National Statistics

Table **4.13**

Employee jobs[1]: by gender and industry

United Kingdom

Percentages

	Males			Females		
	1981	1991	2001	1981	1991	2001
Manufacturing	32	25	22	17	12	8
Distribution, hotels, catering and repairs	17	20	22	26	26	27
Financial and business services	11	15	19	12	17	18
Transport and communication	9	9	9	3	3	4
Construction	9	8	8	2	2	1
Agriculture	2	2	2	1	1	1
Energy and water supply	4	3	1	1	1	–
Other services	17	19	18	38	40	41
All employee jobs (=100%)(millions)	13.2	12.1	12.8	10.0	11.5	12.7

1 At June each year.

Source: Short-term Turnover and Employment Survey, Office for National Statistics

Table **4.14**

Employees[1]: by gender and occupation[2], Spring 2001

United Kingdom

Percentages

	Males	Females
Managers and senior officials	18	8
Professional occupations	13	11
Associate professional and technical	13	13
Administrative and secretarial	6	24
Skilled trades	17	2
Personal service	2	13
Sales and customer service	5	13
Process, plant and machine operatives	13	3
Elementary occupations	13	12
All employees[3] (=100%)(millions)	13.0	11.0

1 Males aged 16 to 64, females aged 16 to 59.

2 Data not comparable with previous years. See Appendix,
   Part 4: Standard Occupation Classification

3 Includes a few people who did not state their occupation.
   Percentages are based on totals which exclude this group.
   Part 4: Standard Occupation Classification.

Source: Labour Force Survey, Office for National Statistics

age but no-one is in employment. Although this proportion was virtually the same in 1984, during the early 1990s it rose to reach 19 per cent in Spring 1994 to Spring 1996, but has since been decreasing gradually. Among lone parent households with dependent children, the proportion who are workless is much higher, at 44 per cent in Spring 2001. This proportion also peaked in the early 1990s, at 54 per cent.

The proportion of working age people living in households with no one in employment has decreased from a peak of 14 per cent in Spring 1995 to 12 per cent in Spring 2001. In Spring 2000 the number of children living in workless households fell below 2 million for the first time since spring 1990, to 1.9 million, and has since fallen again slightly. The proportion of children in workless households peaked at 20 per cent in Spring 1994 and has since dropped to 15 per cent in Spring 2001. The changes in all these proportions can be attributed partly to changes in economic activity and partly to changes in household size and structure over time.

Patterns of employment

It is well-known that the UK economy has experienced structural change in the post-war period with a decline in the manufacturing sector and an increase in service industries. Table 4.13 illustrates the impact this change has had on the labour market. In 1981, one in three male employee jobs were in manufacturing but this had fallen to just over one in five in 2001. The proportion of female employee jobs in the manufacturing sector has also fallen, from just under one in five to under one in ten. The largest increase in both male and female jobs has been in financial and business services, which now account for about one in five of both male and female jobs. The proportion of both male and female jobs in 'other services', an umbrella category including health, education and public administration services, has remained broadly stable since 1981. The total number of jobs done by men is now virtually the same as the number done by women –12.8 million compared with 12.7 million – whereas in 1981 there were 3.2 million more male than female employee jobs. Note that this chart is based on jobs rather than people – one person may have more than one job, and jobs may vary in the number of hours' work they involve.

Table 4.14 uses a revised occupational classification compared with previous editions of Social Trends. Brief details of the Standard Occupation Classification 2000 may be found in the Appendix, Part 4: Standard Occupation Classification.

The pattern of occupations followed by men and women are quite different. About a quarter of women employees are in administrative and secretarial work, whilst men are most likely to be employed as managers and senior officials or in skilled trades. These occupations are among the least likely to be followed by women. Only the associate professional and technical and the elementary occupations are equally likely to be followed by both men and women: about one in eight were employed in each of these occupations.

Of course not all people in employment work as employees: about 3.0 million people in Spring 2001 were self-employed in their main job, of whom 2.2 million or 73 per cent were men (Table 4.3). Evidence from the Labour Force Survey in Spring 2000 indicated that the main reason people became self-employed was that they wanted to be independent (31 per cent of respondents). It was the most important reason for both men and women. Over one-fifth of both men and women said they were self-employed because of the nature of their occupation.

Chart 4.15 shows that people from certain ethnic groups are more likely to be self-employed than others. Around one-fifth of Pakistani/Bangladeshi people in employment were self-employed in Spring 2000 to Winter 2000–01, compared with only one in ten White people and less than one in ten Black people. Chinese and Indian people are also more likely than White or Black people to be self-employed.

People also vary considerably in the type of self-employed work they undertake. Overall, around a fifth of self-employed people work in the construction industry, and similar proportions work in distribution, hotels and restaurants and in banking, finance and insurance. However, two-thirds of self-employed

Chart **4.15**

Self-employment[1]: by ethnic group, 2000-01[2]

Great Britain

Percentages

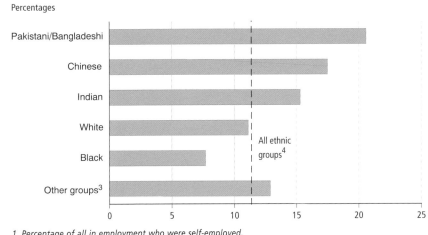

1 Percentage of all in employment who were self-employed.
2 Combined quarters: Spring 2000 to Winter 2000-01.
3 Includes those of mixed origin.
4 Includes those who did not state their ethnic group.

Source: Labour Force Survey, Office for National Statistics

Chinese people and over half of the Indian self-employed work in distribution, hotels and restaurants. Two-fifths of the Pakistani/Bangladeshi self-employed also work in this industry, and only slightly fewer work in transport and communication.

A fairly common reason for women opting for self-employment is family commitments. It is perhaps therefore not surprising that seven in ten of self-employed women working part-time and one in two of those working full-time do so either at home, with home as a base, or in the same grounds or building as

Table **4.16**

People in employment: by location of work, Spring 2001

United Kingdom

Percentages

	Self-employed					Employees				
	Males		Females			Males		Females		
	Full-time	Part-time	Full-time	Part-time	All	Full-time	Part-time	Full-time	Part-time	All
Own home	4	18	21	35	12	1	2	1	2	1
Same grounds or building as own home	6	5	10	3	6	1	..	0	0	0
Different places with home as a base	45	51	20	33	38	4	5	2	2	3
Separate from home	45	26	49	29	44	95	93	97	95	95
All (=100%)(millions)	2.0	0.3	0.4	0.4	3.1	11.9	1.1	6.5	5.1	24.7

Source: Labour Force Survey, Office for National Statistics

Table **4.17**

Employees with flexible working patterns[1]: by gender, Spring 2001

United Kingdom

Percentages

	Males	Females	All employees
Full-time employees			
Flexible working hours	8.9	13.9	10.7
Annualised working hours	5.0	4.8	4.9
Four and a half day week	1.8	1.4	1.7
Term-time working	0.9	5.4	2.5
Nine day fortnight	0.3	0.2	0.3
Any flexible working pattern[2]	17.0	25.9	20.1
Part-time employees			
Flexible working hours	6.5	8.1	7.8
Annualised working hours	3.2	4.0	3.8
Term-time working	4.6	10.2	9.2
Job sharing	–	2.5	2.3
Any flexible working pattern[2]	15.2	25.0	23.3

1 Percentages are based on totals which exclude people who did not state whether or not they worked a flexible working arrangement.

2 Includes other categories of flexible working not separately identified.

Source: Labour Force Survey, Office for National Statistics

Chart **4.18**

Distribution of usual weekly hours[1] of work: by gender, Spring 2001

United Kingdom

Thousands

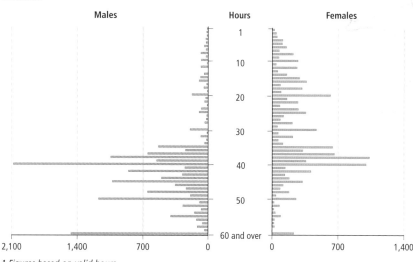

1 Figures based on valid hours.

Source: Labour Force Survey, Office for National Statistics

their home (Table 4.16). Such people are usually termed 'homeworkers'. Much lower proportions of self-employed men work at home or in the same grounds or building as their home, but are much more likely to use their home as a base. In contrast, very low proportions of men or women employees are homeworkers.

Homeworking is most common in the administrative and secretarial occupations and the personal services occupations: one in 20 of all those employed in these sectors were homeworkers in Spring 2001. These are also the occupations in which homeworking is most common among women, but among men it is the associate professional and technical occupations where homeworking is most common.

The low proportion of employee homeworkers is confirmed by analysis of the 1998 Workplace Employee Relations Survey by the Centre for Labour Market Studies at the University of Leicester. This showed that only 9 per cent of workplaces reported that more than 5 per cent of their workforce worked at home on a regular basis. Around a fifth of workplaces that offered their employees the opportunity to work at home were in business services (this includes computer-related activities, management consultancy, accounting and the provision of legal advice), although this sector was no more likely to provide this option than other sectors.

A further family-friendly option is to allow employees to arrange their work schedules to suit their family commitments. Around 20 per cent of employees working full-time and 23 per cent of those working part-time were able to adopt some type of flexible working arrangement in Spring 2001 (Table 4.17). The most common such arrangement for full-time employees was flexible working hours, and the most common for those working part-time was term-time working. Women were more likely than men to have a flexible working pattern.

Table 4.3 showed that there were 5.8 million employees of working age working part-time in Spring 2001, of whom 4.8 million were women. However, to distinguish only between 'part-time' and 'full-time' masks a wide variety of patterns of working hours which people experience. Chart 4.18 therefore shows the distribution of usual weekly hours of work, including regular paid and unpaid overtime, for both men and women in Spring 2001.

The most common length of working week for men was 40 hours followed by 60 hours and over, and for women the most common length was only slightly shorter at 38 hours but the second most common was 40 hours. Men were more likely than women to work in excess of 60 hours per week – nearly 1.5 million did so. However, note that there is a tendency for LFS respondents' reported hours to be bunched around 5 hour marks and so the distribution of hours worked has to be treated with some caution.

The chart clearly illustrates that women are more likely to work part-time than men, but it also shows the wide range of working hours which they undertake. Nearly 2 million women worked 15 hours or fewer, and a further 1.5 million worked between 16 and 20 hours.

Unemployment

The number of people unemployed is linked to the economic cycle, albeit with a time lag. Broadly speaking, as the country experiences economic growth so the number of jobs grows and unemployment falls, though any mismatches between the skill needs of the new jobs and the skills of those available for work may slow this process. Conversely as the economy slows and goes into recession so unemployment tends to rise. The latest peak in unemployment (on the ILO measure – see Appendix, Part 4: ILO Unemployment and Glossary of terms on page 86) occurred in 1993, when it reached just under 3 million (Chart 4.19). This recession had a much greater effect on unemployment among men than among women. Since then, the number of people unemployed has fallen to 1.4 million in Spring 2001, a rate of 4.9 per cent. This compares with an average for the EU of 7.6 per cent in May 2001 and was lower than all EU countries except Austria, Denmark, Luxembourg, Ireland, the Netherlands and Portugal.

The ILO measure of unemployment shown in Chart 4.19 is based on Labour Force Survey estimates of the number of people without a job who are seeking work (see Glossary of terms on page 86). It is based on internationally agreed definitions and is the ONS preferred measure of unemployment. An alternative indicator of unemployment is available, known as the claimant count. This is a count of the number of people claiming unemployment-related benefits. While there is significant overlap between ILO unemployment and the claimant count, not all people who claim unemployment-related benefits are ILO unemployed and not all people who are ILO unemployed claim unemployment-related benefits. For example, ILO unemployment includes women who are often not entitled to claim benefits because their partner is also a claimant. Similarly some people claim

Job Seekers' Allowance but carry out a small amount of part-time work and so would not be counted as ILO unemployed. A key strength of the claimant count is that it can provide small area estimates at a lower level of geographic disaggregation than is possible from the LFS, and it is also more timely.

The ILO and claimant measures both tend to move in the same direction. In times of economic downturn, the claimant count tends to rise faster than the ILO measure so that at the trough of the last recession in 1993 the two measures were very close together. However, in times of economic upturn the claimant count tends to fall faster than the ILO measure. This is because economically inactive people become more optimistic about their employment prospects, start looking for work and hence become ILO unemployed.

Unemployment is not equally distributed across the UK labour force. Age, qualifications, gender, ethnicity and location all have an impact on whether or not people become unemployed and on the length of time people spend out of work.

Chart **4.19**

Unemployment[1]: by gender

United Kingdom

Millions

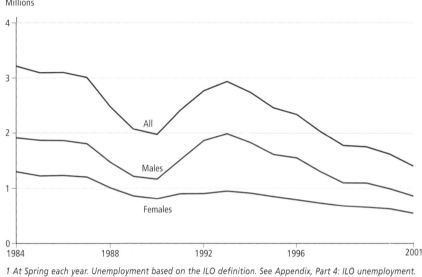

1 At Spring each year. Unemployment based on the ILO definition. See Appendix, Part 4: ILO unemployment.

Source: Labour Force Survey, Office for National Statistics

A higher proportion of young people than older people are unemployed, and a higher proportion of men are unemployed than women. In Spring 2001, 18 per cent of economically active 16 to 17 year old men were unemployed as were 13 per cent of economically active women in the same age group, compared with only 5 per cent of men and 2 per cent of women within 5 years of state pension age (Table 4.20). Over the last ten years, the gap between the unemployment rates for 16 and 17 year olds and the rates for other age groups has widened for both men and women, as the rates for young people have remained relatively stable whilst those for older groups have declined.

Age and gender also influence the length of time that people spend unemployed. Young unemployed people are less likely to have been so for a long period compared with older people, and women are less likely than men to have been unemployed for a long period. In Spring 2000, over half of unemployed women aged between 16 and 29 had been out of work for less than three months, and less than one in

ten had been unemployed for a year or more. However, around a fifth of unemployed men in their thirties and forties had been unemployed for three years or more and this rose to nearly a quarter among those aged 50 to 64.

People from minority ethnic groups had higher unemployment rates than White people in Spring 2000 to Winter 2000–2001 (Table 4.21). Unemployment rates for Black and Pakistani/Bangladeshi people were three times greater than that for White people, and the rate for other minority ethnic groups was more than twice that for White people. For all ethnic groups, unemployment is much higher amongst young people aged 16 to 24 than for other age groups. Nearly one third of young Black people were unemployed, and only a slightly lower proportion of Pakistani/Bangladeshi young people. However, the unemployment rates among Indians were only slightly higher than those for White people at all ages.

Table **4.20**

Unemployment rates[1]: by gender and age

United Kingdom

Percentages

	1992	1993	1994	1995	1996	1997	1998	1999	2000	2001
Males										
16–17	17.7	18.5	18.8	19.2	21.3	19.4	18.1	21.5	20.1	17.7
18–24	19.0	21.1	19.3	17.7	17.2	14.8	13.1	12.6	11.8	10.9
25–44	10.5	10.9	10.2	8.9	8.7	6.9	5.7	5.6	4.8	4.3
45–54	8.4	9.4	8.6	7.5	6.4	6.1	4.7	4.9	4.8	3.5
55–59	11.2	12.3	11.6	10.3	9.8	8.0	6.7	6.4	5.4	3.9
60–64	10.2	14.2	11.6	9.9	8.9	7.6	6.9	6.4	5.8	5.2
65 and over	4.9	4.6	3.7	..	4.0	4.1	..	..	..	..
All aged 16 and over	11.5	12.4	11.4	10.1	9.6	8.1	6.8	6.7	6.1	5.3
Females										
16–17	14.0	15.1	16.9	15.5	15.3	16.0	15.3	14.0	16.9	12.5
18–24	11.0	12.9	11.8	11.6	10.2	9.8	9.4	9.3	8.5	7.8
25–44	7.3	7.3	7.0	6.7	6.3	5.4	5.1	4.8	4.5	4.1
45–54	5.0	5.0	5.0	4.5	4.1	3.7	3.1	3.2	2.9	2.4
55–59	4.5	6.0	6.5	4.7	4.3	4.8	3.5	3.5	3.1	2.0
60 and over	3.1	3.9	2.9	..	..	2.1	2.0	1.9	..	..
All aged 16 and over	7.3	7.6	7.3	6.8	6.3	5.7	5.3	5.1	4.8	4.2

1 At Spring each year. Unemployment based on the ILO definition as a percentage of all economically active. See Appendix, Part 4: ILO unemployment.
Source: Labour Force Survey, Office for National Statistics

The unemployed can be assigned a social class based on their previous occupation. Unemployment rates for people from minorities ethnic in the top four social classes were, on average, more than twice those for White people in 1998–2000. The differential was less for the partly skilled, at 6 percentage points and among the unskilled the difference was 4 percentage points.

Three-quarters of unemployed men looking for work as an employee were seeking a full-time job in Spring 2001 (Table 4.22). However, two-thirds of unemployed women with dependent children were seeking part-time work, as were a third of those with no dependent children. The preference for part-time work is most common among women with pre-school children – nearly three-quarters of them preferred this type of work – but their preference becomes less strong as the age of their youngest child increases.

Table 4.22 is based on those people who are unemployed according to the ILO definition. Table 4.11 showed that there is a further group of people who, although they want to work, were not available to start work in the next week and/or were not looking for work at the time of interview in the Labour Force Survey and were therefore classified as economically inactive. In Spring 2001, about 24 per cent of economically inactive women, and a slightly higher proportion of economically inactive men (27 per cent), said they would like to work. The most common reason that men gave for not seeking work at the time of interview was long term sickness or disability. For women the most common reason was their family commitments.

The Government has adopted a Welfare to Work strategy, which targets the reduction of unemployment amongst lone parents with dependent children, people from minority ethnic groups, people aged over 50, and people with disabilities, as well as those living in disadvantaged areas. The New Deal for unemployed people forms part of this strategy. The impact of the New Deal is discussed in the next section on Labour market dynamics.

Table **4.21**

Unemployment rates[1]: by ethnic group and age, 2000–01[2]

United Kingdom   Percentages

	16–24	25–34	35–44	45–59/64[3]	All aged 16–59/64[3]
White	11	5	4	4	5
Black	32	14	11	10	15
Indian	13	5	7	6	7
Pakistani/Bangladeshi	28	14	12	..	17
Other groups[4]	24	9	11	7	12
All ethnic groups[5]	12	5	4	4	6

1 Unemployment based on the ILO definition as a percentage of all economically active. See Appendix, Part 4: ILO unemployment.
2 Combined quarters: Spring 2000 to Winter 2000–01.
3 Males up to the age of 64, females up to the age of 59.
4 Includes those of mixed origin.
5 Includes those who did not state their ethnic group.
Source: Labour Force Survey, Office for National Statistics

Table **4.22**

Unemployed people[1] seeking work as an employee: by type of work sought, gender and age of youngest dependent child, Spring 2001

United Kingdom   Percentages

	Males	Females				
		Age of youngest dependent child				
		Under 5	5–10	11–15	All[2]	No dependent children
Looking for						
Full-time work	75	15	16	22	18	52
Part-time work	12	73	69	53	66	33
No preference	14	12	15	25	17	15
All unemployed (=100%)(thousands)	851	102	82	57	255	284

1 Based on the ILO definition. See Appendix, Part 4: ILO Unemployment.
2 Includes those with youngest dependent child aged 16–18, for whom the sample size is too small for a reliable estimate.
Source: Labour Force Survey, Office for National Statistics

Table **4.23**

Length of service of employees[1]

United Kingdom   Percentages

	1986	1991	1996	2001
Less than three months	5	5	5	5
Three months but less than six months	4	4	5	5
Six months but less than one year	9	10	9	10
One year but less than two years	11	13	12	13
Two years but less than five years	20	24	19	21
Five years but less than ten years	21	16	21	15
Ten years but less than twenty years	20	19	19	20
Twenty years or more	9	9	11	11
All employees[2] (=100%)(millions)	20.8	21.9	22.1	24.1

1 At Spring each year, males aged 16 to 64, females aged 16 to 59.
2 Includes those who did not state length of time in current employment, but percentages are based on totals that exclude this group.
Source: Labour Force Survey, Office for National Statistics

Labour market dynamics

Information about the labour market experiences of individuals over the course of their working lives complements the sort of 'snap-shots' which other sections in this chapter provide. It enables us to build up a dynamic, as opposed to static, picture.

Table 4.23 gives some indication of how long people stay in a job. In Spring 2001, one in ten employees had been in their current job for less than six months, but a similar proportion had been in the same job for over 20 years. Most people – four out of five – had been in the same job for a year or more, and this proportion changes little between the years shown in the table. Although in 1986 unemployment was more than twice as high as in 2001, the proportion of people who had been in their job for more than a year was virtually the same.

Research using the Labour Force Survey by Paul Gregg and Jonathan Wadsworth indicates that in the late 1990s, typically when someone started a new job it lasted about 15 months, but that the average job in progress lasted around 5.5 years. This is because most employees eventually find a long-term job match. Average job tenure has remained relatively stable since 1975. However, this masks sharp contrasts across gender. Job tenure has risen among women with children, partly as a result of the increased provision and use of maternity leave. However, it has fallen for men and for women without dependent children. The largest fall in job tenure has been among men aged 50 and over.

The British Household Panel Survey provides longitudinal information about how the labour market position of a fixed sample of individuals changes from year to year. Evidence from the first five waves of this survey, covering the period 1991–95, shows that promotion plays a substantial role in workers' mobility, accounting for about 36 per cent of position changes each year. The promotion rates of younger workers are higher than those of older workers, but the gender differences are small. This research finds that men and women who are married, have a full-time job, are employed in large establishments and in high-level occupations are more likely to achieve promotion.

The frequency with which people experience spells of unemployment during their working lives can be traced through the number of times they make a new claim for unemployment related benefits. The Claimant Count cohort data file is a longitudinal dataset which records those who claim unemployment-related benefit at any one period of time, and traces their successive periods of unemployment based on their national insurance number. The database contains a historical record of 5 per cent of claims along with a variety of personal characteristics such as gender, date of birth and occupation, as well as geographic information. At present, the cohort data is the only source of information on length of time between spells and the number of times a person becomes unemployed.

Of those men who began claiming unemployment-related benefit between mid-April and mid-July 2001 statistical count dates, 18 per cent had not done so before during the previous ten years, whilst 46 per cent had claimed on four or more occasions over this period (Chart 4.24). Women were more likely to be claiming for the first time – 34 per cent of those claiming had not done so before during the previous ten years – and only 21 per cent had claimed on four or more occasions.

Research based on the British Household Panel Survey has been carried out to investigate how the experience of unemployment affects an individual's future job tenure. This suggests that 20 per cent of men and women who find work following a spell of unemployment re-enter unemployment within 12 months. Temporary jobs and layoffs account for the termination of the largest proportion of jobs that follow unemployment among men, while voluntary quits account for a greater proportion among women. Individuals who enter a job from unemployment are four times more likely to be laid off from their subsequent job, and are three times more likely to (re)enter unemployment than those entering from another job. However, the longer the duration of the previous unemployment spell the less likely the subsequent job is to end. This would indicate that those who spend more time unemployed and searching for work are likely to achieve a better worker/firm match.

Participation in the Government's New Deal scheme is mandatory for 18 to 24 year olds who have claimed Jobseeker's Allowance continuously for six months. Initially there is a Gateway period which includes intensive careers advice and guidance and help with jobsearch skills. The aim is to find unsubsidised jobs for as many as possible. Those who do not find a job then move onto one of four options: subsidised employment; work experience with a voluntary organisation or on an environmental task force, both with training; or full-time education. For those reaching the end of their option without keeping or finding work, there is a follow-through period of support and further training if needed. The New Deal scheme also covers the long-term unemployed and lone parents.

Of those young people in Great Britain leaving the New Deal during the period January 1998 to August 2001, 59 per cent went into unsubsidised and sustained jobs (Table 4.25). Among those leaving the New Deal programme for those 25 and over, a much lower proportion moved into employment – only 23 per cent – though the employment they find is more likely to be sustained.

Working lives

Most people spend a large proportion of their lives at work. The quality of their working lives therefore has a major influence on their well-being more generally.

Any job is made up of a wide range of different characteristics. However, they can be divided into two main groups: those which are agreed parts of the contract between employer and employee such as financial rewards, working time, job security and opportunities for advancement; and those aspects which tend not to be written down but are nevertheless essential in making the employer/ employee relationship work, for example the interest the worker finds in their job, relationships with others in the workplace, the pace of work and so on. All these aspects will play a part in how an employee views their job, but because each person will value each aspect differently, it is virtually impossible to devise an objective measure of 'job quality'.

It is possible however to measure job satisfaction. In 1998 the Workplace Employee Relations Survey asked employees in Great Britain how satisfied they were with their jobs. The answers can be interpreted as a summary assessment by the individual of all the different characteristics of their job. Overall, 54 per

Chart **4.24**

New claims for unemployment benefit: by number of previous claims[1] and gender, 2001[2]

Great Britain

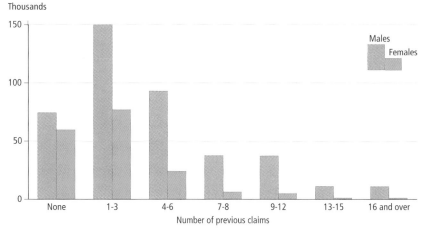

1 Previous claims after 11 April 1991.
2 Males aged 16 to 64, and females aged 16 to 59 who started claiming between 13 April and 12 July 2001 inclusive.
Source: Office for National Statistics

Table 4.25

People entering employment through the New Deal: by age and type of employment, January 1998 to July 2001

Great Britain			Percentages
	18–24	25 and over	All aged 18 and over
Sustained employment			
Unsubsidised	72	63	70
Subsidised	7	17	9
All	78	83	79
Other employment			
Unsubsidised	20	15	19
Subsidised	1	2	2
All	22	17	21
All entering employment			
(=100%)(thousands)	320	76	396
Those entering sustained employment as a percentage of all leavers	59	23	46

Source: Employment Service

Table **4.26**

Reasons[1] full-time employees were looking for a new job: by gender and presence of dependent children, Spring 2001

United Kingdom   Percentages

	Males	Females		
		With dependent children	Without dependent children	All
Pay unsatisfactory in present job	23	18	21	20
Wants longer hours than in present job/other reasons	21	25	21	22
Present job may come to an end	11	..	11	10
In present job to fill time before finding another	6	..	8	7
Wants shorter hours than in present job	6	9	5	6
Journey unsatisfactory in present job	5	..	5	5
Other aspects of present job unsatisfactory	29	34	30	31
All looking for a new job (millions)	0.7	0.1	0.3	0.4
All full-time employees (millions)	11.9	1.8	4.7	6.6
Percentage of full-time employees looking for a new job	6.2	5.3	6.5	6.2

1 More than one reason could be given.
Source: Labour Force Survey, Office for National Statistics

Table **4.27**

Employees'[1] perceived job security: by type of employment, 1998

Great Britain   Percentages

	Strongly agree	Agree	Neither agree or disagree	Disagree	Strongly disagree
Full-time employment	13	45	22	15	6
Part-time employment	14	53	18	11	4
Permanent employment	14	48	21	13	5
Temporary employment	7	33	24	20	16
Fixed term contract	7	32	22	26	13
All	13	47	21	14	5

1 Employees in workplaces with 10 or more employees. Respondents were asked 'Do you feel your job is secure in this workplace?'
Source: Workplace Employee Relations Survey, Department of Trade and Industry

cent of employees were satisfied or very satisfied with their job. Women had higher levels of job satisfaction than men, and part-time employees had higher levels of satisfaction than those working full time. Also, temporary and fixed term contract employees recorded higher levels of job satisfaction than those in permanent jobs.

An important aspect of job satisfaction is the degree to which people feel they are able to achieve the right balance between work and the rest of their lives. A number of practices which contribute to a satisfactory work-life balance have already been discussed elsewhere in this chapter: for example, flexibility of working hours (Table 4.17) and being able to work from home (Table 4.16). A number of other employer policies and practices are also relevant: for example, granting leave arrangements which allow people to meet their non-work commitments or goals, and providing workplace facilities to assist employees to attend work. The aim of the Work-Life Balance Baseline Study, conducted in 2000, was to assess the extent to which employers operate such practices and whether employees felt existing practices met their needs. It found a high level of support for work-life balance amongst employers. Employers and employees agreed that while organisational goals have priority, employers have a responsibility to help people balance work and other aspects of their lives. Employees were less concerned about any potential unfairness arising from work-life balance than employers – 43 per cent of employers thought work-life balance practices were unfair to some staff, but only 26 per cent of employees thought such practices were unfair to people like them.

Dissatisfaction with aspects of their current job is the main reason that prompts people to start looking for another one. In Spring 2001, about 6 per cent of both male and female full-time employees in the United Kingdom were looking for a new job (Table 4.26). For 23 per cent of these men and 20 per cent of the women, unsatisfactory pay in their current job was the main trigger for looking for another one, and similar proportions wanted to work longer hours or stated other reasons. These reasons were also the most common given by women employees working part-time who were looking for a new job. For men working part-time, filling in time before finding another job and wanting to work longer hours were the two main reasons.

Table 4.26 shows that about one in ten full-time employees were looking for a new job because they felt their present job might come to an end. Table 4.27 shows that in 1998, about one in five employees did not feel that their job was secure in their current workplace. Not surprisingly, those in temporary employment or on fixed term contracts were most likely to feel that their job was not secure, though more than half did not feel insecure. However, as already noted, temporary and fixed term contract workers in fact reported higher levels of job satisfaction than those in permanent employment, perhaps because they felt they could change jobs more easily if they wished.

Chart 4.28 shows that the number of employees with temporary work of some kind increased during the early 1990s and has since stabilised at around 1.7 million people. The increase in temporary work has been in fixed period contracts, which form about half of all temporary employment, and in agency temping. In percentage terms, the growth in agency temping has been the greatest, at 200 per cent since 1992.

Compared to many other European Union countries however, the proportion of people in temporary employment, at about 7 per cent in the United Kingdom in 2000, is relatively low (Table 4.29). In 2000, the European Union average was 13 per cent and the proportions for France, Finland, Netherlands, Portugal, Sweden and Spain were all more than twice the United Kingdom figure.

Chart **4.28**

Temporary employees: by type of employment

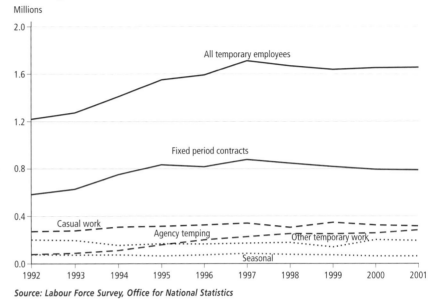

United Kingdom

Millions

Source: Labour Force Survey, Office for National Statistics

Chart **4.29**

Temporary employment[1]: by gender, EU comparison, 2000

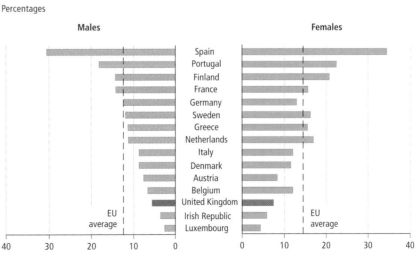

Percentages

1 Percentage of employees in temporary work. People aged 15 to 64, except for United Kingdom where data refer to those aged 16 to 64.

Source: Labour Force Survey, Results 2000 from Eurostat

Glossary of terms

Employees (Labour Force Survey measure) – a measure, obtained from household surveys, of people aged 16 and over who regard themselves as paid employees. People with two or more jobs are counted only once.

Self-employed – a measure, obtained from household surveys, of people aged 16 and over who regard themselves as self-employed, i.e. who in their main employment work on their own account, whether or not they have employees.

In employment – a measure, obtained from household surveys and censuses, of employees, self-employed people, participants in government employment and training programmes, and people doing unpaid family work.

Government employment and training programmes – a measure, obtained from household surveys, of those who said they were participants on Youth Training, Employment Training, Employment Action or Community Industry or a programme organised by TEC/LEC.

ILO unemployed – an International Labour Organisation (ILO) recommended measure, used in household surveys such as the Labour Force Survey, which counts as unemployed those aged 16 and over who are without a job, are available to start work in the next two weeks, who have been seeking a job in the last four weeks or are waiting to start a job already obtained.

Economically active (labour force) – those in employment plus those ILO unemployed.

ILO unemployment rate – the percentage of the economically active who are ILO unemployed.

The economically inactive – people who are neither in employment nor ILO unemployed. For example, all people under 16, those looking after a home or retired, or those permanently unable to work.

Economic activity rate – the percentage of the population in a given age group which is economically active.

Websites

National Statistics	www.statistics.gov.uk
National Centre for Social Research	www.natcen.ac.uk
Department of Trade and Industry	www.dti.gov.uk
Department for Work and Pensions	www.dwp.gov.uk
Cabinet Office Women's Unit	www.womens-unit.gov.uk
Employment Service	www.employment.gov.uk
EUROSTAT	www.europa.eu.int\comm\eurostat\
Labour Market Trends	www.statistics.gov.uk/products/p550.asp

Contacts

Office for National Statistics

Chapter author	020 7533 5283
Labour market enquiry helpline	020 7533 6094
Cabinet Office Women's Equality Unit	020 7273 8880
Department of Trade and Industry	020 7215 6160
Employment Service (New Deal)	020 7549 9571
EUROSTAT	00 352 4301 33209

Chapter 5

Income and Wealth

Household income

■ Household disposable income per head of population, adjusted for inflation, doubled between 1971 and 2000. (Chart 5.1)

■ Average income for pensioner families, adjusted for inflation, grew by an average of 2.9 per cent per year between 1979 and 1999–00. (Chart 5.4)

■ Men's incomes outstripped those of women in all age groups in 1999–00: the median gross income of women was 49 per cent of that of men. (Chart 5.5)

Earnings

■ In April 2000, treasurers and company financial managers headed the earnings league, averaging £1,059 per week: at the other end of the scale, kitchen porters and bar staff had weekly earnings averaging less than a fifth of this. (Table 5.9)

Income distribution

■ During the 1980s, the distribution of household incomes became more unequal: it appeared to stabilise in the early 1990s but in the most recent period there appears to have been a further small increase in inequality. (Chart 5.15)

Low incomes

■ In 1999–00, 18 per cent of the population of Great Britain lived in households with low income (below 60 per cent of median equivalised disposable income, before housing costs), having fallen from a peak of 21 per cent in 1992. (Chart 5.20)

■ Over one in five children in Great Britain in 1999 did not have a holiday away from home once a year because their parents could not afford it. (Chart 5.25)

Wealth

■ In 1999, the most wealthy 1 per cent of individuals owned 23 per cent of total marketable wealth, and half the population owned between them only 6 per cent of total wealth. (Table 5.27)

Chart **5.1**

Real household disposable income per head[1] and gross domestic product per head

United Kingdom

Index (1971=100)

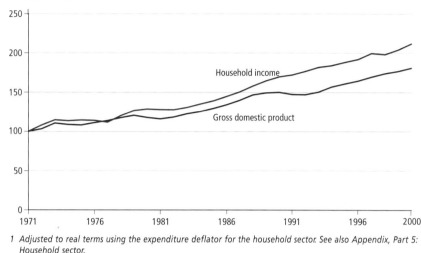

1 Adjusted to real terms using the expenditure deflator for the household sector. See also Appendix, Part 5: Household sector.

Source: Office for National Statistics

Table **5.2**

Composition of household income[1]

United Kingdom

Percentages

	1987	1991	1996	1998	1999	2000
Source of income						
Wages and salaries[2]	59	58	54	55	56	57
Operating income[3]	11	11	12	12	12	11
Net property income	8	8	9	8	8	8
Social benefits[4]	19	21	23	22	22	21
Other current transfers[5]	3	2	3	3	3	3
Total household income						
(=100%) (£ billion at 2000 prices[6])	631	724	809	855	883	929
Taxes etc as a percentage of						
total household income						
Taxes on income	11	11	10	11	11	11
Social contributions	16	17	18	18	18	18
Other current taxes	2	2	2	2	2	2
Other current transfers	2	2	2	3	3	2
Total household disposable income						
(=100%) (£ billion at 2000 prices[6])	427	495	562	584	605	631

1 See Appendix, Part 5: Household sector.
2 Includes employers' social contributions.
3 Includes self-employment income for sole-traders and rental income. See Appendix, Part 5 Household sector.
4 Comprises pensions and benefits.
5 Mostly other government grants, but including transfers from abroad and non-profit making bodies.
6 Adjusted to 2000 prices using the expenditure deflator for the household sector.

Source: Office for National Statistics

People's income has a major influence on their well-being: it determines how much they are able to spend and save. Income levels depend on the level of activity within the economy as a whole – the national income – and on the way in which national income is distributed. Wealth, on the other hand, represents the ownership of assets valued at a point in time.

Household income

The amount of income available for distribution to households depends on the overall level of economic activity. The most commonly used measure of economic activity is gross domestic product (GDP), sometimes also referred to as the amount of 'value added' generated within the economy of a country. The total income generated is divided between individuals, companies and other organisations (for example in the form of profits retained for investment), and government (in the form of taxes on production). Analysis of the trends in GDP may be found in the final section of this chapter.

Household income is derived not only directly from economic activity in the form of wages and salaries and self-employment income but also through transfers such as social security benefits. It is then subject to a number of deductions such as income tax, local taxes, and contributions towards pensions and national insurance. The amount of income remaining is referred to as household disposable income – the amount people have available to spend or save – and it is this measure which is commonly used to describe people's 'economic well-being'.

Household disposable income per head, adjusted for inflation, doubled between 1971 and 2000 (Chart 5.1). During the 1970s and early 1980s growth was somewhat erratic, and in some years there were small year-on-year falls, such as in 1974, 1976, 1977, 1981 and 1982. However, since then there has been growth each year, with the exception of 1998 when there was a very slight fall when adjusted for inflation. Over the period since 1971, a comparison of the patterns of growth of household disposable income and GDP per head shows that there has been a small shift between the shares of households and organisations in GDP in favour of households. Between 1999 and 2000, real household disposable income per head grew by 3.9 per cent compared with GDP per head growth of 2.4 per cent.

Table 5.2 illustrates how the shares of the various components of household income have changed since 1987. This shows a fall in the proportion derived from wages and salaries (including employers' social contributions for pensions and national insurance) from 59 per cent to 54 per cent in 1996, but since then a slight rise to 57 per cent in 2000. The proportion of income derived from social benefits shows the converse pattern, rising when wages and salaries fall and falling when they rise. More information about social benefits and the characteristics of their recipients may be found in Table 8.5 in the Social Protection chapter.

Taxes on income as a proportion of household income have remained stable over this period at around 11 per cent, and social contributions have also remained stable at 18 per cent of household income since 1996, though the proportion rose from 16 per cent in 1987. More information on taxes may be found in the third section of this chapter.

The data in Chart 5.1 and Table 5.2 are derived from the UK national accounts (see Appendix, Part 5: Household sector). In the national accounts the household sector is defined as including a variety of non-profit making institutions such as universities, charities and clubs, and people living in institutions such as nursing homes, as well as people living in private households. In most of the remainder of this chapter, the tables and charts are derived directly from surveys of households (such as the Family Resources Survey, the Family Expenditure Survey, the Labour Force Survey, and the British Household Panel Survey)

and surveys of businesses (such as the New Earnings Survey). Data from these surveys cover the population living in households and some cover certain parts of the population living in institutions, but all exclude non-profit making institutions. They can be used to analyse the distribution of household income between different sub-groups of the population, such as pensioners.

Survey sources differ from the national accounts not only in their population coverage but also in the way that household income is defined. One of the main differences is that the national accounts include the value of national insurance contributions made on behalf of employees by their employer as part of total household income, whereas survey sources do not. Survey sources are also subject to under-reporting and non-response bias. In the case of household income surveys, investment income is commonly underestimated, as is income from self-employment.

All these factors mean that the survey data on income used hereafter in this chapter are not entirely consistent with the national accounts household sector data, and so for example the overall composition of income shown in Table 5.3 differs from that in Table 5.2.

Table **5.3**

Sources of gross weekly household income: by region, 1999–00

Great Britain   Percentages

	Wages and salaries	Self-employment income	Investment income	State retirement pension plus any income support	Other Social security benefits	Private pensions	Other income	Gross household income (=100%) (£ per week)
North East	62	5	2	8	16	6	2	370
North West and Merseyside	63	8	3	7	10	6	2	440
Yorkshire and the Humber	63	8	3	7	11	7	2	410
East Midlands	67	8	3	6	9	6	2	450
West Midlands	65	9	3	7	10	6	2	450
East	65	11	3	6	6	7	2	510
London	66	12	3	4	8	4	2	570
South East	68	9	4	5	5	7	2	580
South West	58	10	4	8	8	10	2	430
England	64	9	3	6	8	7	2	480
Wales	57	8	2	8	13	9	2	400
Scotland	64	6	3	6	12	7	3	420
Great Britain	64	9	3	6	9	7	2	470

Source: Family Resources Survey, Department for Work and Pensions

The main sources of household income differ considerably in their importance between different types of households, particularly according to their family and employment circumstances. Table 5.3 from the Family Resources Survey shows how these differences result in turn in varying levels of household income between the regions of Great Britain. In 1999–00 wages and salaries were within two percentage points of the Great Britain average of 64 per cent in the majority of regions, but in Wales and the South West the proportion was much lower at 57 and 58 per cent respectively. These are areas with high concentrations of retired people as evidenced by the relatively high proportion of income derived from both state and private pensions (17 and 18 per cent respectively, compared with the Great Britain average of 13 per cent). Income from self-employment as a proportion of household income was highest in London and lowest in the North East, whilst the North East had the highest proportion of income derived from social security benefits other than the state retirement pension. The overall level of income was highest in the South East, at £580 per week, and lowest in the North East at £370 per week, less than two-thirds of that in the South East.

The largest source of income for pensioner families in Great Britain, not surprisingly, is social security benefits, which include the state retirement pension (Table 5.4). In 1999–00, the average pensioner family received just over half its gross income from social security benefits. Occupational pensions accounted for 26 per cent of gross income while a further 14 per cent came from investment income.

The average income of pensioner families has grown in real terms, i.e. adjusted for inflation, by over 60 per cent between 1979 and 1996–97, an average annual growth rate of 2.9 per cent. This compares with growth of 36 per cent in average earnings deflated by the Retail Price Index (all items) over the same period (see Chart 5.6).

These data are derived from the Family Expenditure Survey: estimates for more recent years from the Family Resources Survey suggest that this growth rate has been maintained between 1994–95 and 1999–00, and that it has continued to outpace the growth in earnings. Some sources of income have contributed more than others to this overall growth. Between 1979 and 1996–97, the fastest growing sources of income were occupational pensions, which increased by 162 per cent in real terms, and investment income (110 per cent), though average investment income fell slightly in the mid 1990s. The proportional growth in benefit income (41 per cent) is lower, though in absolute terms benefits have contributed just as much to overall growth (up £33 in July 1999 prices) as occupational pensions (up £35) and more than investment income (up £16). Data from the Family Resources Survey suggest that income from occupational pensions continued to grow relatively strongly between 1994–95 and 1999–00, as did income from benefits. Note that this growth is a result of both the increase in the proportion of recipients and in the amount per recipient.

Table **5.4**

Pensioners'[1] gross income: by source[2]

United Kingdom

£ per week[3]

	1979	1981	1987	1990–1991	1994–95	1994–95	1996–97	1999–00
Benefit income	81	87	96	95	110	109	113	122
Occupational pension	21	23	38	42	53	51	56	61
Investment income	14	19	31	39	32	28	28	32
Earnings	15	12	10	14	15	16	17	19
Other income	1	1	1	1	1	1	1	2
Gross income	132	141	176	191	211	205	215	235

1 Pensioner units – single people over the state pension age (65 for males, 60 for females) and couples where the man is over state pension age.
2 Data between 1979 and 1994–95 are from FES and cover the United Kingdom. Data between 1994–95 and 1999–00 are from the FRS and cover Great Britain.
3 Adjusted to July 1999 prices using the retail prices index less local taxes.
Source: Pensioners' Income series, Department for Work and Pensions

Incomes tend to be higher for younger pensioners than for older pensioners, for both singles and couples. Differences in income by age can be caused in different ways. First, older pensioners are less likely to work, purely due to their age. But second, there is influence from historical factors: for example, the rapid rise in occupational pension coverage in the 1950s and 1960s will have been more beneficial to someone born in 1930 than in 1910. A third reason is that whereas before retirement the accrued value of occupational and other earnings-related pensions is broadly linked to earnings growth, the value of these pensions when they are paid is usually linked to prices. Thus all other things being equal, the value of such a pension to someone who has been retired for longer will be less than for the equivalent younger pensioner.

The information presented in this section so far has been in terms of household or family income, since these are generally considered to be the units across which resources are shared (see Appendix Part 2: Households for definition of a household). Thus total household income can be taken as representing the (potential) standard of living of each of its members. The assumption of equal sharing of resources between each member of the household is very difficult to test. Using certain assumptions it is possible to use household survey data to derive estimates of the income accruing to individuals, but it is not possible to infer their living standards from these.

The results of such an exercise are shown in Chart 5.5 which compares the median gross incomes of men and women by age group. (See Appendix Part 5: Individual income for details of how these estimates were derived, and Box on page 96 for explanation of median). Men's incomes outstripped those of women in all age groups in 1999–00: the median gross income of women was 49 per cent of that of men. However, the gap varied according to age. In the youngest age group, incomes were very close (£83 per week for 16 to 19 year old males, £76 per week for females). For women aged between 35 and 64, incomes were less than half those of men of the same age. The proportional difference in median gross income was largest for men and women aged 55 to 59: in this age group women's incomes were only 38 per cent of those of men. The gap between men's and women's incomes was lower for pensioners, and women aged 85 or over had income levels which were 83 per cent of those of men in the same age band. Median income was higher for women aged 80 and over than for women in their 70s, mainly because the older age band includes a higher proportion of widows who have higher individual incomes than women in pensioner couples. Median gross income was highest for men in their mid to late thirties, whereas women's incomes were highest for those in their mid to late twenties.

Chart **5.5**

Median individual gross income[1]: by gender and age, 1999-00

Great Britain

£ per week

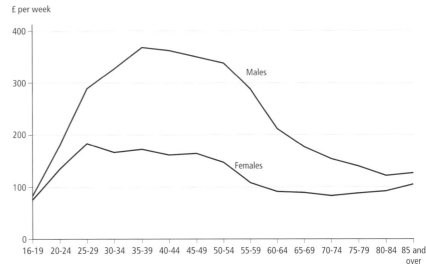

1 See Appendix, Part 5: Individual income.

Source: Family Resources Survey, Department for Work and Pensions

The data in Chart 5.5 are derived from the Family Resources Survey and therefore represent a 'snapshot' of the various age groups in 1999–00 rather than a longitudinal perspective: thus they do not purport to describe the trajectory of income over the life cycle for men and women.

Earnings

Income from employment is the most important component of household income. The average earnings index (AEI), a monthly measure of the pay of a representative sample of all employees across all sectors of the economy, is one of the indicators used to judge the state of the UK economy. If the index rises rapidly, this may indicate that the labour market is under-supplied with employees in the right numbers and with the right skills to meet the level of demand within the economy. In addition, a rapid rise may indicate that wage settlements are higher than the rate of economic growth can sustain and thus create inflationary pressures. A fall in the index may be a reflection of reduced demand within the economy and may presage a fall in GDP and an increase in unemployment. The relationship between the AEI and the retail prices index (RPI) is also of importance. If the AEI rises faster than the RPI, this means that employees' pay is increasing faster than the prices they have to pay for goods and services and that therefore, all things being equal, their purchasing power will rise and they will feel 'better off'.

Chart **5.6**

Average earnings index[1,2] and retail prices index[3]

Percentage change over 12 months

1 Data are for Great Britain.
2 Data for August 2001 are provisional.
3 Data are for United Kingdom.
Source: Office for National Statistics

During the two decades from 1971, the AEI and RPI showed similar patterns of change, but with the RPI generally showing slower growth (Chart 5.6). For example, the peak in earnings growth over this period occurred in February 1975 when it reached an annual rate of 32 per cent. The peak in the RPI occurred in August that year at 27 per cent. During most of the 1990s, the AEI outpaced the RPI. This was made possible mainly through increases in productivity, enabling employers to pay higher wages while not increasing their prices to the same extent to finance their wage bill. The periods during which prices have risen faster than earnings – for example in the latter half of 1995 – have been times of economic downturn when a fall in demand for labour depressed earnings growth.

A wide variety of factors influence the level of earnings which an employee receives such as their skills and experience, their occupation, the economic sector in which they work, the hours they work, and so on. The area of the country in which they work and their gender may also have an impact. The remainder of this section explores some of these factors. However, it should be borne in mind that they are all very much interlinked, and it is not possible here to disentangle the effect that any single factor may have.

Government legislation may also have an effect on wages. The *Equal Pay Act 1970* and subsequent revisions, together with the *Sex Discrimination Act*, established the principle of equal pay for work which can be established to be of equal value to that done by a member of the opposite sex, employed by the same employer, under common terms and conditions of employment. The impact of this legislation, together with other important factors such as the opening up of higher paid work to women, has been to narrow the differential between the hourly earnings of men and women (Chart 5.7). In 1986, the hourly earnings of women working full-time in Great Britain were 74 per cent of those of men, whereas in 2000 they had risen to 82 per cent. The differential between men and women working part-time is smaller, for example women's hourly earnings were 88 per cent of those of men in 2000. However, this proportion fluctuates from year to year and shows no clear trend over the last 15 years: partly because there are relatively few men working part-time (see Table 4.3 on page 71 of the Labour Market chapter) and so these figures are subject to a higher level of sampling error.

Chart **5.7**

Gross earnings[1]: by gender and whether working full-time or part-time

Great Britain

£ per hour

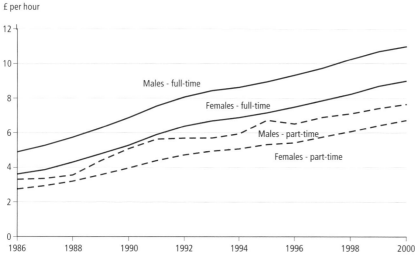

1 Average gross hourly earnings for employees on adult rates at April each year.
Source: New Earnings Survey, Office for National Statistics

Although average hourly pay provides a useful comparison between the earnings of men and women, it does not necessarily indicate differences in rates of pay for comparable jobs. Such averages reflect the different employment characteristics of men and women, such as the proportions in different occupations and their length of time in jobs. The fact that women are more likely than men to be in non-manual occupations raises their overall average pay relative to that of men: the average hourly earnings of non-manual women is higher than that of men in manual work. However, among both manual and non-manual workers, women are concentrated in lower paid occupations which reduces their relative pay.

Wage rates can vary considerably between industrial sectors. Agriculture has traditionally been a relatively low-paid sector and this is still the case, with 65 per cent of employees on wage rates of less than £6 per hour in Spring 2000. The hotel and restaurant sector is also relatively low paid, with 75 per cent earning less than £6 per hour and 34 per cent earning less than £4 per hour. At the other end of the scale, 39 per cent of those in financial intermediation earned more than £12 per hour. Averaged over all industries, 6 per cent of employees earned less than £4 per hour.

Wage rates also vary according to occupation. Table 5.8 shows the highest and lowest paid occupations in Great Britain. Treasurers and company financial managers, earning on average £1,059 per week, topped the earnings league in April 2000, the only occupational group whose average weekly earnings exceeded £1,000. The next highest paid occupation was medical practitioners, with average weekly earnings of £964. The lowest paid of all full-time adult employees were kitchen porters and bar staff, both with earnings of around £184 per week, less than a fifth of the earnings of the highest paid occupational group.

Another picture of the occupational distribution of weekly earnings can be obtained by considering each decile group (see Box on page 96 for explanation) separately and selecting an occupation whose average earnings fall within that range and who can therefore be considered typical of that decile group. Data for 2000 indicate that bar work is a typical occupation in the lowest tenth of the earnings distribution; skilled manual occupations such as bricklaying and welding are typical of the middle of the distribution; and professional and managerial occupations are typical of the upper part, with solicitors a typical occupation in the highest tenth of the distribution.

For some workers, the value of income 'in kind' forms an important part of their overall remuneration package. Such benefits may include a company car, free fuel, or private medical insurance. Information is available from the Inland Revenue on those benefits whose value to the recipient is liable to taxation. In 1999–00, the average value of taxable benefits was £2,530 per recipient, but increased with income. The average value of a company car was £3,350 per recipient.

Table **5.8**

Highest and lowest paid occupations, April 2000

Great Britain	Average gross weekly pay (£)
Highest paid	
Treasurers and company financial managers	1,059
Medical practitioners	964
Organisation and methods and work study managers	813
Management consultants, business analysts	812
Underwriters, claims assessors, brokers, investment analysis	775
Police officers (inspector or above)	766
Computer systems and data processing managers	757
Solicitors	748
Marketing and sales managers	719
Advertising and public relations managers	690
Lowest paid	
Educational assistants	212
Other childcare and related occupations	205
Counterhands, catering assistants	196
Launderers, dry cleaners, pressers	196
Hairdressers, barbers	190
Waiters, waitresses	189
Petrol pump, forecourt attendants	189
Retail cash desk and check-out operators	185
Bar staff	184
Kitchen porters, hands	184

Source: New Earnings Survey, Office for National Statistics

Table 5.9 (see overleaf), taken from the Family Resources Survey, shows a wider range of employee benefits, covering those which are not liable to taxation as well as some that are. A third of male employees and rather less than a third of women in Great Britain received at least one of these benefits in 1999–00. Nearly a fifth of employees benefited from free or subsidised meals or canteen, twice as high a proportion than for any other benefit. Men were more likely than women to benefit from free or subsidised medical insurance or from shares or share options. Negligible proportions of men and women received childcare provision or vouchers from their employer.

Table **5.9**

Availability of employers' packages, 1999–00

Great Britain   Percentages[1]

	Males	Females
Free or subsidised meals/canteen	18	17
Free or subsidised medical insurance	9	4
Shares or share option	8	5
Free or subsidised goods	5	6
Mileage allowances	3	2
Refunds of motoring expenses	1	1
Luncheon vouchers	1	1
Refunds of household expenditure	1	–
Payment of school fees	–	–
Childcare provisions/vouchers	–	–
Any allowance/benefit	33	29

1 Percentage of those in employment.

Source: Family Resources Survey, Department for Work and Pensions

Table **5.10**

Income tax payable: by annual income[1], 2001–02[2]

United Kingdom

	Number of taxpayers (millions)	Total tax payable (£ million)	Average rate of tax payable (percentages)	Average amount of tax payable (£)
£4,535–£4,999	0.5	10	0	20
£5,000–£7,499	3.3	500	3	170
£7,500–£9,999	3.3	2,000	6	550
£10,000–£14,999	6.2	8,500	10	1,260
£15,000–£19,999	4.6	11,000	13	2,270
£20,000–£29,999	5.4	20,700	15	3,690
£30,000–£49,999	3.0	20,800	18	6,810
£50,000–£99,999	1.0	16,700	26	17,400
£100,000 and over	0.3	21,400	34	71,500
All incomes	27.6	101,700	17	3,590

1 Total income of the individual for income tax purposes including earned and investment income. Figures relate to taxpayers only.

2 Based on projections in line with the March 2001 Budget.

Source: Inland Revenue

Taxes

Table 5.2 showed that in 2000, 11 per cent of household income was paid out in taxes on income and 18 per cent in social contributions. Since every taxpayer is entitled to a personal allowance, which in 2001–02 is £4,535, those with income below this do not pay any tax. If they are aged over 65 they may be entitled to further allowances. The income tax regime for 2001–02 includes three different rates of tax. Taxable income of up to £1,880 (i.e. after the deduction of allowances and any other tax relief to which the individual may be entitled) is charged at 10 per cent. Taxable income above £1,880 but less than £29,400 is charged at 22 per cent, while income above this level is charged at 40 per cent. Special rates apply to savings income.

The Inland Revenue estimates that in 2001–02 there will be around 27.6 million taxpayers in the United Kingdom, over half the adult population (Table 5.10). Because of the progressive nature of the income tax system, the amount of tax payable increases both in cash terms and as a proportion of income as income increases, averaging £20 per year for taxpayers with annual incomes under £5,000 and £71,500 for those with incomes of £100,000 and above.

National insurance (NI) contributions are paid according to an individual's earnings rather than their total income, and for employees payments are made both by the individual and by their employer. Employees' contributions tend to be slightly smaller as a proportion of earnings for those on higher weekly earnings compared with those on lower earnings because there is a ceiling on contributions: in 2001–02 contributions were levied only on the first £575 of weekly earnings.

In addition to direct taxes such as income tax households also pay indirect taxes through their expenditure. Indirect taxes include value added tax (VAT), customs duties and excise duties and are included in the prices of consumer goods and services. These taxes are specific to particular commodities: for example, in 2000–01 VAT was payable on most consumer goods at 17.5 per cent of their value, though not on most foods nor on books and newspapers and at a reduced rate on heating and lighting. Customs and excise duties on the other hand tend to vary by the volume rather than value of goods purchased. Because high income households are more likely to devote a larger proportion of their income to investments or repaying loans, and low income households may be funding their expenditure through taking out loans or drawing down savings, the proportion of income paid in indirect taxes tends to be higher for those on low incomes than for those on high incomes.

A further means of raising revenue from households is through local taxes. Local taxes in 1999–00 comprised council tax in Great Britain and domestic rates in Northern Ireland. These taxes are raised by local authorities to part-fund the services they provide. For both council tax and domestic rates, the amount payable by a household depends on the value of the property they occupy. However, for those on low incomes assistance is available in the form of council tax benefits (rates rebates in Northern Ireland). In 1999-00, estimates from the Family Expenditure Survey indicate that local taxes as a percentage of gross income varied within Great Britain between 2.4 per cent in London and 3.7 per cent in the North East (Chart 5.11). Although the percentage was highest in the North East, the net amount of council tax payable in the region at £680 per year was the lowest in Great Britain. The highest amounts payable were in the South East (£880), South West (£870) and the East (£860). Net domestic rates in Northern Ireland, which are based on a quite different valuation system, averaged £330 per year, representing 1.7 per cent of household gross income.

Income distribution

We have already seen how the various components of income differ in importance for different household types and how the levels of earnings vary between individuals. The result is an uneven distribution of total income between households, though the inequality is reduced to some extent by the deduction of taxes and social contributions and their redistribution to households in the form of social security benefits and other payments from government.

During the 1970s, there was relatively little change in the distribution of disposable income among households (Chart 5.12). However, the 1980s were characterised by a large increase in inequality: between 1981 and 1989, whereas average (median) income rose by 27 per cent when adjusted for inflation, income at the ninetieth percentile rose by 38 per cent and that at the tenth percentile rose by only 7 per cent. During the first half of the 1990s, the income distribution appeared to stabilise, but in the most recent period there appears to have been a further small increase in inequality.

Chart **5.11**

Net local taxes[1] as a percentage of gross income: by region, 1999-00

United Kingdom

Percentages

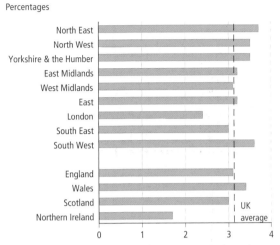

1 Council tax net of council tax benefit in Great Britain; domestic rates net of rates rebate in Northern Ireland.

Source: Office for National Statistics

Chart **5.12**

Distribution of real[1] houshold disposable income[2]

United Kingdom

£ per week

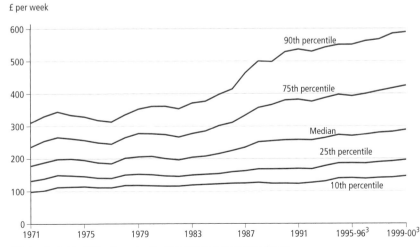

1 Data adjusted to 2001 prices using the Retail Prices Index less local taxes.

2 Before housing costs. See Appendix, Part 5: Households Below Average Income.

3 Data from 1993-94 onwards are for financial years; data for 1994-95 onwards exclude Northern Ireland.

Source: Institute for Fiscal Studies

Table **5.13**

Distribution of equivalised disposable income[1]: by economic status of family, 1999–00

Great Britain

Percentages

	Quintile group					All
	Bottom quintile	Second quintile	Third quintile	Fourth quintile	Top quintile	(=100%) (millions)
Self-employed[2]	22	14	18	18	28	5.2
Single/couple all in full-time work	3	8	19	32	39	13.7
Couple, one in full-time work, one in part time work	4	17	29	28	22	8.5
Couple, one in full-time work, one not working	16	23	23	21	16	6.5
One or more in part-time work	29	26	20	12	13	4.7
Head or spouse aged 60 or over	27	32	21	13	8	9.8
Head or spouse unemployed	67	21	7	3	2	2.1
Other inactive[3]	48	31	12	6	3	6.2
All individuals	20	20	20	20	20	56.7

1 Equivalised household disposable income, before housing costs, has been used for ranking the individuals into quintile groups. See Appendix, Part 5: Equivalisation scales and Households below average income.

2 Those in benefit units which contain one or more adults who are normally self-employed for 30 or more hours a week.

3 Includes long-term sick and disabled people and non-working single-parents.

Source: Households Below Average Income series, Department for Work and Pensions

Equivalisation – in analysing the distribution of income, household disposable income is usually adjusted to take account of the size and composition of the household. This is in recognition of the fact that, for example, to achieve the same standard of living a household of five would require a higher income than would a single person. This process is known as equivalisation (see Appendix, Part 5: Equivalisation scales). Adjustments may also be made to deduct housing costs but these have not been made in the estimates in this chapter.

Quintile and decile groups – the main method of analysing income distribution used in this chapter is to rank units (households, individuals or adults) by a given income measure, and then to divide the ranked units into groups of equal size. Groups containing 20 per cent of units are referred to as 'quintile groups' or 'fifths'. Thus the 'bottom quintile group' is the 20 per cent of units with the lowest incomes. Similarly, groups containing 10 per cent of units are referred to as 'decile groups' or tenths.

Percentiles – an alternative method also used in the chapter is to present the income level above or below which a certain proportion of units fall. Thus the ninetieth percentile is the income level above which only 10 per cent of units fall when ranked by a given income measure. The median is then the midpoint of the distribution above and below which 50 per cent of units fall.

The Institute for Fiscal Studies has investigated some of the possible explanations for the changes in inequality seen over the last two decades, and in particular why the trends are different over the economic cycles of the 1980s and 1990s. They found that wage growth played a part: inequality tends to rise during periods of rapid wage growth because the poorest households are the most likely to contain non-working individuals (see Table 4.12, Workless households on page 75 of the Labour Market chapter). The economic recovery in the 1980s was characterised by large increases in wages in each of the years from 1984 to 1988 (see Chart 5.6 above) matching the period when inequality increased rapidly. In contrast wage growth was very slow to return in the recovery of the 1990s – a time of stable or falling inequality. Growth in self-employment income and in unemployment were also found to be associated with periods of increased inequality. However, this research did not examine the role of tax and benefit policy or the contribution of changing household composition and demographic factors.

People in single and couple households where all members are in full-time work were nearly twice as likely as the population as a whole to be in the top quintile group of disposable income in 1999–00, and only 3 per cent of such people were in the lowest quintile group (Table 5.13). Also over-represented in the highest income group are the self-employed. At the other end of the distribution, people in households where the head or spouse was unemployed were more than three times as likely as all individuals to be in the bottom quintile group. The section below on low incomes examines the characteristics of those at the lower end of the income distribution in more depth.

An alternative approach to the analysis of income distribution is to compare the share of total income received by each quintile group: if income is evenly distributed across all individuals each of these shares would be 20 per cent. Chart 5.14 shows the shares of disposable income received by each quintile group of individuals in Great Britain in 1999-00. The ratio of the share of the top quintile group (42 per cent) to that of the bottom quintile group (7.6 per cent) was 5.5, slightly higher than the ratio of 5.2 in 1994–95. Between 1994–95 and 1999–00, median disposable income rose by 10 per cent in real terms, but for individuals in the bottom quintile it rose by 9 per cent compared with 11 per cent for the fourth and top quintile groups. This evidence indicates a slight, but not statistically significant, increase in overall income inequality over the period.

The Department for Work and Pension's Households Below Average Income analysis from which Table 5.13 and Chart 5.14 are derived, provides an annual cross-sectional snapshot of the distribution of income based on the Family Resources Survey. The British Household Panel Survey (BHPS) complements this by providing longitudinal information about how the incomes of a fixed sample of individuals change from year to year. This enables us to track how people move through the income distribution over time, and to identify the factors associated with changes in their position in the distribution.

One of the major factors contributing to changes in an individual's position in the income distribution is change in the composition of the family in which they live. For women over the period 1991 to 1999, setting up home with a male partner was more than twice as likely to result in an increase in household income of one or more quintile groups as it was to result in a fall of one or more quintile groups (Table 5.15). Conversely, when they separated from a male partner about half experienced a fall of one or more quintiles whereas only about one-fifth experienced a rise. For men, joining with a female partner is more likely to result in stable household income and separating from them is more likely to result in a rise; in general, changes in family composition have less effect on men's position in the income distribution than on the position of women. These results reflect the higher individual incomes of men compared to women (see Chart 5.5 above).

As discussed earlier in this chapter, households initially receive income from various sources such as employment, occupational pensions, investments, and transfers from other households. The state then intervenes both to raise taxes and national insurance contributions from individuals and to redistribute the revenue thus raised in the form of cash benefits to households and in the provision of services which are free or provided at a subsidised price at the point of use. Some households will pay more in tax than they receive in benefits, while others will benefit more than they are taxed. Overall, this process results in a redistribution of income from households with higher incomes to those on lower incomes.

Chart **5.14**

Shares of equivalised disposable income[1], 1999-00

Great Britain

Percentages

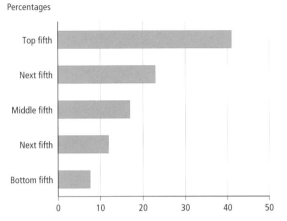

1 Equivalised disposable income before housing costs has been used to rank the individuals into quintile groups. See Appendix, Part 5: Equivalisation scales.

Source: Households Below Average Income Series, Department for Work and Pensions

Table **5.15**

Effects of changes in family composition on household income[1]: by gender, 1991 to 1999[2]

Great Britain   Percentages

	Income fell 1 or more quintile groups	Income stable[3]	Income rose 1 or more quintile groups	All
Joined with partner				
Males	31	42	27	100
Females	20	34	45	100
Separated from partner				
Males	23	40	36	100
Females	49	31	19	100

1 Gross equivalised household income has been used for ranking households into quintile groups.

2 Changes in living arrangements and income between individual years have been analysed separately and then combined in this table.

3 Income did not change by one quintile group.

Source: British Household Panel Survey, Institute for Social and Economic Research

Table **5.16**

Redistribution of income through taxes and benefits[1], 1990–00

United Kingdom   £ per year

	Quintile group of households[2]					All house-holds
	Bottom quintile	Next quintile	Middle quintile	Next quintile	Top quintile	
Average per household						
Wages and salaries	1,700	5,480	13,360	22,150	38,510	16,240
Imputed income from benefits in kind	–	30	120	330	950	290
Self-employment income	350	550	1,130	1,840	8,400	2,450
Occupational pensions, annuities	400	1,110	1,730	2,440	2,840	1,700
Investment income	240	360	650	920	3,500	1,130
Other income	160	160	180	250	190	190
Total original income	2,840	7,680	17,170	27,920	54,400	22,000
plus Benefits in cash						
Contributory	2,100	2,710	1,970	1,190	730	1,740
Non-contributory	2,770	2,410	1,860	930	410	1,680
Gross income	7,720	12,810	21,010	30,040	55,540	25,420
less Income tax[3] and NIC[4]	360	1,170	3,010	5,490	12,030	4,410
less Local taxes[5] (net)	530	640	790	910	1,060	790
Disposable income	6,830	11,000	17,210	23,640	42,450	20,230
less Indirect taxes	2,310	2,720	4,050	4,990	6,380	4,090
Post-tax income	4,520	8,280	13,160	18,650	36,060	16,130
plus Benefits in kind						
Education	2,040	1,280	1,380	1,120	730	1,310
National Health Service	2,130	2,250	1,970	1,740	1,450	1,910
Housing subsidy	60	60	30	20	10	30
Travel subsidies	50	50	50	50	80	60
School meals and welfare milk	70	30	10	10	–	20
Final income	8,870	11,960	16,610	21,590	38,330	19,470

1 See Appendix, Part 5: Redistribution of income.

2 Equivalised disposable income has been used for ranking the households. See Appendix, Part 5: Equivalisation scales.

3 After tax relief at source on mortgage interest and life assurance premiums.

4 Employees' National Insurance contributions.

5 Council tax net of council tax benefits, rates and water charges. Rates net of rebates in Northern Ireland.

Source: Office for National Statistics

The average taxes paid and benefits received by each quintile group in 1999–00 are set out in Table 5.16. The distribution of 'original' income – before any state intervention – is highly unequal, with the average income of the top quintile group over 19 times greater than that of the bottom quintile group. Payment of cash benefits reduces this disparity so that the ratio of gross income in the top group compared with the bottom is 7:1, and deduction of direct and local taxes reduces the ratio further to around 6:1. Based on people's expenditure patterns it is then possible to calculate an estimated payment of indirect taxes such as VAT and excise duties, which are deducted to produce a measure of post-tax income. Finally, an estimate is made for value of the benefit they receive from government expenditure on services such as education and health. (It is not possible to estimate the benefit to households of some items of government expenditure, for example defence and road-building). Addition of these estimates gives a household's final income. Taken together with cash benefits, around 55 per cent of general government expenditure is allocated to households in this analysis. The ratio of average final income in the top quintile group to that in the bottom quintile group is 4:1.

Low incomes

The incidence of low incomes, the factors contributing to low income and the ways of mitigating their effects have been an enduring focus of attention of governments from the introduction of the first poor laws in the 16th century up to the present day. The concerns of investigators such as Charles Booth in the latter part of the 19th century were taken up by governments in the 20th century, from the introduction of the first old age pensions in 1909 to the welfare state of Beveridge some forty years later.

Being disadvantaged, and thus 'excluded' from many of the opportunities available to the average citizen, has often been seen as synonymous with having a low income. While low income is clearly central to poverty and social exclusion, it is now widely accepted that there is a wide range of other factors which are important. People can experience poverty of education, of training, of health, and of environment, as well as poverty in purely cash terms. Nevertheless, the prevalence of low income remains an important indicator of social exclusion. Information on many of the other aspects may be found in other chapters of *Social Trends*.

The definition of 'low' income has always been a source of debate and to some extent has to be arbitrary. Only in countries at a very low level of economic development is it sensible to take an absolutist, 'basic needs' approach, which costs the bare essentials to maintain human life and uses this as the yardstick against which incomes are measured. All other approaches are to a greater or lesser extent relative: 'low' income is defined in terms of what is generally considered adequate to maintain an acceptable standard of living given the norms of a particular society at a particular time. With such approaches, it is possible and indeed perfectly acceptable for 'low' income to differ both temporally and spatially. So for example, while in one country the possession of sufficient income to pay for central heating might be considered a necessity, this might not have been the case in the same country a generation ago and nor might it be so for a different country today.

In this section, the threshold generally adopted to define low income is 60 per cent of median equivalised household disposable income. This is one of a set of indicators in the *Opportunity for All* report used to monitor the Government's strategy to tackle poverty and social exclusion. It has also been agreed by the Statistical Program Committee of the European Union as the basis for making international comparisons of numbers of people on low incomes. In 1999–00, 18 per cent of the population in Great Britain lived in households with income below this level (Chart 5.17). This proportion was fairly static during the 1960s, 1970s and early 1980s, fluctuating between 10 and 15 per cent. It then rose steeply from 1985 to reach a peak of 21 per cent in 1992. There was then a slight drop and the proportion has remained at around 18 per cent over the last four years. This pattern is also reflected in the proportions of people with incomes less than 50 per cent and 40 per cent of the median.

Table 5.18 illustrates the likelihood of individuals in particular family types being in low income households, and the way in which these risks have changed over the last twenty years. In 1999–00, people living in lone parent families, pensioner couples and single pensioners were all more likely than the population as a whole to be living in a low income household. For people in lone parent families the likelihood was nearly twice that for all individuals. The pattern was similar in 1981, though as we have already seen from Chart 5.17 the overall risk of low income was lower at that time.

Chart **5.17**

Percentage of people whose income is below various fractions of median income[1]

United Kingdom

Percentages

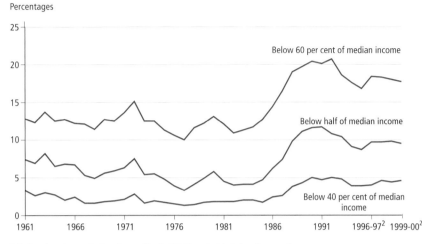

1 Before housing costs. See Appendix, Part 5: Households Below Average Income.
2 Data from 1993–94 onwards are for financial years; data for 1994–95 onwards exclude Northern Ireland.
Source: Institute for Fiscal Studies

Table **5.18**

People in households below 60 per cent median income[1]: by family type

United Kingdom and Great Britain[2]   Percentages

	1981	1991–1992	1996–97	1998–99	1999–00
Single people without children	8	18	16	15	16
Single pensioners	15	29	23	23	23
Lone parents	22	46	38	36	35
Couples without children	5	10	10	10	10
Pensioner couples	17	29	20	23	21
Couples with children	15	20	19	18	17
All individuals	13	21	18	18	18

1 Equivalised disposable income before housing costs. See Appendix, Part 5: Households below average income.
2 Data for 1981 and 1991–1992 are based on the Family Expenditure Survey which covers the United Kingdom. Data for 1996–97 to 1999–00 are based on the Family Resources Survey which covers Great Britain only.
Source: Households Below Average Income series, Department for Work and Pensions

Table **5.19**

Proportion of individuals experiencing periods of persistent low income[1], 1991 to 1999

Great Britain		Percentages
	Below 60% median income	Below 70% median income
Number of years spent below specified income threshold		
At least one year	46	57
At least 5 years	13	22
At least 7 years	6	13
All 9 years	2	4

1 Equivalised disposable income before housing costs. See Appendix Part 5: Households below average income.

Source: Households Below Average Income series, Department for Work and Pensions

Table **5.20**

Low paid jobs: by age of employee and employment status[1]

United Kingdom			Percentages
	1998	1999	2000
Age			
18–21	7.7	2.7	3.1
22 and over	6.4	2.4	1.1
Male employees			
Full-time	2.3	1.1	0.5
Part-time	15.8	7	4.2
All	3.4	1.6	0.8
Female employees			
Full-time	4.3	1.5	0.6
Part-time	16.3	5.5	3
All	9.7	3.3	1.7

1 Table is based on £3.00 per hour for those aged 18–21, £3.60 per hour for those aged 22 and over, the National Minimum Wage rates at Spring 2000.

Source: Office for National Statistics

For some people, for example students and those unemployed for only a brief period, the experience of low income may be a relatively transient one, whereas for others it may be a more-or-less permanent state through their life-times. The British Household Panel Survey provides longitudinal data which allow income mobility and the persistence of low income to be analysed. Table 5.19 shows that although around half of individuals had had some experience of low income over the period 1991 to 1999, only 2 per cent were on low incomes throughout the period.

The government's *Opportunity for All* indicators use alternative definitions of 'persistence' of low incomes to that used in Table 5.19, taking those individuals with incomes below 60 per cent and those below 70 per cent of the median in at least three out of four years. Based on the first of these definitions and again using BHPS data, over the period 1996–99, 16 per cent of children experienced persistent low income compared with 18 per cent of pensioners and only 7 per cent of working age adults. Between 1991 and 1999 there are indications of a decrease in the risk of persistent low incomes for children, and an increased risk for pensioners, though neither change is large in relation to possible measurement error.

Although the incidence of low income is often associated with not working, as Table 5.13 indicated, the existence of income from employment is not always sufficient to lift a household out of low income. For people in some occupations and industries, wage rates may be so low that their household income may still be insufficient for them to support a family adequately. The aim of Working Family Tax Credit, which replaced Family Credit from 5 October 1999, is to guarantee a minimum income to working families with children. In April 2001 this minimum was £214 per week.

The national minimum wage (NMW), which came into force in April 1999, is another measure to combat the phenomenon of the 'working poor'. The minimum wage rates were set at £3.00 per hour for 18-21 year olds and £3.60 for those aged 22 or over, with some exceptions for workers receiving training during the first six months of employment. (As of 1 October 2001, the rate for 18–21 year olds was increased to £3.50 per hour and the rate for those aged 22 and over was raised to £4.10 per hour.)

The NMW has had an impact on the earnings distribution. The number of jobs paid at less than these rates fell from 1, 500 thousand in Spring 1998 to 300 thousand in Spring 2000. Overall, these jobs represented 6.4 per cent of the total in 1998 but only 1.2 per cent in 2000. However, the likelihood of being paid less than the NMW varies according to age, employment status and gender (Table 5.20). Overall, women are twice as likely as men to have a job with hourly pay below the NMW, but the group most at risk is males working part-time, followed by female part-timers.

Note that these estimates cannot be used as a measure of non-compliance because it is not possible to discern from the data sources whether an individual is eligible for minimum wage rates.

Children are disproportionately present in low income households: in 1999–00, 23 per cent of children (3 million) were living in households with below 60 per cent of median income in Great Britain. However, the proportion of children in low income households has fallen slightly over the last five years, from 26 per cent in 1996–97. The risk of a child living in a low income household is increased by the presence of disabled people (Table 5.21). Over one in three of children living with one or more disabled adults were in low income households in 1999–00, and over two in five of those living in families with both disabled adult(s) and disabled child(ren). However, in households with a disabled child but no disabled adult, the risk of children being in a low income household was similar to that for children as a whole.

Low income may lead to material deprivation. The 1999 Poverty and Social Exclusion Survey, supported by the Joseph Rowntree Foundation, sought to identify the items that a majority of the general public perceive to be necessities which all adults should be able to afford and which they should not have to do without. The next step was to find out how many people lacked these because they could not afford them rather than because they did not want them. Similar methods were used to establish a list of 'necessities' that all parents considered that they should be able to afford for their children and then to find out how many children lacked them because their parents could not afford them.

Chart 5.22 shows those necessities defined in this way which the highest proportions of children do not have because their parents cannot afford them. Over one in five did not have a holiday away from home once a year, and more than one in fifteen could not go swimming at least once a month. About 18 per cent of all children lacked two or more items which parents considered to be necessities but which their own parents said that they were unable to afford, and are defined as 'necessity deprived'.

Table **5.21**

Proportion of children living in low income households: by presence of disabled[1] people in the family, 1999–00

Great Britain — Percentages

	Proportion of children living in households below 60 per cent of median income[2]	All children (=100%) (millions)
No disabled adults	21	10.6
One or more disabled adults	34	2.3
No disabled child	23	11.5
One or more disabled child:	31	1.4
of which:		
No disabled adults	23	0.9
One or more disabled adults	44	0.5

1 See Appendix, Part 5: Disability.
2 Equivalised disposable income before housing costs. See Appendix, Part 5: Households below average income.
Source: Households Below Average Income series, Department for Work and Pensions

Chart **5.22**

Proportion of children lacking selected necessities[1] through inability of their parents to afford them, 1999[2]

Great Britain

Percentages

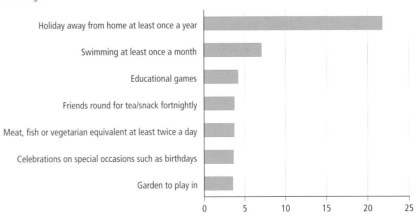

1 Items considered by over 50 per cent of all parents as 'necessary', which all parents should be able to afford to provide their children and their children should not have to do without.
2 Fieldwork was carried out in September and October.
Source: Poverty and Social Exclusion Survey of Britain, Joseph Rowntree Foundation

Table **5.23**

Composition of the net wealth[1] of the household sector

United Kingdom

£ billion at 2000[2] prices

	1987	1991	1996	1998	1999	2000
Non-financial assets	1,651	1,781	1,606	1,880	2,103	2,206
Financial assets						
Life assurance and pension funds	634	769	1,162	1,485	1,683	1,658
Securities and shares	259	319	444	589	771	750
Currency and deposits	407	481	533	583	609	642
Other assets	68	81	78	80	83	87
Total assets	3,019	3,431	3,824	4,617	5,249	5,343
Financial liabilities						
Loans secured on dwellings	298	399	439	466	497	535
Other loans	89	103	94	111	120	135
Other liabilities	50	56	54	58	57	56
Total liabilities	440	562	595	643	685	738
Total net wealth	2,580	2,870	3,229	3,974	4,565	4,605

1 See Appendix, Part 5: Net wealth of the household sector.
2 Adjusted to 2000 prices using the expenditure deflator for the household sector.
Source: Office for National Statistics

Table **5.24**

Distribution of wealth[1]

United Kingdom

Percentages

	1976	1981	1986	1991	1996	1997	1998	1999
Marketable wealth								
Percentage of wealth owned by[2]:								
Most wealthy 1%	21	18	18	17	20	22	23	23
Most wealthy 5%	38	36	36	35	40	43	43	43
Most wealthy 10%	50	50	50	47	52	54	55	54
Most wealthy 25%	71	73	73	71	74	75	75	74
Most wealthy 50%	92	92	90	92	93	93	94	94
Total marketable wealth (£ billion)	280	565	955	1,711	2,092	2,248	2,594	2,752
Marketable wealth less value of dwellings								
Percentage of wealth owned by[2]:								
Most wealthy 1%	29	26	25	29	26	30	32	34
Most wealthy 5%	47	45	46	51	49	54	58	58
Most wealthy 10%	57	56	58	64	63	66	70	71
Most wealthy 25%	73	74	75	80	81	83	85	86
Most wealthy 50%	88	87	89	93	94	95	96	97

1 See Appendix, Part 5: Distribution of personal wealth. Estimates for individual years should be treated with caution as they are affected by sampling error and the particular pattern of deaths in that year.
2 Adults aged 18 and over.
Source: Inland Revenue

The employment status of the household has a large impact on levels of child 'necessity deprivation'. The proportion of such children in households where there are no workers are double those for children as a whole: nearly two-fifths of children in jobless households are 'necessity deprived'. However, having working parents does not necessarily protect children from deprivation, particularly when the work is part-time where, as Table 5.20 showed, wage rates are more likely to be below the National Minimum Wage. About three in ten children with one or both parents working part-time lack two or more necessities.

Wealth

Although the terms 'wealthy' and 'high income' are often used interchangeably, in fact they relate to quite distinct concepts. 'Income' represents a flow of resources over a period, received either in cash or in kind. 'Wealth' on the other hand describes the ownership of assets valued at a particular point in time. These assets may provide the owner with a flow of income, for example interest payments on a building society account, or they may not, for example the ownership of works of art – unless of course the asset is sold. However, not all assets can be sold and their value realised. In particular, an individual's stake in an occupational pension scheme often cannot be 'cashed in'. The distinction is therefore usually made between 'marketable wealth' which the owner can sell if they so desire, and 'non-marketable wealth'. Wealth may be accumulated either by the acquisition of new assets, or by the increase in value of existing assets.

The wealth of the household sector in the United Kingdom, net of any loans outstanding on the purchase of assets such as housing, has shown strong growth in recent years increasing by an average of 4.6 per cent per year between 1987 and 2000 after adjusting for inflation (Table 5.23). Non-financial assets such as the value of residential dwellings formed the most important component of the wealth of the household sector in 2000, though the largest category of liability is loans secured on dwellings. The second most important component of household sector wealth was holdings in life assurance and pension funds. The strong growth in this component of wealth has resulted both from increases in the contributions paid into occupational pension schemes as well as increased take-up of personal pension provision. There has also been strong growth in the value of the assets underlying these funds. Table 8.24 on page 147 of the Social Protection chapter shows how pension provision for those of working age varies between age groups and type of work. Stocks and shares have grown in importance between 1987 and 2000, to exceed the value of currency and deposits from 1998. The growth in the value of residential dwellings has been more modest, having only recently recovered from falls seen in the first half of the 1990s.

Table **5.25**

Household savings: by household type and amount, 1999–00

Great Britain
Percentages

	No savings	Less than £1,500	£1,500 but less than £10,000	£10,000 but less than £20,000	£20,000 or more	All households (base=100%)
One adult above pensionable age, no children	26	20	27	9	17	3,888
Two adults one or both over pensionable age, no children	16	16	24	13	31	3,739
Two adults below pensionable age						
No children	19	22	29	12	18	4,340
One or more children	28	29	26	8	10	5,325
One adult below pensionable age						
No children	37	26	23	6	8	3,363
One or more children	68	23	7	1	1	1,834
Other households	19	25	28	12	16	2,499
All households	27	23	25	9	15	24,988

Source: Family Resources Survey, Department for Work and Pensions

Wealth is considerably less evenly distributed than income. Life cycle effects mean that this will almost always be so: people build up assets during the course of their working lives and then draw them down during the years of retirement with the residue passing to others at their death. It is estimated that the most wealthy 1 per cent of individuals owned between a fifth and a quarter of the total wealth of the household sector in the late 1990s (Table 5.24). In contrast, half the population shared between them only 6 per cent of total wealth. If the value of housing is omitted from the wealth estimates, the resulting distribution is even more skewed indicating that this form of wealth is rather more evenly distributed than the remainder.

This analysis of the aggregate data available on the distribution of wealth is borne out by information available from the Family Resources Survey based on individuals' own estimates of their savings. In 1999–00, 50 per cent of households in Great Britain reported having less than £1,500 in savings, with about half of these reporting no savings at all (Table 5.25). Savings patterns vary with household type. Couples without dependent children where one or both are over pension age are the most likely to have substantial savings – about three in ten had savings of £20,000 or more, twice the proportion in the population as a whole. This is perhaps not surprising since they may have been able to build up their savings over their lifetime. However, the pattern of savings for single pensioners is similar to that for population in general. Lone parent families are the least likely to have any savings.

Chart **5.26**

Annual growth in gross domestic product at constant prices[1]

United Kingdom

Percentages

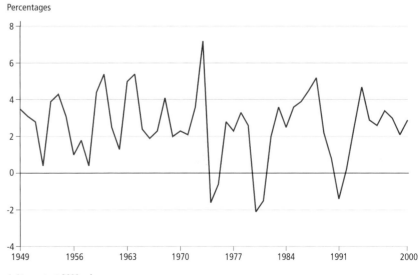

1 At constant 2000 prices.
Source: Office for National Statistics

Table 5.27

Gross domestic product per head at basic prices[1]: by region

Indices (UK[2]=100)

	1991	1992	1993	1994	1995	1996	1997	1998	1999
North East	84	85	85	83	83	81	78	78	77
North West	91	91	91	91	90	89	88	87	87
Yorkshire and the Humber	90	89	89	88	88	89	89	88	88
East Midlands	95	94	94	94	94	95	96	94	94
West Midlands	91	91	92	92	93	92	91	91	92
East	112	113	111	113	112	112	115	116	116
London	129	129	129	129	126	126	129	132	130
South East	111	111	112	112	112	114	115	116	116
South West	92	93	92	92	93	93	93	91	91
England	102	102	102	102	101	102	102	102	102
Wales	84	83	82	83	84	83	81	80	81
Scotland	99	100	99	100	102	100	96	97	96
Northern Ireland	76	78	79	80	82	80	80	78	77

1 Excludes Extra-Regio and statistical discrepancy.
2 United Kingdom less that part of GDP that cannot be allocated to a specific region.
Source: Office for National Statistics

Table 5.28

Gross domestic product[1] per head: EU comparison, 1991, 1996 and 1999

Index (EU=100)

	1991	1996	1999
Luxembourg[2]	161	169	183
Denmark	110	119	119
Netherlands[2]	104	107	115
Austria	109	112	110
Belgium	107	111	111
Irish Republic	77	94	112
Germany	107	110	105
United Kingdom	97	99	104
Finland	94	95	101
Sweden[2]	106	101	102
Italy	106	103	103
France	110	102	99
Spain[2]	81	79	80
Portugal[2,3]	65	71	75
Greece[3]	61	67	67

1 Gross domestic product at current market prices using current purchasing power standard and compiled on the basis of the European System of Accounts 1995. Latest update September 2001.
2 Figure for 1991 is an estimate.
3 Population figure for 1999 is a forecast.
Source: Eurostat

The term 'financial exclusion' has been coined to describe those people who do not use financial services at all. Data from the Family Resources Survey indicate that in 1999–00, 8 per cent of households did not have any kind of current account (including Post Office account) or investments such as savings accounts or premium bonds. This proportion rises to 18 per cent of households whose total weekly income is less than £100. Since the options for operating a household budget without mainstream financial services are more expensive and often unregulated, this is of policy concern.

National income and expenditure

Gross domestic product (GDP) measures the level of income generated by economic activity in the United Kingdom in accordance with international conventions. Chart 5.1 at the beginning of this chapter showed that when adjusted for inflation, the trend in GDP per head since 1971 has generally been one of steady growth. However, within this long-term trend the United Kingdom is nevertheless subject to cycles of weaker and stronger growth usually referred to as the economic or business cycle.

The year on year growth rates for GDP, adjusted to remove the effects of inflation, shown in Chart 5.26 suggest that the United Kingdom's economy contracted in the mid-1970s, at the time of the OPEC oil crisis, and again in the early 1980s and early 1990s. However, growth has exceeded 4 per cent per year 10 times in the post-war period, most recently in 1994. The long-term average annual growth rate was 2.5 per cent between 1948 and 2000. In 1995, the base year for these figures, two-thirds of gross value added was from the services sector, compared to a quarter from the production sector. Agriculture accounted for less than 2 per cent, and construction for about 5 per cent.

GDP per head of population shows marked variations between the regions of the United Kingdom. During the early 1990s, GDP per head was lower in Northern Ireland than anywhere else in the United Kingdom, at more than a fifth below the United Kingdom average (Table 5.27). However, in the latter part of the 1990s, the North East, Northern Ireland and Wales were at very similar levels. GDP per head in London has remained considerably higher than the United Kingdom average. The South East and the East have also maintained above average levels of GDP per head over the same period.

A comparison of GDP per head across the countries of the European Union (EU) in 1999 shows that Luxembourg, where the financial sector dominates the economy, had the highest level of economic activity, around 83 per cent higher than the EU average (Table 5.28). The gap between Luxembourg and the rest of the EU has grown during the 1990s. At the other end of the scale, Portugal and Greece had GDP per head about a quarter and a third below the EU average respectively, though in both countries it has grown relative to the EU average during the 1990s. Other countries were clustered more closely around the EU average in 1999, with the United Kingdom, France, Finland, Germany, Italy and Sweden all lying within five percentage points of the average in 1999. The most dramatic increase between 1991 and 1999 in GDP per head was for the Irish Republic, which rose from 77 per cent of the EU average in 1991 to 12 per cent above average in 1999. These estimates have been converted to a common basis making adjustments for the relative purchasing power of national currencies.

Government receives income primarily through transfers from individuals, companies and other organisations in the form of taxes, national insurance contributions and other payments, though they may also engage in economic activity from which income is derived. This revenue is then spent on the provision of goods and services such as health care and education, on servicing government debt, and on transfer payments such as social security benefits. There are various ways in which public expenditure can be defined at a detailed level: the present government's main measure of public expenditure is total managed expenditure (TME), which includes all current and capital expenditure and excludes privatisation proceeds. TME as a proportion of GDP rose during the economic downturn in the first half of the 1970s, and reached nearly 50 per cent in 1975 and 1976 (Chart 5.29). The proportion fell between 1983 and 1989, but there was a slight rise in the early 1990s as economic downturn kicked in again. However, since 1993 it has been falling and reached 38 per cent in 2000.

As well as expenditure for purely domestic purposes, total managed expenditure also includes the contributions made by the United Kingdom to the EC budget. In 1998 the United Kingdom contributed £8.4 billion and had receipts amounting to £4.6 billion. Germany was the largest net contributor, with contributions exceeding receipts by £7 billion. The only net recipients from the EU budget in 1998 were the Irish Republic, Portugal, Greece and Spain.

Of total EU expenditure of £55 billion in 1999, just under half was spent in support of agriculture in the form of Agricultural Guarantee (Table 5.30). Although still substantial, this proportion has fallen by 15 percentage points since 1981, whilst structural funds expenditure has risen in importance. Structural funds aim to reduce regional disparities and thus to achieve a more even social and economic balance across the EU. The areas within the United Kingdom currently eligible for EU Structural Funds include Cornwall, West Wales and the Valleys, South Yorkshire and Merseyside.

Chart **5.29**

Total managed expenditure as a percentage of gross domestic product

United Kingdom
Percentages

Source: Office for National Statistics

Table **5.30**

European Union expenditure[1]: by sector

Percentages

	1981	1986	1991	1996	1997	1999
Agricultural Guarantee	62	64	58	51	51	47
Structural funds						
Agricultural guidance	3	2	4	4	4	5
Regional policy	14	7	12	14	14	17
Social policy	3	7	8	8	8	9
Other	.	.	3	6	6	6
All structural funds	20	16	26	32	33	36
Research	2	2	3	4	4	3
External action	4	3	4	5	5	6
Administration	5	4	5	5	5	5
Other	6	10	4	3	3	3
All expenditure (=100%)(£ billion)	9.8	23.3	37.5	61.8	55.0	55.0

1 At current prices. See also Appendix, Part 5: European Union expenditure.
Source: European Commission

Websites

Inland Revenue	www.inlandrevenue.gov.uk
Institute for Fiscal Studies	www.ifs.org.uk
Institute for Social and Economic Research	www.iser.essex.ac.uk
National Statistics	www.statistics.gov.uk
National Centre for Social Research	www.natcen.ac.uk
EUROSTAT	www.europa.eu.int/comm/eurostat
Department for Work and Pensions	www.dwp.gov.uk
Women and Equality Unit	www.womens-unit.gov.uk
NOMIS	www.nomisweb.co.uk

Contacts

Office for National Statistics

Chapter author	020 7533 5283
Effects of taxes and benefits	020 7533 5770
National accounts	020 7533 5938
New Earnings Survey	01633 819024
Regional accounts	020 7533 5809
Retail Prices Index	020 7533 5874

Department for Work and Pensions

Family Resources Survey	020 7962 8092
Households Below Average Income	020 7962 8232
Individual Income	020 7712 2258
Pensioners' Incomes	020 7962 8975
Inland Revenue	020 7438 7370
Institute for Fiscal Studies	020 7291 4800
Institute for Social and Economic Research	01206 872957
National Centre for Social Research	020 7549 9571

Eurostat

Data Shop Luxembourg	00 352 4335 2251
Data Shop London	020 7533 5676

Chapter 6

Expenditure

Overview

- Total household expenditure in the United Kingdom in 2000 was approximately £595 billion, more than double the 1971 level, in real terms. (Table 6.2)

- Expenditure on tobacco has fallen by 40 per cent since 1971, although it remained level between 1999 and 2000. (Page 108)

- Households in London spent over 40 per cent more than the UK average on housing due to higher house prices and rents. (Table 6.3)

Household and personal expenditure

- In 2000–01 single pensioners spent a fifth of their weekly budget on food and a further fifth on housing. (Table 6.4)

- Households where the head of the household was in a professional occupation spent almost £150, 23 per cent of their total weekly expenditure, on leisure goods and services in 2000–01. Households where the head was in an unskilled occupation spent over £30, 14 per cent of their total weekly expenditure. (Table 6.8)

Transactions and credit

- There has been a decline in the use of cheques: since 1990 the volume of payments made by cheque has fallen by 40 per cent, from 2.4 billion to 1.4 billion payments a year in 2000. (Chart 6.13)

- The average value of cash purchases in the United Kingdom in 2000 was £11, the average value of credit card purchases was £56, whilst for debit card purchases it was £33. (Page 115)

Prices

- Inflation measured by the retail prices index stood at 1.6 per cent in October 2001, after a general decline from the peak level in August 1975 of 26.9 per cent. (Chart 6.15)

Chart **6.1**

Household expenditure at constant prices[1]

United Kingdom

£ billion

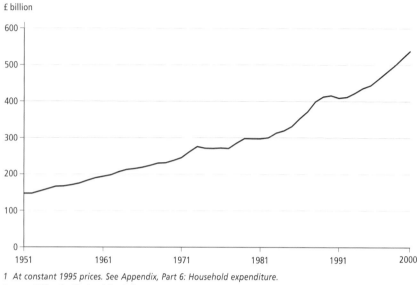

1 At constant 1995 prices. See Appendix, Part 6: Household expenditure.

Source: Office for National Statistics

Table **6.2**

Household expenditure[1]

United Kingdom   Indices[2] (1971=100)

	Indices at constant prices[2]					£ billion (current prices)
	1971	1981	1991	1999	2000	2000
Household goods	100	134	211	294	306	145.3
Rent, water and sewerage charges[3]	100	121	140	155	157	82.0
Food	100	104	116	133	137	58.3
Transport and communication	100	144	214	312	328	57.8
Clothing and footwear	100	129	197	302	322	33.6
Alcohol	100	128	135	143	144	34.5
Recreational and cultural activities	100	142	184	234	228	29.3
Financial services	100	135	348	443	467	26.9
Fuel & power	100	119	145	138	141	31.2
Tobacco	100	89	72	60	60	15.1
Other services	100	131	211	284	296	73.9
Less expenditure by foreign tourists, etc	100	152	187	238	237	-14.7
Household expenditure abroad	100	193	298	586	648	21.6
All household expenditure	100	121	167	211	220	594.8

1 See Appendix, Part 6: Household expenditure.

2 At constant 1995 prices.

3 Includes rents, rates and water charges, but excludes expenditure on home improvements, insurance, community charge and council tax.

Source: Office for National Statistics

Overview

The amount households spend on goods and services provides an indication of their standard of living and material wellbeing. How people choose to spend their income has changed over time; this reflects changes in society and consumer preferences and the growth in choices available to the consumer. Patterns of expenditure also vary within society; the region in which people live, their age, sex and income are just some of the factors that influence levels and patterns of spending.

There has been a gradual increase in household expenditure in the United Kingdom over the last 50 years. In real terms (after allowing for inflation by comparing expenditure levels as if at 1995 prices), total household expenditure in 2000 was over three and a half times the level recorded in 1951 (Chart 6.1). Although the long term growth in household expenditure has been relatively steady there have been several periods where downturns in the economic cycle have led to a decrease in household spending. This occurred most recently in the early 1990s.

In 2000 total household expenditure in the United Kingdom was approximately £595 billion (Table 6.2) more than double the 1971 level (in real terms). Since 1971 household expenditure increased in all of the broad categories of expenditure shown in Table 6.2, with the exception of tobacco. Expenditure on tobacco has fallen by 40 per cent since 1971, although it has remained level between 1999 and 2000. This decrease can partly be explained by a decrease in the number of people who smoke (see Table 7.17 on page 128 in the Health chapter). Over the last 30 years the level of expenditure increased more rapidly for some items than for others. For example, UK tourists' expenditure abroad increased more than six-fold since 1971. This can largely be attributed to the increasing numbers of people who are travelling abroad (see Table 12.21 on page 206 in the Transport chapter). Expenditure on financial services increased almost five-fold while expenditure on food increased by only 37 per cent since 1971. Higher levels of disposable income have allowed people to increase their spending on services and durable goods, such as motor vehicles and personal computers, and so proportionally less is spent on essential non-durable items such as food, and fuel and power.

There are regional variations in patterns of expenditure. Over the three-year period 1998–2001 households in London and the South East had the highest average weekly expenditure, £440 and £420 per week respectively, whilst those in the North East had the lowest at £300 per week (Table 6.3). Households in London spent 40 per cent more than

Table **6.3**

Household weekly expenditure[1]: by region, 1998–01

£ per week[2]

	Leisure goods and services	Motoring and fares	Food and non-alcoholic drink	Housing	Alcohol and tobacco	Fuel, light and power	All expenditure[3]
United Kingdom	64.20	62.10	60.20	59.40	20.70	11.60	365.80
North East	48.50	43.40	52.20	46.60	22.60	11.30	297.20
North West	60.60	58.00	56.20	51.50	22.40	11.90	340.40
Yorkshire and the Humber	60.50	60.90	56.30	53.60	22.20	11.50	347.50
East Midlands	61.60	61.30	58.90	53.50	20.50	11.60	347.90
West Midlands	61.30	62.70	58.70	54.80	20.50	12.00	353.20
East	64.70	73.90	62.50	63.50	17.50	11.00	386.60
London	82.50	66.00	68.50	83.00	21.80	10.90	435.70
South East	74.90	72.90	64.20	73.30	18.90	11.30	417.80
South West	61.90	62.50	57.60	57.60	18.80	11.30	354.10
England	66.20	64.00	60.40	62.10	20.50	11.40	373.80
Wales	55.90	49.60	55.10	45.30	19.90	12.00	315.40
Scotland	54.00	54.10	59.00	49.60	23.20	12.40	330.70
Northern Ireland[4]	50.50	50.40	65.60	31.50	22.40	15.70	323.50

1 See Appendix, Part 6: Household Expenditure. Combined data from the 1998–99, 1999–00 and 2000–01 surveys.

2 Expenditure rounded to the nearest 10 pence.

3 Includes other expenditure not separately listed.

4 Northern Ireland data are calculated from an enhanced sample for 1998–99 and 1999–00, but the United Kingdom figures are calculated from the main Family Expenditure Survey sample. The data from the main Family Expenditure Survey include expenditure by children; the Northern Ireland data relate to adults only.

Source: Family Expenditure Survey, Office for National Statistics and Northern Ireland Statistics and Research Agency

the UK average on housing and those in the South East spent almost a quarter more, due to the higher house prices and rents in these areas. Households in Northern Ireland spent 47 per cent less than the UK average on housing, but spent 9 per cent more on food and non-alcoholic drink and 35 per cent more on fuel. Higher levels of spending on leisure goods and services in London and the South East reflect the higher levels of income in these areas in comparison to the average UK income.

Household and personal expenditure

The size and composition of a household influences the expenditure patterns within that household. Larger households have higher expenditure and the presence or absence of children has a great influence on household size and so on expenditure. Couples with children spend more on average than those without children. In 2000–01 a household composed of two adults with children had an average weekly

expenditure of £530, whilst a couple household without children spent approximately £460 per week, 13 per cent less (see Table 6.4 overleaf).

In 2000–01 single parent families in the United Kingdom spent an average of £260 per week, less than half the amount spent by couples with children. The greatest proportion of single parent families' expenditure was on food, almost 20 per cent of their total budget. Lone parents spent less on housing compared with couples with children; this is a reflection of their tendency to live in social sector housing. Lone parents and single pensioners spent a smaller proportion on motoring than other family types; reflecting the fact that they are less likely to own a car.

Retired households have lower weekly expenditure than non-retired households, mirroring the pattern of income; households where the head is retired have lower incomes than households where the head is of working age. In 2000–01 pensioner couples spent an

Table **6.4**

Household expenditure[1]: by selected family type and type of expenditure, 2000–01

United Kingdom

£ per week[2]

	Couple[3]		Single[3]			
	With children	No children	With children	No children	Pensioner couple	Single pensioner
Leisure goods and services	97.50	87.10	43.20	47.60	54.30	23.30
Motoring	79.70	75.60	24.10	35.30	37.00	9.80
Food and non-alcoholic drinks	86.10	66.50	50.90	32.00	51.90	26.40
Housing	92.40	77.40	38.80	56.50	37.10	26.30
Household goods and services	73.90	66.30	42.40	34.00	49.10	24.50
Clothing and footwear	34.40	22.50	22.20	9.90	11.10	5.60
Alcohol	14.80	20.40	5.70	11.30	9.40	2.80
Fuel and power	14.50	11.90	11.20	8.30	12.00	9.40
Tobacco	6.70	6.10	5.90	4.90	3.20	2.00
Personal goods and services	18.80	18.90	10.20	7.50	12.50	6.60
Fares and other travel costs	10.90	11.00	6.30	7.10	4.40	1.90
Other goods and services	1.20	0.70	1.00	0.60	0.20	0.10
All household expenditure (=100%) (£ per week)	530.80	464.40	261.70	255.00	282.30	138.60

1 See Appendix, Part 6: Household expenditure.
2 Expenditure rounded to the nearest 10 pence.
3 Non-retired households.
Source: Family Expenditure Survey, Office for National Statistics

Table **6.5**

Household expenditure[1] on selected items: by family type[2], 2000–01

United Kingdom

£ per week

	Couples		Singles	
	Dependent children	No children	Dependent children	No children
Restaurant meals	11.60	14.00	4.80	6.50
Take away meals	5.60	3.60	3.30	2.20
Confectionery	1.00	0.30	0.90	0.20
Ice cream	0.40	0.10	0.30	0.10
Holiday abroad	16.40	19.50	6.20	6.70
National Lottery and scratchcards	2.80	3.30	1.20	1.50
Newspapers	1.80	2.10	0.70	1.20
Cinema and theatre	1.60	1.20	1.10	0.70
Total	41.20	44.20	18.40	19.00
All household expenditure	530.80	464.40	261.70	255.00

1 Expenditure rounded to nearest ten pence.
2 Excludes retired families.
Source: Family Expenditure Survey, Office for National Statistics

average of £280 per week, approximately 40 per cent less than non-retired childless couples. Single pensioners spent £140 per week, 45 per cent less than their non-retired childless counterparts. Single pensioners spend a large proportion of their income on essential items, for example a fifth of their weekly budget went on food, and a further fifth was spent on housing. The majority of their remaining weekly expenditure was on household goods and services, such as cleaning products and telephone bills, and on leisure goods and services, such as newspapers and cinema admissions (18 per cent and 17 per cent respectively).

There are differences in spending on luxury, non-essential items in non-retired households. Both single parent families and couples with children spend less on restaurant meals than their childless counterparts, 26 per cent and 17 per cent less per week respectively (Table 6.5). Families with children, though, spend more than those without children on take away meals, sweets, ice cream and the cinema.

Overall lone parent families spend less on non-essential items than couples with children. Single parent families spend approximately £5 per week on restaurant meals, whilst couples with children spend over twice that amount at almost £12 per week. Similarly single parent families spend 62 per cent less than couples with children on holidays abroad and 57 per cent less on the National Lottery.

Although the majority of expenditure on items for children is made by their parents, many children receive pocket money and are able to make their own decisions as to how they spend it. The Wall's Pocket Money Monitor, an annual survey that asks parents about their children's income and expenditure patterns, found that in the United Kingdom in 2001 the average amount of pocket money received by children was £3.19 per week. The average amount of pocket money received increases with age; in 2001 children aged 5–7 received an average of £1.46 per week, whilst children aged 14–16 received £5.48. Pocket money is not the only source of children's income, particularly for older children. They may earn money through paid work and may receive cash gifts from parents and relatives.

The Family Expenditure Survey (FES) collects information about the expenditure patterns of children in the United Kingdom. Children aged 7–15 are asked to keep diaries in which they record their expenditure over a two week period. In 2000–01 children spent an average of £12.30 per week. A third of this money was spent on food and non-alcoholic drink and almost a quarter was spent on leisure goods (Table 6.6). Only 4 per cent, or 50 pence, of children's weekly expenditure is on transport and fares; children's public transport costs are subsidised and tend to be paid for by their parents, as are the costs of car journeys.

There are gender differences in children's spending; in total girls spent £2 per week more than boys. Boys spent substantially more on leisure goods and services such as computer games, CDs, videos and sports admissions, £4.70 compared to £3.30. Girls spent almost three times the amount spent by boys on clothes and footwear, £2.90 compared to £1.00, and four times the amount spent by boys on personal goods, such as jewellery, toiletries and cosmetics.

Children may remain financially dependent upon their parents for some time, particularly if they continue on to higher education. In 1998/99, half of all expenditure by students (aged under 26) in the United Kingdom was on living expenses such as accommodation and food and on course expenditure, including text books and the cost of travel to college (Table 6.7). The amount spent on course items, excluding essential travel, fell by 27 per cent, in real terms (after allowing for inflation by comparing expenditure levels as if at 1999 prices), from £515 per year in 1996/96 to £378 per year in 1998/99.

Since the early 1990s the maintenance grant has been phased out and replaced by student loans, changing the way that young people's education is funded. University tuition fees were first introduced in 1998 and are included under course expenditure in Table 6.7 for 1998/99. In 1998/99 only first year students were liable to pay tuition fees, and most students' fees were paid by their parents or their Local Education Authority, so the average amount spent by students themselves on tuition fees was only £40 a year per person.

An increasing number of students are choosing to attend universities near to their parental home, due to the costs of living independently. As Table 6.7 indicates those students who lived at home, spent approximately £1000 less in 1998/99 than those living independently; most of this difference is accounted for by living expenses. Students who lived at home spent less on accommodation, around a quarter of the amount spent by those living independently, and two-thirds of the amount spent on food and bills as such costs are subsidised by their parents. However, they spent approximately double the amount on essential travel; students who live independently can move to accommodation close to their University, thereby reducing their travel expenses.

Table **6.6**

Children's[1] expenditure: by gender and type of purchase, 2000–01

United Kingdom   Percentages

	Males	Females	All aged 7–15
Leisure goods	31	17	23
Leisure services	10	8	9
Food and non-alcoholic drinks	37	30	33
Household goods and services	6	9	8
Clothing and footwear	9	22	16
Personal goods	3	9	6
Transport and fares	4	4	4
Other goods and services	–	–	–
All expenditure (=100%) (£ per week)[2]	11.20	13.20	12.30

1 Children aged 7 to 15.
2 Expenditure rounded to the nearest 10 pence.
Source: Family Expenditure Survey, Office for National Statistics

Table **6.7**

Student[1] expenditure, 1995/96 and 1998/99

United Kingdom   Percentages

	Lives independently		Lives with parents		All students	
	1995/96	1998/99	1995/96	1998/99	1995/96	1998/99
Essential expenditure						
Accommodation	26	23	4	7	23	20
Food, bills, household goods	21	19	15	15	20	18
Course expenditure	10	6	15	10	10	7
Essential travel	3	4	4	11	3	6
Children	1	–	1	–	1	–
All essential expenditure	60	53	40	42	58	51
Other expenditure						
Entertainment	26	30	32	35	26	31
Non-essential travel	3	3	7	4	4	3
Other[2]	11	15	21	19	12	16
All other expenditure	40	47	60	58	42	49
All expenditure (=100%) (£ per student per year at July 1999 prices[3])	5204	5550	3991	4583	5031	5403

1 Students under the age of 26 in higher education.
2 Includes non-essential consumer items and credit repayments.
3 Adjusted to July 1999 prices using the retail prices deflator (excluding mortgage interest payments).
Source: Student Income and Expenditure Survey, Department for Education and Skills

Table **6.8**

Household expenditure[1]: by social class of head of household, 2000–01

United Kingdom   £ per week[2]

	Professional	Managerial and technical	Skilled non-manual	Skilled manual	Partly skilled occupations	Unskilled occupations
Leisure goods and services	145.90	111.80	64.80	67.00	47.30	32.50
Motoring	92.00	84.50	56.00	64.40	43.10	23.10
Food and non-alcoholic drink	87.20	79.50	59.80	70.40	57.90	48.60
Housing	112.40	100.50	69.50	65.40	50.90	38.50
Household goods and services	86.80	79.20	53.10	50.40	46.60	29.50
Clothing and footwear	34.20	30.90	24.70	26.70	20.50	14.70
Alcohol	23.90	20.80	15.80	17.90	14.50	11.30
Fuel and power	14.70	13.40	10.70	12.10	10.90	9.60
Tobacco	4.20	5.40	6.80	8.60	9.40	8.70
Personal goods and services	22.50	21.40	16.80	13.90	11.00	7.90
Fares and other travel costs	17.50	14.90	14.20	8.60	7.10	6.70
Other goods and services	1.10	1.20	0.80	0.80	1.00	0.20
All household expenditure (=100%)(£ per week)	642.40	563.50	393.10	406.10	320.40	231.50

1 See Appendix, Part 6: Household expenditure.
2 Expenditure rounded to the nearest 10 pence.
Source: Family Expenditure Survey, Office for National Statistics

Table **6.9**

Household expenditure[1]: by income grouping, 1999–2000

United Kingdom   £ per week

	Quintile groups of households[2]					
	Bottom fifth	Next fifth	Middle fifth	Next fifth	Top fifth	All house-holds
Leisure goods and services	27.20	36.10	55.30	74.50	119.40	62.50
Motoring and fares	25.60	32.10	54.40	80.10	116.40	61.70
Food	41.80	46.80	60.70	68.50	80.30	59.60
Housing	31.90	36.50	52.40	67.40	100.20	57.70
Household goods and services	26.40	31.80	46.20	58.30	85.50	49.60
Clothing and footwear	11.00	13.10	21.20	24.50	34.90	21.00
Alcohol	7.40	9.40	16.50	19.30	23.80	15.30
Fuel, light and power	9.90	10.40	11.20	11.90	13.30	11.30
Tobacco	6.20	6.00	6.50	6.40	4.80	6.00
Other goods and services	8.10	10.20	14.30	18.80	25.10	15.30
All household expenditure (=100%)(£ per week)	195.60	232.40	338.90	429.70	603.80	360.10

1 See Appendix, Part 6: Household expenditure.
2 Equivalised disposable income has been used for ranking the households into quintile
 groups. See Appendix, Part 5: Equivalisation scales.
Source: Family Expenditure Survey, Office for National Statistics

Expenditure varies with the socio-economic characteristics of the head of the household. In 1999–2000 those households where the head was in employment had a weekly expenditure more than double that of households where the head was retired or unemployed. Households where the head is in a professional occupation spent the most per week, £640 in 2000–01, whilst those households where the head was in an unskilled occupation spent the least, £230 per week (Table 6.8).

Households headed by an individual in an unskilled occupation spent the greatest proportion, a fifth, of their weekly expenditure on food and non-alcoholic drinks. Those in professional occupations spent almost a quarter of their total expenditure on leisure goods and services and those in managerial and technical positions spent a fifth, higher proportions than other occupational groups as well as significantly greater amounts. This spending is linked to the level of income that a household has at its disposal; those in professional occupations earn more than those in manual and unskilled occupations and so can afford to spend more on services and non-essential items.

There are differences in the expenditure patterns of households with different levels of equivalised income, that is income after the size and composition of households has been taken into account to recognise their differing demands on resources. (See page 96 of the Income and Wealth chapter for a more detailed explanation of equivalisation). In 1999–2000 households in the top fifth of the equivalised income distribution had the highest expenditure, £600 per week (Table 6.9). Households in the bottom two quintiles spent around 20 per cent of their expenditure on food, a higher proportion than those towards the top of the income distribution. A fifth, £119, of the top quintile's expenditure was on leisure goods and services. Expenditure on motoring and fares rose with income, from 13 per cent (£26 per week) of the expenditure of those in the bottom income quintile to 19 per cent (£116 per week) of the expenditure of the top quintile.

Different groups of people are over-represented at different points of the income distribution, for example lone parents and pensioners are over-represented in the bottom quintile and as previously discussed these groups tend to have low levels of expenditure.

Retired households that are mainly dependent on a state pension have lower incomes than those pensioners with other sources of income and this is reflected in their expenditure patterns. In 2000–01 the expenditure of both single pensioners and pensioner couples mainly dependent on a state pension was approximately 55 per cent of the value of the expenditure of pensioners with other sources of income (Table 6.10). Almost half of the total weekly expenditure of those dependent upon state provision is on essential items, such as housing, fuel and food and non-alcoholic drink. While pensioners with other sources of income spent more on these essential items, this expenditure constituted a smaller proportion of their total expenditure (41 per cent for single pensioners and 34 per cent for pensioner couples). The expenditure of retired households also varies with age: as their age increases their expenditure decreases. Older pensioners tend to have lower incomes than their younger counterparts as they have run down their savings during their retirement and are less likely to be receiving earnings from paid work.

Transactions and credit

Households may spend more than their income by running down their savings, or by borrowing money. Borrowing by consumers, net of repayments, provides the best measure of current growth in consumer credit in the United Kingdom and it reflects changes in the economic cycle. For example, increasing interest rates make borrowing more expensive and so may lead to a fall in the levels of borrowing. Chart 6.11 shows that

Table **6.10**

Expenditure of retired households[1]: by whether or not mainly dependent on state pension, 2000–01

United Kingdom
£ per week[2]

	1 adult		2 adults	
	State pension[3]	Other	State pension[3]	Other
Leisure goods and services	13.60	34.70	26.30	63.50
Motoring	3.60	17.10	19.50	42.80
Food and non-alcoholic drink	23.60	29.70	40.80	55.60
Housing	18.10	35.90	28.90	39.90
Household goods and services	18.80	31.30	28.20	56.10
Clothing and footwear	4.50	6.90	6.60	12.60
Alcohol	1.90	3.90	5.40	10.70
Fuel and power	8.80	10.00	10.80	12.40
Tobacco	1.90	2.00	3.60	3.10
Personal goods and services	4.90	8.50	6.30	14.50
Fares and other travel costs	1.20	2.70	2.30	5.10
Other goods and services	0.10	0.10	0.10	0.20
All household expenditure (=100%)(£ per week)	101.00	182.90	178.90	316.40

1 Households where the head of household is over state retirement age and is retired. See also Appendix, Part 6: Retired households and Household Expenditure.
2 Expenditure rounded to the nearest 10 pence.
3 At least three-quarters of the total household income is derived from state pensions and other benefits.
Source: Family Expenditure Survey, Office for National Statistics

Chart **6.11**

Net borrowing by consumers in real terms[1]

United Kingdom
£ billion at 2000 prices[1]

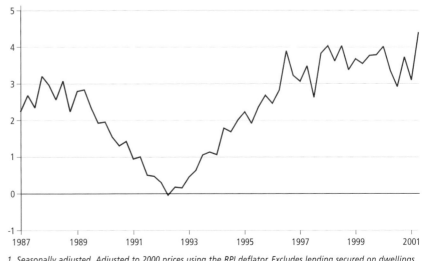

1 Seasonally adjusted. Adjusted to 2000 prices using the RPI deflator. Excludes lending secured on dwellings.
Source: Bank of England; Office for National Statistics

Table **6.12**

Plastic card holders[1]: by gender

Great Britain

Percentages

	1990		1995		2000	
	Males	Females	Males	Females	Males	Females
Any credit/charge card	43	34	43	36	57	50
Debit card	45	35	59	55	84	81
Store/retailer card	12	18	19	26	28	40
Cheque guarantee card	49	46	65	60	73	67
ATM debit card[2]	53	47	75	68	87	85
Any plastic card	73	67	85	80	90	89

1 Percentage of all adults over 16 holding each type of card.

2 Cards used in an ATM for cash withdrawals and other bank services. Includes single function ATM cards and multi-function debit cards, but excludes credit/charge cards, most of which can be used to access ATMs.

Source: Association for Payment Clearing Services; RSGB (1990 & 1995), IPSO-RSL (2000)

Chart **6.13**

Non-cash transactions[1]: by method of payment

United Kingdom

Billions

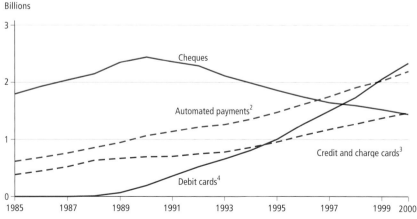

1 Figures are for payments only, cheque encashments and cash withdrawals from ATMs and branch counters using credit/charge and debit cards are not included.

2 Includes direct debits, standing orders, direct credits, inter-branch automated items.

3 Visa, Mastercards, travel/entertainment cards and store cards.

4 Visa Debit and Switch cards in all years; includes Electron cards from 1996 and Solo cards from 1997.

Source: Association for Payment Clearing Services

net borrowing fell, in real terms, from approximately £3.2 billion in the fourth quarter of 1987 to around zero during 1992. Since 1992 there has been a general trend for increased borrowing, although there have been some fluctuations during this period. Consumers borrowed approximately £4.4 billion in the second quarter of 2001.

One way that consumers borrow money is to make purchases using credit, which is then repaid in stages, over time, rather than in a single transaction, for example purchases made using a credit card. The total number of plastic cards, such as debit and credit cards, in circulation has increased steadily over time. Data from the Association for Payment Clearing Services (APACS) shows that in 2000, 90 per cent of the adult population in Great Britain held at least one plastic card, the most commonly held cards being ATM and debit cards.

There are sex differences in the types of cards held. In 2000 the difference between the proportion of men and women in Great Britain who held any type of plastic card was only 1 per cent, a gap which had narrowed slightly since 1990 (Table 6.12). However, store cards are held by a higher proportion of women than men, a trend that has been evident for the last 10 years. Men have a higher level of card holding for all other types of plastic card, although the gap between the sexes has been narrowing over time for each of these card types. Similarly there are age differences in the types of cards held; for example young adults, aged 16–24, are more likely to hold an ATM card than any other type of plastic card.

With the increase in the number of payment methods available has come a decline in the use of cheques; since the peak of their usage in 1990 the volume of payments made by cheque has fallen by 40 per cent, to 1.4 billion payments a year in 2000 (Chart 6.13). In 2000, debit card payments accounted for the largest number of non-cash payments, 2.3 billion. The number of automated payments, such as direct debits and standing orders, has more than doubled in the last 10 years to approximately 2.2 billion a year by 2000. Despite the increasing use of non-cash methods of payment approximately 72 per cent of all payments are still made using cash; a "cashless society" is still some way off.

Plastic cards can also be used as a method of acquiring cash from accounts held with banks or building societies, for example, cash withdrawals from Automated Teller Machines (ATMs) or cashback from supermarkets. The majority, 80 per cent, of cash acquisition transactions in the United Kingdom in 2000 were through ATMs. Cashback accounts for a small amount of cash acquisition, 8 per cent in 2000, although this is the fastest growing method of cash acquisition, with an increase of 23 per cent between 1999 and 2000. There are differences in the value of cash acquired by these methods; the average ATM withdrawal in Great Britain in 2000 was £56, whilst the average cashback amount was £24.

Different methods of payment are used in different ways by consumers; for example direct debits are generally used to pay household bills. Whilst cash is most commonly used to make small value purchases, the average value of cash payments in the United Kingdom in 2000 was £11. Credit cards tend to be used to purchase more expensive items than debit cards; in the United Kingdom in 2000, the average value of credit card purchases was £56, whilst for debit card purchases it was £33.

Figures from the Credit Card Research Group (CCRG) indicate that food and drink purchases from supermarkets, off licences and general food stores dominated debit card expenditure, accounting for over £24 billion in 2000 (Chart 6.14). This was over twice the debit card expenditure in any other category and approximately a third of all debit card expenditure. However, included in the food and drink category is the use of cashback services as detailed earlier. Expenditure on travel, which includes aeroplane and train tickets and foreign currency, and expenditure on hotels is more likely to be made using a credit card than a debit card. In 2000 expenditure on travel comprised 12 per cent of all credit card expenditure, around twice the amount spent on travel using a debit card, and expenditure on hotels accounted for 5 per cent of all credit card expenditure, almost five times the amount spent on hotels using a debit card.

There is little reliable information on transactions made over the Internet. However, current figures indicate that the majority of purchases made over the Internet are paid for using credit cards, 80 per cent of purchases in 1999, and the most commonly purchased items are CDs and books. However, Internet spending only accounts for a small percentage of all plastic card turnover, approximately 2 per cent in 1999.

Chart **6.14**

Credit[1] and debit[2] card spending: by type of purchase, 2000

United Kingdom

£ billions

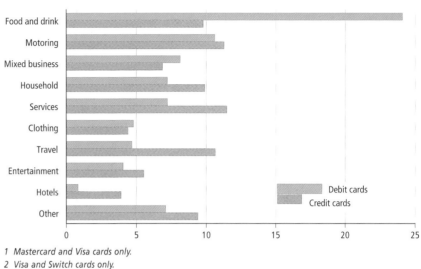

1 Mastercard and Visa cards only.
2 Visa and Switch cards only.
Source: Credit Card Research Group

Prices

How people and households choose to spend their money is affected by the price of the goods and services that they want to buy. The retail prices index (RPI) is the main domestic measure of inflation in the United Kingdom. The RPI measures the average change, from month to month, in the prices of the goods and services purchased by most households in the United Kingdom.

The current RPI collects prices for around 650 specified types of goods and services. The majority are collected from retail outlets in 147 different areas of the United Kingdom. The remainder, over 100 goods and services, are collected centrally by the ONS. These prices are then analysed to produce a monthly figure, comparing the percentage change from the previous 12 months to give the RPI all items 12 month percentage change. This is sometimes known as the 'all items' inflation rate or 'headline rate'. This figure is used to uprate many payments such as pensions and social security benefits, wages and allowances, rent and alimony payments; consequently it affects the lives of nearly everyone in the country.

Chart **6.15**

Retail prices index[1]

United Kingdom

Percentage change over 12 months

1 See Appendix, Part 6: Retail prices index.

Source: Office for National Statistics

Table **6.16**

Percentage change in retail prices index: 1995 and 2000

United Kingdom	Percentage change
Tobacco	50.6
Housing	28.8
Leisure services	24.0
Catering	20.5
Motoring expenditure	19.0
Personal goods and services	17.3
Fares and other travel costs	15.9
Alcoholic drink	13.9
Household services	10.9
Household goods	5.3
Food	4.7
Clothing and footwear	−6.9
Fuel and light	−7.9
Leisure goods	−7.9

Source: Office for National Statistics

There have been periods of both high and low inflation in the United Kingdom over the last 40 years; these fluctuations are illustrated in Chart 6.15. Over this period, inflation was at its lowest level in July 1963 at 0.8 per cent. It reached its highest level in August 1975 when it was 26.9 per cent. Since then, there has been an overall decline in the level of inflation, which stood at 1.6 per cent in October 2001.

The movement of the inflation rate reflects the price movements of the goods and services that the RPI is composed of, such as food, clothing and footwear, housing and fuel and light. Each component is given a different weight, to represent the amount of expenditure by households on that item. For example, the average household spends ten times the amount on electrical appliances as it does on postage. An increase in the price of electrical appliances would have a greater effect on the total cost of all items in the RPI than a similar increase in the price of postage. In 2001, the housing group had the largest weight of 205 parts per 1,000 whilst the fares and other travel group carried the lowest weight of 23 parts per 1,000.

Table 6.16 shows the average percentage change over the last 5 years for the main components of the RPI in the United Kingdom in 2000. The largest change was in tobacco, an increase of over 50 per cent; this was mainly due to regular increases in Budgets in the duty levied on tobacco. Housing increased by 29 per cent, house prices have risen sharply in recent years due to low mortgage rates, high employment and increased income. The biggest decreases were in fuel and light, leisure goods (both by 8 per cent) and clothing and footwear (7 per cent), reflecting 'price wars' over items within these groups by the companies who provide these goods and services.

The goods and services for which prices are collected are altered over time to reflect changes in consumer tastes and technological developments. New items added for 2001 include organic fruit and vegetables, gym membership, DVDs and mini-disc players. Similarly items are removed from the RPI if spending on them falls and they are no longer representative of what the average household purchases. Items dropped for 2001 include streaky bacon, salad cream and jigsaw puzzles.

Although some items are dropped and added each year some items have remained in the RPI since it began in 1947 and were also in the Board of Trade Cost of Living Index which began in 1914, so price comparisons can be made over time. Some of these items are illustrated in Table 6.17. In 2000 the items necessary to make cheese sandwiches (with butter) would cost £2.60, 43 times the amount the same ingredients would have cost in 1914. However, many of the items listed in Table 6.17 form a smaller proportion of total household expenditure in the year 2000 than they did the past. For example, in the 1950s food accounted for 35 per cent of a household's expenditure, whilst today it accounts for only 12 per cent. Similarly butter accounted for 2 per cent of a household's expenditure in 1950, whilst today it is 0.2 per cent.

Table 6.17

Cost of groceries

United Kingdom

Pence

	1914[1]	1950[1]	1975	2000
250g cheddar cheese	2	3	25	126
500g margarine	3	5	23	80
250g butter (home produced)	3	6	18	82
Half dozen eggs (size 2)	3	11	21	84
125g loose tea	2	5	11	81
1 kg granulated sugar	2	5	25	55
800g white sliced bread	1	2	16	52
1 kg old potatoes	1	1	12	67
1 pint pasteurised milk	1	2	7	34

1 Prices and weights are given to the nearest decimal equivalents.
Source: Office for National Statistics

Websites

National Statistics	www.statistics.gov.uk
Association for Payment Clearing Services	www.apacs.org.uk
Bank of England	www.bankofengland.co.uk
Credit Card Research Group	www.ccrg.org.uk
Department for Education and Skills	www.dfes.gov.uk
Joseph Rowntree Foundation	www.jrf.org.uk

Contacts

Office for National Statistics

Chapter author	020 7533 5773
Household expenditure	020 7533 5999
Family Expenditure Survey	020 7533 5756
Retail prices index	020 7533 5853
Financial inquiries	01633 812782
Association for Payment Clearing Services	020 7711 6200
Bank of England	020 7601 4878
Credit Card Research Group	020 7436 9937
Department for Education and Skills	020 7925 5875

Chapter 7

Health

The nation's health

- In 1971 in the United Kingdom life expectancy at birth was 69 years for males and 75 years for females; this had reached 75 and 80 respectively by 2000. (Chart 7.1)

- Around half of the 3.4 thousand people who were diagnosed with HIV in the United Kingdom in 2000 contracted the virus through heterosexual sex, compared with a fifth ten years earlier. (Chart 7.8)

Trends in deaths

- In 2000 just under 6 children per 1,000 live births died before the age of one in the United Kingdom compared with 18 per 1,000 live births in 1971. (Chart 7.10)

- In 2000, death rates from sudden infant death syndrome in England and Wales were 0.47 per 1,000 live births for boys and 0.33 for girls, a fall of around 40 per cent since 1996. (Page 125)

Health-related behaviour

- In 2000, almost a fifth of boys and girls aged 13 years old reported that they had drunk alcohol in the previous week; for 14 year olds, this rose to a third and to a half for 15 year olds. (Chart 7.16)

- Cannabis was the most commonly used illegal drug among young people in 2000; 29 per cent of men and 23 per cent of women aged 16 to 24 in England and Wales reported using it in the previous year. (Table 7.19)

Prevention

- In the United Kingdom, 95 per cent of children under the age of two are now immunised against diphtheria, tetanus, whooping cough and polio. (Table 7.22)

- Concerns over the safety of the MMR vaccine have led to a fall in the number of children in England immunised against MMR by their second birthday, from 91 per cent in 1997–98 to 88 per cent in 1999–00. (Table 7.22)

Chart **7.1**

Expectation of life[1] at birth: by gender

United Kingdom

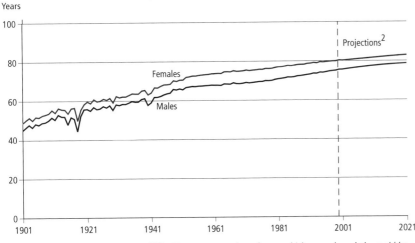

1 See Appendix, Part 7: Expectation of life. The average number of years which a new born baby could be expected to live if its rates of mortality at each age were those experienced in that calendar year.

2 2000-based projections.

Source: Government Actuary's Department

Table **7.2**

Self-reported sickness[1]: by type of complaint, gender and age, 2000–01

Great Britain

Percentages

	Poor general health	Longstanding illness	Limiting longstanding illness	Restricted activity[2]
Males				
0–4	4	14	4	11
5–15	3	23	9	10
16–44	6	23	11	10
45–64	18	45	27	17
65–74	22	61	38	20
75 and over	29	63	44	23
All	11	33	18	13
Females				
0–4	3	13	4	7
5–15	3	18	8	11
16–44	8	22	11	12
45–64	16	42	27	19
65–74	21	54	35	21
75 and over	26	64	48	27
All	12	32	19	15

1 See Appendix, Part 7: Self-reported sickness.

2 In the 14 days before interview.

Source: General Household Survey, Office for National Statistics

The patterns of health in the United Kingdom are continually changing, in terms of which diseases people experience, how they act in relation to their own health, and how illness is prevented. Advances in medical and scientific knowledge and services, screening, and improved standards of living have all contributed to gradual improvements in people's health. However the same developments also play a part in raising our knowledge of new and existing health problems.

The nation's health

A widely used indicator of the nation's health is life expectancy, a measure of mortality. Over the last century, the number of years which people born in the United Kingdom could expect to live rose gradually, from around 45 years for males and 49 years for females in 1901 to over 75 and 80 years respectively in 2000 (Chart 7.1). Life expectancy for adults did not, however, start improving until later in the 20th century. Over recent years, the increase in life expectancy among older adults has been particularly dramatic. For example, between 1970 and 2000 in England and Wales, life expectancy at age 65 increased by three years for both men and women. By 2000, men aged 65 could expect to live for a further 15 years, while women could expect another 19 years of life. The latest (2000-based) projections suggest that these expectations will increase by a further two years by 2021.

Inequality in life expectancy between social classes has widened over the last 20 years. Life expectancy at birth for all men in England and Wales rose by nearly five years between 1972–1976 and 1992–1996. The rise for men in social class I, the 'professional' class, was above this, at almost six years, while the rise for men in social class V, 'unskilled manual', was less than two years. By 1992–1996 the gap between the professional and unskilled manual classes was almost 10 years. For women, the social class difference has been less marked; however, life expectancy for professional women rose by four years between 1972–76 and 1992-96, while for unskilled women it increased by only three years.

The General Household Survey (GHS) collects a range of information about self-perceived health. There is little difference between males and females on these measures, but as people get older, they tend to be more likely to report both longstanding illness and restricted activity. These problems can begin at an early age – parents in Great Britain reported that around 14 per cent of 0 to 4 year olds had a longstanding illness and almost 10 per cent had restricted activity in the two weeks before the interview in 2000–01. Around 45 per cent of people aged between 45 and 64 and 60 per cent of those aged 65 to 74 reported a longstanding illness. Limiting longstanding illness (see Appendix, Part 7: Self-reported sickness) increased even more steeply - almost half of men and women aged 75 and over reported such a problem, compared with around a tenth of people up to the age of 44 (Table 7.2). Restricted activity (see Appendix, Part 7: Self-reported sickness) varied less with age, but around a quarter of men and women aged 75 and over reported having their activity restricted in the last two weeks, compared with around a fifth of people aged between 45 and 64. The Continuous Household Survey (CHS) reports similar trends for Northern Ireland in 1998–99; 67 per cent of men aged 65–74 and 60 per cent of women of the same age reported a longstanding illness. Those aged over 75 in Northern Ireland were more likely to experience limiting longstanding illness than their British counterparts, over 65 per cent compared with approximately 46 per cent in Great Britain.

During the last two years, the Department of Health, the National Assembly for Wales, the Scottish Executive and the Northern Ireland Assembly have all published major health strategies. Although there were differences between the documents, all four focused on the same three clinical priorities: coronary heart disease, cancer and mental health. In 2000 the Office for National Statistics (ONS) carried out a survey of psychiatric morbidity of people aged 16 to 74 years living in private households in Great Britain, and it found that about one in six adults aged between 16 and 74 living in private households had a neurotic disorder, such as depression, anxiety or a phobia. These mental health problems tend to affect women more than men: 19 per cent of women and 14 per cent of men were assessed as having a neurotic disorder. Table 7.3 shows the proportion of people reporting lifetime experiences of highly stressful life events. Such events, as well as contributing to mental health problems, can also lead to physical illnesses such as coronary heart disease and diabetes. More women than men reported having experienced the death of a relative or close friend, separation from a relationship, domestic violence and sexual abuse at some time in their lives, while more men reported having undergone redundancy, serious illness or injury, bullying, violence at work and serious money problems.

Data from the General Practice Research Database (GPRD) indicate that the prevalence of treated anxiety is much higher among females than males. In 1998, 54 per 1,000 female patients in England and Wales were recorded as having treated anxiety by their GP, compared with 24 per 1,000 male patients. A sign that mental health issues are a growing concern – perhaps because of increased awareness – is that just four years earlier, the prevalence of treated anxiety was 42 per 1,000 female and 18 per 1,000 male patients.

Table **7.3**

Lifetime experience of stressful life events: by type of event and gender, 2000

Great Britain　　　　　　　　　　　　　　　　Percentages[1]

	Males	Females
Death of a close friend or other relative	68	73
Death of a close relative[2]	51	55
Being sacked or made redundant	40	19
Serious or life threatening illness/injury	30	22
Separation due to marital difficulties or breakdown of steady relationship	25	29
Bullying	19	17
Serious money problems	14	8
Violence at work	6	2
Running away from home	5	5
Violence at home	4	10
Being homeless	4	3
Being expelled from school	2	1
Sexual abuse	2	5

1 Percentage of males/females aged 16–74 who reported experiencing each event.
2 Parent, spouse or partner, child or sibling.
Source: Psychiatric Morbidity Survey, Office for National Statistics

Table **7.4**

Prevalence of treated coronary heart disease: by deprivation category[1] and gender, 1994–1998[2]

England & Wales		Rates per 1,000 patients[3]
	Males	Females
Q1: least deprived	31.3	17.4
Q2	33.8	19.0
Q3	35.6	21.3
Q4	36.3	21.7
Q5: most deprived	40.9	26.0
All	35.8	21.3

1 Based on the Townsend Material Deprivation Score. See Appendix, Part 7: General Practice Research Database.
2 Data are recorded in general practice.
3 Directly age-standardised to the European standard population. See Appendix, Part 7: Standardised rates.
Source: Office for National Statistics, from data supplied by the Medicines Control Agency

Chart **7.5**

Age-specific incidence of all cancers[1]: by gender and age, 1997

United Kingdom

Rates per 100,000 population

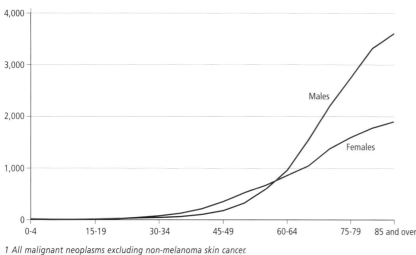

1 All malignant neoplasms excluding non-melanoma skin cancer.

Source: Office for National Statistics; Welsh Cancer Intelligence and Surveillance Unit; Scottish Cancer Registry, NHS in Scotland; Northern Ireland Cancer Registry

Prevalence increases with age – among females, 21 per 1,000 patients aged between 16 and 24 were recorded as having treated anxiety in 1998, compared with 102 per 1,000 females aged 65–74 and 110 per 1,000 aged 75–84. However, this pattern was not observed in the psychiatric morbidity survey of adults in private households. It found that older people were less likely to be assessed as having a neurotic disorder in the past week than the population in general.

Circulatory diseases are the biggest killers of both men and women in the United Kingdom. A major circulatory disease is coronary heart disease (CHD). In 1998, the prevalence of treated CHD was 36 per 1,000 male patients and 21 per 1,000 female patients in England and Wales (Table 7.4). Table 7.4 also presents the prevalence of CHD by deprivation category. The deprivation categories are derived using the Townsend Material Deprivation Score. This is a composite score calculated using information on unemployment, overcrowding, car availability and home ownership from 1991 Census data to categorise areas according to the level of deprivation. There is a clear relationship between treated CHD and deprivation – the prevalence rate for male patients living in the least deprived areas was 31 per 1,000, compared with almost 41 per 1,000 males in the most deprived areas. Despite the fact that overall CHD rates are much lower for females than for males, the difference between the prevalence rates in the least and most deprived areas is of a similar magnitude. Twenty six per 1,000 female patients from the most deprived areas were recorded as having treated CHD, compared with 17 per 1,000 in the least deprived areas.

The prevalence of heart disease is strongly associated with age. The prevalence of treated CHD for patients aged under 35 is negligible, and rates then rise with increasing age. Between the age groups 55–64 and 65–74 the age-specific treated prevalence rates double, from 95 per 1,000 male patients and 49 per 1,000 female patients, to 184 per 1,000 and 112 per 1,000 respectively.

People of all ages are affected by cancer, but tend to develop different diseases. Among young people, the incidence of cancer is low, with males slightly more likely than females to develop a cancer. But between the ages of 25 and 59, women are more likely than men to develop a cancer. For instance, in 1997 the incidence of all cancers for women aged 45 to 49 in the United Kingdom was 357 per 100,000 population – twice the rate for men of the same age (178 per 100,000) (Chart 7.5). Cancer is much more commonly diagnosed among the older members of the population. Unlike at younger ages, it is older men who are more at risk of developing a cancer – the incidence of all cancers for men aged 70 to 74 was 2,204 per 100,000 population in 1997, compared with

1,378 per 100,000 for women. These differences are principally due to the particular types of cancers that occur in men and women, and the age profiles of those cancers. The most common cancers among men are of the lung and prostate, and they occur predominantly in older age. By contrast, breast cancer, the most common cancer among women, has high rates of incidence among middle aged women.

The incidence of malignant melanoma of the skin has shown a sharp rise in recent years. As this is strongly linked to exposure to the sun's rays, generally people themselves can take an active role in preventing the disease. Over the last 30 years, there has been a four-fold rise in the incidence of melanoma among males and a three-fold rise among females (Chart 7.6).

Trends in infectious diseases have changed significantly over the last 30 years (Chart 7.7). Although the occurrence of these illnesses fluctuates far more than for other types of health problems, as a result of epidemics, occurrence of the types of infectious diseases which children tend to suffer from has declined. While in 1971 there were around 155 thousand cases of measles in the United Kingdom, by 2000 there were only 3 thousand. Similarly, there were 900 cases of whooping cough in 2000, compared with the peak incidence of 71 thousand in 1978 and 1982. In the case of measles, there is a link with immunisation. In the mid-1970s, the uptake of the measles vaccine was around 50 per cent; by 1988 this had risen to 80 per cent, and after that point the number of notifications of measles fell dramatically. The measles vaccine is now a part of the MMR vaccine for measles, mumps and rubella. There was no immunisation for the latter two diseases before MMR; after its introduction in 1988, notifications of both diseases fell. Chart 7.7 also shows a rise in the occurrence of tuberculosis (TB), from 6 thousand in 1990 to 7 thousand in 2000. This may be linked to recent problems with the availability of the TB vaccine. (More information on immunisation can be found in Table 7.22.)

Figures from the Public Health Laboratory Service (PHLS) indicate that by June 2001, 46.1 thousand diagnoses of Human Immuno-deficiency Virus (HIV) had been reported in the United Kingdom. In contrast to the patterns for whooping cough, measles and TB, infections that can be sexually transmitted, such as HIV, have been increasing in recent years. However, this rise may be partly due to an increasing awareness of the disease and the consequent increase in testing. The way that those with HIV contracted the infection has also changed. In the late 1990s, diagnoses of infections acquired through sex between men were overtaken in number by diagnoses of infections due to sex between men and women (see Chart 7.8 overleaf). Forty nine per cent of the 3.4 thousand people who

Chart 7.6

Incidence of malignant melanoma of the skin: by gender

United Kingdom

Rates per 100,000 population[1]

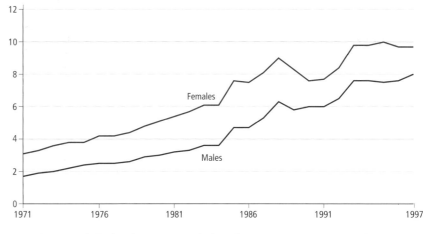

1 Directly age-standardised to the European standard population. See Appendix, Part 7: Standardised incidence rates.

Source: Office for National Statistics; Welsh Cancer Intelligence and Surveillance Unit; Scottish Cancer Registry, NHS in Scotland; Northern Ireland Cancer Registry

Chart 7.7

Notifications of selected infectious diseases

United Kingdom

Thousands

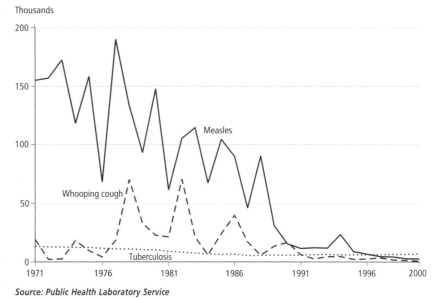

Source: Public Health Laboratory Service

Chart **7.8**

HIV infections[1]: by year of diagnosis and route of transmission

United Kingdom

Thousands

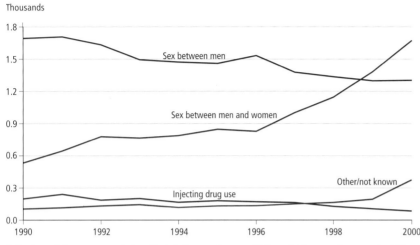

1 Numbers of diagnoses recorded, particularly for recent years, will rise as further reports are received. Those where the probable route of infection was not known, particularly for recent years, will fall as follow-up continues.

Source: Public Health Laboratory Service

Table **7.9**

New episodes of gonorrhoea: by gender and age

England & Wales

Numbers

	1995	1996	1997	1998	1999	2000
Males						
0–15	42	29	47	37	44	58
16–19	690	915	1,064	1,009	1,392	1,854
20–24	1,709	2,095	2,184	2,153	2,767	3,562
25–34	3,222	3,714	3,791	3,558	4,300	5,315
35–44	836	990	1,165	1,357	1,762	2,318
45–64	253	315	322	434	560	828
65 and over	12	9	26	21	43	32
All ages	6,764	8,067	8,599	8,569	10,868	13,967
Females						
0–15	128	136	142	158	168	224
16–19	1,025	1,411	1,462	1,509	1,854	2,350
20–24	1,124	1,309	1,198	1,222	1,429	1,882
25–34	908	974	1,001	952	1,152	1,269
35–44	169	186	208	255	331	410
45–64	38	55	55	70	70	86
65 and over	3	2	5	6	2	2
All ages	3,395	4,073	4,071	4,172	5,006	6,223

Source: Public Health Laboratory Service

were diagnosed with HIV in 2000 contracted the virus through heterosexual sex, compared with 21 per cent ten years earlier. Three-quarters of these heterosexually-acquired infections probably occurred abroad, with over 800 attributed to infection in Africa. Meanwhile, the number of people becoming infected as a result of the use of injected drugs has more than halved since 1993, to less than 100. It should be noted that numbers for all of these categories for recent years will rise as the PHLS receives delayed notifications of new cases.

More generally, data from the PHLS indicate that sexually transmitted infections are still a real problem for the nation's health. As Table 7.9 shows, the number of new cases of gonorrhoea (a disease that can cause infertility) diagnosed at genitourinary medicine clinics has risen every year since 1995. Between 1998 and 1999 the number of cases in England and Wales rose by 25 per cent, and between 1999 and 2000 there was a further 27 per cent increase. Although men were much more likely than women to be diagnosed with gonorrhoea, the rise in incidence occurred in both sexes. The biggest rises have occurred among teenagers – between 1995 and 2000, the number of cases of gonorrhoea among young people aged 19 and under more than doubled. But the disease has become more common among every single age group over the period. The trends for another STI, chlamydia, are very similar, with an 18 per cent rise between 1999 and 2000, a rise in each age group, and a doubling of reports of the illness among teenage females.

Trends in deaths

A major advance over the 20th century has been the massive fall in infant mortality and this has been a major contributor to the rise in life expectancy discussed earlier in the chapter. In 1921, 84.0 children per 1,000 live births died before the age of one in the United Kingdom (Chart 7.10). There was a sharp fall after the Second World War, from 48.8 deaths before the age of one per 1,000 live births in 1945 to exactly half that only 11 years later in 1956. This decline has continued, so that in 2000 the rate was 5.6. This is likely to have been largely due to improvements in nutritional intake of children, in sanitary and hygiene improvements, better antenatal and postnatal care, the development of an immunisation programme and other improvements in medical care, changes in medical technology – which have played a large part in improving the survival and life chances of premature and low birthweight babies – and, more recently, the fall in the rate of cot deaths.

In 2000, death rates from sudden infant death syndrome (SIDS) in England and Wales were 0.47 per 1,000 live births for boys and 0.33 for girls. SIDS has been in decline over the last few years – in 1996 the death rates were 0.75 per 1,000 live births for boys and 0.55 per 1,000 for girls. Since then they have declined by 37 per cent among boys and 40 per cent among girls (although it should be noted that some of the fall in SIDS between 1997 and 1998 may have been due to a diagnostic transfer from SIDS to other causes, particularly for post neonatal deaths). While the death rates are low, SIDS is more common in boys than in girls – in the period 1996–2000, boys comprised 51 per cent of all live births, but accounted for 60 per cent of deaths from SIDS.

Some social and biological factors affect the likelihood of SIDS occurring. One such factor is the mother's age at birth of the child. Compared with an overall SIDS rate of 0.40 per 1,000 live births in 2000, the death rate from SIDS for babies born to mothers aged under 20 was 1.05 per 1,000 live births, while the rate for mothers aged between 30 and 34 was 0.21 per 1,000 live births, and the rate for mothers aged 40 and over was 0.13 per 1,000. Another factor to consider is social class based on the father's occupation. The death rates from sudden infant death syndrome for babies born into families in the manual social classes were 0.29 per 1,000 live births inside marriage and 0.57 per 1,000 live births outside marriage, compared with 0.13 per 1,000 live births inside marriage and 0.30 per live births outside marriage in the non-manual social classes.

In 1911 there were 2.8 thousand deaths per million population from respiratory diseases among males aged 15 to 74 in Great Britain. There were just under 2 thousand deaths per million population among females in the same age group (Chart 7.11). By 1999 death rates from respiratory diseases had fallen to under 600 deaths per million men and around 400 deaths per million women. Respiratory disease and infections caused 11 per cent of deaths among those aged 15–74 in 2000 in England and Wales.

Death rates from cancer among men in Great Britain rose from 1.9 thousand per million population in 1911 to a peak of 2.7 thousand per million in the late 1960s, before falling to 2.0 thousand per million in 1999. For women, cancer death rates were steadier, falling from a peak of 2.1 thousand per million population in 1926 to 1.5 thousand per million in 1999. However, as a result of the greater falls in death rates from other types of illness, the proportion of deaths caused by cancer has risen, so that in 2000 cancers were responsible for 33 per cent of male deaths and 42 per cent of female deaths among 15–74 year olds in England and Wales.

Chart **7.10**

Infant mortality[1]

United Kingdom

Rate per 1,000 live births

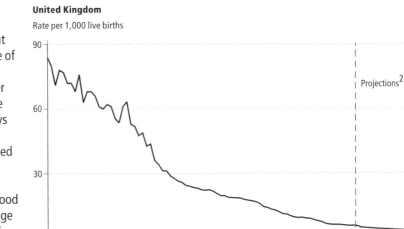

1 Deaths within one year of birth.
2 2000-based projections.

Source: Office for National Statistics; General Register Office for Scotland; Northern Ireland Statistics and Research Agency; Government Actuary's Department

Chart **7.11**

Mortality[1]: by gender and major cause

Great Britain

Rates per million population

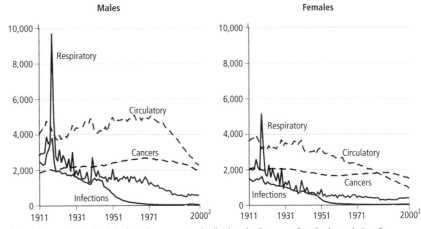

1 People aged 15 to 74. Data have been age standardised to the European Standard population. See Appendix, Part 7: Standardised death rates and International Classification of Diseases.
2 England and Wales only. Data for Scotland not comparable due to changes in classification.

Source: Office for National Statistics

Chart **7.12**

Premature deaths from circulatory diseases, 1998[1]

Rates per 100,000 population[2]

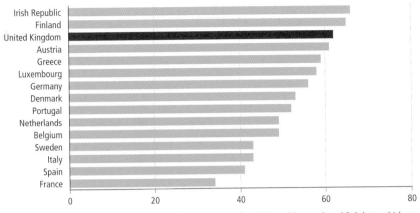

1 Data are for 1998, except for Germany and Italy, which are for 1997, and Denmark and Belgium, which are for 1996.

2 Death rates for those aged under 65 standardised to the European standard population. See Appendix, Part 7: Standardised death rates.

Source: Eurostat

Chart **7.13**

Death rates from selected cancers: by gender

United Kingdom

Rates per 100,000 population[1]

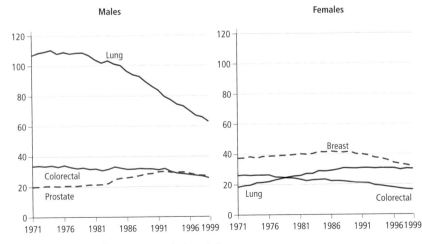

1 Age-standardised to the European standard population.

Source: Office for National Statistics; Welsh Cancer Intelligence and Surveillance Unit; Scottish Cancer Registry, NHS in Scotland; Northern Ireland Cancer Registry

While circulatory diseases are the main cause of death for males, the death rate for men aged 15–74 has fallen from around 5 thousand per million for most of the 1960s and early 1970s to just over 2 thousand deaths per million. However, the United Kingdom has one of the highest premature death rates from circulatory disease (which includes heart disease and stroke) in Europe, after the Irish Republic and Finland (Chart 7.12). For those aged under 65, the rate for the United Kingdom in 1998 was almost twice the rate in France, the country with the lowest death rate. A number of risk factors known to increase a person's risk of circulatory disease have been identified, including drinking alcohol, smoking, obesity and the lack of regular exercise. These are discussed later in this chapter.

Death rates from cancer have also fallen over the past 30 years. By 1999 there were 63 deaths per 100,000 men from lung cancer compared to 111 deaths per 100,000 men in 1974 (Chart 7.13). However, for women, lung cancer deaths rose from 1971 to 1988, and since then there have been around 30 deaths per 100,000 women each year. The disease is principally caused by smoking (information on the decline in smoking can be found in Table 7.17).

After lung cancer, the cancers that cause most deaths are colorectal, breast and prostate cancers. The death rate for breast cancer among women has fallen by 24 per cent since 1986, so that in 1999 there were 32 deaths per 100,000 women. For prostate cancer, which only affects men, there has been a slight fall since the early 1990s, but this was preceded by a 51 per cent rise in the death rate between 1971 and 1992. The death rates for prostate cancer and breast cancer are now very similar. Colorectal cancer deaths have been gradually declining – from 34 deaths per 100,000 men and 26 deaths per 100,000 women in 1971 to 26 deaths per 100,000 men and 16 deaths per 100,000 women in 1999.

Accidents are the most common cause of death among people aged between 16 and 24. In 2000 there were more than 13 thousand accidental deaths in the United Kingdom, representing 2 per cent of all deaths. Of these, 9 per cent occurred to young people aged 16 to 24 (Table 7.14). Since 1971 the number of accidental deaths has fallen by over a third. Moreover, the number of deaths caused by transport accidents has fallen at an even faster rate, to 3.2 thousand in Great Britain in 2000. Further information on road accidents is contained in Table 12.16 in the Transport chapter.

Trends in suicide rates by age group and gender have shown some marked differences in the last 25 years. For men aged 15 to 24, there were 16 suicides per 100,000 population in 2000, compared with a rate of 9 per 100,000 in 1974 and 10 per 100,000 a decade later (Chart 7.15). Suicide is now the cause of 22 per cent of deaths of men in this age group. The suicide rate for men aged 25 to 44 has increased considerably since the mid-1970s reaching a peak of almost 25.6 per 100,000 population in 1998; in 2000 the rate for that age group was 23.4 per 100,000. Conversely, the suicide rate for men aged 45 and over has fallen since the mid-1980s. Suicide rates among women are significantly lower than among men. The rate for 15–24 year old women has remained relatively stable, at around 4 per 100,000 population since the mid-1970s, while the rates for older age groups have fallen. In the case of women aged 45 and over the rates have more than halved.

Health-related behaviour

The way people choose to live can have a direct impact on their health. The consumption of alcohol in excessive amounts can lead to ill health, and an increased likelihood of problems such as high blood pressure, cancer and cirrhosis of the liver. The current Department of Health (DH) advice on alcohol is that consumption of between three and four units a day for men and two to three units a day for women will not accrue significant health risks. Consistently drinking four or more units a day for men, and three units or more for women, is not advised because of the progressive health risks.

For adults in the United Kingdom, around a quarter of men and women had exceeded the recommended amount of alcohol on their heaviest drinking day in the week prior to being interviewed in 2000–01. The proportions for 16 to 24 year olds were higher than for any other age group, with 51 per cent of young men having consumed more than four units and 42 per cent of young women having consumed more than three units.

Table **7.14**

Accidental deaths: by age and gender, 2000

United Kingdom		Numbers
	Males	Females
0–15	282	157
16–24	943	241
25–34	1,125	207
35–44	985	264
45–54	732	289
55–64	658	319
65–74	755	524
75 and over	2,001	3,551
All ages	7,481	5,552

Source: Office for National Statistics; General Register Office for Scotland; Northern Ireland Statistics and Research Agency

Chart **7.15**

Death rates from suicide[1]: by gender and age

United Kingdom

Rates per 100,000 population[2]

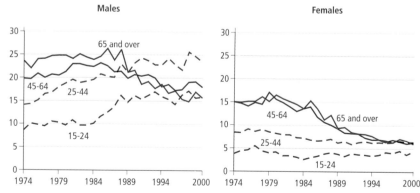

1 Figures are based on suicides registered in the year. Includes deaths undetermined whether accidentally or purposely inflicted.

2 Directly age-standardised to the European standard population. All data are based on ICD9 apart from the Scotland data for 2000, which are based on ICD10. See Appendix, Part 7: International Classification of Diseases.

Source: Office for National Statistics; General Register Office for Scotland; Northern Ireland Statistics and Research Agency

Chart **7.16**

Percentage of children drinking alcohol at least once a week[1]: by gender and age, 2000

England

Percentages

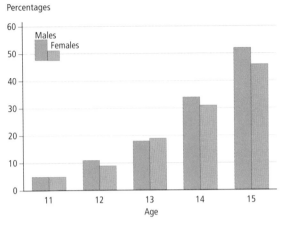

1 Percentage who reported usually drinking alcohol almost every day, about twice a week or about once a week.

Source: Survey of drug use, smoking and drinking among young teenagers, National Centre for Social Research

Table **7.17**

Prevalence of regular cigarette smoking: by gender and age

United Kingdom				Percentages
	1986	1990–91	1994–95	1998–99
Men				
16–19	30	28	28	30
20–24	41	37	40	42
25–34	37	36	34	37
35–49	37	34	31	32
50–59	35	28	27	27
60 and over	28	24	18	16
All men aged				
16 and over	34	31	28	28
Women				
16–19	30	31	27	31
20–24	38	38	38	39
25–34	35	34	30	33
35–49	34	33	28	29
50–59	35	29	26	27
60 and over	22	19	17	16
All women aged				
16 and over	31	29	26	26

Source: General Household Survey, Office for National Statistics; Continuous Household Survey, Northern Ireland Statistics and Research Agency

There is evidence that drinking by young people starts at earlier ages. According to the 2000 survey of drug use, smoking and drinking among young teenagers in England, commissioned by DH, drinking becomes much more common as children move towards and through the mid-teen years. Among 13 year olds, almost 20 per cent of both boys and girls reported drinking at least once a week; for 14 year olds this rose to 34 per cent and 31 respectively, and around half of 15 year olds reported drinking at least once a week (Chart 7.16).

Examining the trends over time, there has been only a small rise in the proportion of children who drink alcohol. In 2000, 25 per cent of boys aged between 11 and 15 and 23 per cent of girls of the same age reported having had a drink in the last week, compared with 22 per cent and 20 per cent respectively ten years earlier. However, the amounts of alcohol drunk by children have risen over the last few years. Among those who had had a drink in the seven days prior to interview, the average number of units consumed during that week was 11.7 units for boys and 9.1 units for girls in 2000. The number of units consumed has doubled for both boys and girls since 1990, when the average consumption was 5.7 units for boys and 4.7 for girls.

More cancer deaths in the United Kingdom can be attributed to smoking tobacco than to any other single risk factor. In 2000, 72 per cent of smokers said that they wanted to give up, and nine out of ten of those cited at least one health-related motivation behind this. As shown in Chart 7.13, lung cancer deaths have been falling, and this is due largely to the reduction in the proportion of people who smoke. In 1974, 51 per cent of men and 41 per cent of women in Great Britain reported that they were regular cigarette smokers. These figures have fallen steadily since then, in 1998-99 in the United Kingdom 28 per cent of men and 26 per cent of women were regular smokers (Table 7.17). The biggest declines have been among older men: for example among those aged 60 and over, 44 per cent were smokers in 1974 compared with 16 per cent in 1998–99. However, more recent trends in smoking prevalence indicate a levelling off, and moreover, smoking has risen over the last ten years among women aged 16 to 19, from 27 per cent in 1994–95 to 31 per cent in 1998–99. Since 1982 there has been no real fall in smoking by young people in England aged between 11 and 15. Nine per cent of boys and 12 per cent of girls reported being regular cigarette smokers in 2000 compared with 11 per cent amongst both boys and girls in 1982. Prevalence has fluctuated over this period, and there is currently no clear trend amongst this age group.

Smoking during pregnancy can have harmful effects on the health of the child, and although it is now less common, women from the manual social classes remain more likely to smoke than those in the non-manual groups (Table 7.18). In 2000, 4 per cent of women in the 'professional class' reported smoking while pregnant, compared with 26 per cent in the 'unskilled' group. In 1985, 8 per cent of professional women and 46 per cent of unskilled women reported smoking while pregnant. Smoking in pregnancy overall declined by almost a third in the last 15 years.

Drugs can also damage people's health. Results from the 2000 British Crime Survey indicate that 8 per cent of 16 to 29 year olds in England and Wales had used Class A drugs in the previous 12 months, and 4 per cent in that age group had done so during the last month. Young people are more likely than older people to use drugs. The most commonly used illegal drug in 2000 among young people was cannabis, which had been used by 29 per cent of men and 23 per cent of women aged 16 to 24 in England and Wales in the previous year (Table 7.19). In Scotland, figures on reported drug use are considerably lower – in 2000, 13 per cent of both males and females aged between 16 and 24 reported having used cannabis in the last year.

Some drug use also occurs among those under the age of 16. According to the survey of smoking, drinking and drug use among young teenagers in England in 2000, 14 per cent of children aged between 11 and, 15 in England said that they had taken illegal drugs in the last year – this represents a rise of 3 percentage points on two years earlier. Cannabis was again the most commonly taken drug: 12 per cent of this age group had taken cannabis, 4 per cent had tried a stimulant and 3 per cent had sniffed glue/gas.

Increasingly, dietary concerns have shifted from the early 20th century problems of under-nutrition towards the problems of over-nutrition and obesity, and the health-related properties of particular foods and diets. There is also concern about the impact sedentary lifestyles have on the prevalence of obesity.

Table **7.18**

Cigarette smoking by women during pregnancy: by social class

United Kingdom				Percentages
	1985	1990	1995	2000[1]
Professional	8	8	7	4
Employers and managers	18	13	12	8
Intermediate and junior non-manual	19	16	14	11
Skilled manual	31	29	23	20
Semi-skilled manual	32	34	28	21
Unskilled manual	46	39	37	26
All women	30	28	24	20

1 The smoking questions asked in the Infant Feeding Survey were redesigned in 2000 to improve the reliability of the information provided. As a result, percentages from the 2000 survey are for 'women who continued to smoke during pregnancy' and are not directly comparable with data from previous surveys.

Source: Infant Feeding Survey, Department of Health

Table **7.19**

Percentage of 16 to 24 year olds who had used selected drugs in the past year: by gender, 2000

England & Wales			Percentages
	Males	Females	All
Cannabis	29	23	26
Amphetamines	7	5	6
Ecstasy	7	4	5
Cocaine	7	3	5
Poppers	5	3	4
LSD	4	1	2
Magic mushrooms	4	1	2
Glue	1	1	1
Crack	1	0	1
Heroin	1	0	1
Any drug	33	25	29

Source: British Crime Survey, Home Office

Chart **7.20**

Obesity[1] among people aged 16 and over: by social class of head of household and gender, 1998

England

Percentages

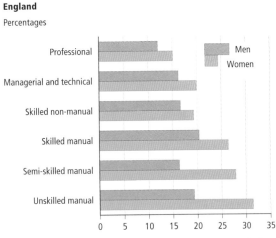

1 Percentage who had a BMI score of 30 or more, age-standardised to the European standard population.

Source: Health Survey for England, Department of Health

Chart **7.21**

Changing patterns in the consumption of food at home

Great Britain

Grams per person per week

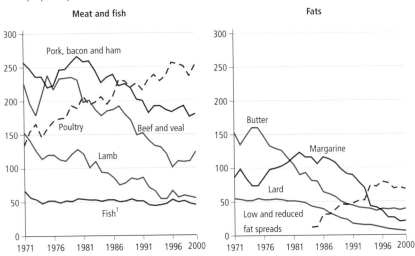

1 Includes fresh and frozen fish, excludes processed fish and fish products.

Source: National Food Survey, Department for Environment, Food and Rural Affairs

Obesity, a major risk factor for cardiovascular disease, diabetes, hypertension and premature death, is increasing in most industrialised countries. A common measure of obesity is body mass index (BMI, see Appendix, Part 7: Body mass index), a measurement which allows for differences in weight due to height. Between 1993 and 1999 the proportion of men in England who were classified as being of 'desirable' weight fell, and in 1999, 63 per cent men were either overweight or obese. There has also been an increase in the prevalence of obesity among women, with more than half either overweight or obese in 1999. The likelihood of becoming obese increases with age – those over the age of 45 were more likely to be either overweight or obese in 1999, than those in younger age groups.

Obesity is strongly linked to social class – it is more common in the manual social classes (Chart 7.20). While 12 per cent of men in the professional class were obese, 20 per cent in the skilled manual group and 19 per cent in the unskilled class were obese. For women the link is even stronger: 15 per cent of professional women were obese in England in 1999, compared with 31 per cent of unskilled women.

A diet which is rich in complex carbohydrates (such as bread, cereals and potatoes) and wholegrain cereals, fruit and vegetables, and low in total fat and salt can help to reduce risk of weight gain, diabetes, hypertension, cardiovascular disease and some cancers.

Data from the National Food Survey suggest that household consumption of some foods is increasingly in line with dietary recommendations, although this is not true for all food types and population groups. For example, consumption of both butter and margarine is now only about a quarter of the level of 1971. This is linked to a sharp rise in consumption of low and reduced fat spreads, from 12 grams per person per week in 1984 to 79 grams in 1996. Since then consumption of low and reduced fat spreads has levelled off, and was 68 grams per person per week in 2000. Purchases of lard (6 grams per person per week) in 2000 were only one-tenth of the 1971 level while purchases of vegetable and salad oils rose nearly three-fold to 47 millilitres per person per week. In addition, consumption of fruit and vegetables has increased from approximately 200 grams to 300 grams per person per day since the 1950s. Consumption of red meat has fallen over the last 30 years – for example consumption of beef and veal in Great Britain was 124 grams per person per week in 2000, compared with 226 grams in 1971 (Chart 7.21). In contrast, consumption of poultry, at 253 grams per person per week in 2000, was approaching twice the level of 1971 (134 grams).

There are differences in diet between social groups. In 1998, according to the Health Survey for England (HSE), 19 per cent of men in the professional class and 7 per cent of women in the same group had a high fat intake. By contrast, two-fifths of men and a fifth of women in the unskilled class had a high fat intake. Furthermore around a fifth of professional men and women had a high fibre intake (defined as 30 grams or more a day) compared with only a tenth of men and women classified as unskilled. According to data from the National Food Survey, unskilled groups tend to eat around 50 per cent less fruit and vegetables than professional groups.

Physical activity is another key determinant of good health; it helps to reduce the chances of developing coronary heart disease, stroke and osteoporosis. It also has beneficial effects on weight control, blood pressure and diabetes, all of which are cardiovascular disease risk factors. The Department of Health recommends that people engage in at least 30 minutes of physical activity at moderate intensity on five or more days of the week. The Health Survey for England in 1998 found that 37 per cent of men and 25 per cent of women were active at recommended levels. Participation in activity fell steadily with age, from 58 per cent of men aged 16–24 to 7 per cent of those aged 75 and over. Among women, the decline was less marked, from around 30 per cent in women aged 16–54, before falling with age to 4 per cent among women aged 75 and over. A total of 24 per cent of men and 28 per cent of women were classed as being inactive – having done no physical activity in the last four weeks.

Prevention

An important preventative measure which people receive at an early age is immunisation against key diseases, which has been one of the main factors contributing to the fall in deaths from infectious disease (see Chart 7.11). For example, diphtheria was a leading cause of death in children until 1941 when immunisation was introduced; by the end of the 1950s the disease had almost disappeared and in the 1980s only 30 cases were reported. Over the years there have been a number of campaigns to encourage parents to have their children immunised against major infectious diseases. Most children under the age of two are now immunised against diphtheria, tetanus, whooping cough and polio (Table 7.22).

Pertussis (whooping cough) immunisation started in the 1950s, and this led to a sharp decline in deaths and notifications. In 1970, however, a study suggested that encephalopathy and brain damage might be a rare complication of immunisation. By 1978, only

Table **7.22**

Immunisation of children[1] by their second birthday

United Kingdom Percentages

	1981[2]	1991–92	1997–98	1998–99	1999–00
Tetanus	83	94	96	96	95
Diphtheria	83	94	96	95	95
Poliomyelitis	82	94	96	95	95
Whooping cough	45	88	94	94	94
Measles, mumps, rubella[3]	54	90	91	89	88

1 See Appendix, Part 7: Immunisation.
2 Data exclude Scotland.
3 Includes measles only vaccine for 1981. Combined vaccine was not available prior to 1988.
Source: Department of Health; National Assembly for Wales; National Health Service in Scotland; Department of Health, Social Services and Public Safety, Northern Ireland

30 per cent of children under two years were immunised and large outbreaks of whooping cough followed in 1978 and 1982. New evidence showed that the association between immunisation and encephalopathy was not causative; vaccine coverage rates have increased and, by 1999–00, 94 per cent of children in the United Kingdom had been immunised by their second birthday against whooping cough.

Measles immunisation was introduced in 1968 and, although immunisation was slow to gain general acceptance, notifications fell in the early 1980s in the United Kingdom (see Chart 7.7). In 1988, the measles/mumps/rubella (MMR) vaccine was introduced. Notifications of measles fell to their lowest recorded annual total of under 3 thousand in 2000. Concerns by some over the safety of the MMR combined vaccine has led to a fall in the number of children immunised against MMR by their second birthday in England, from 91 per cent in 1997–98 to 88 per cent in 1999–00.

The National Health Service (NHS) provides screening programmes for breast and cervical cancer with the aims of preventing mortality (in the case of breast cancer) and incidence (of cervical cancer). There are no known primary prevention measures that men can take to minimise the risk of developing prostate cancer. However, a prostate cancer risk management programme was introduced in 2001, including an informed choice project for men contemplating being tested for prostate cancer. The programme also includes the development of a standardised testing system and a systematic and standardised follow-up procedure. In addition, a pilot study into the feasibility of screening for colorectal cancer is due to be completed in 2002, and trials into ovarian cancer screening are also underway.

Table **7.23**

Cervical screening[1]: by age[2] and country, March 2001[3]

Percentages

	England	Wales	Scotland
25–34	80	79	80
35–44	86	88	92
45–54	85	86	92
55–64	80	77	87
All aged 25–64	83	82	87

1 Women in the target age group who are within five years of their most recent cervical screening test. Target population in England excludes those no longer eligible for clinical reasons.

2 For Wales the age groups are 20–34, 35–44, 45–54, 55–64 and 20–64 respectively. For Scotland they are 20–34, 35–44, 45–54, 55–59 and 20–59 respectively.

3 March 2000 for Wales and Scotland.

Source: Department of Health; National Assembly for Wales; National Health Service in Scotland

Table **7.24**

Breast cancer screening[1]: by region, 1999–00

Percentages

United Kingdom	76
Northern and Yorkshire	78
North West	75
Trent	81
West Midlands	77
Eastern	77
London	62
South East	77
South West	78
England	76
Wales	77
Scotland	74
Northern Ireland	74

1 As a percentage of women aged 50–64 invited for screening.

Source: Department of Health; National Assembly for Wales; National Health Service in Scotland; Department of Health, Social Services and Public Safety, Northern Ireland

National policy for cervical screening is that women should be screened every three to five years (three and a half to five and a half years in Scotland). In order to reduce the incidence of the disease, the test identifies cervical intraepithelial neoplasia, a pre-cancerous stage which after a long developmental period may sometimes proceed to invasive cancer. The programme invites women aged 20 to 64 (20 to 59 in Scotland) for screening. However, since many women are not invited immediately when they reach their 20th birthday, the age group 25 to 64 is used to give a more accurate estimate of coverage of the target population in England. At 31st March 2000, more than four-fifths of women in the target population had been screened in England, Scotland and Wales (Chart 7.23). This is a considerable improvement on the figures for 1989, when 44 per cent of the target population in England had undergone a smear test in the previous five years.

Breast cancer accounts for around a quarter of all new cases of cancer in women, and more deaths than any other cancer (see Charts 7.5 and 7.13). Around three-quarters of women in both England and Scotland with breast cancer survive for at least five years after diagnosis. At present, breast cancer screening is offered to all women aged between 50 and 64 (and women aged 65 and over on request). This will be extended to all women aged 65 to 70 by 2004 (and women aged over 70 on request). The proportion of those who are invited for screening who attend has remained fairly constant over the last three years. In 1999–00, around three-quarters of the women invited from the target population in the United Kingdom underwent screening for breast cancer (Table 7.24). Some regional variation does exist, however; while the proportion screened in most regions and countries of the United Kingdom was between 74 and 78 per cent, in the Trent region it reached 81 per cent, and in London it was only 62 per cent.

It is not just through NHS services that health problems can be prevented. Another cancer that has been focused on in this chapter is skin cancer (see Chart 7.6), and this is one cancer which people themselves can help to prevent, by taking precautions before exposing their skin to the sun, to avoid being harmed by its ultra-violet radiation. In 1999, more women than men in Great Britain saw taking such preventative measures as very important (79 per cent compared with 57 per cent) (Table 7.25). Furthermore, a tenth of men thought that it was not important.

Another way that people can take action to protect their own health is by using condoms – this drastically reduces their chance of contracting sexually transmitted infections. Results from the ONS's Omnibus Survey suggest that around a third of sexually active people use condoms (Table 7.26). From the age of 25 onwards, condom use declines with age; in 1999, two-thirds of men aged 20–29 in Great Britain reported using a condom in the previous year, and half of women of the same age reported having sexual intercourse where a condom was used. Among 45 to 49 year olds, the oldest group of whom the questions were asked of both men and women, 28 per cent of men and 20 per cent of women said that they had used a condom in the last 12 months.

Table **7.25**

Attitudes to protecting self from sun exposure[1]: by gender, 1999

Great Britain		Percentages
	Males	Females
Very important	57	79
Fairly important	30	18
Not important	11	3
Don't know	1	–

1 Among people aged 16 and over.

Source: Omnibus Survey, Office for National Statistics

Table **7.26**

Use of condoms in the previous year: by age and gender, 1998 and 1999[1]

Great Britain				Percentages
	Males		Females	
	1998	1999	1998	1999
16–19	48	53	45	37
20–24	77	66	59	50
25–29	57	68	43	51
30–34	53	54	29	29
35–39	38	43	27	30
40–44	33	32	19	20
45–49	27	28	17	20
50–64	18	16	..	..
65–69	8	6	..	..
All males aged 16–69	37	36	.	.
All females aged 16–49[2]	.	.	31	33

1 For 1998, interviews took place over four months between June 1998 and February 1999; for 1999, interviews took place over four months between June 1999 and March 2000.

2 Women aged 50 and over were not interviewed.

Source: Omnibus Survey, Office for National Statistics

Websites

National Statistics	www.statistics.gov.uk
Department of Health	www.doh.gov.uk
Department of Health, Social Services and Public Safety, Northern Ireland	www.dhsspsni.gov.uk/iau
General Register Office for Northern Ireland	www.groni.gov.uk
General Register Office for Scotland	www.gro-scotland.gov.uk
Government Actuary's Department	www.gad.gov.uk
Information and Statistics Division (Scotland)	www.show.scot.nhs.uk/isd
Department for Environment, Food and Rural Affairs	www.defra.gov.uk
National Assembly for Wales	www.wales.gov.uk
Northern Ireland Cancer Registry	www.qub.ac.uk/nicr
Northern Ireland Statistics and Research Agency	www.nisra.gov.uk
Public Health Laboratory Service	www.phls.co.uk
Scottish Executive	www.scotland.gov.uk
Welsh Cancer Intelligence &Surveillance Unit	www.velindre-tr.wales.nhs.uk/wcisu
Eurostat	http: europa.eu.int/comm/eurostat

Contacts

Office for National Statistics

Chapter author	020 7533 5081
Cancer statistics	020 7533 5230
Condom use	020 7533 5391
General Household Survey	020 7533 5444
General Practice Research Database	020 7533 5240
Life expectancy by social class	020 7533 5186
Mortality Statistics	01329 813758
Psychiatric morbidity survey	020 7533 5305
Sudden Infant Death Syndrome	020 7533 5198

Department of Health

Health Survey for England	020 7972 5718/5660
Immunisation and cancer screening	020 7972 5533
Smoking, misuse of alcohol and drugs	020 7972 5551

Department for Environment, Food and Rural Affairs	020 7270 8547
Department of Health, Social Services and Public Safety, Northern Ireland	028 9052 2800
General Register Office for Northern Ireland	02890 252031
General Register Office for Scotland	0131 314 4227
Government Actuary's Department	020 7211 2635
Home Office	020 7273 2084
National Assembly for Wales	029 20825080
National Health Service in Scotland	0131 551 8899
Northern Ireland Statistics and Research Agency	028 9034 8132
Continuous Household Survey	028 9034 8243
Northern Ireland Cancer Registry	028 9026 3136
Welsh Cancer Intelligence & Surveillance Unit	029 2037 3500
Eurostat	00 352 4301 32 056
Public Health Laboratory Service	020 8200 6868

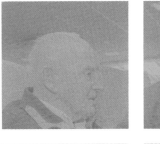

Chapter 8

Social Protection

Overview

■ In 1999–00, expenditure by the state on social protection benefits in the United Kingdom was £230 billion. (Chart 8.2)

■ Between 1981 and 2000, the number of GPs in Great Britain rose by 37 per cent, from 27 thousand to 37 thousand. The number of nurses, midwives and health visitors fell by 7 per cent over the same period. (Table 8.7)

Sick and disabled people

■ At 31 March 2001, 10.4 thousand people had been on NHS in-patient waiting lists in England for 15 months or more, compared to 11.7 thousand in 2000. (Chart 8.15)

■ The median time people in England waited for NHS in-patient treatment was 2.9 months at 31 March 2001. (Page 143)

■ In February 2001, more than 3.1 million people in the United Kingdom were receiving benefits for sickness or disability, such as incapacity benefit and severe disablement allowance. (Table 8.17)

Children and families

■ In 2000, around 2,800 children were adopted in England and Wales, compared with around 2,000 in 1995. (Chart 8.19)

■ There were 35 thousand children on child protection registers in England, Wales and Northern Ireland in 2000, a fall of 29 per cent since 1991. (Page 145)

■ There has been an increase in the proportion of babies delivered by Caesarean section. In 1999–00, 20 per cent of deliveries in England were Caesareans, compared with 11 per cent in 1989–90. (Page 146)

Chart **8.1**

Expenditure[1] on social protection benefits per head: EU comparison, 1998

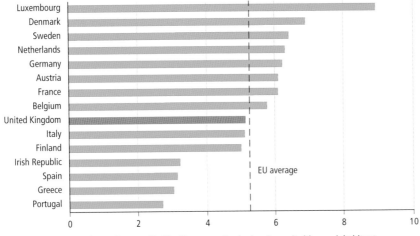

£ thousand per head

1 Before deduction of tax, where applicable. Figures are Purchasing Power Parities per inhabitant.

Source: Eurostat

To compare expenditure between countries, expenditure must be expressed in the same currency. However, this takes no account of differences in the general level of prices of goods and services within each country. Thus in order to make direct comparisons in real terms between countries, expenditure is expressed in purchasing power standards. The differences shown in Chart 8.1 between countries therefore reflect differences in the social protection systems, demographic structures, unemployment rates and other social, institutional and economic factors.

Social protection is a term used to describe help given to those who are in need or at risk, whether it is provided by the state, the private sector, voluntary groups or individuals. Such need or risk may arise through a variety of circumstances, such as illness, low income, family circumstances or age. This chapter focuses on the support provided for these groups and individuals, many of whom are identified in the other chapters of *Social Trends*.

Overview

State social care and welfare services have developed significantly over the last 60 years. At the beginning of the 20th century these services hardly existed, with the exception of the Poor Law which provided some assistance to those with very low incomes. The major development in social security came in 1942 with the Beveridge report that introduced the concept of the welfare state. This included the development of family allowances, the National Health Service (NHS) and the 'maintenance of employment' through a scheme based on employee contributions. Today a large proportion of expenditure on social protection is funded by the Government on similar programmes, including social security benefits, training programmes and the NHS. These are designed specifically to protect people against common sources of hardship such as the problems associated with old age, sickness, unemployment and disability. Benefits can be direct cash payments, such as jobseeker's allowance; payments in kind, for example free prescriptions; or provision of services, such as NHS GP consultations. Non-government expenditure is aimed principally at elderly people or survivors (for example, widows) in the form of occupational pensions, but also at sick and disabled people in the form of sick pay and compensation for occupational accidents and expectant mothers in the form of maternity pay. Unpaid care and other voluntary activity also play a part in helping people in need (see Table 8.12).

It is difficult to quantify with one number the amount of social protection in the UK. In order for spending on social protection to be compared across the member countries of the European Union (EU), Eurostat has designed a framework for the presentation of information on such expenditure which has been adopted by member states as the European System of Integrated Social Protection Statistics (ESSPROS). For this purpose programmes which are specifically designed to protect people against common sources of hardship, and which are funded by either general government contributions or social security contributions (from government, employers or employees) are collectively described as expenditure on social protection benefits. These programmes are those from which households can readily perceive a direct benefit, whether in cash or kind. The expenditure level in the United Kingdom was £5,138 per head in 1998, slightly below the EU average of £5,315 but considerably lower than Luxembourg, the country with the highest spending (£8,925 per head) (Chart 8.1).

In 1999–00, state social protection benefit expenditure in the United Kingdom was £230 billion. This represents a rise of 8 per cent since 1994–95, in real terms (after allowing for inflation by comparing expenditure levels as if at 1999–00 prices). During that time the breakdown of this social protection spending has changed. As the Population chapter shows, the country has an ageing population, and this is reflected in patterns of social protection spending (Chart 8.2). Between 1994–95 and 1999–00, expenditure on 'old age and survivors (widows and widowers)' rose by 16 per cent, and it now represents nearly half of the total expenditure. Expenditure on children and families has risen by 9 per cent and expenditure on ill-health and disability has risen by 7 per cent. Spending on unemployment has fallen to around 3 per cent of total state social protection spending, from 6 per cent in 1994–95.

A large proportion of social protection expenditure in the United Kingdom is taken up by spending on the social security programme and on the National Health Service (NHS). Around a third of the Government's total managed expenditure is spent on social security. In the late 1970s, social security spending was around twice the level of spending on the NHS. This gap has remained roughly the same, because over the intervening years spending on both in real terms has doubled. Between 1977–78 and 2000–01 social security spending rose from £50 billion (at 2000–01 prices) to £104 billion; and NHS spending rose from £26 billion to £59 billion over the same period (Chart 8.3). However, the growth patterns of the two are distinct: spending on social security has tended to be cyclical, in line with the general economic pattern, while NHS expenditure has risen more steadily. The NHS is financed mainly through general taxation with an element of National Insurance contributions paid by employees, their employers and the self-employed. The remainder is financed through charges, such as drugs prescribed by family doctors, receipts from land sales and the proceeds of income generation schemes.

Chart **8.2**

Expenditure on social protection benefits in real terms[1]: by function, 1994–95 and 1999–00

United Kingdom

£ billion at 1999-00 prices[1]

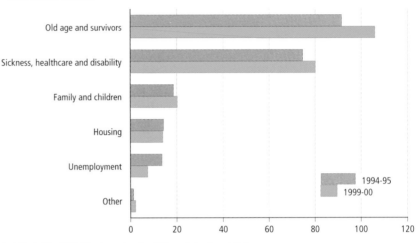

1 Adjusted to 1999–00 prices using the GDP market prices deflator.
Source: Office for National Statistics

Chart **8.3**

Real[1] growth in social security benefits and National Health Service expenditure

United Kingdom

£ billion at 2000-01 prices[1]

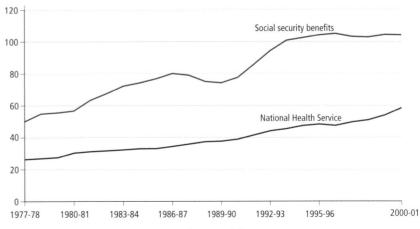

1 Adjusted to 2000–01 prices using the GDP market prices deflator.
Source: Department of Health; Department for Work and Pensions; Department for Social Development, Northern Ireland

Chart **8.4**

Social security benefit expenditure: by recipient group[1], 1999–00

Great Britain

Percentages

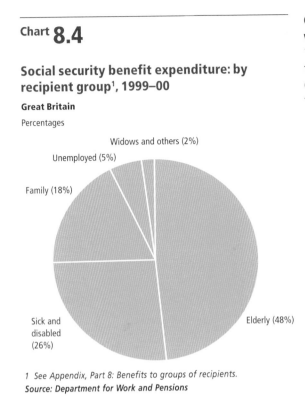

1 See Appendix, Part 8: Benefits to groups of recipients.

Source: Department for Work and Pensions

Chart 8.4 shows how social security benefit spending was divided amongst the main groups of recipients in 1999–00. Benefit expenditure is classified according to the main reasons a benefit is paid, for example, a disability benefit paid to an elderly person is allocated to the sick and disabled rather than to the elderly. Nevertheless, benefits for the elderly account for nearly half of all expenditure. This proportion has been rising gradually over the last few years, as the proportion of the population that are aged 65 and over continues to increase. Sick and disabled people are the second largest recipient group, receiving over a quarter of all benefit expenditure; this includes benefits such as incapacity benefit, severe disablement allowance, disability working allowance and statutory sick pay.

Table **8.5**

Receipt of selected social security benefits: by family type[1], 1999–00

Great Britain

Percentages

	Family credit or income support[2]	Housing benefit	Council tax benefit	Job-seeker's allowance	Retirement pension	Incapacity or disablement benefits[3]	Child benefit	Any benefit
Pensioners[4]								
Couple	6	10	17	.	99	24	1	100
Single								
Male	12	29	35	.	97	20	.	99
Female	24	29	42	.	96	20	.	99
Couples								
Dependent children	11	8	11	3	0	9	98	98
No dependent children	4	5	7	2	9	16	.	28
Single person								
Dependent children	73	57	62	1	0	8	98	99
No dependent children								
Male	7	11	11	9	0	8	.	23
Female	9	10	12	4	0	8	.	23
All family types[5]	12	14	18	3	24	13	23	59

1 See Appendix, Part 8: Benefit units.

2 Family credit replaced by working families tax credit from October 1999.

3 Incapacity benefit, disability living allowance (care and mobility components), severe disablement allowance, industrial injuries disability benefit, war disablement pension, attendance allowance and disability working allowance. Replaced by disabled persons tax credit from October 1999.

4 Females aged 60 and over, males aged 65 and over; for couples, where head is over pension age.

5 Components do not add to the total as each benefit unit may receive more than one benefit.

Source: Family Resources Survey, Department for Work and Pensions

Fifty nine per cent of the families in Great Britain received a social security benefit of some sort in 1999–00, and the majority of people will receive one at some point in their lives (Table 8.5). A variety of different benefits are available to people, depending on their circumstances. Overall, the benefit that is received by the highest proportion of the population is the retirement pension, which is received by almost a quarter of families – this reflects the high proportion of social security spending which goes towards older people. Subject to a normal history of National Insurance contributions, most pensioners are eligible to receive a state pension (from the age of 65 for men and currently from the age of 60 for women) and most of them claim. However, single pensioners were much more likely than those living as a couple to also receive income support, housing benefit and council tax benefit.

Child benefit is received by virtually all families with children. In 1999–00, almost three-quarters of lone parents were in receipt of family credit (working families tax credit from October 1999) or income support, and around three-fifths received housing benefit and council tax benefit. In February 2000, there were more than 10 thousand children in Great Britain living in families who were receiving at least one of the following benefits: jobseeker's allowance, incapacity benefit, severe disablement allowance, disability living allowance and income support.

Older people receive a large proportion of health expenditure as well as social security spending. In 1999–00, around £28 billion was spent on hospital and community health services (HCHS), and nearly two-fifths of this was spent on people aged 65 and over. Expenditure on that age group was £1,371 per head of population (Chart 8.6), whilst expenditure on people aged between 16 and 44 was around a quarter of this amount. Total spending on children aged between 0 and 4 was around a quarter the amount spent on older people. However, in terms of spending per head, the youngest children received far more health spending than any other age group apart from those aged 65 and over; £1,085 per head was spent on children aged 0 to 4, compared with £184 for those aged between 5 and 15.

Between 1981 and 2000, the number of GPs in Great Britain rose by more than a third, from 27 thousand to 37 thousand (Table 8.7) and the number of general dental practitioners increased by two-fifths, from 15 thousand to 21 thousand. Conversely, the number of nurses, midwives and health visitors fell by 7 per cent over the same period. The main reasons for this fall were the changes to the training regime and funding for student nurses in the early 1990s which meant that they were no longer directly employed by the NHS. The NHS is not the only provider of healthcare,

Chart **8.6**

Hospital and community health service expenditure[1]: by age of recipient, 1999–00

England

£ per head of population

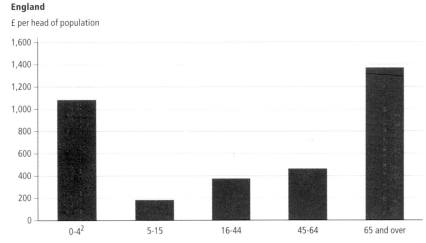

1 Figures for 1999-00 are estimates based on distribution of expenditure on 1998–99 and total expenditure on 1999–00. These figures are not directly comparable with expenditure figures for previous years.
2 Includes birth.
Source: Department of Health

Table **8.7**

Health and personal social services staff[1]

Great Britain

Thousands

	1981	1991	2000
NHS hospital and community health service staff			
Direct care staff			
Medical and dental	48	56	74
Nursing, midwifery and health visitors	458	470	425
Other non-medical staff	95	113	176
All direct care staff	601	639	676
General medical practitioners	27	31	37
General dental practitioners	15	18	21
Personal social services	241	288	269

1 See Appendix, Part 8: Health and personal social services staff.
Source: Department of Health; National Assembly for Wales; National Health Service in Scotland

Chart **8.8**

Gross personal social services expenditure: by type of provision, 1990–00

England and Wales

Percentages

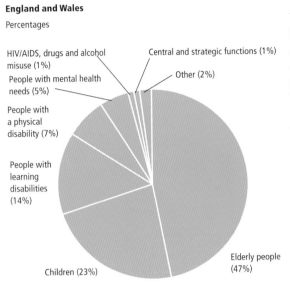

HIV/AIDS, drugs and alcohol misuse (1%)

Central and strategic functions (1%)

People with mental health needs (5%)

Other (2%)

People with a physical disability (7%)

People with learning disabilities (14%)

Children (23%)

Elderly people (47%)

Source: Department of Health; National Assembly for Wales

Table **8.9**

Places available in residential care homes: by client group

United Kingdom

Percentages

	1996[1]	1998	1999	2000
Older people[2]	78	76	76	75
Younger physically/sensorily disabled adults	2	3	3	3
People with mental illness	5	5	5	5
People with learning disabilities[3]	14	14	15	15
Alcohol/drug misusers and other people	1	2	1	1
All (=100%)(thousands)	353.8	400.1	395.7	395.8

1 Data for Wales not available for 1996.
2 People aged 65 and over.
3 Excludes children.
Source: Department of Health; National Assembly for Wales; Scottish Executive; Department of Health, Social Services and Public Safety, Northern Ireland

the private sector is of growing importance in this regard, and the trend in nurse staffing levels were very different to that in the public sector. In England in 2000 there were 141 thousand nurses employed by the private sector, a rise of 81 per cent since 1990.

The personal social services group in Table 8.7 includes local authority social work staff, home helps and those working in residential homes, day centres and special locations. In 1999–00, £12.8 billion was spent on personal social services (PSS) in England and Wales, of which almost half was spent on the elderly, and nearly a quarter was spent on children (details of this expenditure can be found later in the chapter) (Chart 8.8). People with physical and learning disabilities and those with mental health needs also receive assistance from personal social services. In addition, £72 million was spent on services for people with drug and alcohol misuse or HIV/AIDS in 1999–00.

Just under half of the total spent on personal social services in England in 1999–00 was spent on residential care. In total there were 396 thousand places available in residential care homes in 2000 in the United Kingdom (Table 8.9). The majority (298 thousand, or 75 per cent) of these were places for older people, consistent with the high proportion of state social protection spending on this group. This majority is consistent across all of the years shown in Table 8.9. In 2000 there were 61 thousand places available for people with learning disabilities, 15 per cent of the total number of places available.

Although there has been little change in the overall number of residential care places since 1998, there has been some change in the division of these places between the different types of providers. The number of residential care places provided by local authorities – that is, by the public sector – fell by 12 per cent between 1998 and 2000, from 81 thousand to 71 thousand (Table 8.10). Local authorities provided only 18 per cent of the total number of residential care places in 2000, compared with 24 per cent in 1996.

Local authorities provided approximately 398 thousand households with home help and home care in 2000. However, over the last decade there has been a change of emphasis in the provision of this assistance. Chart 8.11 shows that in England, the households which received home help or home care in 2000 received 2.8 million hours of help in the survey week, an increase of two-thirds on the 1992 figure of 1.7 million hours of contact. However over the same period, the number of households that received this help decreased by 6 per cent. In 2000 a smaller number of households received a more intense level of care in comparison to 1992. The other change in local authorities' provision of home care is that a declining proportion of the help is delivered directly by local authorities. In 2000, 1.6 million of the contact hours (56 per cent) were provided by independent sector providers (private sector plus voluntary sector), who were commissioned to carry out the care by local authorities. In 1992, just 2 per cent of home help was administered this way. Consequently, in absolute terms, although the number of hours of home help rose over the 1990s, the amount provided directly by local authorities fell by a quarter, while the amount provided by the independent sector rose dramatically.

The chapter so far has concentrated on institutional providers of social protection – the state, private companies, and the voluntary sector. However, there has been growing awareness and recognition of the role played by informal carers; individuals who provide care for family members, friends, or others in their community. The Family Resources Survey (FRS) collects information on this type of care, and found that in 1999–00, 9 per cent of people in Great Britain had some informal care responsibilities. Of these people most were in the older working age groups, almost a half of both male and female informal carers were aged between 45 and 64 (Table 8.12). Older people often carry out informal care as well – nearly a quarter of male carers and almost a fifth of female carers were aged 65 and over. In addition, some children also had informal care responsibilities, 2 per cent of male informal carers and 1 per cent of female carers were aged between 5 and 15. The most common recipients of informal care were family members. Almost a quarter of male informal carers and a seventh of female informal carers reported that the person they cared for was their partner, spouse or cohabitee, and around two-fifths of carers said that they cared for a relative who was not living in the same household.

Table **8.10**

Places available in residential care homes: by type of accommodation

United Kingdom Percentages

	1996[1]	1998	1999	2000
All staffed residential homes[2]	95	92	92	91
Local authority staffed	24	20	19	18
Registered homes				
Voluntary	19	19	18	19
Private	48	48	50	49
Small homes[3]	3	5	5	5
Dual registered homes[4]	5	8	8	9
Total all homes (=100%)(thousands)	353.8	400.1	395.7	395.8

1 Data for Wales not available for 1996.
2 Excludes dual registered homes.
3 For England and Wales only.
4 For England only before 2000, and for England and Northern Ireland from 2000. Dual registered homes provide both residential and nursing care.

Source: Department of Health; National Assembly for Wales; Scottish Executive; Department of Health, Social Services and Public Safety, Northern Ireland

Chart **8.11**

Number of contact hours of home help and home care: by sector

England

Millions

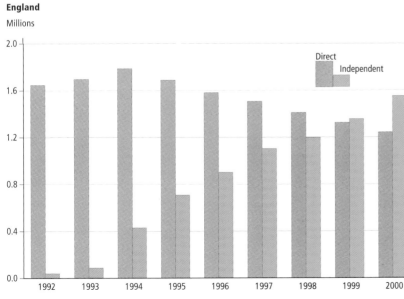

Source: Department of Health

Table **8.12**

Informal carers[1]: by age and gender, 1999–00

Great Britain Percentages

	Males	Females
0–4	0	–
5–15	2	1
16–24	5	5
25–34	9	12
35–44	15	18
45–54	23	25
55–64	23	22
65–74	15	12
75–84	7	5
85 and over	1	–
All	100	100

1 The proportions of males and females that provided informal care to a person or persons in their household.

Source: Family Resources Survey, Department for Work and Pensions

Table **8.13**

National Health Service activity for sick and disabled people[1]: in-patients

United Kingdom

	1981	1991–92	1997–98	1998–99	1999–00
Acute[2]					
Finished consultant episodes[3] (thousands)	5,693	6,729	7,425	7,946	7,999
In-patient episodes per available bed (numbers)	31.1	45.9	54.6	58.5	63.5
Mean duration of stay (days)	8.4	6.0	5.5	4.9	5.6
Mentally ill					
Finished consultant episodes[3] (thousands)	244	281	296	276	271
In-patient episodes per available bed (numbers)	2.2	4.0	5.9	5.7	6.5
Mean duration of stay (days)	..	114.8	58.5	75.2	60.6
People with learning disabilities[4]					
Finished consultant episodes[3] (thousands)	34	62	65	45	42
In-patient episodes per available bed (numbers)	0.6	2.2	5.2	4.0	4.8
Mean duration of stay (days)	..	544.1	163.6	101.9	104.8

1 Excludes NHS beds and activity in joint-user and contractual hospitals.

2 Wards for general patients, excluding elderly, maternity and neonate cots in maternity units.

3 See Appendix, Part 8: In-patient activity.

4 Excludes mental handicap community units.

Source: Department of Health; National Assembly for Wales; National Health Service in Scotland; Department of Health, Social Services and Public Safety, Northern Ireland

Table **8.14**

National Health Service activity for sick and disabled people: accident and emergency, acute out-patients and day cases

United Kingdom   Thousands

	1981	1991–92	1997–98	1998–99	1999–00
Accident and emergency services					
New attendances	11,321	13,397	15,569	15,603	16,035
Total attendances	15,957	16,289	17,598	17,492	17,928
Out-patient services					
New attendances	8,619	9,862	12,703	13,173	14,578
Total attendances	36,160	38,944	44,535	46,148	52,031
Day case finished consultant episodes[1]	817	1,772	3,818	4,195	4,059

1 Excludes Wales in 1981 and Northern Ireland in 1981 and 1986. Data for Northern Ireland from 1991–92 are for day case admissions.

Source: Department of Health; National Assembly for Wales; National Health Service in Scotland; Department of Health, Social Services and Public Safety, Northern Ireland

Sick and disabled people

In Chapter 7: Health, the illnesses and other health problems faced by the population were discussed, and earlier in this chapter, an overview was provided of some of the social protection that is available for people with health problems. This section focuses on the support provided for sick and disabled people.

The number of hospital in-patient episodes (see Appendix, Part 8: In-patient episodes) in all NHS hospitals in the United Kingdom has risen since 1981. The number of in-patient episodes for acute cases rose by 41 per cent between 1981 and 1999–00 to 8.0 million, and the number of episodes for mental health cases increased by 11 per cent to 271 thousand, probably reflecting the growing awareness of this type of health problem (Table 8.13). For people with learning disabilities, the number of cases rose by 82 per cent between 1981 and 1991–92 to 62 thousand; but in 1999–00 the number of cases was 42 thousand. While the number of hospital in-patient episodes has risen over the last two decades an overall decline in the mean duration of stay in NHS hospitals has occurred across all specialities, although there is some evidence of a recent increase in average stay. For example, for acute cases, the mean duration of stay was 4.9 days in 1998–99, compared with 8.4 days in 1981; in 1999–00 mean stay for acute cases was 5.6 days, but it is too early to say if this indicates a new trend.

As well as an increase in the number of in-patient episodes, the number of people being treated as an accident and emergency patient, an out-patient or a day case has also increased (Table 8.14). The number of day case episodes was five times higher in 1999–00 than in 1981, although this number is slightly lower than in 1998–99. The total number of out-patient attendances also increased over the same period by over two-fifths.

A source of much public and media attention in the NHS are waiting lists and waiting times. Chart 8.15 shows the number of people who had been on in-patient waiting lists in England for 15 months or more – these are the people who have been waiting longest for treatment. At 31 March 2001 there were 10.4 thousand people who had been on the list for 15 months or more. This compares with 19.8 thousand in 1994, the earliest year for which comparable figures are available. However, the pattern has not been one of continuous decline between those two points, in fact the list shrank to as small as 0.6 thousand in 1996, before rising again to 16.5 thousand two years later. For the last three years between 10 thousand and 12 thousand people have been waiting for in-patient treatment for 15 months or more.

In 2001, the Government announced that it was switching from waiting lists to waiting times as its top priority in terms of cutting waiting for NHS in-patient treatment. The median waiting time for people on in-patient waiting lists was 2.9 months at 31 March 2001. Across the country there was relatively little variation – the South East had the highest median waiting time at 3.4 months.

As discussed in the Overview section, the private sector is an important and growing provider of healthcare. One type of private health provision that many people take up is private medical insurance. In 2000, 6.9 million people were covered by such insurance, more than three times the number in 1971 (2.1 million) (Chart 8.16). Most of this rise occurred in the late 1970s and 1980s. However, after a stable period in the 1990s, the number of people with private medical insurance rose by 5 per cent between 1999 and 2000. This rise was entirely due to company paid business, as the number of individual private medical insurance subscribers fell between 1999 and 2000. But people's reliance on private insurance continues to rise. The overall cost of claims to private medical insurers rose by 5.5 per cent between 1999 and 2000, to £1,934 million.

Chart **8.15**

People on in-patient waiting lists for 15 months or more[1]

England

Thousands

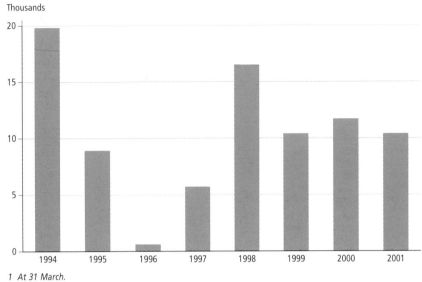

1 At 31 March.
Source: Department of Health

Chart **8.16**

People insured by private medical insurance[1]

United Kingdom

Millions

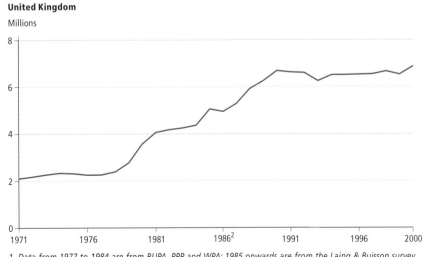

1 Data from 1977 to 1984 are from BUPA, PPP and WPA; 1985 onwards are from the Laing & Buisson survey of private medical insurance.
2 The apparent decrease in the number of people insured in 1986 and 1993 is an artefact of re-estimation of BUPA's multiplier which converts subscribers to persons covered.
Source: BUPA; PPP; WPA; Laing & Buisson

Table **8.17**

Working age claimants of sickness and/or disability benefits: by type of benefit[1]

United Kingdom   Thousands

	1998	1999	2000	2001
Incapacity only[2]	1,678	1,661	1,674	1,697
Incapacity and disability	1,082	1,097	1,121	1,164
Disability only[2]	222	231	237	249
All sick and disabled	2,981	2,989	3,032	3,110

1 In February of each year.
2 Incapacity benefits include invalidity benefit payments, invalidity benefit credits, income support on grounds of sickness and severe disablement allowance. Disability benefit is disabled living allowance. Some of these claimants may also be working. See Appendix, Part 8: Recipients of benefits.
Source: Department of Work and Pensions; Department for Social Development, Northern Ireland

Table **8.18**

Day care places for children[1]

England, Wales & Northern Ireland   Thousands

	1987	1992	1998	1999	2000
Day nurseries					
Local authority provided[2]	29	24	19	16	18
Registered	32	98	216	235	261
Non-registered[3]	1	1	1	12	2
All day nursery places	62	123	236	262	281
Childminders					
Local authority provided[2]	2	2	4	9	3
Other registered person	159	275	403	360	349
All childminder places	161	277	407	369	353
Playgroups					
Local authority provided	4	2	2	3	2
Registered	434	450	423	383	391
Non-registered[2]	7	3	1	3	1
All playgroup places	444	455	426	389	394
Out of school clubs	..	..	97	119	153

1 Under the age of eight. Under the age of 12 in Northern Ireland.
2 England and Wales only.
3 England only before 2000; England and Wales only from 2000.
Source: Department for Education and Skills; National Assembly for Wales; Department of Health, Social Services and Public Safety, Northern Ireland

Social protection for sick and disabled people does not just come from public and private health services. Some help provided by the government for sick and disabled people comes in the form of cash benefits. In February 2001 more than 3.1 million people in the United Kingdom were receiving some sort of cash benefit, for sickness, disability, or both. The main benefits available in this context are incapacity benefit (which replaced invalidity benefit, and, unlike its predecessor, is withdrawn when claimants reach retirement age), severe disablement allowance for sickness and the disability living allowance. While the overall number of people of working age who were claiming these benefits has not changed much over the last few years, there has been a shift towards disability benefits; between 1998 and 2001 there was a 12 per cent rise in the number of people claiming benefits for disability only (Table 8.17).

Children and families

Around 9 per cent of social protection expenditure in the United Kingdom is spent on children and families (see Chart 8.2). Much of this goes on services specifically designed for children, who are among the more vulnerable groups in society. Especially with the changes in the labour market which have occurred over the last few years (see Chapter 4: Labour Market), there has been a rise in demand for day care places for young children. Day care is provided by childminders, voluntary agencies, private nurseries and local authorities as well as nannies and relations. In 2000 there were over 1 million places with childminders, in playgroups and day nurseries for children under the age of eight in England and Wales and under the age of 12 in Northern Ireland, an increase of over 50 per cent since 1987 (Table 8.18). In 2000 there were more than four times as many day nursery places as there were in 1987, and the number of childminder places more than doubled over the same period. Out of school clubs have been introduced in recent years and in 2000 there were 153 thousand such places in England, Wales and Northern Ireland. The exception to the trend of rising provision is in playgroups, in which the number of places fell by 11 per cent between 1987 and 2000.

Looking at day care places by type of provider, there has been a decrease in state provision. The number of places in day nurseries, with childminders and in playgroups combined which were provided by local authorities fell by 34 per cent between 1987 and 2000. The rise in overall places has largely been due to a dramatic increase in provision of day nursery and childminder places by non-state bodies.

In cases where parents are unable to provide proper care for their children, for example due to illness or disability, local authorities can take the child into their care. The term in general use to describe such care is being 'looked after'. In some instances this will be a temporary arrangement, while social services intervene to improve the care available in the child's home environment. Becoming looked after therefore does not always mean that a child is permanently taken away from its original home environment. There tend to be slightly more boys than girls who are being looked after by local authorities; 55 per cent of the 61 thousand children being looked after by local authorities in England and Northern Ireland in 2000 were boys.

After a fall in the first half of the 1990s, the number of children being looked after by local authorities in England, Wales and Northern Ireland rose by 15 per cent between 1995 and 2000 (Chart 8.19). Of the looked after children in 2000, 62 per cent were in foster homes. Some children who are being looked after by a local authority go on to be adopted. In 2000, around 2,800 children were placed for adoption in England and Wales, compared with around 2,000 three years earlier.

Scotland has a different definition of looked after children, so data are not comparable with the rest of the United Kingdom. In Scotland, children who have committed offences or are in need of care and protection may be brought before a Children's Hearing, which can impose a supervision requirement if it thinks that compulsory measures are appropriate. Under these requirements, most children are allowed to remain at home under the supervision of a social worker, but some may live with foster parents or in a residential establishment while under supervision. Children under a supervision order in Scotland are considered to be in the care of their local authority, whilst in the rest of the United Kingdom they are not. Supervision requirements are reviewed at least once a year until ended by a Children's Hearing. In 2000 there were around 11 thousand looked after children in Scotland, of whom almost half were living with their parents and around a quarter were living in foster placements.

Chart **8.19**

Children looked after by local authorities[1]: by type of accommodation, 1995 and 2000

England, Wales and Northern Ireland

Thousands

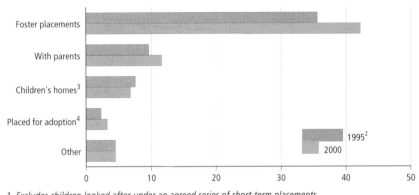

1 Excludes children looked after under an agreed series of short-term placements.
2 1994 for Wales.
3 In England and Wales includes local authority, voluntary and private children's homes.
4 Not collected for Northern Ireland.
Source: Department of Health; National Assembly for Wales; Department of Health, Social Services and Public Safety, Northern Ireland

Children who have more serious problems and are considered to be at risk of abuse may be placed on a local authority child protection register. Registration takes place following a case conference in which decisions are made about the child's welfare, and subsequently the child's name may be placed on a register and a plan set out in order to protect the child. The Children Act 1989, which was implemented in 1991, aimed to enable local authorities to work with families to promote and protect the child's welfare while keeping the families together. The number of children on child protection registers has fallen. In 2000 there were 35 thousand children on such registers in England, Wales and Northern Ireland, compared with 49 thousand in 1991.

Chart 8.20 shows the number of children on child protection registers in England and Wales according to the reason for their placement. Neglect was the most common reason, for both boys and girls, in 2000, accounting for 37 per cent and 35 per cent of cases respectively. However, there are differences between the sexes in terms of the types of problems these children have encountered (or are at risk of encountering). More girls were placed on a register as a result of sexual abuse – 2.4 thousand girls compared with 1.6 thousand boys. However, 3.5 thousand boys were placed on a register as a result of physical injury, compared with 2.9 thousand girls.

Chart **8.20**

Children on child protection registers: by gender and category of abuse, 2000

England and Wales

Thousands

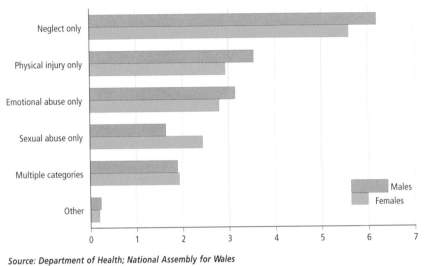

Source: Department of Health; National Assembly for Wales

Table **8.21**

Calls and letters to Childline: by type of concern and gender, 1999–00

United Kingdom		Numbers
	Males	Females
Physical abuse	5,316	8,965
Bullying	5,267	17,105
Family relationship including divorce/separation	3,719	14,828
Sexual abuse	2,648	7,388
Facts of life	1,535	6,873
Runaway/homelessness	1,190	1,860
Concern for others	1,106	9,639
Sexuality	1,023	1,041
Emotional or physical health	836	3,773
Smoking/alcohol/drug/solvent abuse	687	1,515
Partner relationship	686	4,302
School problem	634	1,540
Pregnancy	573	7,374
Other abuse: risk/neglect/emotional	500	1,626
Problem with friends	498	5,538
In care	216	455
Other[1]	1,663	4,989
Total (=100%)	28,097	98,811

1 *Includes a range of problems which add up to less than one per cent such as bereavement, domestic violence, offending, legal, adoption, racism, financial, cultural and religious.*

Source: Childline

It is not just the state that provides help to children who have problems – voluntary organisation and charities also play a role. In 1999–00 Childline, which runs a 24-hour free telephone counselling service for children, received around 127 thousand calls and letters. Almost four-fifths of these were from girls (Table 8.21). The most common reasons for boys using the service were physical abuse and bullying, each of which was responsible for more than 5 thousand calls or letters. For girls, bullying and family relationship problems were the most common reasons, representing 17 per cent and 15 per cent of the requests for help from girls. However, almost a tenth of all of the calls and letters to Childline (more than 10 thousand) were about sexual abuse.

An important part of the social protection provided for families is maternity care, and several aspects of fertility and birth have changed in recent years. The length of new mothers' post-natal stay in hospital is declining (Chart 8.22). In 1997–98, the mean duration of post-natal stay in England was 2.2 days, compared with 3.2 days in 1989–90 and 5.5 days in 1981. Another notable trend in maternity care has been the rise in the proportion of deliveries that are performed by Caesarean section. In 1999–00, 20 per cent of deliveries were Caesareans, compared with 11 per cent ten years earlier.

Chart **8.22**

Mean duration of postnatal stay[1]

England

Days

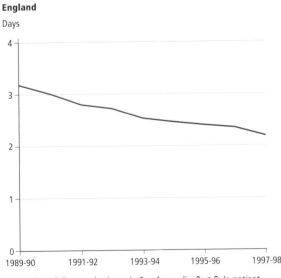

1 *Based on delivery episodes only. See Appendix, Part 8: In-patient activity.*

Source: Department of Health

Older people

As has been discussed earlier in the chapter, older people receive almost a half of social protection expenditure in the United Kingdom, including roughly the same proportion of social security benefit and health spending. The main benefit for older people is the retirement pension, which was received by around 7.4 million people in the United Kingdom at 31 March 2001 (Table 8.23). Older people may also receive other benefits; in 2000 2.5 million older people received sickness and disability benefits and 627 thousand were in receipt of non-disabled income support to boost their low incomes. Since invalidity benefit was replaced by incapacity benefit, which ceases to be paid when recipients retire, the retirement pension has become a more central benefit for older people. The state pension is currently set at £72.50 for single pensioners and £115.90 for married couples. Since 1991, these figures have risen by £20.50 and £32.65 respectively.

An increasing proportion of people are making their own provision for their old age. Two ways of doing this are through occupational and personal pension schemes. Occupational pensions are schemes set up and provided through people's employers, while personal pension schemes are pensions which people set up independently, into which they make payments prior to their old age. According to the FRS, among employees, three-fifths of men and half of women in Great Britain contributed to either an occupational pension or a personal pension (or both) in 1999–00 (Table 8.24). Occupational pensions are not available to the self-employed who are less likely than employees to contribute to a private pension – around half of self-employed men and three-tenths of self-employed women contributed to a pension scheme.

There is a strong generational pattern in the contribution to these pension schemes. Those aged between 45 and 54 were the most likely to contribute to one, for both employees and the self-employed. However, even among 16 to 24 year olds, around a fifth of adults were paying in to a pension scheme. Overall, and in the vast majority of age groups, men were more likely than women to contribute to a pension scheme, although in the 16 to 24 and 25 to 34 age groups women were as likely as men to contribute to one. People of state pension age were unlikely to still be contributing to a scheme but to be using the pensions as a source of income.

Table 8.23

Claimants of state pension age receiving key benefits[1]: by type

United Kingdom			Thousands
	1998	**1999**	**2000**
Sick and disabled	2,374	2,429	2,530
Non-disabled income support	669	614	627
Retirement pension only	7,419	7,437	7,367
All claimants	10,462	10,481	10,522

1 Key benefits are jobseeker's allowance, disability living allowance, incapacity benefit, income support, retirement pension and severe disablement allowance. See Appendix, Part 8: Recipients of benefits.

Source: Department for Work and Pensions; Department for Social Development, Northern Ireland

Table 8.24

Pension provision: by selected employment status[1], gender and age, 1999–00

Great Britain								Percentages
	16–24	25–34	35–44	45–54	55–59	60–64	All aged 65 and over	All aged 16 and over
Males								
Employees								
Occupational pension only	15	44	57	59	53	35	3	46
Personal pension only	4	15	15	15	14	13	1	13
Either occupational or personal pension or both	19	61	75	77	70	51	4	61
No pension scheme	81	39	25	23	30	49	96	39
Self-employed								
Personal pension only	11	46	56	57	57	44	9	48
No pension scheme	89	54	44	43	43	56	91	52
Females								
Employees								
Occupational pension only	19	48	49	49	45	30	2	43
Personal pension only	3	9	9	9	8	7	0	8
Either occupational or personal pension or both	22	58	59	60	55	37	2	52
No pension scheme	78	42	41	40	45	63	98	48
Self-employed								
Personal pension only	5	31	33	38	20	16	0	29
No pension scheme	95	69	67	62	80	84	100	71

1 The table includes employees and self-employed people, but not 'others'.

Source: Family Resources Survey, Department for Work and Pensions

Websites

National Statistics	www.statistics.gov.uk
Department of Health	www.doh.gov.uk
Department for Work and Pensions	www.dwp.gov.uk
Department for Education and Skills	www.dfes.gov.uk
Department of Health, Social Services and Public Safety, Northern Ireland	www.dhsspsni.gov.uk/iau/index.html
Department for Social Development, Northern Ireland	www.dsdni.gov.uk
National Assembly for Wales	www.wales.gov.uk
NHS in Scotland	www.show.scot.nhs.uk/isd
Northern Ireland Statistics and Research Agency	www.nisra.gov.uk
Scottish Executive	www.scotland.gov.uk
Eurostat	www.europa.eu.int/comm/eurostat
Childline	www.childline.co.uk
Laing & Buisson	www.laingbuisson.co.uk

Contacts

Office for National Statistics	
Chapter author	020 7533 5081
General Household Survey	020 7533 5444
Department of Health	
Acute services activity	0113 254 5522
Adults' services	020 7972 5585
Children's services	020 7972 5581
Community and cross-sector services	020 7972 5524
General dental and community dental service	020 7972 5392
General medical services statistics	0113 254 5911
Mental illness/handicap	020 7972 5546
NHS expenditure	0113 254 6012
NHS medical staff	0113 254 5892
NHS non-medical manpower	0113 254 5744
Non-psychiatric hospital activity	020 7972 5529
Personal social services expenditure	020 7210 5699
Residential care and home help	020 7972 5600
Social services staffing and finance data	020 7972 5595
Waiting lists	0113 254 5200
Department for Work and Pensions	020 7962 8000
Family Resources Survey	020 7962 8092
Number of benefit recipients	0191 225 7373
Department for Education and Skills	
Day care for children	01325 392827
Department of Health, Social Services and Public Safety, Northern Ireland	
Health and personal social services activity	028 9052 2800
Health and personal social services manpower	028 9052 2468
Department for Social Development, Northern Ireland	028 9052 2280
National Assembly for Wales	029 2082 5080
National Health Service in Scotland	0131 551 8899
Northern Ireland Statistics and Research Agency	028 9034 8243
Scottish Executive	
Children's social services	0131 244 3551
Adult community care	0131 244 3777
Social work staffing	0131 244 3740
Eurostat	00 352 4301 34122
Childline	020 7239 1098
Laing & Buisson	020 7833 9123

Chapter 9

Crime and Justice

Offences

- Overall incidents of crime in the British Crime Survey fell by 12 per cent between 1999 and 2000 in England and Wales and have declined by a third since the peak in 1995. (Table 9.2)

- In 2000–01 there were 5.2 million crimes recorded by the police in England and Wales, 130 thousand fewer than in the previous year. Recorded crime in Scotland fell by 3 per cent between 1999 and 2000. (Table 9.3)

- When comparing 1995 with 1999, crime rates recorded by the police fell by 10 per cent in England and Wales and by 8 per cent in Scotland, compared with an average 1 per cent fall in EU member states. (Chart 9.5)

- Over one in three burglaries with loss committed in England and Wales in 2000 involved the theft of cash. (Table 9.6)

Offenders

- Of the 475 thousand people cautioned or found guilty for an indictable offence in England and Wales in 2000, the vast majority, around eight in ten, were male. (Table 9.11)

- In 2000, in England and Wales, 151 thousand cautions for indictable offences were given, over 40 thousand fewer than in 1998. (Table 9.12)

Police and courts action

- There were 31 thousand complaints completed against the police in England and Wales in 2000–01, around the same number as in the previous year. Of these, less than 1,000 (3 per cent) were substantiated. (Table 9.16)

- In England and Wales, overall detection rates were 24 per cent in 2000–01, a 1 per cent decrease on the previous year. Scotland had a clear-up rate of 44 per cent in 2000. (Table 9.17)

Chart **9.1**

Offenders[1] as a percentage of the population: by gender and age, 2000

England & Wales

Percentages

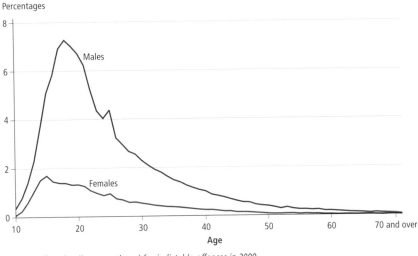

Age

1 People found guilty or cautioned for indictable offences in 2000.
Source: Home Office

Overview

Most individuals are relatively untroubled by crime and do not regularly come into direct contact with police, judges and other authorities connected with the Criminal Justice System. Crime and its consequences are nonetheless a perpetual problem for government and society at large. Tackling crime is a priority for the government; being able to lead lives free from crime and free from the worry of crime remain the wishes of most family groups and households.

Data showing offenders as a percentage of the population give a good indication of how criminal activity varies with gender and age. According to recorded crime figures based on administrative data collected by the police, the proportion of offenders rises sharply in young people (between the ages of 10 and 18 for boys and 10 and 15 for girls). In 2000 in England and Wales, 7 per cent of all eighteen year old boys were found guilty of indictable offences, by far the highest rate for any age group, and six times the corresponding rate for girls. As men and women enter their thirties, the proportions who are offenders decline gradually with age (Chart 9.1). For those over the age of 40, less than 1 per cent of the population were found guilty or cautioned for an indictable offence, with negligible proportions of offenders aged 70 and above.

Crime data collected by the police is a by-product of the administrative procedure of completing a record for crimes which they investigate. While this provides detailed data on crime, many crimes are never reported to the police and some that are reported are not recorded. Major changes in methods of recording crime were adopted by the police from April 1998. The new rules have increased the coverage of offences and have also increased the emphasis on measuring one crime per victim rather than one crime per offender. An additional explanation of these changes is contained in Appendix: Part 9, Types of offences in England and Wales – recorded crime statistics.

Police recording rates – whether a reported crime is considered of sufficient seriousness to go 'on the record' – depend to a certain extent on the discretion of the police officers concerned and will vary from force to force. Sixty per cent of British Crime Survey crimes reported to the police are recorded by them, a proportion which has fluctuated from a high of 62 per cent in 1981 to a low of 50 per cent in 1995. A new National Crime Standard, taking effect from April 2002 in every police force in England and Wales, aims to achieve greater harmonisation of recording rates. Reporting rates vary according to the crimes committed. A high proportion of car thefts are reported to the police as police involvement is required for insurance purposes. There is some evidence to suggest that shop theft is less likely to be reported to the police, with some thefts being absorbed by the businesses as overheads, and some shop owners either not wishing to attract publicity or else believing that reported crimes are unlikely to be detected.

The British Crime Survey provides an alternative measure of crime to the data on offenders in Chart 9.1. BCS data is derived from households and individuals surveyed, and the results are therefore based on reports of victims of crimes rather than on police recording. Survey data are then combined with population data to give estimates of the total number of crimes in England and Wales. There are some differences in the coverage of police recorded crime and BCS measured crime. Unlike crime data recorded by the police, the BCS is restricted to crimes against adults (aged 16 or more) living in private households and their property and does not include some types of crime (for example, fraud, murder and so-called victimless crimes). Since 1992 the BCS has been carried out in England and Wales every two years but has moved to an annual cycle from 2001. In 1982, the BCS also covered Scotland, with Scottish results being reported separately. Scotland and Northern Ireland have their own surveys. The number of crimes measured by the Scottish Crime Survey (SCS) fell by 13 per cent between 1995 and 1999. Overall, since 1981, the number of crimes estimated by the SCS has fallen by nearly a third.

According to the British Crime Survey, overall incidents of crime in England and Wales fell 12 per cent between 1999 and 2000 and have declined by a third since the peak in 1995 (Table 9.2). Large falls in burglary, and theft of and from vehicles have contributed to the recent overall reductions. The proportion of people who were victims of some type of crime once or more during the year fell from 30 per cent in 1999 to 27 per cent in 2000, the lowest overall victimisation rate ever recorded by the BCS. Around one in five BCS crimes involved violence, a proportion that has remained relatively unchanged since 1981. Among individual violent crime categories, wounding incidents fell by 34 per cent between 1999 and 2000.

The total number of crimes recorded by the police provides another way of looking at the extent of criminal activity in the country (Table 9.3). Recent figures show there were 5.2 million crimes committed in England and Wales in the year ending March 2001 – a slight decrease on the previous year when 5.3 million crimes were committed. The decrease follows a 4 per cent rise in recorded crime in the 12 months to March 2000.

Table **9.2**

Violent crimes as a percentage of all BCS[1] crimes: by year[2]

England & Wales			Millions
	All BCS crime	All violence	All violence as a percentage of all BCS crime
1981	11.0	2.2	20
1983	11.9	2.1	18
1987	13.3	2.3	17
1991	15.1	2.7	18
1993	18.6	3.6	19
1995	19.2	4.1	21
1997	16.4	3.4	21
1999	14.7	3.2	22
2000	12.9	2.6	20

1 All incidents of crime measured by the British Crime Survey, whether or not they were recorded by the police.
2 Surveys were not carried out in 1985 or 1989.

Source: British Crime Survey, Home Office

Table **9.3**

Recorded crime: by type of offence[1]

	England & Wales		Scotland		Northern Ireland		
	1999–00[2]	2000–01	1999	2000	1999–00	2000–01	
Theft and handling stolen goods,	2,224	2,145	196	183	37	37	
of which: theft of vehicles	375	339	30	26	10	11	
theft from vehicles	669	630	49	43	6	6	
Criminal damage	946	960	80	83	31	32	
Burglary	906	836	54	49	16	16	
Violence against the person	581	601	18	19	21	21	
Fraud and forgery	335	319	24	26	8	8	
Drugs offences[3]	122	113	32	31	2	1	
Robbery	84	95	5	4	1	2	
Sexual offences,	38	37	4	4	1	1	
of which: rape	8	9	1	1	0	0	
Other notifiable offences[4]	66	63	23	23	1	1	
All notifiable offences	5,301	5,171	436	423	119	120	

Thousands

1 See Appendix, Part 9: Types of offences in England, Wales and Northern Ireland and Offences and crimes.
2 No longer includes assault on police and communicating false information regarding a bomb hoax. These offences have been removed from the categories 'Violence against the person' and 'Other notifiable offences'.
3 From 1 April 1998 a new 'drug offence' group was created. Included within it are drug trafficking, possession of controlled drugs and other drugs offences.
4 In Northern Ireland includes 'offences against the state'. In Scotland excludes 'offending while on bail' from 1991 onwards.

Source: Home Office; Scottish Executive; Royal Ulster Constabulary

Map **9.4**

Recorded crime: by police force area[1,2], 1999–00 – 2000–01

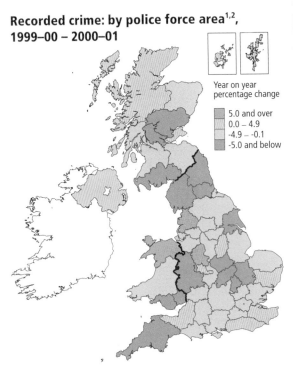

Year on year percentage change

- 5.0 and over
- 0.0 – 4.9
- -4.9 – -0.1
- -5.0 and below

1 Data for Scotland relate to 1999 and 2000.
2 For the Metropolitan Police, Surrey, Essex and Hertfordshire, the percentage changes are based on figures for the new force areas.
Source: Home Office; Scottish Executive; RUC

Chart **9.5**

Crimes recorded by the police in selected EU countries

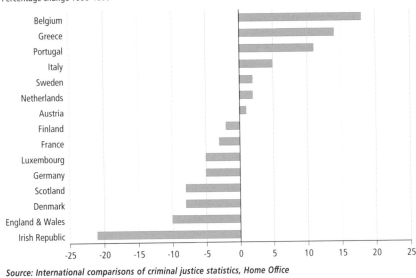

Percentage change 1995-1999

Source: International comparisons of criminal justice statistics, Home Office

Distinctions between different types of crime are often less than straightforward. Street thefts, for instance, are recorded as thefts from the person if pockets are picked or items snatched. However, the incident becomes a robbery if there is any resistance from the victim, or violence or threat of violence used. Recorded violent crime in England and Wales in the year ending March 2001 rose, but at a slower rate than the previous year. All offences of violence against the person rose by 3 per cent. The largest increases in recorded violent crime were in the racially aggravated offences of harassment (up 16 per cent); common assault (up 11 per cent) and other wounding (up 18 per cent). Robberies rose 13 per cent, but sexual offences fell by 1 per cent in the 12 months to March 2001.

Due to difference in the legal systems, recording practices and classifications, comparisons between countries within the UK should only be made with care. In Scotland the term 'crimes' is used for the more serious criminal acts (roughly equivalent to 'indictable' and 'triable-either-way' offences in England and Wales.) Less serious crimes are termed 'offences'. Scottish figures are given for crimes only, unless otherwise stated. In Northern Ireland the definitions used are broadly comparable with those in England and Wales. Recorded crime in Scotland decreased by 3 per cent between 1999 and 2000 to a total of 423 thousand crimes. Recorded crime in Northern Ireland increased slightly (by less than 1 per cent) between 1999–2000 and 2000–01.

Since 1998, 376 crime and disorder reduction partnerships have been established, bringing together the police local authorities and other relevant agencies to develop strategies for dealing with local crime problems. New initiatives carried out at this level have helped to focus attention on the large regional variations in patterns of recorded crime. Initial research generated by the crime reduction partnerships has indicated that two types of regions are more vulnerable to higher levels of crime: university towns with large numbers of students living in privately rented accommodation; and seaside towns with a large transient population and higher than average levels of drug-related activity.

In 2000–01, there were decreases in the total number of recorded crimes in 34 of the 43 police forces in England and Wales. South Wales and Cumbria both recorded falls of almost 13 per cent (Map 9.4). Ten other forces recorded falls in crime exceeding 5 per cent. Of the forces recording increases, the largest in percentage terms was Lancashire with an 8 per cent increase. This was followed by North Wales with an increase of 7 per cent.

Periodic surveys are carried out giving international comparisons of crime in different countries. Making direct comparisons is complicated by a number of factors: laws are different across international boundaries, and methods of collecting crime data vary enormously from country to country, with some relying more on administrative data collected by the police and others relying more on surveys. For these reasons, international crime comparisons are invariably given in terms of percentage changes within each country rather than absolute rates. When comparing 1995 with 1999, crime recorded by the police in England and Wales fell by 10 per cent compared with a 1 per cent fall in EU member states (Chart 9.5). Recorded crime in Scotland fell by 8 per cent over the same period. Since the agreed definition of homicide is similar in most countries, absolute comparisons are easier to make. For a three-year period, 1997 to 1999, the average homicide rate (number of homicides per 100,000 of the population) was 1.7 in EU member states with the highest rates in Northern Ireland (3.1), Finland (2.6), Spain (2.6) and Scotland (2.1). The rate in England and Wales (1.5) was below the average. Austria had the lowest rate of EU member states, at 0.8 homicides per 100,000 of the population.

The nature of crime may change over time. Some crime, such as burglary, may stay the same in that it involves the breaking and entering of households and theft of goods, but the type of articles stolen in a burglary will change, reflecting amongst other things fashions, technological developments, and the desirability and availability of various household goods. Between 1994 and 2000 the proportion of burglaries in England and Wales with loss involving the theft of jewellery and videos fell from over one in three to just over one in four; those involving theft of a television fell from one in five to one in eight; while those involving theft of computer equipment rose from one in twelve to one in seven (Table 9.6). The flexibility and versatility of money has kept it a favourite target for those committing burglary – over one in three burglaries with loss committed in 2000 involved the theft of cash.

In 1999, the number of drugs seizures fell by 13 per cent over the previous year to a total of 132 thousand (Table 9.7). Much of the overall decline can be attributed to sharp falls in the number of seizures by police and customs involving Class B drugs such as cannabis – the most widely available and regularly used illegal substance in the UK. There were falls too in the amounts seized of these drugs. The number of heroin seizures stayed roughly the same between 1998 and 1999 but with around a 75 per cent rise in the quantity seized. Drug use is higher among younger than older age groups, and more prevalent in urban than rural areas. The British Crime Survey in 2000 for England and Wales showed that 16 to 29 year olds in affluent urban areas were the most regular users, with

Table **9.6**

Items stolen in burglary[1]

England & Wales				Percentages
	1994	1996	1998	2000
Jewellery	38	36	34	28
Video	36	33	35	28
Cash	33	33	41	36
Stereo/HiFi Equipment	24	27	25	20
Television	21	21	16	12
Camera	17	14	13	11
Clothes	13	8	9	10
Documents	9	7	6	6
Computer equipment	8	7	9	14
Purse/wallet	7	10	16	11
Briefcase/bag	7	5	5	6
Credit cards/cheque book	7	8	15	9
Other	35	35	33	36

1 Excludes don't knows.
Source: British Crime Survey, Home Office

Table **9.7**

Seizures[1] of selected drugs

United Kingdom					Numbers
	1981	1991	1995	1998	1999
Cannabis	17,227	59,420	91,325	114,667	97,356
Heroin	819	2,640	6,468	15,188	15,108
Ecstasy-type	..	1,735	5,513	4,849	6,438
Cocaine	503	1,401	2,210	5,207	5,619
Crack	..	583	1,444	2,488	2,436
Methadone	402	427	941	1,584	1,176
LSD	384	1,636	1,155	623	465
Amphetamines	1,117	6,821	15,443	18,629	13,194
All seizures	19,428	69,805	114,539	151,719	132,194

1 Seizures by the police and HM Customs. A seizure can include more than one type of drug.
  See Appendix, Part 9: Drugs seizures.
Source: Home Office

Chart **9.8**

Levels of disorder[1], 2000

England & Wales

Percentages

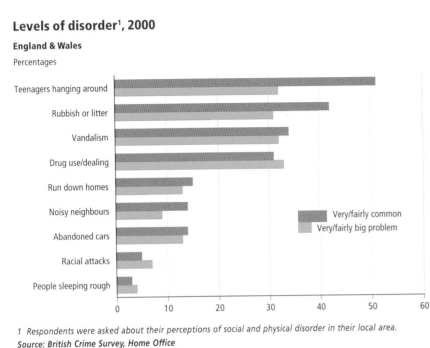

1 Respondents were asked about their perceptions of social and physical disorder in their local area.

Source: British Crime Survey, Home Office

around 40 per cent of this group estimated to have taken any form of drug in the previous year. The number of drugs related offences recorded can be affected by certain police priorities and practices, such as an increased focusing on Class A drugs by law enforcement agencies. More information on the classification of drugs can be found in Appendix: Part 9, Drugs seizures. Additionally, following Home Office research to identify good practice of, and enable improvements, in the use of 'Stop and Search', the number of 'Stop and Searches' for drugs fell from 362 to 274 thousand between 1998–9 and 1999–00. The number of drug related arrests arising from 'Stop and Searches' also fell over the same period, from 44 thousand to 37 thousand.

Victims

Any form of disorder can have impact on the quality of people's lives. The degree of disruption caused by the disorder will vary according to the type of disorder experienced. Some, such as excessive noise from neighbours are undesirable and a nuisance; other acts of disorder such as vandalism are prosecutable offences. In a research study carried out in England and Wales in 1999 by the British Crime Survey, teenagers hanging around was judged by respondents to be the most common 'disorder' issue in their local area; people sleeping rough the least (Chart 9.8) Whether or not the identified issue represented a 'problem' or not produced different results, with four issues: teenagers hanging around; rubbish or litter, vandalism and drug use/drug dealing constituting very big or fairly big problems for roughly equal numbers of respondents (around a third of those surveyed). The unemployed, students, and those in low income and local authority housing were groups most likely to say that disorder had a negative impact on their quality of life. Those under the age of 65 were more likely to say that disorder had a detrimental impact on their quality of life than older people.

Older people are also less at risk than younger people of directly falling victim to crime. According to the 2000 British Crime Survey, around 1 per cent of adults where the head of household was over 60 were the victim of some violent crime in 1999 in England and Wales. The group most likely to be subjected to violent crime was single adult and child households – 11 per cent of this group were subject to some form of violence. Around three-quarters of the assaults committed against single adult and children households were of a domestic nature (Table 9.9) The type of area in which people live can affect their likelihood of being a victim of violent crime. In general, those households located in council estates

Table **9.9**

Proportion of adult victims of violent crime[1]: by household characterisics, 1999

England & Wales

Percentages

	No children	Adults and children	Single adult and children	Head of household over 60	All adults
Domestic	0.8	0.8	7.3	0.2	0.8
Acquaintance	2.0	2.4	2.2	0.4	1.7
Stranger	2.1	1.5	1.1	0.5	1.5
Mugging	0.7	0.8	1.2	0.3	0.6
All violence	5.2	5.1	10.7	1.4	4.2

1 Percentage victimised once or more.

Source: British Crime Survey, Home Office

and low-income areas were the most likely to have been victims of violent crimes – around twice the rate of those living in affluent suburban and rural areas. Single adult and child households were most likely to fall victim of burglary – burglary rates for this group were over twice as high as the corresponding rates for all households.

Concern about crime depends on a number of complex factors, including disorder and actual and perceived levels of risk. Individuals and households from Black and Asian groups have consistently shown higher levels of concern about crime than individuals from other ethnic groups. According to the British Crime Survey, Black and Asian adults in England and Wales in 2000 were roughly twice as likely to be worried about suffering some form of personal attack, or some form of car theft than White adults (Table 9.10). Asian adults were also three times as likely to be worried about being insulted or pestered than White adults. Females of all ages and ethnic groups were more likely to be concerned about all kinds of crime than males. Perceptions of risk show variations across the various ethnic groups, with Asians more than three times as likely to say they were very or fairly likely to be a victim of mugging than Whites. Differences in perceptions of risk for car-related theft was not so pronounced, with just under one in two Asian adults saying they thought they were very or fairly likely to fall victim to this crime in the coming year, compared with one in three White adults.

Offenders

In 2000, 475 thousand people were cautioned or found guilty for an indictable offence in England and Wales (Table 9.11). The vast majority of these, around eight in ten, were male. For both males and females it was young adults who offended the most. In 2000, 597 per 10,000 population of 16 to 24 year old men were found guilty of, or cautioned for, an indictable offence, compared with a rate of 123 per 10,000 women in the same age group. Theft was the most common offence committed by both male and female offenders. Over half of all female offenders were found guilty or cautioned for theft-related offences compared with 37 per cent of all male offenders. A relatively small number of offenders are responsible for a disproportionately high number of offences. Research into the number of offenders who re-offend has shown that in England and Wales, for males born in 1953, two-thirds of all court appearances were attributable to a quarter of offenders. Conversely, the criminal careers of many offenders are comparatively short lived: half of male offenders and three-quarters of female offenders born in 1953 had, by 2001, only been convicted once.

Table **9.10**

Worry about crime[1]: by ethnic group, 2000

England & Wales				Percentages[2]
	White	Black	Asian	All adults
Theft of car[3]	20	37	37	21
Theft from car[3]	15	33	30	16
Burglary	18	37	41	19
Mugging	16	32	38	17
Physical attack	17	35	38	18
Rape	18	34	34	19

1 Percentage of people who were 'very worried' about each type of crime.
2 Aged 16–59.
3 Percentage of car owners.
Source: British Crime Survey, Home Office

Table **9.11**

Offenders found guilty of, or cautioned for, indictable offences[1]: by gender, type of offence and age, 2000

England & Wales				Rates per 10,000 population
	10–15	16–24	25–34	35 and over	All aged 10 and over (thousands)
Males					
Theft and handling stolen goods	113	205	89	16	142.1
Drug offences	14	143	53	8	76.5
Violence against the person	29	68	28	7	47.1
Burglary	32	53	16	2	31.0
Criminal damage	13	17	6	1	12.0
Robbery	6	11	2	–	5.9
Sexual offences	3	4	2	2	5.2
Other indictable offences	11	96	52	11	66.4
All indictable offences	221	597	250	47	386.2
Females					
Theft and handling stolen goods	65	72	30	6	53.5
Drug offences	2	15	8	1	9.3
Violence against the person	9	11	5	1	8.1
Burglary	3	3	1	–	1.8
Criminal damage	2	2	1	–	1.4
Robbery	1	1	–	–	0.6
Sexual offences	–	–	–	–	0.1
Other indictable offences	3	20	12	2	14.3
All indictable offences	85	123	57	11	88.9

1 See Appendix, Part 9: Types of offences in England, Wales and Northern Ireland.
Source: Home Office

Table **9.12**

Offenders cautioned for indictable offences[1]: by type of offence

England & Wales   Thousands

	1971[2]	1981	1991	1995	1998	1999	2000
Theft and handling stolen goods	53.5	79.2	108.5	104.9	83.6	75.4	67.6
Drug offences[2]	..	0.3	21.2	48.2	58.7	49.4	41.1
Violence against the person	2.3	5.6	19.4	20.4	23.5	21.2	19.9
Burglary[3]	12.4	11.2	13.3	10.5	8.4	7.7	6.6
Fraud and forgery	1.0	1.4	5.6	7.9	7.4	7.2	6.2
Criminal damage	3.6	2.1	3.8	3.8	2.7	3.0	3.2
Sexual offences	3.9	2.8	3.3	2.3	1.7	1.5	1.3
Robbery	0.2	0.1	0.6	0.6	0.6	0.6	0.6
Other	0.3	1.3	4.1	4.0	5.0	4.6	4.4
All offenders cautioned	77.3	103.9	179.9	202.6	191.7	170.6	150.9

1 Excludes motoring offences.
2 Adjusted to take account of the Criminal Damage Act 1971. Drug offences data for 1971
  are included in 'Other'.
3 See Appendix, Part 9: Offenders cautioned for burglary.
Source: Home Office

In England and Wales a formal caution may be given by a senior police officer when an offender has admitted their guilt, there is sufficient evidence for a conviction and it is not in the public interest to institute criminal proceedings. Details of cautions given remain on an individual's record. In 2000, 151 thousand cautions for indictable offences in England and Wales were given – over 40 thousand fewer than in 1998 (Table 9.12). Between 1971 and 1995 the number of cautions rose steadily. The number of cautions for drug offences rose sharply in the 1980s and continued to a peak of 59 thousand in 1998. Between 1999 and 2000 the number of people cautioned for drug offences fell further, from 49 thousand to 41 thousand. The declining number of cautions for possession of drugs mirrors the decline in drug-related offences noted in Table 9.7 and reflects new priorities in a UK-wide anti-drugs strategy, aiming to move the attentions of the relevant authorities away from punishing users and towards restricting the availability of illegal drugs on the streets.

When an offender has been charged or summoned and then found guilty, the court will impose a sentence. Sentences in England, Wales and Northern Ireland can include immediate custody, a community sentence, a fine or, if the court considers that no punishment is necessary, a discharge. In 2000, 325

Table **9.13**

Offenders sentenced for indictable offences[1]: by type of offence and type of sentence[2], 2000

England & Wales   Percentages

	Discharge	Fine	Community sentence	Fully suspended sentence	Immediate custody	Other	All sentenced (=100%) (thousands)
Theft and handling stolen goods	22	23	32	0	20	2	127.6
Drug offences	16	46	18	1	18	1	45.0
Violence against the person	13	11	40	2	32	3	35.5
Burglary	6	3	38	0	51	1	26.7
Fraud and forgery	18	17	42	2	20	2	19.1
Criminal damage	24	17	40	0	12	7	10.2
Motoring	5	48	23	1	23	1	7.7
Robbery	1	0	23	0	73	1	5.9
Sexual offences	5	3	27	2	62	2	3.9
Other offences	11	41	18	1	19	10	43.2
All indictable offences	16	25	30	1	25	3	324.9

1 See Appendix, Part 9: Types of offences in England and Wales.
2 See Appendix, Part 9: Sentences and orders.
Source: Home Office

thousand people were sentenced for indictable offences in England and Wales (Table 9.13). The form of sentence varied according to the type of offence committed. Those sentenced for motoring offences were the most likely to be fined, with 48 per cent receiving this form of sentence. Offenders sentenced for robbery were the most likely to be sentenced to immediate custody, while those sentenced for fraud and forgery were the most likely to receive a community sentence. Tagging, where the whereabouts of the offender is made known to the relevant authorities by means of an electronic monitoring device, has been used since 1995 as an alternative means of sentencing. Preliminary research has found that offenders 'tagged' tended to be male, in their mid-twenties and criminally active since their late teens. In February 2001 the use of tagging was extended to offenders under curfew and young offenders under the age of 17.

Police and courts action

The confidence of the community in the Criminal Justice System (CJS) is one measure of how well the CJS is performing. Research from the British Crime Survey in 1999 showed that more people thought that the CJS respects the rights of people committing a crime and treats them fairly than believed that the CJS system meets the needs of victims of crime (Chart 9.14). Minority ethnic groups were more confident than White people that the system was effective in bringing people to justice, dealing with cases promptly and efficiently and meeting the needs of victims of crime. However, they were less confident that the criminal justice system respects the rights of, or treated fairly, people accused of committing a crime. Black respondents had particularly low confidence in this respect, with only just over half believing that the system respects the rights of accused people.

Police are often the first point of contact with the criminal justice system, with public initiated contact around a third higher than police initiated contact. To report a crime remains the most frequent reason for the public contacting the police (Table 9.15). Stopping for questioning in a vehicle remains the most frequent reason for police initiated contact. Young men aged 16–29 are particularly likely to be stopped by the police. In the 2000 BCS, a quarter of respondents from this group said they had been stopped while in a vehicle and 15 per cent while on foot. In spring 2001, a new Internet facility, **www.police.uk** enabled individuals wishing to   report non-urgent crimes to make 'online' contact with the police.

Chart **9.14**

Confidence in the Criminal Justice System: by ethnic group, 1999

England & Wales

Percentages

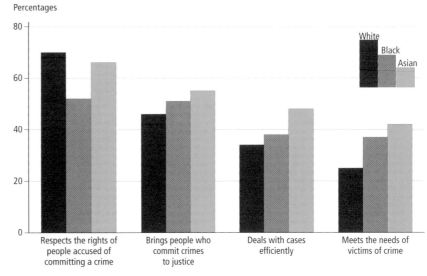

Source: British Crime Survey, Home Office

Table **9.15**

Contacts with the police

England & Wales   Percentages

	1992	1994	1996	1998	2000
Police initiated	31	30	33	31	26
Stopped while in a vehicle	16	14	14	14	12
Returned missing property[1]	14	14	17	15	11
Required to show documents	4	5	4	3	3
Investigate a disturbance[2]	4	4	5	5	3
Questioned on foot	3	3	3	3	3
Public initiated	39	43	41	37	35
To report a crime	16	20	17	15	15
Report a suspicious person[3]	14	19	16	15	12
To report an accident[4]	14	17	14	13	12
To ask for advice or information	6	7	6	5	4
For a social chat	2	2	2	1	2

1 Also includes dealing with ringing alarms, asking information about a crime, or other reason.

2 Also includes investigate traffic accident or offence, search a home, make an arrest, asked to move on.

3 Also includes suspicious circumstances, a disturbance or other nuisance or problem (including alarms).

4 Also includes emergencies, missing people or property, or to give information.

Source: British Crime Survey, Home Office

Table 9.16

Complaints against the police[1]: by outcome

England & Wales   Thousands

	1981	1986	1991	1995–96	1998–99	1999–00	2000–01
Substantiated	1.5	1.1	0.8	0.7	0.7	0.7	0.9
Unsubstantiated	14.7	12.7	11.3	7.9	8.5	7.3	8.9
Informally resolved	.	4.0	9.0	11.7	11.0	11.1	10.6
Withdrawn/not proceeded with	16.2	11.3	14.2	15.5	11.4	11.7	10.6
All complaints	32.4	29.2	35.3	35.8	31.7	30.8	31.0

1 Complaints are counted in the year in which they are completed.
Source: Home Office

Police behaviour towards individuals has come under scrutiny in recent years. Individuals and organisations who feel they have been badly treated in some way may make a formal complaint against the police. In England and Wales there were around 31 thousand complaints in 2000–01, around the same as in the previous year (Table 9.16). Over 800 complaints, representing the more serious cases, were supervised by the Police Complaints Authority. A third of all complaints were not proceeded with. Similar proportions were informally resolved. The proportion of complaints which were substantiated is small – only 3 per cent of complaints were substantiated in 2000–01, a slight increase on the previous year.

In England, Wales and Northern Ireland, following an arrest the police may release the suspect without further action, issue a formal or informal caution, or charge. Offences are said to be cleared up for example where someone is cautioned, charged or summoned to appear in court or a prisoner admits to further offences. The new counting rules introduced on 1 April 1998 (see Appendix 9) had an effect on the clear-up figures, making longer term comparisons less straightforward.

Table 9.17

Clear-up rates for notifiable offences[1]: by type of offence, 2000–01

United Kingdom   Percentages

	England & Wales	Scotland[2]	Northern Ireland
Drug offences	95	100	88
Violence against the person	62	81	60
Sexual offences,	53	77	68
of which: rape	46	77	68
Fraud and forgery	29	82	35
Robbery	18	38	13
Theft and handling stolen goods,	17	33	19
of which: theft of vehicles	13	30	11
theft from vehicles	6	17	4
Burglary	12	24	14
Criminal damage	14	24	14
Other notifiable offences[3]	73	99	62
All notifiable offences	24	44	27

1 See Appendix, Part 9: Types of offences in England and Wales, Types of offences in Northern Ireland, and Offences and crimes.
2 Scottish figures refer to 2000 crimes.
3 In Northern Ireland includes 'offences against the state'.
Source: Home Office; Scottish Executive; Royal Ulster Constabulary

Detection rates, known as clear-up rates in Scotland, vary according to the type of offence. Of the main categories of offence in the United Kingdom, drug offences were the most likely to be detected in 2000–01 and theft from vehicles the least likely (Table 9.17). Detection rates for violent crimes were generally higher than those for property crimes. In England and Wales, overall detection rates were 24 per cent in 2000–01, under counting rules introduced in 1998–99, a 1 per cent decrease on the previous year. Fifty-nine per cent of all detections resulted in a charge or summons. Scotland had a clear-up rate of 44 per cent in 2000 and Northern Ireland had a comparable rate of 27 per cent in 2000–01. Often, there may be a time lapse between the committing of an offence and the police clearing it up.

Probation and prisons

Custodial sentences are normally given by courts to the most serious, dangerous and persistent offenders. In court a defendant may choose to either plead guilty or go on to contest the case by pleading not guilty. Appeals against decisions made at magistrates courts are heard in the crown court, while those against crown court decisions are made at the Court of Appeal. In 2000, just under 8 thousand appeals were started in England and Wales by the Court of Appeal (Criminal Division); 2 thousand appeals (against sentencing and conviction) were granted and over 5 thousand refused.

Prisons are the usual and eventual destination for offenders receiving custodial sentences. Offenders initially given non-custodial sentences who break the terms of their sentence are then liable to receive custodial sentences. Sentenced prisoners are classified into different risk-level groups for security purposes. Women prisoners are held in separate prisons or in separate accommodation in mixed prisons. Young offenders receiving custodial sentences have traditionally been separated from adult offenders, enabling them to receive additional educational and rehabilitative treatment.

Aspects of the Criminal Justice System (CJS) come under periodic review. The Halliday Review, published in England in 2001, has helped stimulate debate on the sentencing of convicted offenders. In a survey commissioned by the Halliday Review, rehabilitation of offenders was thought to be the most important purpose of sentencing by the largest proportion of those surveyed. Just under half of respondents chose this. When asked what they considered to be the second most important purpose, one in four thought it was deterring others and a similar proportion thought it was punishment. Expressing society's disapproval of a particular type of behaviour was thought to be the least important aim of sentencing (Chart 9.18). Previous research has indicated that individuals surveyed often endorse several objectives for sentencing at once and think sentencing should depend on the nature of the crime under consideration, and the kind of offender being sentenced. Sentences to deter the individual were favoured for more minor offences, and custodial sentences favoured for the more serious offences.

Figures on the population in custody give a snapshot of the size of the prison population at any one time; receptions under sentence show how many offenders start custodial sentences over the course of a given year. Receptions under sentence in England and Wales fell from a previous peak in 1985 and fluctuated throughout the late 1980s and 1990s. In 2000 there were around 94 thousand receptions in all Prison Service establishments in England and Wales, a slight

Chart **9.18**

Purposes of sentencing[1], 2000

England & Wales

Percentages

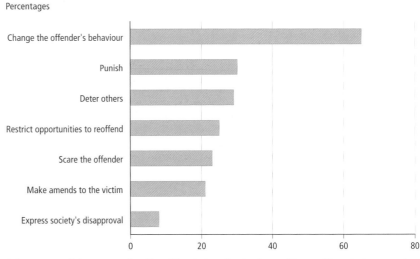

1 Percentages of those surveyed ranking different aims of sentencing as either most important or second most important.

Source: Home Office

Chart **9.19**

Receptions under sentence

England & Wales

Thousands

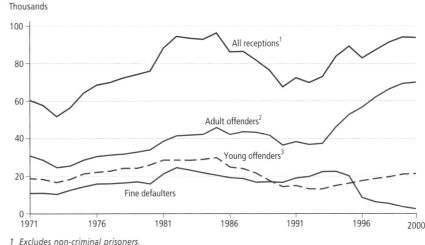

1 Excludes non-criminal prisoners.
2 Includes approved places; excludes fine defaulters.
3 Excludes fine defaulters.

Source: Home Office

Table **9.20**

Receptions of adults into prison under sentence of immediate imprisonment: by length of sentence and gender

England & Wales

Percentages

	Males		Females	
	1990	**2000**	**1990**	**2000**
12 months or less	57	71	66	79
Over 12 months up to 4 years	35	23	28	16
Over 4 years up to 10 years	7	5	5	4
Over 10 years	1	1	–	1
All sentences (=100%)	34,737	64,103	1,734	5,770

Source: Home Office

Table **9.21**

People commencing criminal supervision orders[1]

England & Wales

Thousands

	1981	**1986**	**1991**	**1998**	**1999**	**2000**
Probation	36	40	45	55	56	54
Community service	28	35	42	50	51	52
Combination	.	.	.	21	21	19
Under the Children and Young Persons Act 1969	12	6	2	3	2	–
Other	8	7	8	7	7	7
All[2]	79	83	91	127	127	122

1 Supervised by the probation service. See Appendix, Part 9: Sentences and orders.
2 Individual figures do not sum to the total because each person may have more than one type of order.

Source: Home Office

decrease on the previous year (Chart 9.19). Young offenders accounted for roughly a quarter of the total. Fine defaulters (those in prison for non-criminal offences) numbered less than 2,500. The average daily prison population in Scotland decreased by 3 per cent in 2000 to just under 6 thousand. In Northern Ireland the prison population in custody declined by 29 per cent between 1995 and 1999.

Most prisoners serve sentences of comparatively short duration. In 2000, male and female adults in England and Wales received into prison to serve a sentence of four years or less comprised more than 90 per cent of the total. The vast majority of prisoners are males; compared with males, higher proportions of females serve shorter sentences – there is one female for every ten male prisoners serving sentences of under one year, but one female for every twenty five male prisoners serving sentences of over ten years (Table 9.20). Proportions of adult male and female prisoners serving sentences of one year or less in England and Wales increased between 1990 and 2000, from 57 to 72 per cent of the total prison population. Numbers serving life sentences have fluctuated over time – and in June 2000 in England and Wales comprised over 4,500 inmates, up from 4,200 in June 1999. Approximately three-quarters of these were convicted murderers.

Parole and early release schemes mean that many prisoners do not serve the full length of their original sentence. Most prisoners sentenced to at least three months but less than four years are eligible for release up to 60 days early under the Home Detention Curfew (HDC) scheme, introduced in England and Wales in January 1999. In 2000, over 55 thousand prisoners were eligible to be considered for HDC, and over a quarter of the total, over 15 thousand prisoners, were granted early release.

While custodial sentences are given for some of the more serious offences, other crimes are more likely to result in the offender receiving a criminal supervision order. In 2000, some 122 thousand people started a criminal supervision order in England and Wales, a slight decrease from 1999 (Table 9.21). Males starting orders outnumbered females by five to one. As the same people may receive more than one order, the number of orders exceeds the number of persons receiving orders. Non criminal orders, not covered in the table, include anti-social behaviour orders (ASBOs), measures introduced to England and Wales by the Crime and Disorder Act of 1998 which may be applied to individuals or groups whose threatening and disruptive conduct harasses the local community. By the end of March 2001 around 215 ASBOs had been issued.

Civil justice

While this chapter has so far looked at cases where a charge has been made as part of the official legal system, for example by the Crown Prosecution Service in England and Wales, a case may also be brought under civil law by others, including an individual or a company. The majority of these cases are handled by the county courts and High Court in England, Wales and Northern Ireland and by the Sheriff Court and Court of Session in Scotland. The High Court and Court of Session deal with the more substantial and complex cases. Civil cases may include consumer problems, claims for debt, negligence and recovery of land. Smaller cases, such as claims for unfair dismissal and disputes over social security benefits, are held by tribunals.

Following the issuing of a claim, many cases are settled without the need for a court hearing. Claims were once held at county and high courts, now the vast majority of claims are settled at county court level. The total number of claims issued in county courts in England and Wales rose sharply from just under 2.0 million in 1981 to peak at more than 3.7 million in 1991 (Chart 9.22). This rise may be explained, in part, by the increase in lending as a consequence of financial deregulation. This led to an increase in cases concerned with the recovery and collection of debt, so that in 2000 such claims accounted for over half the total number of 1.9 million claims issued in 2000. After debt recovery, the second and third most common types of claims related to recovery of land and personal injury.

The number of applications granted and received for legal aid is another measure of activity levels within the civil justice system. In England and Wales, the Legal Services Commission operates the Community Legal Service (CLS), which funds civil legal and advice services and civil representation. The Commission was launched in April 2000, replacing the Legal Aid Board. Additional information on the new role of the Commission can be found in the Appendix. For clients whose capital and income are within certain financial limits, the Commission funds a range of legal and advice services in civil matters, either on a contributory or a free basis. The number of applications granted in England and Wales has fallen in each of the past five years to 174 thousand in 2000–01. The number of applications received fell at a similar rate to 226 thousand in 2000–01 (Chart 9.23). Civil Legal Aid in Scotland operates on a similar basis to that operating prior to April 2000 in England and Wales.

Chart **9.22**

Writs and summonses issued[1]

England & Wales

Millions

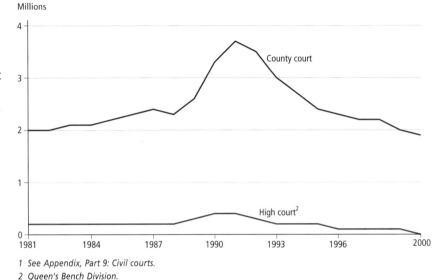

1 See Appendix, Part 9: Civil courts.
2 Queen's Bench Division.
Source: Court Service

Chart **9.23**

Civil legal aid[1]: applications received and granted

England & Wales

Thousands

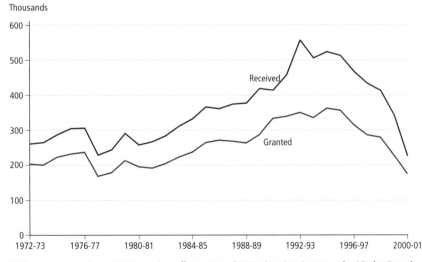

1 The Access to Justice Act 1999 came into effect on 1 April 2000, changing the scope of public funding of legel services. see Appendix, Part 9: Publicly funded legal services.
Source: Lord Chancellor's Department

Table **9.24**

Police officer strength[1]: by ethnic group, gender and rank, at 31 March 2001

England & Wales   Numbers

	Males	Females	All ethnic minorities	White
Chief Constable	43	3	0	46
Assistant Chief Constable	136	13	2	147
Superintendent	1,149	73	15	1,207
Chief Inspector	1,440	111	24	1,527
Inspector	5,612	394	83	5,923
Sergeant	16,770	1,790	339	18,221
Constable	76,988	18,790	2,492	93,286
All ranks	102,139	21,174	2,955	120,358

1 Full-time equivalents employed in the 43 police force areas in England and Wales. With officers on secondment, the total police force strength was 125,519.
Source: Home Office

Resources

A large share of expenditure in the Criminal Justice System has traditionally been spent on the police force, with smaller amounts being spent on prisons and the courts (administered in England and Wales by the Lord Chancellor's Department). In 2001–02, around £14 billion was allocated for expenditure on the criminal justice system.

In 1999, the government set employment targets for the recruitment, retention and progression of minority ethnic officers in England and Wales. The targets are intended to ensure that by 2009, forces will reflect their minority ethnic population. On 31 March 2001, in England and Wales there were almost three thousand officers from minority ethnic backgrounds (up from around 2,700 a year previously) representing 2.4 per cent of the police service. Eighty-five per cent of these officers were constables (Table 9.24). Scotland had 15,149 police officers in 2001, with female officers making up 17 per cent of total police numbers and 20 per cent of constables.

Websites

National Statistics	www.statistics.gov.uk
Lord Chancellor's Department	www. lcd.gov.uk
Court Service	www.courtservice.gov.uk
Home Office	www.homeoffice.gov.uk
Home Office (Criminal Justice System)	www.criminal-justice-system.gov.uk
National Assembly for Wales	www.wales.gov.uk
Scottish Executive	www.scotland.gov.uk
Northern Ireland Executive Information Service	www.nics.gov.uk
Northern Ireland Office	www.nio.gov.uk
Police Service of Northern Ireland	www.psni.police.uk

Contacts

Office for National Statistics	
Chapter author	020 7533 5776
Home Office	020 7273 2084
Lord Chancellor's Department	020 7210 8500
National Assembly for Wales	029 2082 5625
Northern Ireland Office	028 9052 7534/8
Royal Ulster Constabulary	028 9065 0222 ext. 24135
Scottish Executive Justice Department	0131 244 2227

Chapter 10

Housing

Housing stock and housebuilding

■ In 1951 there were 14 million dwellings in Great Britain, by 2001 there were 25 million, an increase of 80 per cent over 50 years. (Chart 10.1)

■ Private sector enterprises were responsible for 154 thousand housebuilding completions – 86% of all dwellings completed in the United Kingdom in 2000–01. (Chart 10.3)

Types of tenure and accommodation

■ In the two decades between 1981 and 2001 the number of owner-occupied dwellings in the United Kingdom increased by more than 40 per cent, while the number of rented dwellings fell by around 15 per cent. (Chart 10.5)

Homelessness

■ In 2000, 30 per cent of all households accepted as homeless in England were in their situation because parents, other relatives or friends were no longer able or willing to accommodate them. (Chart 10.13)

Housing conditions and satisfaction with area

■ Eighty three per cent of all households in England had central heating in all living rooms and bedrooms in 2000–01, compared with 73 per cent in 1994–95. (Page 171)

Housing mobility

■ In 2000–01 the most common tenure for new heads of households in England was privately rented accommodation, with just over 40 per cent opting to rent furnished or unfurnished accommodation. (Chart 10.18)

Housing costs and expenditure

■ In 2000 the average dwelling price in England and Wales was £110,200, an increase of 12 per cent on 1999. (Table 10.24)

■ There were marked regional variations in house prices, with the average amount paid for a detached house in London (£447,000) over four times the amount in Wales (£103,000). The annual rise in dwelling price between 1999 and 2000 ranged from 3 per cent in the North East to 19 per cent in the South East. (Page 176)

Chart **10.1**

Stock of dwellings[1]

Great Britain

Millions

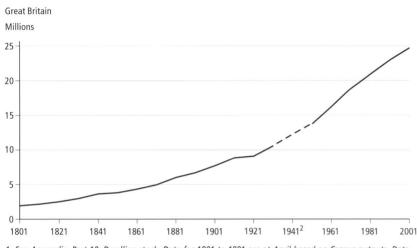

1 See Appendix, Part 10: Dwelling stock. Data for 1801 to 1981 are at April based on Census outputs. Data for England and Wales are at 31 March for 1991 and 2001. Data for Scotland are at April based on census outputs for 1991 and 31 December 2000 for 2001.

2 No census was undertaken in 1941.

Source: Census; Department for Transport, Local Government and the Regions; National Assembly for Wales; Scottish Executive

Throughout life one of the main human requisites is adequate shelter. Housing and its environment can contribute to the quality of our physical and mental well being. A household's requirements, in terms of housing location, size and tenure, can change over time. Housing costs form a significant proportion of household expenditure.

Housing stock and housebuilding

The last two centuries have seen a substantial increase in the number of dwellings in Great Britain together with an increase in population over the same period. This increase in population (see Table 1.1 of the Population chapter for increases from 1901), together with changes in the nature and composition of households, have had a direct impact on demand for accommodation. There were 25 million dwellings at the start of the 21st century compared to just under 2 million at the start of the 19th century, a twelve-fold increase (Chart 10.1). During the same period the population increased five-fold from around 10.5 million to just under 60 million. In all censuses up to 1951 there were more households than dwellings in Great Britain but by 2001 it was estimated from the Labour Force Survey that there were approximately 24 million households: around 1 million fewer households than dwellings. The number of households has increased at a faster rate than the population because the average size of households is declining, partly because of the increasing number of people living alone. It is estimated that the number of one person households in England grew by 2.85 million between 1971 and 1996, an increase of 97 per cent and this increase is projected to continue.

Much of the current housing stock reflects over 100 years of housebuilding, with a fifth of houses in England having been built before the end of the First World War (Table 10.2). The type of dwellings that are built, however, has changed over time. Over a third of the current stock of terraced houses was built before 1919. Between the two World Wars there was a shift in the emphasis in the type of home that was being built in favour of semi-detached dwellings and since 1965 there has been a shift towards the building of detached houses and purpose-built flats. Almost two-thirds of the current stock of purpose-built flats or maisonettes were built after 1964 and very few before 1919.

Table **10.2**

Type of accommodation: by construction date, 2000–01

England

Percentages

	Before 1919	1919– 1944	1945– 1964	1965– 1984	1985 or later	All
House or bungalow						
Detached	13	14	18	31	23	100
Semi-detached	11	29	33	19	8	100
Terraced	35	20	15	20	10	100
Flat or maisonette						
Purpose-built	4	9	24	42	21	100
Other	68	18	8	4	2	100
All dwellings[1]	20	20	22	24	13	100

1 Includes other types of accommodation, such as mobile homes.

Source: Survey of English Housing, Department for Transport, Local Government and the Regions

Chart 10.3 shows trends in housebuilding in the United Kingdom since 1951. The peak for housebuilding was in 1968 when total completions amounted to 426 thousand dwellings, 226 thousand being completed by private enterprises and 200 thousand from the remaining sectors. In the early post-war years local authorities undertook the majority of housing construction. They undertook a massive housebuilding programme between the wars and after the Second World War with peaks in the mid-1950s, mid-1960s and mid-1970s, but they are no longer major developers of new housing, although they still play an important role as landlords. Private housebuilding began to take off in the 1950s and has been the dominant sector since 1959. In the 1970s housing associations became active in acquiring and renovating rented stock from private landlords, while in recent years they have tended to build new homes. Registered social landlords (predominantly housing associations) now dominate building in the social sector, completing 25 thousand dwellings in 2000–01. In the same period private sector enterprises were responsible for 154 thousand completions – 86 per cent of all dwellings completed.

Another influence on housebuilding is an increasing awareness of environmental issues. The government has made commitments to the protection of the countryside by recycling previously developed land – 'brownfield' and empty properties – as opposed to building on 'greenfield' sites. It has set a target that by 2008, 60 per cent of new homes in England should be built on this previously developed land. The redevelopment of brownfield sites allows more efficient use to be made of available land, helps to reduce transport needs and allows economic development to take place without excessive urbanisation of the countryside.

In 1998, 57 per cent of all new dwellings in England were provided on previously developed land. In the same year, 47 per cent of land changing to residential use was previously developed, compared with 38 per cent in 1985. In 1996 the percentage of dwellings built on previously developed land varied from 82 per cent in London to 35 per cent in the South West.

The last 30 or so years of the 20th century witnessed a change in the number of bedrooms contained in houses constructed in England and Wales. In England 1 in 10 houses completed in 1971 had four or more bedrooms; by 2000–01 this had increased to almost 2 in 5 (Table 10.4). At the same time there was a reduction in the proportion of one bedroom houses that were completed. In Wales one in 20 houses or flats completed in 1971 had four or more bedrooms; by 2000 this had also increased to almost 2 in 5. This rise reflects householders' aspiration to purchase houses with an extra room(s), for purposes such as a

Chart **10.3**

Housebuilding completions[1]

United Kingdom

Thousands

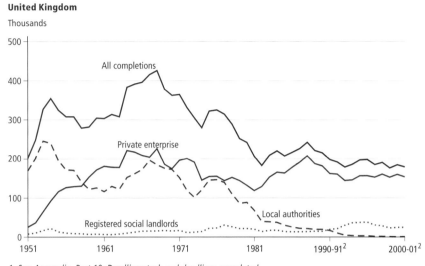

1 See Appendix, Part 10: Dwelling stock and dwellings completed.
2 From 1990–91 data are financial year.
Source: Department for Transport, Local Government and the Regions; National Assembly for Wales; Scottish Executive; Department for Social Development (Northern Ireland)

Table **10.4**

Housebuilding completions: by number of bedrooms

England   Percentages

	1971	1981	1990–91	1995–96	2000–01[1]
1 bedroom	3	5	6	2	1
2 bedrooms	17	22	28	29	19
3 bedrooms	70	53	39	41	40
4 or more bedrooms	10	20	28	28	40
All houses (=100%) (thousands)	213	119	115	127	135

1 Provisional figures.
Source: Department for Transport, Local Government and the Regions

Chart **10.5**

Stock of dwellings[1]: by tenure

United Kingdom

Millions

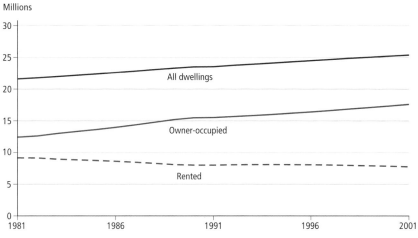

1 See Appendix, Part 10: Dwelling stock. Data are at 31 December from 1981–1990. Data for England and Wales are at 31 March from 1991–2001. Data for Scotland and Northern Ireland are at April based on Census outputs for 1991 and at 31 December of the previous year for 1992–2001.

Source: Department for Transport, Local Government and the Regions; National Assembly for Wales; Scottish Executive; Department for Social Development (Northern Ireland)

Chart **10.6**

Owner-occupied dwellings: EU comparison, 1996

Percentages

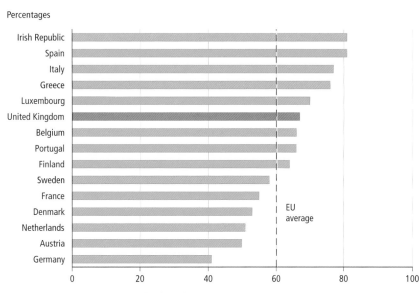

Source: European Community Household Panel, Eurostat

spare bedroom, a storage room or a home-office rather than an increase in family sizes. There is also an increased expectation that each child should have a separate bedroom. The private sector remained the main providers of larger dwellings throughout the period in England. In 1971, around four-fifths of new houses with four or more bedrooms were completed by the private sector and by 2000–01 this had increased to 98 per cent.

Types of tenure and accommodation

From 1951 there were changes in the tenure of dwelling stock in Great Britain. Private renting decreased from 52 per cent in 1951 to 20 per cent in 1971. The period also saw an increase in the number of dwellings rented from local authorities as a result of the major housebuilding programme they had undertaken between the wars and after the Second World War. Renting from local authorities increased from 19 per cent in 1951 to 30 per cent in 1971. Owner-occupation increased from 29 per cent in 1951 to 50 per cent in 1971 and has continued to rise since. In 2000–01, 70 per cent of households owned their homes, either with a mortgage or outright; 21 per cent rented from the social sector, and 9 per cent rented privately.

In the two decades between 1981 and 2001 the number of owner-occupied dwellings in the United Kingdom increased by more than 40 per cent, while the number of rented dwellings fell by around 15 per cent (Chart 10.5). By 2001 the number of owner-occupied dwellings was over 17 million, which was more than double the number of rented dwellings.

Owner occupation in the UK is just above the average for all EU countries (Chart 10.6). In the Irish Republic and Spain just over 8 in 10 households owned their homes in 1996, the highest of any EU country. Germany had the lowest where only one in four owned their own homes.

Table **10.7**

Age of household reference person[1]: by tenure, 2000–01

Great Britain   Percentages

	Under 25	25–34	35–44	45–54	55–64	65–74	75 and over	All ages
Owner-occupied								
Owned outright	1	2	7	19	47	66	59	29
Owned with mortgage	17	57	68	60	32	8	3	41
Rented from social sector								
Local authority	28	16	12	11	13	17	23	15
Housing association	10	6	5	5	4	6	9	6
Rented privately								
Furnished	23	7	2	1	1	1	1	3
Unfurnished[2]	21	12	6	6	4	3	5	6
All tenures	100	100	100	100	100	100	100	100

1 See Appendix, Part 10: Household reference person.
2 Privately unfurnished or not known whether furnished.
Source: General Household Survey, Office for National Statistics

Housing tenure varies with the age of the 'household reference person' (see Appendix, Part 10: Household reference person). Data from the General Household Survey in Great Britain showed that in 2000–01 over 40 per cent of households where the household reference person was under 25 were living in privately rented accommodation. This was more than twice the proportion for those aged 25 to 34 and far greater than for any other age group (Table 10.7). Private renters in furnished accommodation were particularly likely to be young: over the age of 24 there were very few renters of private rented, furnished property. Around a fifth of household reference persons aged under 25 owned their own property with a mortgage and very few, only 1 per cent, owned the property outright. With an increase in age, there was an increase in the proportion of households that owned their property outright. In 2000–01 over half of 25–34 year olds and over two-thirds of 35 to 44 year olds were buying their property with a mortgage. In the 45–54 age group 19 per cent owned their property outright while 60 per cent were buying with a mortgage. People aged 65 and over were most likely to own their property outright, many having repaid their mortgage in its entirety by the time they had retired.

Tenure also varies according to the type of household. In Great Britain in 2000–01, households consisting of lone parents with dependent children were much more likely to rent their property than to own it (Table 10.8).

Table **10.8**

Selected household types: by tenure, 2000–01

Great Britain   Percentages

	Owned outright	Owned with mortgage	Rented from social sector	Rented privately	All tenures[1]
One person					
Under pensionable age	15	43	23	18	100
Over pensionable age	53	5	35	6	100
Single family households[2]					
Couple					
No children	45	38	10	7	100
Dependent children[3]	7	72	15	6	100
Non-dependent children only	31	53	13	2	100
Lone parent					
Dependent children[3]	6	28	52	15	100
All households[4]	29	41	21	9	100

1 Includes other types of accommodation, such as mobile homes.
2 Other individuals who were not family members may also be included.
3 May also include non-dependent children.
4 Also includes 'two or more unrelated adults', 'lone parents with non-dependent children' and 'multi-family households'.
Source: General Household Survey, Office for National Statistics

Table **10.9**

Ethnic group of head of household: by tenure, 1998–01

England   Percentages

	Owned outright	Owned with mortgage	Rented from social sector	Rented privately[1]	All tenures (=100%) (millions)
White	28	43	20	10	19.2
Black Caribbean	12	34	47	6	0.3
Indian	24	57	9	11	0.3
Pakistani	22	48	16	14	0.2
Bangladeshi	4	30	54	11	0.1
Other or mixed	9	30	38	23	0.6
All heads of household	27	42	21	10	20.6

1 Includes rent-free accommodation

Source: Survey of English Housing, Department for Transport, Local Government and the Regions

Table **10.10**

Socio-economic group[1] of household reference person[2]: by type of accommodation, 2000–01

Great Britain   Percentages

	House or bungalow			Flat or maisonette		
	Detached	Semi-detached	Terraced	Purpose-built	Other	All dwellings[3]
Economically active						
Professional	37	27	21	9	7	100
Employers and managers	36	30	21	8	4	100
Intermediate non-manual	23	31	31	10	6	100
Junior non-manual	15	31	32	17	5	100
Skilled manual	19	38	32	9	4	100
Semi-skilled manual	10	37	35	14	4	100
Unskilled manual	7	41	35	12	4	100
All economically active	23	33	29	11	5	100
Economically inactive						
Retired	26	32	24	16	2	100
Other	10	29	33	23	5	100
All economically inactive	21	31	26	18	3	100
All socio-economic groups	22	32	28	13	4	100

1 Excludes members of the armed forces, economically active full-time students and those who were unemployed and had never worked.

2 See Appendix, Part 10: Household reference person.

3 Excludes those living in mobile homes.

Source: General Household Survey, Office for National Statistics

In contrast, 72 per cent of households containing a couple with dependent children were buying their home with a mortgage. Over half of one person households consisting of a person over pension age owned their home outright, compared with only 15 per cent of those under pension age.

Tenure patterns also vary markedly with the ethnic group of the household head. Data from the Survey of English Housing (SEH) for 1998–01 show that a high proportion of households headed by someone of Bangladeshi or Black Caribbean ethnic origin were living in the social rented sector (54 per cent and 47 per cent respectively). These figures compare with 20 per cent of households headed by a White person and just 9 per cent of households headed by someone of Indian descent (Table 10.9). On the other hand, 57 per cent of Indian heads of household and 48 per cent of Pakistanis were buying their home with a mortgage. White heads of household were still the most likely to own their home outright (28 per cent).

Traditionally, housing tenure in Great Britain has been closely related to social class and economic status, as has the type of accommodation people live in. Table 10.10 shows how the type of accommodation in which people live varies with socio-economic group. Among the economically active, more than a third of both professional households (37 per cent) and employer and manager households (36 per cent) lived in detached houses, compared with 7 per cent of unskilled manual households. The economically inactive under retirement age were twice as likely as the economically active to live in purpose-built flats or maisonettes.

To some extent these patterns reflect the availability of housing in the areas where previous generations from minority groups originally settled and also difficulties experienced in gaining access to council housing. However, choice of tenure is also driven by people's economic circumstances and by their own aspirations.

Overall, 82 per cent of households in Great Britain lived in a house or bungalow in 2000–01 (Table 10.11). The type of home in which people live is often a reflection of the size and type of their household as well as what they can afford. Of one person households, those over pension age were more likely to live in a detached house (19 per cent) than those under pension age (8 per cent).

There was a far higher percentage of one person households living in flats and maisonettes than family households. The majority of family households lived in detached or semi-detached houses. Forty one per cent of couples with non-dependent children lived in semi-detached housing compared to 3 per cent who lived in purpose built flats. However 18 per cent of lone parents with dependent children lived in purpose-built flats, the highest percentage of family households, and only 7 per cent lived in detached houses. Flats and maisonettes were much more common for lone parents with dependent children (21 per cent) than for couples with dependent children (6 per cent).

Homelessness

When a household makes a homelessness application the local housing authority must decide whether the applicant is eligible for assistance (certain persons from abroad are not), unintentionally homeless and in a priority need group. Where all these criteria are met, a main homelessness duty will be owed. In England and Wales, if other suitable accommodation is available in the district (for example, in the private rented sector) the authority must provide sufficient advice and assistance to enable the applicant to obtain this accommodation. Where such accommodation is not available, the authority must itself ensure that suitable accommodation is provided for up to two years. In either case the household is entitled to be placed on the housing register and given reasonable preference in the allocation of a long-term social tenancy. The duty, discharged by the provision of temporary accommodation, is likely to recur until a settled housing solution can be found; in most cases this is likely to be the allocation of a secure council tenancy or an assured tenancy with an RSL.

In 2000, local authorities in England made a total of 251.5 thousand decisions on applications for housing from households eligible under the homelessness provisions of the 1985 and 1996 Housing Acts. They accepted 111.5 thousand households as meeting the criteria for assistance. This represents 5.4 homeless acceptances for every 1,000 resident households (Table 10.12). London had the highest number of households in need with 28.6 thousand being accepted as homeless. This represented 9.2 homeless acceptances per 1,000 households, the highest rate in any region. The region with the smallest number of acceptances was the North East where 5.1 thousand were accepted as in priority need, a rate of 4.7 per 1,000 households. Three regions – East of England, East Midlands and Yorkshire and the Humber – shared the lowest rate of 4.2 per 1,000 households.

Table **10.11**

Selected household types: by type of dwelling, 2000–01

Great Britain   Percentages

	House or bungalow			Flat or maisonette		
	Detached	Semi-detached	Terraced	Purpose-built	Other	All dwellings[1]
One person						
Under pensionable age	8	22	30	27	13	100
Over pensionable age	19	26	25	26	4	100
Single family households[2]						
Couple						
No children	31	35	23	8	3	100
Dependent children[3]	28	38	28	5	1	100
Non-dependent						
children only	30	41	26	3	0	100
Lone parent						
Dependent children[3]	7	31	41	18	3	100
All households[4]	22	32	28	14	4	100

1 Includes other types of accommodation, such as mobile homes.
2 Other individuals who were not family members may also be included.
3 May also include non-dependent children.
4 Also includes 'two or more unrelated adults', 'lone parents with non-dependent children' and 'multi-family households'.
Source: General Household Survey, Office for National Statistics

Table **10.12**

Homeless households in priority need accepted by local authorities[1]: by region[2], 2000

	Total acceptances	Acceptances per 1,000 households
North East	5,130	4.7
North West	13,110	4.6
Yorkshire and the Humber	8,950	4.2
East Midlands	7,280	4.2
West Midlands	13,700	6.3
East	9,410	4.2
London	28,610	9.2
South East	14,310	4.3
South West	11,050	5.3
England	111,550	5.4

1 Figures include decisions taken under both the 1985 and 1996 Housing Acts.
2 Government Office Region.
Source: Department for Transport, Local Government and the Regions

Chart **10.13**

Households accepted as homeless[1] by local authorities[2]: by main reason for loss[3] of last settled home

England

Percentages

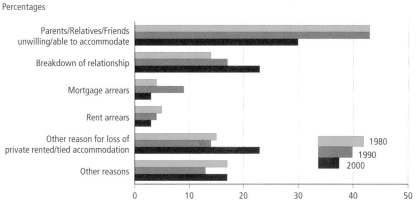

1 See Appendix, Part 10: Homeless households.

2 2000 totals represent unintentionally homeless households in priority need: earlier years also include those found intentionally homeless, and a small number of non-priority homeless.

3 Because of changes in 'reasons for loss' classifications, some categories presented in this table may not be fully consistent throughout the twenty year period.

Source: Department for Transport, Local Government and the Regions

Table **10.14**

Under-occupation[1] and overcrowding[2]: by selected types of household, 2000–01

Great Britain		Percentages
	Under-occupied	Overcrowded
One person		
Under pensionable age	34	0
Over pensionable age	40	0
Single family households[3]		
Couple		
No children	65	0
Dependent children[4]	17	4
Non-dependent children only	20	3
Lone parent		
Dependent children[4]	4	9
All households[5]	36	2

1 Two or more above bedroom standard. See Appendix, Part 10: Bedroom standard.

2 One or more below bedroom standard. See Appendix, Part 10: Bedroom standard.

3 Other individuals who were not family members may also be included.

4 May also include non-dependent children.

5 Also includes 'two or more unrelated adults', 'lone parents with non-dependent children' and 'multi-family households'.

Source: General Household Survey, Office for National Statistics

In 2000 111.6 thousand households in England were accepted as homeless by their local authority compared to 105.5 thousand in 1999. In Wales 3.7 thousand households were accepted as homeless in 1999–00, a reduction from 4.3 thousand households in 1998–99. In the same period in Northern Ireland there was a slight increase with 5.2 thousand households being accepted as homeless in 1999–00 compared to 5.0 thousand in 1998–99. Scotland had 16.8 thousand acceptances in 1998–99, an increase from 15.6 thousand in 1997–98.

Homelessness often results from changes in personal circumstances. In 2000, 30 per cent of all households accepted as homeless in England were in their situation because parents, other relatives or friends were no longer able or willing to accommodate them. Although this is lower than in 1990 and 1980 when over 40 per cent gave this as the reason for their situation, this continues to be the biggest single reason for households becoming homeless in England. In 2000, 23 per cent gave the breakdown of a relationship with a partner as their main reason for the loss of their last settled home, compared to 17 per cent in 1990 and 14 per cent in 1980 (Chart 10.13). Mortgage and rent arrears made small contributions to the number of homeless households in England, each accounting for 3 per cent of the total in 2000. Fewer people have been made homeless as a result of mortgage arrears since 1990. Research has shown that older homeless people also identified family crises, such as widowhood and marital breakdown, alongside eviction, redundancy and mental illness as reasons for homelessness.

Housing conditions and satisfaction with area

Over the years the provision of basic facilities available in our homes has gradually improved. In 1996 the English House Condition Survey (EHCS) identified dwellings in England which lacked the basic amenities of a kitchen sink, a bath or shower in a bathroom, a wash-hand basin, hot and cold water to each of these and an indoor toilet. The survey found that the number of dwellings lacking these basic amenities had dropped from 3 million in 1971 to 207 thousand in 1996, amounting to less than 1 per cent of the stock. Properties that lacked amenities were likely to be lived in by elderly people who had lived in the same home for many years and to be privately owned. Around half of the dwellings lacking amenities were vacant, either long-term or in the process of renovation. A proportion of the occupied stock may also lack an amenity purely on a temporary basis as repair work is carried out.

There has been a steady improvement over the last decade in the energy related aspects of housing (such as the provision of central heating and double glazing) and in other aspects of the comfort and security of occupants (such as modernisation of bathrooms and the installation of smoke alarms).

According to the Survey of English Housing 83 per cent of all households had central heating in all living rooms and bedrooms in 2000–01, compared with 73 per cent in 1994–95. In 2000–01 86 per cent of owner-occupiers had central heating, compared with 81 per cent of social sector tenants and 71 per cent of private tenants.

The concept of bedroom standard (see Appendix, Part 10: Bedroom standard) is used as an indicator of occupation density and hence of overcrowding and under-occupation. The standard compares the number of bedrooms a household needs in order to avoid undesirable sharing and the number of bedrooms it actually has. In 2000–01, 2 per cent of households in Great Britain were below the bedroom standard and hence defined as overcrowded (Table 10.14). Overcrowding was most common among lone parents with dependent children. Under-occupation was most common, by far, for couples with no children. This category includes many people whose children have grown up and left home.

In 2000–01, according to the SEH, under-occupation was commonest in the owner occupied sector, where 55 per cent of households that owned their property outright and 35 per cent of those buying with a mortgage were two or more bedrooms above the bedroom standard. Overcrowding was most common among those renting in the social sector were 6 per cent of households were below the bedroom standard. Of private renters 17 per cent of households were under-occupying and 4 per cent were overcrowded.

The SEH found that around 9 in 10 households were 'very satisfied' or 'fairly satisfied' with their accommodation and the area they lived in. Those living in 'affluent family', 'mature home-owning' and 'affluent suburban and rural areas' were more likely to be satisfied with both their accommodation and area than people who lived elsewhere. The lowest levels of satisfaction were found in 'council estates and low-income areas' although here too over 80 per cent were satisfied with their accommodation, and three-quarters with their area. Those living in 'new home-owning areas' were more satisfied with their accommodation than their area (Table 10.15). Generally, older heads of households expressed higher levels of satisfaction with their accommodation than younger heads of households. At all ages, owners were more likely to be satisfied with their accommodation.

Table **10.15**

Satisfaction[1] with accommodation and area: by type of area[2], 2000–01

England		Percentages
	Accommodation	Area
Affluent family areas	93	92
Mature home-owning areas	93	89
Affluent suburban and rural areas	95	94
New home-owning areas	90	83
Council estates and low income areas	84	74
Affluent urban areas	87	85
All types of areas	91	86

1 Heads of household or partners who replied that they were 'very satisfied' or 'fairly satisfied'.
2 Based on the ACORN classification. See Appendix, Part 10: Area type.
Source: Survey of English Housing, Department for Transport, Local Government and the Regions

Table **10.16**

Problems[1] with aspects of the area: by type of area[2], 1999–00

England							Percentages
	Affluent family areas	Mature home-owning areas	Affluent suburban rural areas	New home-owning areas	Council and low income areas	Affluent urban areas	All types of area
Crime	51	54	49	57	66	59	56
Litter and rubbish	31	41	26	47	58	49	42
Vandalism and hooliganism	32	38	25	44	58	42	40
Dogs	25	29	22	33	37	25	29
Noise	17	21	16	25	31	35	23
Graffiti	16	18	11	23	36	32	22
Neighbours	9	11	7	15	18	17	13
Racial harassment	2	3	1	4	8	9	4

1 Proportion of heads of household or partners who said the issue was 'a serious problem' or 'a problem, but not serious' in the local area.
2 Based on the ACORN classification. See Appendix, Part 10: Area type.
Source: Survey of English Housing, Department for Transport, Local Government and the Regions

Table **10.17**

Difficulty in accessing various amenities[1]: all households, 1997–98

England   Percentages

	Corner shop	Super-market	Post Office	Doctor	Hospital
One person					
Under pensionable age	3	6	6	8	22
Over pensionable age	13	17	12	18	35
Two or more unrelated adults	4	6	6	8	23
Single family households[2]					
Couple					
No children	4	4	4	6	20
Dependent children[3]	2	3	2	4	19
Non-dependent children only	3	3	2	4	18
Lone parent					
Dependent children[3]	4	8	4	8	32
Non-dependent children only	4	10	5	9	27
Multi-family households	2	3	2	5	15
All households	5	7	5	8	23

1 Heads of household or partners who replied that they found access to amenity either 'very difficult' or 'fairly difficult'.

2 Other individuals who were not family members may also be included.

3 May also include non-dependent children.

Source: Survey of English Housing, Department for Transport, Local Government and the Regions

Chart **10.18**

Tenure of new heads of household and all heads of households, 2000–01

England

Percentages

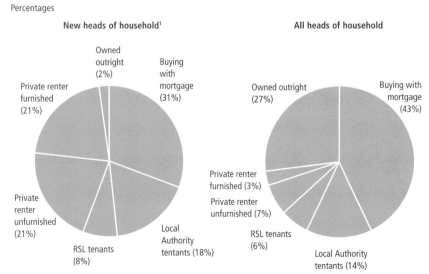

New heads of household[1]

Owned outright (2%)

Buying with mortgage (31%)

Private renter furnished (21%)

Private renter unfurnished (21%)

RSL tenants (8%)

Local Authority tentants (18%)

All heads of household

Owned outright (27%)

Buying with mortgage (43%)

Private renter furnished (3%)

Private renter unfurnished (7%)

RSL tenants (6%)

Local Authority tentants (14%)

1 Head of household who was not a head of household at their last previous permanent address.

Source: Survey of English Housing, Department for Transport, Local Government and the Regions

People were asked in the 1999–00 SEH whether various problems occurred in their area and, if so, whether or not they were serious (Table 10.16). Fifty six per cent of all householders said that crime was a problem. Two-thirds of households living in 'council estates and low income areas' reported this as a problem compared with just under half of those in 'affluent suburban and rural areas'. Litter and rubbish and vandalism and hooliganism were also common problems, particularly in 'council estates and low income areas' (reported by 58 per cent of the group). Racial harassment was mentioned by 4 per cent of households overall – similar to levels in 1997–98, but by 8 per cent in 'council estate and low income areas' and by 9 per cent in 'affluent urban areas'.

A key factor that contributes to satisfaction with an area is accessibility to amenities. In 1997–98 the SEH considered five everyday services which people require and asked whether they were easily accessible (Table 10.17). It is perhaps not surprising that it was mainly households over pension age who considered access to the various amenities to be either 'fairly difficult' or 'very difficult'. Of all the amenities, access to the local hospital was considered by all groups to be the most difficult, with around one third of those over pension age and of lone parents with dependent children reporting access fairly or very difficult. Seventeen per cent of one person households over pension age found access to the supermarket either fairly or very difficult, together with 8 per cent of lone parents with children. Where people live is one factor helping to determine how easily they can access amenities; what transport they use is another factor, examined in more detail in Table 12.13 in the Transport chapter.

Housing mobility

One aspect of housing mobility involves changes between tenures. In 2000–01 the Survey of English Housing estimated that 2.3 million households (11 per cent of all households) had moved into their present accommodation in the year prior to the interview. Around 18 per cent of these were new households which were headed by someone who was not previously a household head, such as an adult child who had been living with their parents. Chart 10.18 compares the tenure of new heads of households with all heads of households in 2000–01. It shows that the most common tenure for new heads of households was privately rented accommodation, with just over 40 per cent renting furnished or unfurnished accommodation. This compares to around 10 per cent of all heads of household. Thirty one per cent of new household heads were buying their home with a mortgage, compared with 43 per cent of all households, while not surprisingly far fewer new heads owned their own property outright (2 per cent, compared with 27 per cent of all households).

Another aspect of mobility – the length of time people remain living in the same home – is related to tenure. In 2000–01, 57 per cent of outright owner-occupiers in Great Britain had lived in their home for more than twenty years (Table 10.19). The second least mobile group was local authority tenants, where 25 per cent had been in their present accommodation for over twenty years. This compares with 13 per cent of housing association tenants: a difference which may reflect not only the types of household provided for but also the growth of the housing association sector in recent years. The most mobile group is those renting furnished accommodation, which are mainly young people. Around fifty per cent of 16–24 year olds had been at their current address for less than a year.

Information from the British Household Panel Survey suggests that the average length of time households remain in the same house is between five and ten years. Data for 1996–99 show that of those adults who move with the whole of their household, 10 per cent of those who move from owner-occupied accommodation go into the the private-rented sector (Table 10.20). There are various reasons for this such as elderly people moving into sheltered accommodation, moves resulting from evictions and repossessions and moves for employment reasons. When part of the household moves there is an even greater shift with 36 per cent of those moving from owner-occupation going into privately rented accommodation. This can be attributed to the characteristics of those moving, who are mainly children leaving home for the first time or separating couples, one of whom in many cases moves into rented accommodation. To a certain extent private renting is a transitory tenure status, so shifts from this tenure into owner-occupation are fairly common: about 40 per cent of private renters who moved with their whole household became owner-occupiers.

Mobility can also involve geographical relocation and distance moved in relocating varies with tenure. Of those who rented privately in England in 2000–01 and had moved in the previous year, over a third had moved more than 20 miles away from their previous home compared with just over a tenth of those who rented from the social sector (see Table 10.21 overleaf). One reason for this is that opportunities for social rented tenants to move to another local authority area can be fairly limited, whereas private tenants are free to move long distances, provided they can afford the rent in the new area. Of all moves two-thirds were under 10 miles from the previous home, and one in twenty were from abroad.

Table **10.19**

Tenure: by length of time at current address of household reference person[1], 2000–01

Great Britain   Percentages

	Under 1 year	1–4 years	5–9 years	10–19 years	20 years or more	All
Owner-occupied						
Owned outright	3	10	9	21	57	100
Owned with mortgage	8	30	22	28	12	100
Rented from social sector						
Local authority	10	28	17	20	25	100
Housing association	11	33	24	20	13	100
Rented privately						
Furnished	48	35	9	5	3	100
Unfurnished[2]	28	43	12	7	11	100
All tenures	9	25	17	22	27	100

1 See Appendix, Part 10: Household reference person.
2 Privately unfurnished or not known whether furnished.
Source: General Household Survey, Office for National Statistics

Table **10.20**

Adults moving house each year: by tenure before and after move, 1996–99[1]

Great Britain   Percentages

	Tenure after move			
	Owner-occupied	Rented from social sector	Rented privately	All movers
Tenure before move				
Whole household moves				
Owner-occupied	86	4	10	100
Rented from social sector	23	63	14	100
Rented privately	39	13	48	100
Part of household moves				
Owner-occupied	51	13	36	100
Rented from social sector	33	43	24	100
Rented privately	40	9	51	100

1 Changes in tenure for the periods 1996 to 1997, 1997 to 1998 and 1998 to 1999 have been analysed separately and then combined in this table.
Source: British Household Panel Survey, ESRC UK Longitudinal Study Centre

Table **10.21**

Tenure: by distance moved[1], 2000–01

England   Percentages

	Owner-occupied	Rented from social sector	Rented privately	All movers
Under 1 mile	19	35	16	21
1 but not 10 miles	52	52	36	46
10 but not 20 miles	9	5	7	8
20 but not 50 miles	7	2	7	6
50 miles or more	11	5	23	14
Abroad	2	2	10	5
All moves	100	100	100	100

1 Distance of head of household's present home from previous home.
Source: Survey of English Housing, Department for Transport, Local Government and the Regions

In 2000–01, over a fifth of owners buying with a mortgage who had moved in the previous year reported wanting a larger or better house or flat as the main reason for doing so. More than a fifth of those that owned outright reported that the main reason for moving had been the desire for a smaller or cheaper house or flat (Table 10.22). One-quarter of those who rented privately reported job-related reasons as being the main reason for moving. The consequences of marriage or cohabitation and divorce or separation accounted for 17 per cent of all moves during the previous 12 months. Nine per cent of those surveyed said that wanting their own home or independence was their main reason for moving – many of these people were young people who no longer lived with their parents. Reasons for moving also vary with household type. In 2000–01 about one in seven recently moving couples with dependent children reported job related reasons, as the main reason. This compares with only one in twenty lone parents with dependent children.

Table **10.22**

Main reasons for moving[1]: by post-move tenure, 2000–01

England   Percentages

	Owned outright	Owned with mortgage	Rented from council	Rented from housing association	Rented privately	All tenures
Different size accommodation:						
Wanted larger or better house or flat	7	23	16	15	9	16
Wanted smaller or cheaper house or flat	23	3	5	5	3	5
Personal reasons:						
Divorce or separation	5	9	9	12	9	9
Marriage or cohabitation	7	12	6	6	6	8
Other personal reasons	22	5	15	15	8	9
To move to a better area	10	9	13	9	7	9
Job related reasons	7	9	2	3	25	13
Accommodation no longer available	0	1	5	6	8	4
Wanted to buy	3	16	0	0	0	6
Couldn't afford mortgage or rent	1	0	2	2	2	1
To live independently	4	9	12	12	7	9
Other reasons	13	5	15	16	16	11
All households (=100%) (millions)	0.2	0.8	0.3	0.2	0.8	2.3

1 Current tenure of all household heads who moved in the year before interview.
Source: Survey of English Housing, Department for Transport, Local Government and the Regions

The 'right-to-buy' (RTB) scheme involves a change of tenure without moving home. Normally, secure tenants with at least two years public sector tenancy are entitled to buy their own house or flat at a discount under RTB. This scheme was introduced in Scotland in 1979 and across the rest of Great Britain in 1980. The Northern Ireland Housing Executive operates a voluntary house sales scheme which is comparable to the right to buy schemes in Great Britain. Another type of scheme which aims to increase low-cost home-ownership across the United Kingdom is shared ownership, in which home-owners buy a share of their property from a registered social landlord and pay rent for the remainder. In Northern Ireland the shared ownership scheme is operated by the Northern Ireland Co-ownership Housing Association. Other schemes include discounted sales of empty properties by local authorities, and interest-free equity loans and cash grants to tenants to help them move out and buy a property on the open market. (This scheme is not available in Northern Ireland.) Sales of properties under the right to buy scheme in Great Britain peaked at around 200 thousand in 1982 (Chart 10.23). The following four years saw a decline in the number of sales, but then more buoyant conditions in the housing market and changes in legislation enabled more tenants to buy.

Chart **10.23**

Sales and transfers of local authority dwellings[1]

Great Britain

Thousands

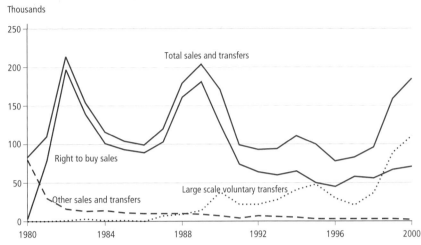

1 Excludes new town and Scottish Homes sales and transfers. See also Appendix, Part 10: Sales and transfers of local authority dwellings.

Source: Department for Transport, Local Government and the Regions; National Assembly for Wales; Scottish Executive

Table **10.24**

Average dwelling prices[1]: by region and type of accommodation, 2000[2]

£

| | House or bungalow | | | Flats/ maisonette | All dwellings | Percentage increase 1999–00 |
	Detached	Semi-detached	Terraced			
England & Wales	167,027	91,826	81,148	113,069	110,221	12.0
North East	111,374	57,417	43,255	47,401	62,945	2.8
North West	130,791	66,623	42,232	67,414	70,837	4.0
Yorkshire and the Humber	114,648	60,984	44,510	67,242	70,007	7.0
East Midlands	118,923	61,879	49,729	53,464	78,780	8.4
West Midlands	150,514	73,653	58,313	60,453	87,719	10.2
East	177,897	102,839	84,540	70,990	114,392	15.2
London	446,615	212,068	194,967	171,771	177,949	12.5
South East	250,531	132,132	104,242	87,581	147,271	18.7
South West	168,963	96,218	80,035	75,163	110,132	15.9
England	171,103	113,908	93,465	83,241	112,388	12.5
Wales	102,985	53,339	60,025	46,353	67,598	4.1

1 Excludes those bought at non-market prices. Averages are taken from the last quarter of the year.

2 There is a time lag between the completion of a house purchase and its subsequent lodgement with the Land Registry. Thus data for the final quarter 2000 are not as complete as those for the final quarter of 1999. The table includes all sales registered up to 31 March 2001.

Source: HM Land Registry

Chart **10.25**

New mortgages: average mortgage repayment[1] as a percentage of average household income

United Kingdom

Percentages

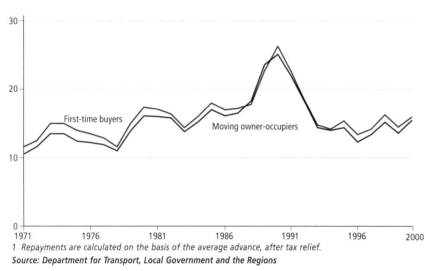

1 Repayments are calculated on the basis of the average advance, after tax relief.

Source: Department for Transport, Local Government and the Regions

Chart **10.26**

Type of mortgage for house purchase[1]

United Kingdom

Percentages

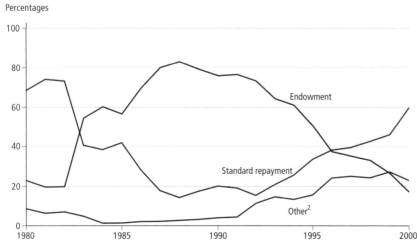

1 Data prior to 1992 are for new mortgages advanced by building societies and Abbey National plc; since 1992 new mortgages advanced by other major lenders have been included. Includes sitting tenants.

2 Includes interest only, PEP/ISA and pension.

Source: Department for Transport, Local Government and the Regions

The number of sales rose again and reached another peak in 1989 at over 180 thousand. In 2000 there were over 70 thousand sales of right to buy properties.

Housing costs and expenditure

In 2000 the average dwelling price in England and Wales was £110,200, although there were marked regional variations in house prices overall and for the type of accommodation that was purchased. House prices in London and the South East are well above the rest of the country. Data from HM Land Registry for England and Wales showed that the amount buyers in London pay for a detached house was over four times the amount paid by buyers in Wales: £447,000 and £103,000 respectively (Table 10.24). A terraced house in the North West of England costs on average £42,000 compared with £195,000 in London. Between 1999 and 2000 house prices in England and Wales increased by 12 per cent overall: ranging from 3 per cent in the North East to almost 19 per cent in the South East.

Taking out a mortgage on a property constitutes a significant proportion of a new home-owner's household budget. In the early 1970s those taking out a new mortgage spent, on average, around 10 per cent of their household income on mortgage repayments and by 1990 this proportion had reached more than 25 per cent (Chart 10.25). The four years of housing recession from 1990 to 1993 saw interest rates falling and real earnings rising such that by 1993, when house prices began to stabilise, mortgage repayments were accounting for about 14 per cent of household incomes for new homebuyers. This proportion has remained fairly stable over the period 1993 to 2000, when homebuyers with a new mortgage were spending around 15 per cent of their income on mortgage repayments.

A feature of home-ownership in the United Kingdom is the relatively high proportion of homes purchased with a mortgage. Approximately three-quarters of all homes are purchased with a mortgage loan facility. In 2000 loans for home purchase were obtained through banks (70 per cent) and building societies (21 per cent), with 9 per cent of loans obtained from other lenders. Lenders differ in the amount that they are willing to lend relative to annual income. In 2000 the ratio of the average advance to income for all borrowers was 2.26; 2.30 for first-time buyers and 2.23 for former owner-occupiers moving to another home. Those who are buying a house can choose from a variety of different types of mortgage; the most common being repayment, endowment and interest-only. In the early 1980s repayment mortgages, which provide for regular monthly payments so that over the life of the mortgage (usually 25 years) the debt and the interest are entirely repaid, accounted for almost three-quarters of all new mortgages (Chart 10.26).

Around 60 per cent of all new mortgages were standard repayment mortgages in 2000. Endowment policies involve paying interest on the loan while contributions are made to an insurance policy designed to repay the outstanding amount at the end of the mortgage term. The popularity of endowment mortgages peaked in 1988 when 83 per cent of new mortgages for house purchase in the United Kingdom were of this type, but by 2000 this had fallen to 17 per cent. These types of policies have become increasingly less popular with borrowers because of the possibility that investments may not grow fast enough to repay the capital borrowed. Interest-only mortgages, which include ISAs (individual savings accounts) and personal pensions, account for the bulk of the other mortgages in Chart 10.26.

In 1999–00 average weekly rents in England varied between the private sector (£90), local authorities (£44) and registered social landlords (£53). London was the most expensive region for private renting with an average weekly rent of £141 compared with £56 in the North East.

The recession in the economy and the slump in the housing market at the end of the 1980s caused widespread falls in house prices in cash terms. The possibility of the property realising 'negative equity' was of concern to many and the number of home-owners losing their homes through mortgage default rose to unprecedented levels. The number of warrants issued for repossession of properties peaked at 134 thousand in 1991; it then fluctuated but overall declined to 111 thousand in 1996 (Chart 10.27). By 1999, the number of warrants issued had reached a new high of 137 thousand but by 2000 had reduced slightly to 134 thousand. Although the number of warrants executed remained fairly steady at around 50 thousand between 1993 and 1997, it rose to 69 thousand in 1999. However the number of warrants executed dropped to 62 thousand in 2000.

Evictions and repossessions may in many cases be the result of a lengthy spell of financial difficulties, as many households will accumulate arrears prior to being evicted. Households with certain characteristics are more likely to experience financial problems with their housing. For example, households with younger heads are at greater risk of having mortgage arrears. Older people will in general have had more time to accumulate savings to cushion against times of unexpected financial hardship.

Chart **10.27**

Repossession of properties[1]: warrants issued and executed

England and Wales

1 Rented and mortgaged.

Source: Court Service

Websites

National Statistics	www.statistics.gov.uk
Department for Transport, Local Government and the Regions	www.dtlr.gov.uk
Court Service	www.courtservice.gov.uk
Department for Social Development, Northern Ireland	www.dsdni.gov.uk
Department for Work and Pensions	www.dwp.gov.uk
National Assembly for Wales	www.wales.gov.uk
Northern Ireland Statistics Research Agency	www.nisra.gov.uk
Scottish Executive	www.scotland.gov.uk
Social Exclusion Unit	www.cabinet-office.gov.uk/seu
Council of Mortgage Lenders	www.cml.org.uk
Eurostat	www.europa.eu.int/comm/eurostat
Institute for Social and Economic Research	www.iser.essex.ac.uk
Land Registry	www.landreg.gov.uk

Contacts

Office for National Statistics	
Chapter Author	020 7533 5807
Family Expenditure Survey	020 7533 5754
General Household Survey	020 7533 5444
Department for Transport, Local Government and the Regions	020 7944 3303
Planning and Land Use Statistics	020 7944 5533
Court Service	020 7210 1773
Department for Social Development, Northern Ireland	028 9052 2762
Department for Work and Pensions	
Family Resources Survey	020 7962 8092
National Assembly of Wales	029 2082 5063
Northern Ireland Statistics and Research Agency	028 9034 8243
Scottish Executive	0131 244 7232
Council of Mortgage Lenders	020 7440 2251
Eurostat	00352 4301 35370
Institute of Social and Economic Research	01206 872957
Land Registry	0151 473 6008

Chapter 11

Environment

Environmental concern and behaviour

- Two-thirds of people in England and Wales said they were 'very worried' about disposal of hazardous waste in 2001, the most frequently mentioned environmental concern. (Table 11.1)

- Over half of people in England regularly take waste paper to a paper bank or separate it for collection. (Table 11.2)

Air and atmospheric pollution

- Road transport accounted for 69 per cent of all carbon monoxide emissions in the UK in 1999, whereas electricity production was responsible for 65 per cent of sulphur dioxide emitted. (Table 11.3)

Pressures on land and wildlife

- Around three-quarters of all land in the UK was used for agricultural purposes in 1999. (Table 11.7)

- Eighty one per cent of domestic waste in England and Wales was disposed by landfill in 1999–00, a lower proportion than in 1997–98, when 85 per cent of domestic waste was disposed of in this way. (Page 186)

Natural resources

- North Sea stocks of haddock, plaice and whiting have all declined since the mid 1980s, although stocks of Atlantic mackerel have increased by over 50 per cent since 1984. (Chart 11.16)

Energy consumption

- UK production of natural gas rose by 140 per cent from 1990 to 2000, whilst production of petroleum increased by 38 per cent over the same period. (Chart 11.19)

- The UK produces 2 per cent of its electricity from hydro and wind power, compared to an EU average of 14 per cent. (Table 11.20)

Table **11.1**

Environmental concerns[1]

England and Wales   Percentages

	1986	1989	1993	1996/7	2001[2]
Disposal of hazardous waste[3]	..	..	63	60	66
Effects of livestock methods (inc. BSE)[4]	..	..	..	33	59
Pollution in rivers and seas[5]	54	64	63	65	55
Pollution in bathing waters and on beaches[6]	37	59	56	61	52
Traffic exhaust fumes and urban smog	23	33	40	48	52
Loss of plants and animals in the UK	38	45	43	45	50
Ozone layer depletion	..	56	41	46	49
Tropical forest destruction	..	44	45	44	48
Climate change/global warming	..	44	35	35	46
Loss of trees and hedgerows	17	34	36	40	46
Losing Green Belt land	26	27	35	38	44
Fumes and smoke from factories	26	34	35	41	43
Traffic congestion	..	..	35	42	43
Use of pesticides, fertilisers and chemical sprays	39	46	36	46	43
Using up the UK's natural resources	..	..	27	23	38
Acid rain	35	40	31	31	34
Household waste disposal	..	..	22	22	33
Decay of inner cities	27	22	26	23	31
Growing genetically modified crops	..	..	..	..	29
Noise	10	13	16	15	22

1 Respondents who replied personally very worried about each issue.

2 England only.

3 Toxic Waste: disposal and import 1993 and 1996/97.

4 1996/97 did not specify BSE.

5 Rivers only 2001.

6 In 1986, 1989 and 1996/7 the wording of this category was sewage on beaches/bathing water.

Source: Department for Environment, Food and Rural Affairs

Human activities affect the physical environment and natural resources at both the local and global level. The move from agricultural communities into industrial towns and now urban conglomerates has lead to huge pressures being put on the land, wildlife, atmosphere and waters. Attempts to reduce these pressures are reflected in the UK-wide strategy for sustainable development. The overall aim of the strategy is to ensure a better quality of life for all now and in the future. To do this four objectives need to be met: social progress which recognises the needs of everyone, maintenance of high and stable levels of economic growth and employment, prudent use of natural resources and effective protection of the environment. To protect the environment and reduce the impact that human activity has upon it, the UK government has developed environment-related policies and regulations.

Environmental concern and behaviour

The fifth Survey of Public Attitudes to the Environment in England, carried out in 2001, found that concerns about the environment have increased across all types of issues in the last 15 years (Table 11.1). People were in general most worried about pollution issues (e.g. hazardous waste, pollution in rivers and bathing waters) and least worried about local environmental issues, although the percentage of individuals who were worried about noise levels doubled between 1986 and 2001. More recently, concerns over the effects of livestock management methods have increased significantly, with the percentage of those worried about the subject rising from 33 per cent in 1996/97 to 59 per cent in 2001. The survey also found that traffic (congestion, noise, and fumes), climate change (and its effects) and air pollution were the three top issues that people thought would cause the most concern in 20 years time.

Concerns about the environment might lead to the adoption of activities that may have a positive environmental impact. Domestic actions that individuals in England take toward the solution of environmental problems are: recycling (e.g. take paper to a paper bank), resource use (e.g. cut down on use of water), car use (e.g. use public transport instead of a car) and other activities (e.g. making sure that your noise does not disturb others). Gender seems to play little part in the degree of participation in domestic activities which have a positive environmental impact (Table 11.2). However, variations do exist between different age groups. The percentage of younger people (18–24 years old) who undertake environmentally friendly activities is in general lower than the percentage of all other age groups. Despite this, the British Social Attitudes Survey (BSA) 2000 found that those aged 18–24 are more likely to sign a petition about an environmental issue than those aged over 65.

The solution of environmental problems depends not only on individuals' activities but also on the activities of business and governments. The BSA found, in 2000, that when told that "some countries in the world are doing more to protect the world environment than other countries are", half of those living in Great Britain believed that Britain was not doing enough.

Air and atmospheric pollution

The impact of air and atmospheric pollution on people and ecosystems is a global environmental concern.

In the UK, the main air pollutants are sulphur dioxide, nitrogen oxide, carbon monoxide, particles (especially those whose diameter is smaller than 10 μm – indicated by PM_{10}) and ground-level ozone. At ground level, ozone occurs naturally, but levels can be increased as the result of the presence of other pollutants. In the summer months, the bright, warm, still weather can lead to ozone concentrations rising substantially above background levels. Ozone production is affected by the weather since either ozone itself or the pollutants that cause it might be blown to the UK from mainland Europe. Ozone is the main cause of air pollution in rural areas. Concentrations recorded at urban sites are generally lower than those reported in rural areas because of the high concentration of nitrogen oxides found there - these react negatively with, and reduce, ozone levels.

Table **11.2**

Domestic actions[1] taken 'on a regular basis' which may have a positive environmental impact: by age and gender, 2001

England   Percentages[1]

	18–24	25–44	45–64	65 and over	Male	Female	All
Recycling							
Taken paper to a paper-bank or separated paper[2]	29	45	59	70	52	54	53
Taken glass to a bottle bank or separated glass[2]	20	37	49	55	43	42	42
Taken cans to a can-bank or separated cans[2]	15	26	34	40	31	29	30
Taken plastic to a recycling facility or separated plastic[2]	13	20	26	28	23	22	23
Made compost out of kitchen waste	8	14	26	30	22	18	20
Resource use							
Cut down the amount of electricity/ gas your household uses	35	39	43	39	40	40	40
Cut down on use of water	21	26	32	36	28	31	29
Car use							
Deliberately used public transport, walked or cycled instead of a car	47	42	42	41	40	45	42
Cut down the use of a car for short journeys (eg school, work etc)	36	39	38	41	39	38	39
Other							
Made sure that your noise did not disturb others	59	75	85	86	76	82	79
Done things to encourage wildlife in garden	31	45	67	71	56	55	56

1 Based on respondents to which the action was applicable.
2 From rubbish so that it could be collected for recycling.
Source: Department for Environment, Food and Rural Affairs

Table **11.3**

Air pollutants: by source, 1999

United Kingdom   Percentages

	Carbon monoxide	Sulphur dioxide	Nitrogen oxides	Volatile organic compounds	PM$_{10}$
Road transport	69	1	44	27	20
Electricity supply	1	65	21	0	10
Domestic	5	4	4	2	20
Other	24	29	30	70	50
All sources (=100%)					
(million tonnes)	4.8	1.2	1.6	1.7	0.2

Source: National Environmental Technology Centre

Chart **11.4**

Emissions of selected air pollutants: by year

United Kingdom

Million tonnes

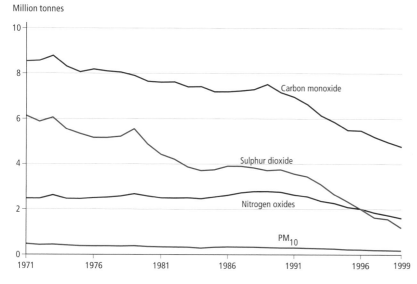

Source: National Environmental Technology Centre

The main sources of air pollution are road transport, the production of electricity and domestic users (Table 11.3). Electricity production accounted for 65 per cent of all sulphur dioxides released into the atmosphere in 1999. In contrast, road transport accounted for 69 per cent of carbon monoxide, 44 per cent of nitrogen oxides and 20 per cent of PM$_{10}$ releases. In urban areas, vehicle emissions constituted the greatest cause of human exposure to nitrogen oxides and carbon monoxide.

The introduction of cleaner fuels and catalytic converters led to reductions in total road traffic emissions for some pollutants (such as particles, nitrogen oxides and volatile organic compounds) between 1989 and 1999, despite a growth of over 15 per cent in road traffic over the same period. However, in the future (beyond 2015), increases in traffic volumes could result in a reversal of these trends unless further technological advances are made.

Air quality has improved over the past 20 years. Between 1971 and 1999 sulphur dioxide emissions, PM$_{10}$ and carbon monoxide emissions fell and emissions of nitrogen oxides were also falling by the 1990s (Chart 11.4). These reductions resulted from the decrease in sulphur dioxide and nitrogen oxide emissions from large combustion plants, the decline of heavy industries, the replacement of coal by natural gas in power stations and houses as well as technological improvements to motor vehicles.

The Air Quality Strategy, which was published in January 2000, sets out air quality objectives, which are to be achieved by 2005, for the following pollutants: sulphur dioxide, PM$_{10}$, carbon monoxide, ozone and nitrogen oxides, lead, benzene and 1,3-butadiene.

There has been some reduction in emissions from energy use in the domestic sector, primarily because of a switch from coal to gas both in homes for heating and by power stations for electricity production. Further scope for reducing emissions from domestic premises in the future is limited as about three-quarters of households in Great Britain are now using gas for heating. People heat their homes to a higher temperature and use more appliances now than in the past, which increases energy use and therefore emission levels, although these factors have been counterbalanced by improved thermal efficiency of housing and improved energy efficiency of individual appliances.

Air emissions in the UK affect not only the quality of local and regional air but also the air quality of other European countries as pollutants are carried from one country to another. Members of the United Nations Economic Council for Europe (UNECE) have been working together since 1979 to set targets for reducing emissions of long range trans-boundary air pollution. The most recent outcome was the 1999 UNECE Gothenburg Protocol, which was designed to address acidification, eutrophication and ground level ozone. Emission ceiling levels have been agreed for 2010 for sulphur dioxide, nitrogen oxides, volatile organic compounds and ammonia.

Climate change is recognised as one of the greatest threats to our environment. Temperatures rose globally and in central England during the 20th century (Chart 11.5). Over this century, increased temperatures are predicted to cause major adverse effects on the world's ecosystems. These effects include increased incidence of extreme weather events and higher sea levels. Large reductions in the emissions of greenhouse gases (i.e. carbon dioxide, methane, nitrous oxide, hydrofluorocarbons, and perfluorocarbons and sulphur hexafluoride) will be necessary to stabilise atmospheric concentrations of these gases.

Under the internationally agreed Kyoto Protocol, EU countries as a unit are committed to reducing emissions of six greenhouse gases by 8 per cent below the 1990 level over the period 2008 to 2012. The United Kingdom has a legally binding target to reduce emissions by 12.5 per cent relative to the 1990 level over that period. Thirty parties of the United Nations Framework Convention on Climate Change (UNFCCC) have ratified the Kyoto Protocol: it will come into force when it has been ratified by at least 50 parties of the UNFCC.

In the period 1990 to 1998, the United Kingdom was one of the three EU countries that succeeded in reducing greenhouse gases emissions (Table 11.6). In 1998, the United Kingdom emitted nine tonnes per capita of carbon dioxide which is the main gas that contributes to climate change. In the EU, the United Kingdom was ninth highest emission of carbon dioxide per capita out of fifteen countries. The United Kingdom aims to move beyond its Kyoto target towards a goal of reducing carbon dioxide emissions by 20 per cent below 1990 levels by 2010. The UK Climate Change Programme, published in 2000, sets out a package of policies to meet its Kyoto target and move towards its domestic goal. For example, although there has been limited success in reducing carbon dioxide emissions from road traffic, major car manufacturers have agreed to reduce emissions from new cars by a quarter by 2008.

Chart **11.5**

Difference in average surface temperature: comparison with 1961-1990 average

Global and Central England

Source: Hadley Centre for Climate Prediction and Research

Table **11.6**

Greenhouse gas emissions: by EU country, 1998[1]

Tonnes per capita

	Carbon dioxide emissions	Total greenhouse gas emissions	Percentage change 1990–1998[2]
Austria	8	10	6
Belgium	12	14	7
Denmark	11	14	9
Finland	12	15	6
France	7	9	1
Germany	11	12	−16
Greece	10	11	15
Ireland	11	17	20
Italy	8	9	5
Luxembourg	12	14	−58
Netherlands	12	15	8
Portugal	5	7	18
Spain	7	9	21
Sweden	6	8	1
United Kingdom	9	11	−9

1 See Appendix Part 11: Greenhouse gas emissions.
2 Change in total greenhouse gas emissions.
Source: United Nations Framework Convention on Climate Change; European Environment Agency

Table **11.7**

Land use[1], 1999

Percentages and thousand hectares

	England	Wales	Scotland	Northern Ireland	United Kingdom
Agricultural					
Crops and fallow	31	3	8	4	20
Grass and rough grazing	36	76	67	76	52
Other	5	1	2	1	4
Forest and woodland	8	12	16	6	10
Urban land and land not elsewhere specified	19	8	11	13	15
All land (=100%)(thousand hectares)[2,3]	12,972	2,064	7,710	1,348	24,093
Inland water (thousand hectares)[2]	76	13	169	67	325

1 See Appendix, Part 11: Land use.
2 At 31st March 1981.
3 Because data come from a number of sources the components do not always add to total.
Source: Department for Environment, Food and Rural Affairs; Ordnance Survey; Forestry Commission; Department of Agriculture for Northern Ireland

Chart **11.8**

Land under organic crop production

United Kingdom

Thousand hectares

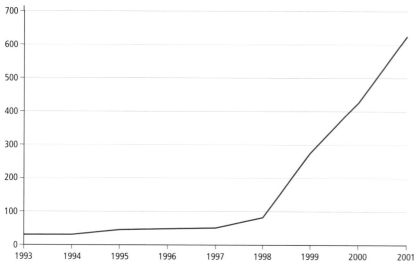

Source: Department for Environment, Food and Rural Affairs

Pressures on land and wildlife

Land use activities – agriculture, industry, housing and tourism – put great pressures on the quality of the soil and landscape features and need to be managed properly in order to retain a diverse environment. Seventy six per cent of all land in the UK was used for agricultural purposes in 1999 (Table 11.7) and agriculture remains an important industry. Although the number of farms has decreased, farms are now larger and agriculture output has risen as a result of increased field sizes and intensive fertiliser usage. The percentage of land used for different purposes has varied little in recent years, although within categories there has been some change. For example, the area under crops fell by over 10 per cent between 1990 and 1995, mainly as a result of Set Aside Schemes run by the (then) European Community, and was still over 6 per cent lower in 1999. It is estimated that around 169,000 hectares or 1.3 per cent of England's area will change from rural uses to urban uses between 1991 and 2016.

In the past 10 years, there has been growing concern about the use of pesticides, the development of genetically modified (GM) crops and the possible impact these may have on people's health. Since 1998, the amount of land used for organic farming has increased seven-fold (Chart 11.8), and there were nearly 4,000 organic holdings in the UK by June 2001. The growth in organic farming reflects not only anxieties about food safety, but also broader environmental concerns (including animal welfare), and increasing interest in health and fitness issues.

A significant outbreak of foot and mouth disease occurred in the UK in 2001. By 11 October 2001, 2,030 cases were identified and 3,902,000 animals were slaughtered. Movement restrictions led to the cancellation of several major sporting events and had a severe impact on the tourist industry.

As described above, atmospheric pollution impacts on air quality in a number of ways. Certain emissions such as sulphur and nitrogen also have an impact on the quality of our soils, vegetation, buildings and waters, in the form of acid deposition. Map 11.9 shows the areas where the acidity levels of the soil and vegetation exceeded acceptable levels during 1995–1997. Wales, Scotland and the North East of England were most affected by excess acid deposition over this period.

A consequence of larger farms and urbanisation has been a decline in traditional linear features such as walls and hedges (Table 11.10). The 1990 Countryside Survey (CS) revealed a net loss of field boundaries such as hedges between 1984 and 1990 as a result of agricultural and other types of development. However, the results of the 2000 Countryside Survey showed no further decline over the 1990s. Hedges, walls, fences and other boundary features are integral parts of the British landscape. They provide important habitats for many animal and plant species and act as important barriers against soil erosion and loss. Further, they act as corridors for dispersal for some species and help maintain bio-diversity.

Map **11.9**

Exceedance for critical load of acidity of soils, 1995–1997[1]

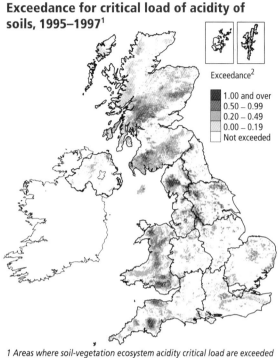

Exceedance[2]

- 1.00 and over
- 0.50 – 0.99
- 0.20 – 0.49
- 0.00 – 0.19
- Not exceeded

1 Areas where soil-vegetation ecosystem acidity critical load are exceeded by net oxidised nitrogen and non-marine sulphur deposition.
2 Exceedance (K_{eq} H$^+$ ha^{-1}year^{-1}). See Appendix: Part 11 Critical load of acidity of soils.
Source: Centre for Hydrology and Ecology; National Environmental Technology Centre

Table **11.10**

Landscape features[1], 1984, 1990 and 1998

England and Wales			Thousand kilometres
	1984	1990	1998
Hedge	577	467	449
Remnant hedge	50	59	52
Wall	220	109	106
Bank/grass strip	50	71	70
Fence	400	300	423

1 See Appendix Part 11: Landscape features.
Source: Countryside Survey 2000; Department for Environment, Food and Rural Affairs

Chart **11.11**

Population of wild birds

United Kingdom
Indices (1970 = 100)

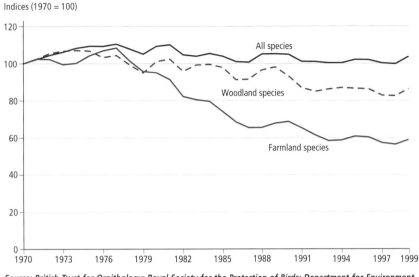

Source: British Trust for Ornithology; Royal Society for the Protection of Birds; Department for Environment, Food and Rural Affairs

Chart **11.12**

New woodland creation: by year

Great Britain
Thousand hectares

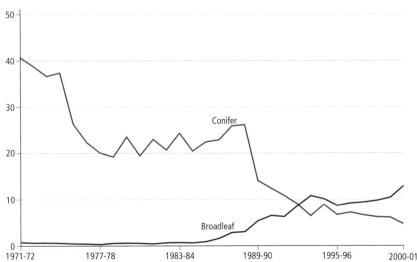

Source: Forestry Commission

The decline in woodland and farmland bird populations seen since the late 1970s is a consequence of the impact of the loss of habitats such as hedges and changes in farming methods (Chart 11.11). Wild bird populations, however, increased in 1999, mainly as a result of the mild winter of 1998–99. In contrast to more common farmland and woodland species, rare bird populations have been stable or started to increase. This is mainly a result of conservation efforts which been have focused on these species.

Forests are important features of the landscape. They serve as habitats for wildlife, are used for recreation and provide timber for wood processing industries. The area covered by forest and woodland in the UK more than doubled over the 20th century. Since the 1980s, forestry policy has encouraged sustainable forest management and more planting of native trees and there has been an increase in the number of broadleaved trees planted, with the result that, since 1993–94, more broadleaved trees have been planted each year than conifer (Chart 11.12).

The disposal of waste also puts great pressures on land, as landfill is the most common form of waste disposal. As more and more waste is produced, the more landfill sites are required raising concerns about the impact on the surrounding soil and waters. At present, the amount of municipal (mostly household) waste going to landfill is still increasing. However, compared with other methods of waste disposal, the proportion of municipal waste going to landfill fell slightly in the late 1990s from 85 per cent in 1997–98 to 81 per cent in 1999–00.

Recycling is a cleaner alternative for the disposal of some waste. One-tenth of all household waste was recycled or composted in 1999–00 in England and Wales. Over half of all waste paper was recycled in 1998 compared with around a quarter in 1990 (Chart 11.13). The proportion of aluminium cans and container glass recycled also increased substantially, to 36 per cent and 22 per cent respectively, over the same period. In 1999–2000, 10 per cent of household waste in England and Wales was recycled. For households, taking paper to a paper bank or separating it for collection is the most common recycling activity (see Table 11.2). Around 43 per cent of households in England and Wales are now served by some form of kerbside recycling scheme.

Water quality

Water is used in a variety of ways and the quality and quantity of our water supplies is paramount to the health and wellbeing of society and the natural environment. Fertiliser run-off, industrial waste and household sewage can each have an impact upon the quality of the water in rivers. While there are regional variations, in the last decade general chemical and biological water quality has improved considerably in the UK (Table 11.14).

Chart **11.13**

Recycling levels: by type of material

United Kingdom

Percentages

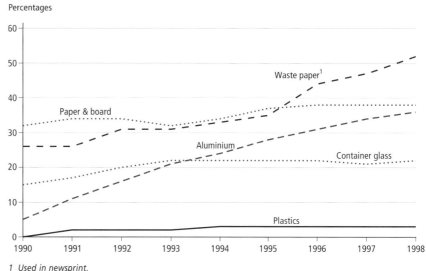

1 Used in newsprint.

Source: Aluminium Can Recycling Association; British Glass Manufacturers' Confederation; British Paper & Board Industry Federation; The Paper Federation of Great Britain; British Plastics Federation

Table **11.14**

Rivers and canals: by biological and chemical quality[1]

United Kingdom

Percentages

	Biological quality				Chemical quality			
	1990		2000		1988–90		1998–00	
	Good/ Fair	Poor/ Bad	Good/ Fair	Poor/ Bad	Good/ Fair	Poor/ Bad	Good/ Fair	Poor/ Bad
Environment Agency Regions[2]								
North West	63	37	84	16	73	27	91	9
North East	83	17	91	9	81	19	93	7
Midlands	82	18	93	7	81	19	94	6
Anglian	93	7	99	1	81	20	92	8
Thames	89	11	95	5	81	19	94	6
Southern	97	3	98	2	88	12	93	7
South West	96	4	99	1	94	6	98	2
England	86	14	94	6	83	17	94	6
Wales	97	3	98	2	98	2	99	1
Scotland[1]	97	3	96	4	97	3	96	4
Northern Ireland[3]	100	–	97	3	95	5	96	4

1 See Appendix Part 11: Rivers and canals.

2 In England. The boundaries of the Environment Agency regions are based on river catchment areas and not county or country borders. Overall figures for England and for Wales relate to political boundaries.

3 Surveys relate to 1991. Biological figures for 2000 relate to the old river network for consistency with 1990.

Source: Environment Agency, Environment and Heritage Service, Northern Ireland; Scottish Environment Protection Agency

Table **11.15**

Bathing water – compliance with EC Bathing Water Directive[1] coliform standards: by coastal region

Numbers and percentages

	Identified bathing waters (numbers)		Percentage complying during the bathing season	
	1991	2001	1991	2001
Environment Agency Regions				
United Kingdom	453	546	76	95
North East	55	55	73	100
North West	34	34	29	88
Midlands	.	.	.	.
Anglian	33	37	88	97
Thames	3	5	67	100
Southern	67	79	67	99
South West	172	187	82	98
England	364	397	73	98
Wales	50	75	90	93
Scotland	23	58	65	84
Northern Ireland	16	16	100	81

1 See Appendix, Part II: Bathing Waters.

Source: Environment Agency; Scottish Environment Protection Agency; Environment and Heritage Service, Northern Ireland

Pollutants such as sewage can also affect bathing water quality. Although regional variations exist, this quality has in general improved since 1991 (Table 11.15), with 95 per cent of beaches in the UK complying with EU standards in 2001. Compliance levels ranged from 81 per cent of beaches in Northern Ireland to 100 per cent in the Thames and North East regions of England. Quality standards used to judge the cleanliness of beaches include the 'Blue Flag' scheme and seaside awards for beaches.

Natural resources

Marine and coastal waters are valuable natural resources for the United Kingdom. They have diverse ecosystems that are influenced by natural factors and commercial exploitation. The latter affects the level and the natural ability of fish stocks to regenerate. Trends vary from species to species and stocks can fluctuate over relatively short periods of time. Although North Sea herring stocks were seriously affected by overfishing during the 1970s, the closure of the North Sea Fishery between 1978 and 1982 allowed them to recover (Chart 11.16). From the late 1980s, there was a further decline in stocks of North Sea herring as well as decreases in the stocks of haddock, whiting and plaice. Herring stocks have increased slightly in recent years. Some stocks are at historically low levels, although stocks of mackerel increased during the 1980s and 1990s.

The last decade has been characterised by substantial variations in overall reservoir stocks for England and Wales due to unusual climatic conditions (Table 11.17). Periods of drought such as in 1990 and 1995 placed stress on water resources in some regions whereas periods of extensive rainfall in 2000 resulted in severe flooding in many regions. The problem of flooding is likely to become an issue for more households in the future if the demand for housing results in more and more homes being built on land in floodplains.

Chart **11.16**

North Sea fish stocks and stocks of North-East Atlantic mackerel[1]

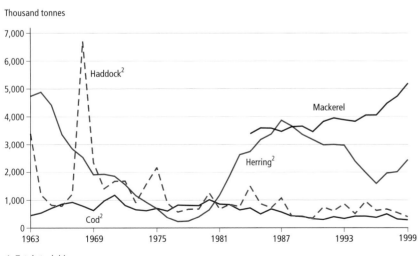

Thousand tonnes

1 Total stock biomass.

2 North Sea stock.

Source: Centre for Environment, Fisheries and Aquaculture Science; International Council for the Exploration of the Sea

Energy consumption

At a time when the UK is committed to reducing its emissions of greenhouse gases and other energy-related pollutants, energy efficiency is playing a major part in achieving this goal. While energy consumption by industries has fallen, consumption increased in the transport sector – this is the biggest energy user in the UK, accounting for over a third of total energy use. This increase in consumption is linked to increases in the distance travelled and number of cars. Similarly, energy consumption by the domestic sector has increased over the past 30 years with households now being responsible for more than a quarter of total energy consumption. The reason for this increase has been the rise in the number of households and subsequently in the energy used for space heating (Chart 11.8).

Production of coal in the UK has been declining since the early 1980s, whilst levels of production of oil and especially natural gas have risen sharply over the same time span (see Chart 11.19 overleaf). The UK has large reserves of fossil fuels, which suggests that the country will be self-sufficient in oil and gas for several years. For example, at the end of 2000, remaining proven, probable and possible oil reserves stood at 1,490 million tonnes. Actual production was 126 million tonnes in the same year. Remaining gas reserves on the same basis were 1,600 billion cubic metres at the end of 2000, and production of gas was 115 billion cubic metres over the year. Since the 1970s fossil fuel dependency for power generation has declined, mainly as a result of the use of nuclear energy.

Chart **11.17**

Reservoir stocks[1]

England and Wales

Percentages

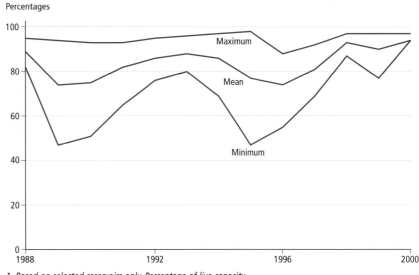

1 Based on selected reservoirs only. Percentage of live capacity.

Source: Centre for Ecology and Hydrology; from Environment Agency and water services companies data

Chart **11.18**

Environmental impacts of households

United Kingdom

Indices (1970 = 100)

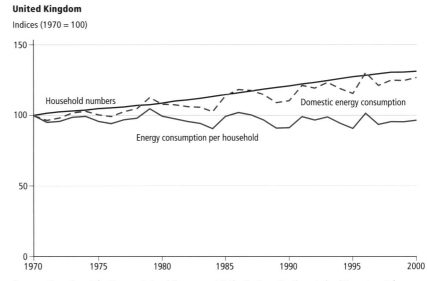

Sources: Department for Transport, Local Government & the Regions; Northern Ireland Department for Social Development; Office for National Statistics; Department of Trade and Industry, Building Research Establishment

Chart **11.19**

Production of primary fuels

United Kingdom

Millions tonnes of oil equivalent

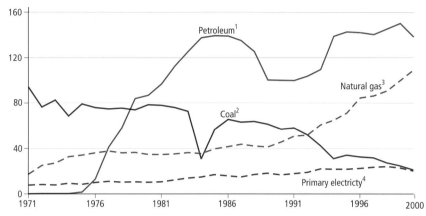

1 Includes crude oil, natural gas liquids and feedstocks.
2 From 1988 includes solid renewables (wood, straw, waste, etc).
3 Includes colliery methane and, from 1988, landfill gas and sewage gas.
4 Nuclear, natural flow hydro-electricity and, from 1988, generation at wind stations.
Source: Department of Trade and Industry

In 2000, three per cent of the electricity generated in the UK was from renewable sources with just under half of this from hydropower (Table 11.20). Generation from renewables other than hydropower in 2000 was, however, twice the level of 1996. A target has been set for 2010 which aims for 10 per cent of UK electricity sales by licensed suppliers to be supplied from sources eligible for the Renewables Obligation (which excludes older very large hydro schemes and energy from certain wastes).

Compared with most other countries in Europe, electricity generation within the UK by alternative, renewable fuels is very small, while the proportion generated by gas, 40 per cent, was among the highest in Europe (Table 11.21).

Table **11.20**

Electricity produced by renewable sources[1]

United Kingdom   Percentages

	1989	1993	1996	1999	2000
Hydro power	87	73	56	52	49
Landfill gas	3	8	12	17	21
Municipal solid waste combustion	5	7	13	13	13
Onshore wind	–	4	8	8	9
Other	5	9	11	10	8
All renewable energy sources (=100%)(GWh)	5,496	5,883	6,102	10,198	10,476

1 See Appendix, Part 11: Electricity produced by renewable sources.
Source: Department of Trade and Industry.

Table **11.21**

Electricity generation: by fuel used, EU comparison, 1999

European Union Percentages

	Nuclear	Coal & Lignite	Petroleum Products	Natural & Derived Gases	Hydro and wind[1]	Biomass and geothermal	Other fuels	All fuels (=100%) (000 GWh)
France	75	6	2	2	15	1	0	524.2
Belgium	58	12	1	26	2	1	–	84.5
Sweden	47	1	2	1	46	2	–	155.4
Finland	33	19	1	16	18	12	–	69.4
Spain	28	35	12	10	13	1	1	209.0
Germany	31	50	1	11	5	1	1	556.8
United Kingdom	26	29	2	40	2	1	0	366.8
Netherlands	4	22	8	61	1	3	1	86.4
Denmark	0	52	13	24	8	5	0	38.9
Irish Republic	0	34	28	32	6	1	0	22.1
Portugal	0	35	25	19	18	3	0	43.3
Italy	0	9	34	34	20	2	0	265.0
Austria	0	7	5	16	69	3	–	60.4
Greece	0	65	16	8	10	0	–	49.9
Luxembourg	0	0	0	20	75	5	0	1.0
EU average	34	25	7	18	14	2	–	2,533.0

1 Includes pumped storage.
Source: Eurostat

Websites

National Statistics	www.statistics.gov.uk
Department for Environment, Food and Rural Affairs	www.defra.gov.uk
Department of Trade and Industry	www.dti.gov.uk/energy
Scottish Executive	www.scotland.gov.uk
National Assembly for Wales	www.wales.org.uk
Northern Ireland Department of Environment	www.nics.gov.uk
Countryside Council for Wales	www.ccw.gov.uk
Environment Agency	www.environment-agency.gov.uk
Environment and Heritage Service (NI)	www.ehsni.gov.uk
Countryside Agency	www.countryside.gov.uk
Forestry Commission	www.forestry.gov.uk/statistics
Joint Nature Conservation Committee	www.jncc.gov.uk
Northern Ireland Statistics and Research Agency	www.nisra.gov.uk
OFWAT	www.ofwat.gov.uk
Centre for Ecology and Hydrology, Wallingford	www.ceh-nerc.ac.uk
National Centre for Social Research	www.natcen.ac.uk
Scottish Environment Protection Agency	www.sepa.gov.uk
Scottish Natural Heritage	www.snh.org.uk
European Environment Agency	www.eea.eu.int

Contacts

Office for National Statistics	
Chapter author	020 7533 5781
Department for Environment, Food and Rural Affairs	020 7944 6497
Department of Trade and Industry	020 7215 2697
Scottish Executive	0131 244 0445
National Assembly for Wales	029 2082 5111
Northern Ireland Department of Environment	028 9054 0540
Centre for Ecology and Hydrology	01491 838 800
Countryside Agency	020 7340 2900
Countryside Council for Wales	01248 385 500
CADW	029 2082 5111
Environment Agency	0645 333 111
National Water Demand Management Centre	01903 832 073
Environment and Heritage Services (Northern Ireland)	028 9023 5000
European Environment Agency	0045 3336 7100
Eurostat	00352 4301 33023
Forestry Commission	0131 314 6337
Joint Nature Conservation Committee	01733 562 626
OFWAT	0121 625 1300
Scottish Environment Protection Agency	01786 457 700
Scottish Natural Heritage	0131 447 4784
National Centre for Social Research	020 7250 1866
Northern Ireland Statistics Research Agency	028 9034 8200

Chapter 12

Transport

Overview

- On average, people in Great Britain travelled about 11,000 kilometres a year in 1998–2000, excluding travel abroad, a 29 per cent increase in the distance travelled when compared to 1985–1986. (Page 194)

Travel by car

- At the end of 2000, there were over 24 million cars registered in the UK. The proportion of British households with access to two or more cars almost doubled from 1981 to 2000, to reach 28 per cent. (Page 198)

- Average car occupancy was 1.56 in 1998–2000. Sixty per cent of people making a trip by car were drivers. (Table 12.9)

Travel by bus and train

- After a long decline, the distance travelled by local buses increased from the mid-1980s to the mid-1990s. Bus journeys accounted for 4.3 billion passenger journeys in 2000–01. (Page 200)

- Over the last 2 decades a number of light railways and metros, such as the Manchester Metrolink, have been built and the passenger journeys made on such systems rose from 14 million in 1981–82 to 120 million in 2000–01. (Table 12.14)

Transport safety

- Casualties from road accidents involving illegal alcohol levels rose for the second year running in 2000, but are still much lower than in earlier periods. (Chart 12.17)

Travel to work and school

- The proportion of children aged 5–10 who walk to school fell from 67 per cent in 1985–86 to 56 per cent in 1998–2000. Forty three per cent of those aged 11–16 now travel to school on foot. (Table 12.19)

Attitudes to transport issues

- Three-quarters of those questioned by the British Social Attitudes Survey in 2000 thought it was very or fairly important to cut the number of cars on Britain's roads. (Page 207)

Chart **12.1**

Distance travelled per person per year: by age, 1985–1986 and 1998–2000

Great Britain

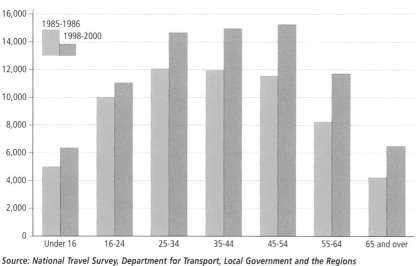

Kilometres

Source: National Travel Survey, Department for Transport, Local Government and the Regions

Although people in the United Kingdom are travelling more often and further than at any time in the past, different sections of the population have different patterns of travel. Some of these differences seem obvious – middle aged men travel the furthest by car each year, and women are more likely to take children to school. Some however are less obvious – older men walk much further on average each year than their sons, although not as far as their grandsons. The ways in which we travel have also changed, and over three-fifths of all trips are now made in the car, either as a driver or passenger, compared to less than half of all trips made as recently as 1985–1986.

Overview

On average, people in Great Britain travelled about 11,000 kilometres a year in 1998–2000 (not including travel abroad). This is a 29 per cent increase in less than 15 years; in 1985–1986, the average was about 8,500 kilometres a year. Cars, vans and taxis accounted for 85 per cent of all passenger kilometres travelled in 2000. Buses and coaches (6 per cent), rail (7 per cent), and pedal cycles and motorcycles (1 per cent each), account for most of the remaining passenger kilometres, and these shares have changed little over the course of the 1990s.

Table **12.2**

Trips per person per year: by main mode and trip purpose[1], 1985–1986 and 1998–2000

Great Britain

Percentages

	Car		Walk		Bus, coach and rail[2]		Other		All modes	
	1985–86	1998–00	1985–86	1998–00	1985–86	1998–00	1985–86	1998–00	1985–86	1998–00
Social/entertainment	28	26	20	19	21	18	24	28	25	23
Shopping	17	20	25	24	26	25	12	12	21	21
Commuting	20	18	8	7	27	26	31	26	17	16
Education	3	3	12	11	11	14	16	11	8	6
Escort education	3	4	5	8	1	2	1	1	3	5
Business	5	4	1	2	1	2	3	4	3	4
Holiday/day trip	4	3	1	1	2	3	4	8	2	3
Other escort and personal business	20	21	15	14	10	10	9	10	17	18
Other, including just walk	–	–	13	15	–	–	–	–	5	4
All purposes (=100%)(numbers)	517	645	350	281	102	78	55	41	1,024	1,046

1 See Appendix, Part 12: National Travel Survey.
2 Includes London Underground.

Source: National Travel Survey, Department for Transport, Local Government and the Regions

The distance travelled each year varies significantly with age (Chart 12.1). Adults aged 45–54 travel the furthest at over 15,000 kilometres a year, almost two and a half times further than children (aged under 16) who travel the least far. Each person spent an average of 360 hours, or 15 days, a year travelling in 1998–2000, only a slight increase on the 1985–1986 figure of 337 hours a year. However, the average length of trips increased by over 2 kilometres over the same period, from 8.4 kilometres in 1985–1986 to 10.7 kilometres in 1998–2000.

Car access has a large impact on the distance a person travels each year. In 1998–2000, the National Travel Survey (NTS) found that the main drivers of a car (see Appendix, Part 12: National Travel Survey) travelled an average of nearly 17 thousand kilometres a year, 90 per cent of which was in a car. In contrast, people living in households without car access travelled just over 4 thousand kilometres a year on average over the same period, with 35 per cent of this distance by car, mainly as a passenger. Another major factor is area of residence – in 1998–2000, people in the south east of England travelled further in a year than those in any other area of Great Britain, at an average of 13 thousand kilometres a year. However, Londoners travelled the least far, averaging less than 9 thousand kilometres a year.

According to the NTS, people in Britain made an average of just over 1,000 trips per year in 1998–2000 (Table 12.2). Over three-fifths of all trips were made by car, while over a quarter were on foot and less than 1 in 10 were by bus, coach or rail. This compares with just over a half of all trips in 1985–1986 being by car, over a third on foot and one in 10 by bus coach or rail. Car travel accounts for a lower proportion of trips made than of distance travelled, as people are more likely to use alternative travel modes like walking or buses for short distances.

Overall, the number of trips made was very similar in 1998–2000 to those in 1985–1986. However, in the 65 and over age group, members of both sexes made on average over 15 per cent more trips in 1998–2000 than in 1985–1986.

An increase in the use of the car has occurred among all age groups and in both sexes since the mid 1980s. Over half of all trips by children under 16 were as car or van passengers in 1998–2000 compared with under two-fifths in 1985–1986. Men make slightly more trips by car than women, although they make many more as car drivers – almost half of all trips made by men are as a car driver, compared to only a third of trips made by women.

Table **12.3**

Trips per person per year: by gender, age and purpose[1], 1998–2000

Great Britain   Percentages

	Under 16	16–24	25–34	35–44	45–54	55–64	65 and over
Males							
Social/entertainment	27	33	24	20	18	21	25
Shopping	12	12	17	17	18	23	34
Other escort and personal business	18	10	14	17	19	20	22
Commuting	1	26	31	28	25	20	3
Business	–	2	6	9	10	6	1
Education	28	12	1	–	–	–	–
Escort education	6	–	2	4	2	1	1
Holiday/day trip	3	2	2	2	3	3	5
Other, including just walk	3	2	3	3	5	6	9
All purposes (=100%)(numbers)	877	994	1,098	1,178	1,203	1,108	919
Females							
Social/entertainment	27	31	23	18	20	26	27
Shopping	13	19	21	21	25	32	37
Other escort and personal business	19	11	17	21	17	16	21
Commuting	1	20	18	18	22	13	1
Business	–	1	2	3	3	2	–
Education	28	10	1	1	–	–	–
Escort education	6	3	13	13	4	2	1
Holiday/day trip	3	2	2	2	3	3	4
Other, including just walk	3	2	3	3	6	6	8
All purposes (=100%)(numbers)	908	1,091	1,225	1,311	1,136	963	663

1 See Appendix Part 12: National Travel Survey.
Source: National Travel Survey, Department for Transport, Local Government and the Regions

The most common reason for travel in 1998–2000 was social and entertainment purposes (23 per cent of all trips made). Different transport modes are used for different purposes: public transport is used more for shopping and commuting trips, whereas the car is used more for social/entertainment trips. The reasons for making trips vary with gender and age, with women making proportionally more trips for shopping and taking children to school than do men, and fewer commuting and business trips (Table 12.3). Most of the gender differences apply to people of working age, however, and reflect different patterns of both employment and work in the home. Among children travel patterns differ little by gender.

Once people pass the age of 65 the number of trips they make each year falls, to about half the number of trips made by the 35–44 year olds. The nature and purpose of their trips also change. Trips to work decline in number and shopping accounts for an ever greater proportion of trips. For example, in 1998–2000 shopping accounted for over a third of all trips made by men aged 65 and over, and almost two-fifths of trips made by women of the same age.

As the use of cars has increased, the distance walked each year has declined. This has largely occurred in the last 10 years – people walked an average of just under 400 kilometres a year in 1985–1986 and 300 kilometres a year in 1998–2000. The steepest fall has come from those aged 11–16, who walked nearly 30 per cent less far in 1998–2000 than in 1985–1986. The smallest changes have come from the very young and the over 65s. The particularly steep decline in walking among secondary school children has caused concerns about the long-term health implications of less exercise, a loss of independence and increasing road congestion as a result of their parents driving them to school (see also Table 12.20). The distances covered by bicycle have also fallen in recent years from just over 70 kilometres per person per year in 1989–1991 to just over 60 kilometres in 1998–2000.

Although both sexes walk approximately the same distance each year, women under the age of 55 generally walk further than men; this includes the 11–16 age range, where girls walk on average around 10 per cent further than boys each year. The most marked contrast, however, can be found in the 65 and over age group. Men of this age walked an average of over 100 kilometres a year further in 1998–2000 than women.

Whilst motoring prices in the UK have roughly kept pace with inflation since 1981, bus and coach and rail fares have increased at a faster rate (Table 12.4). By January 2001, the 'All fares and other travel costs' index of the Retail Prices Index (RPI) had risen by 167 per cent when compared to January 1981; the 'All motoring' index rose by 139 per cent over the same period. These figures compare with an increase in the general RPI of 143 per cent. However, different components of transport costs have seen different price increases. For example, vehicle tax and insurance prices have risen by over 320 per cent since 1981, whereas the cost of purchasing a vehicle has increased by around 50 per cent, and has actually been falling in recent years. Similarly, bus and coach fares have risen by around 210 per cent since 1981, whereas other travel costs, such as the purchase of bicycles, have increased by only 81 per cent.

Household expenditure on motoring increased by over 60 per cent in real terms in the last 20 years, whilst expenditure on fares and other travel costs rose by 14 per cent (Table 12.5). Given that the price of motoring has risen broadly in line with inflation (see above), this increase reflects the higher levels of car ownership in the UK than in the past, and also that a much greater proportion of both trips taken and distance travelled are now by car.

Table 12.4

Passenger transport prices[1], 1981 to 2001

United Kingdom
Indices (1981=100)

	1981	1986	1991	1996	1999	2000	2001
Motoring costs							
Vehicle tax and insurance	100	146	220	299	353	400	429
Maintenance[2]	100	138	195	251	287	300	313
Petrol and oil	100	145	156	213	242	285	293
Purchase of vehicles	100	116	144	165	169	158	152
All motoring expenditure	100	131	163	205	225	236	239
Fares and other travel costs							
Bus and coach fares	100	139	198	261	287	299	313
Rail fares	100	137	201	262	288	294	303
Other	100	107	137	156	169	175	181
All fares and other travel	100	135	186	229	250	258	267
Retail prices index	100	137	185	214	232	237	243

1 At January each year based on the retail prices index. See Appendix, Part 6: Retail prices index.

2 Includes spares and accessories, repairs and motoring organisation membership fees.

Source: Office for National Statistics

Table **12.5**

Household expenditure on transport

United Kingdom						£ per week[1]
	1970	1980	1990	1998–99	1999–00	2000–01
Motoring						
Cars, vans and motorcycle purchase	..	..	22.00	23.80	22.90	22.50
Repairs, servicing, spares and accessories	..	..	6.10	6.40	6.20	6.10
Motor vehicle insurance and taxation	..	..	6.20	7.20	7.40	8.10
Petrol, diesels and other oils	..	..	10.60	13.60	14.60	15.60
Other motoring costs	..	..	1.10	1.80	1.80	1.80
All Motoring Expenditure	28.40	32.90	46.00	52.80	52.80	54.10
Fares and other travel costs						
Rail and tube fares	..	..	1.50	1.70	1.60	1.80
Bus and coach fares	..	..	1.70	1.20	1.40	1.20
Taxis, air and other travel costs[2]	..	..	4.30	4.20	4.60	4.80
All fares and other travel costs[3]	7.10	7.70	8.40	7.90	8.60	8.80
All Transport and Travel	35.50	40.60	54.40	60.70	61.50	62.90
All expenditure groups	260.00	277.90	335.80	362.00	363.90	378.30

1 At 2000–01 prices.

2 Includes combined fares.

3 All fares and other travel costs includes expenditure on bicycles, boats - purchases and repairs.

Source: Family Expenditure Survey, Office for National Statistics

However, if expenditure on travel is calculated as a percentage of overall household expenditure, the trend is much flatter. In 1980, around 15 per cent of total household expenditure was on transport and travel – by 2000–01 this figure had increased to around 17 per cent. Around 14 per cent of that total expenditure was on motoring costs in 2000–01, compared to only around 2 per cent on fares and other travel costs: in 1980 these figures were 12 per cent and 3 per cent respectively.

As with personal travel, freight travel on the roads has grown significantly in the last 20 years, by nearly 60 per cent to 158 billion tonne kilometres in 2000 (Chart 12.6). The amount of goods moved by rail, 18 billion tonne kilometres in 2000, is almost the same as that in 1980; however, it fell to a low of 13 billion tonne kilometres in 1995, and has been increasing since.

The increase in road freight reflects an increase in the distance travelled rather than the amount of goods lifted, which has changed little since the early 1970s. Recent years have seen a decrease in the total freight lifted at the same time as an increase in the tonne kilometres travelled. A total of 1,593 million tonnes of freight was lifted on British roads in 2000,

Chart **12.6**

Goods moved by domestic freight transport: by mode

Great Britain

Billion tonne kilometres

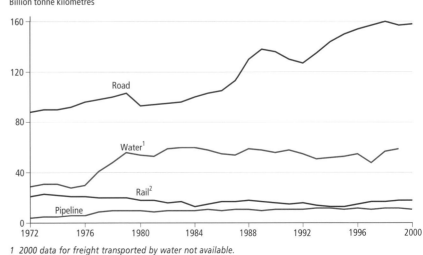

1 2000 data for freight transported by water not available.

2 From 1991 data for rail are financial years.

Source: Department for Transport, Local Government and the Regions

Table **12.7**

Households with regular use of a car[1]: by age of head of household, 1998–2000

Great Britain   Percentages

	Percentage of households with			
	No car	One car	Two or more cars	All
17–24	57	35	8	100
25–34	22	53	26	100
35–44	16	48	36	100
45–54	15	41	43	100
55–64	21	49	30	100
65 and over	51	40	8	100
All	28	45	26	100

1 See Appendix, Part 12: National Travel Survey.
Source: National Travel Survey, Department for Transport, Local Government and the Regions.

Chart **12.8**

Road traffic[1]

Great Britain

Billion vehicle kilometres

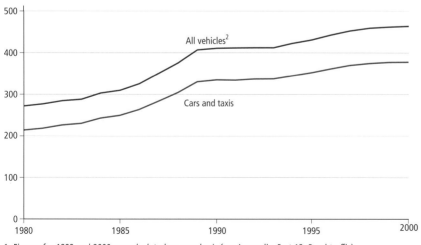

1 Figures for 1999 and 2000 are calculated on new basis (see Appendix, Part 12: Road traffic).
2 Excludes two wheeled traffic.
Source: Department for Transport, Local Government and the Regions

compared to 1,645 million tonnes in 1990. A fifth of this was food, drink and tobacco. The average length of haul for goods lifted by road was 94 kilometres in 2000. This is a considerable increase on the average length in 1990, which was 79 kilometres. For food, drink and tobacco, the average length of haul was 128 kilometres in 2000, compared to 110 kilometres in 1990.

Travel by car

At the end of 2000, there were over 24 million cars registered in the UK, double the number registered in 1975. Over 70 per cent of British households had regular use of a car in 1998–2000, and ownership is well spread amongst different sectors of the population. Only where the head of household is in the youngest or oldest age groups is the rate of car ownership less than 50 per cent (Table 12.7). Equally, only amongst the poorest fifth of households (measured by equivalised household income), do ownership levels fall below 50 per cent. The NTS found that in 1998–2000, 35 per cent of households in the lowest income quintile had regular use of a car, compared to 57 per cent in the next quintile and 81 per cent in the middle quintile. The number of households with the use of one car has remained stable over recent years at about 45 per cent, but the proportion with the use of two or more has risen to 28 per cent, almost doubling from 1981 to 2000.

In 1998–2000, 18 million men and nearly 14 million women held full car driving licences. Men are more likely to drive than women – in 1975–1976, 69 per cent of men held a driving licence compared with only 29 per cent of women. But women are catching up – by 1998–2000 the proportions with a licence were 82 per cent for men and 60 per cent for women, a much smaller difference. The proportion of people holding full driving licences is highest among those aged 30 to 49: about nine in ten males and three in four females in this age group held a full car driving licence in 1998–2000. The proportions holding licences then fall with age and are particularly low for females aged 70 or over – just over one in five held a licence in 1998–2000. The lower proportion of older people holding driving licences is largely because fewer of these people learned to drive when they were younger – very few people gain full licences after the age of 60. As the younger groups grow older, the proportions of those aged 70 or over who hold driving licences can be expected to increase further, even though after the age of 70 drivers have to reapply for their licence at least every three years. In 1998–2000 there were over 2 million licence holders aged 70 or over in Great Britain. Tentative projections suggest that this might double by 2015.

As car ownership has increased, so have road traffic levels. In 1980 cars and taxis travelled a total of 215.0 billion vehicle kilometres in Great Britain. By 2000, this figure was 378.7 billion, an increase of 76 per cent. Overall road traffic increased by slightly less, 71 per cent, over the same period (Chart 12.8).

Average traffic flows rose substantially in the 1980s, particularly on motorways, but grew more slowly in the early 1990s, and have remained largely stable in recent years. In built-up areas the major roads are quite heavily congested, so any growth tends to be on minor roads. In non-built-up areas there is less congestion and so traffic can still use motorways and other major roads without resorting to minor roads. However, road traffic is projected to increase over the next decade. The Government has set targets to reduce road congestion on the inter-urban trunk network and in large urban areas to below 2000 levels by 2010. Proposed methods for achieving this, as part of local authorities' Local Transport Plans, range from park and ride schemes to proposals for introducing congestion charging schemes in town and city centres.

One factor which has a bearing on traffic congestion is car occupancy levels. Since 1985–86, average car occupancy has fallen from 1.63 to 1.56. Overall 64 per cent of people making a car trip were the driver, as opposed to a passenger (Table 12.9). For commuting, this increased to 83 per cent of those travelling by car. Average vehicle occupancy levels only rise above two on education and holiday/day trips. There are several schemes in operation, both Government and private, which are designed to encourage car sharing. For example, there are now a number of car sharing clubs in operation in the UK, where drivers pay a monthly fee and are then billed for the hours they hire a car and the miles driven.

Average traffic speeds are falling as the volume of traffic increases, according to the National Traffic Census. However, when the average speed of vehicles passing a particular point is measured (spot speeds, which tend to be taken where traffic is relatively free flowing), in 2000 cars averaged 70 miles an hour on motorways, compared with 45 miles an hour on single carriageways, the same as in 1993 (Table 12.10). Lorries, in comparison, averaged 55 miles an hour on motorways and 45 miles an hour on single carriageways. Nevertheless, speeding is widespread when roads are not congested, particularly on motorways, dual carriageways and urban roads. In 2000, over half of cars on non-urban motorways and dual carriageways exceeded the speed limit and two-thirds of cars exceeded the 30 mile an hour limit on urban roads.

Table **12.9**

Car occupancy: by trip purpose[1], 1998–2000

Great Britain   Percentage and number

	Driver	Front passenger	Rear passenger	Total	Average vehicle occupancy
Commuting	83	14	3	100	1.2
Business	90	8	3	100	1.1
Education	47	19	34	100	2.1
Shopping	61	25	14	100	1.6
Personal Business	62	24	15	100	1.6
Leisure	53	28	20	100	1.9
Holiday/day trip	43	32	25	100	2.3
Other	78	12	11	100	1.3
Total	64	21	14	100	1.6

1 Each purpose includes the appropriate escort purpose. For example, education includes escort education.

Source: National Travel Survey, Department for Transport, Local Government and the Regions

Table **12.10**

Traffic speeds: by class of road and type of vehicle, 1993 and 2000

Great Britain   Miles per hour

	1993		2000	
	Cars	Buses and coaches	Cars	Buses and coaches
Motorways				
Average speed	70	64	70	60
Speed limit	70	70	70	70
Percentage exceeding limit	56	21	55	4
Dual carriageways				
Average speed	67	53	70	59
Speed limit	70	60	70	60
Percentage exceeding limit	40	29	52	49
Single carriageways				
Average speed	45	40	45	41
Speed limit	60	50	60	50
Percentage exceeding limit	7	14	9	22

Source: Department for Transport, Local Government and the Regions

Travel by Bus and Train

Buses are the dominant form of public transport in terms of journeys, though not distance, accounting for 4.3 billion passenger journeys in 2000–01, more than twice as many as the number of rail journeys (including underground services). After a long period of decline, the distance travelled on all buses increased from the mid-1980s to the mid-1990s.

National targets for reliability and investment have been agreed with the bus industry: no more than 0.5 per cent of scheduled bus mileage should be lost for reasons within an operator's control (including predictable peak hour congestion); and the average age of the bus fleet should be reduced to 8 years by mid-2001. A bus reliability survey in England in the April – June quarter of 2001 found some 1.4 per cent of scheduled local bus mileage lost owing to factors within an operator's control. This figure was 3.2 per cent in London, and just under one per cent outside the capital. The average age of the bus fleet was 8.5 years at the end of June 2001, continuing a downward trend in vehicle age over recent years.

The distance from households to the nearest bus service has remained relatively stable since the mid-1980s – 87 per cent of households in Great Britain were within 6 minutes walk of a bus stop in 1998–2000 (Table 12.11). This proportion was lowest in rural areas, although the proportion of households with good access to a bus service (defined as within 13 minutes walk of a bus stop with a service of at least once an hour) is rising, from 35 per cent in 1985–1986 to 50 per cent in 1998–2000, in such areas.

Easy access to services by foot or public transport is a key aspect of any integrated transport system. In general the time taken to travel by bus to local facilities has remained largely constant over the last 10 years, whereas the time taken to walk to some services has increased. More than four out of five households in urban areas could walk to their nearest food store in 13 minutes or less in 1998-2000 (Table 12.12). In 1989–1991, this figure was almost 9 out of 10. As would be expected, services are more difficult to access in rural areas. For example, although under a third of urban households lived more than 44 minutes by bus away from a general hospital in 1998–2000, this rose to over half of households in rural areas.

Table **12.11**

Time taken to walk to nearest bus stop: by type of area[1], 1985–1986 and 1998–2000

Great Britain   Percentages

	London borough	Metro-politan built-up area	Large urban	Medium urban	Small urban	Rural	All areas
1985–86							
6 minutes or less	86	91	90	90	81	74	86
7–13 minutes	12	8	8	8	13	13	10
14–26 minutes	1	1	2	1	3	7	2
27 minutes or more	–	–	–	–	2	6	1
Accessibility indicator[2]	98	98	96	95	79	35	86
1998–00							
6 minutes or less	88	91	91	89	82	77	87
7–13 minutes	11	7	7	9	12	12	10
14–26 minutes	1	1	1	1	4	6	2
27 minutes or more	–	–	–	–	2	5	1
Accessibility indicator[2]	98	98	98	95	76	50	88

1 See Appendix Part 12: Type of area.
2 Households within 13 minutes walk of a bus stop with a service at least once an hour.
Source: National Travel Survey, Department for Transport, Local Government and the Regions

Table **12.12**

Time taken to walk and travel by bus to local facilities in urban areas, 1998–2000

Great Britain   Percentage of households

	Time taken to walk					Time taken to travel by bus				
	Doctor	Post office	Chemist	Food store	General Hospital	Doctor	Post office	Chemist	Food store	General Hospital
No bus/quicker to walk	.	.	.	.	.	57	80	71	86	10
6 minutes or less	17	41	33	59	2	10	10	11	7	3
7–13 minutes	21	33	29	25	3	14	6	10	4	11
14–26 minutes	31	21	26	13	12	12	2	5	2	23
27–43 minutes	15	3	6	2	14	4	–	1	–	24
44 mins or more	16	2	6	2	69	3	–	1	–	29
Total	100	100	100	100	100	100	100	100	100	100

Source: National Travel Survey, Department for Transport, Local Government and the Regions

Use of local bus services is spread unevenly amongst different sections of the population, with the young, older people and women being far more likely to travel in this way. Those aged 16–24 used buses the most frequently in 1998–2000, making more than twice the number of trip stages (see Appendix Part 12: NTS) each year than the average for all ages combined (Table 12.13). Women use buses more than men, making over a third more trips a year than men in 1998–2000. The reasons for using buses also varied across different sectors of the population. For example, over two-fifths of all shopping trip stages made by bus are made by the over 65s, and over two-thirds by women.

Since June 2001 every pensioner in England has been entitled to a free bus pass to enable them to claim concessionary fares at no more than half the full cost, and similar schemes are being brought forward in Wales and in Scotland. In 1998–2000, before the recent changes, 98 per cent of pensioners in Great Britain had some form of concessionary fare scheme available. The take-up rate has declined from 60 per cent of those with schemes available in 1989–1991 to 48 per cent in 1998–2000 – car use and the holding of a driving licence has increased among older people in recent years. Take-up in areas with a scheme available was highest in London at 81 per cent, and generally decreased with area type down to 29 per cent in rural areas. Dependence on cars is higher in rural areas and where there are few buses there is little incentive to acquire a bus pass.

Table **12.13**

Local bus journey stages[1]: by trip purpose and age, 1998–2000

Great Britain   Percentages and numbers

	Under 16	16–24	25–34	35–44	45–54	55–64	65 and over	All Ages
Commuting and business	1	23	23	21	21	10	1	100
Education	58	34	3	3	2	1	–	100
Shopping	9	9	8	10	10	14	41	100
Other Personal Business[2]	15	10	12	11	10	12	30	100
Leisure	18	17	10	10	8	11	25	100
Other	14	14	8	8	6	12	38	100
Stages per person per year	54	128	53	47	49	56	79	63

1 See Appendix, part 12: National Travel Survey.
2 Includes all escorted journeys.
Source: National Travel Survey, Department for Transport, Local Government and the Regions

Table **12.14**

Rail journeys[1]: by operator

Great Britain

Millions

	1981	1991–92	1995–96	1998–99	1999–00	2000–01
Main line/underground						
National Rail	719	792	761	892	931	957
London Underground	541	751	784	866	927	970
Glasgow Underground	11	14	14	15	15	14
All main line/underground	1,271	1,557	1,559	1,773	1,873	1,941
Light railways and trams						
Tyne and Wear PTE	14	41	36	34	33	33
Docklands Light Railway	.	8	14	28	31	38
Greater Manchester Metro	.	.	13	13	14	17
South Yorkshire Supertram	.	.	5	10	11	11
West Midlands Metro	.	.	.	.	5	5
Croydon Tramlink	.	.	.	.	.	15
All light railways and trams	14	49	68	85	94	120
All journeys by rail	1,285	1,605	1,628	1,858	1,967	2,061

1 Excludes railways operated principally as tourist attractions.

Source: Department for Transport, Local Government and the Regions

Chart **12.15**

Rail complaints: by category, 1998–99 and 2000–01

Great Britain

Percentages

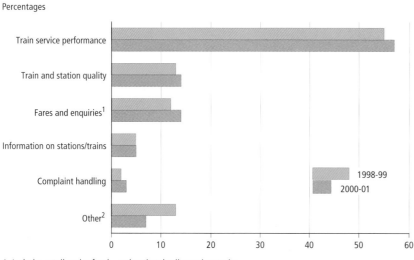

1 Includes retail and refunds, and national rail enquiry service.

2 Includes safety and security, special needs, timetable, connection service and staff conduct.

Source: Strategic Rail Authority

Passenger traffic on the national railways rose by three per cent in 2000–01, when some 957 million passenger journeys were made (Table 12.14). This is the highest number of passenger journeys since 1962, but there had been more than a billion rail passenger journeys a year in 1961 and before. However, passenger kilometres travelled are much higher than the early 1960s, which suggests that people are using the railways for longer journeys than previously. In 2000 the Government set targets for a 50 per cent growth in rail passengers, 80 per cent growth in rail freight and 6 thousand new carriages and trains by 2010.

Travel on underground and light railways has increased rapidly in recent years. Journeys on the London Underground increased by 79 per cent between 1981–82 and 2000–01. A feature of the last two decades has been the development of light railways and metros – Nexus (Tyne and Wear) in 1980, the Docklands Light Railway (1988–89), Manchester Metrolink (1992–93), Sheffield Supertram (1993–94), Centro (West Midlands Metro) (1999) and the Croydon Tramlink (2000). The number of passenger journeys made on light rail systems grew from 14 million in 1981 to 120 million in 2000–01, and further schemes are planned for the future.

Following the Hatfield crash in October 2000, which the Health and Safety Executive believe was due to a fractured rail, temporary speed restrictions (TSRs) were imposed by Railtrack on around one thousand sites throughout the national rail network. Placed on locations previously identified as having similar problems to those which caused the accident, the TSRs meant that revised timetables had to be issued for many services, and these, coupled with severe flooding in some areas, had an adverse affect on service timelines. For example, between July and September 2000, 80 per cent of long distance trains arrived on time (within 10 minutes of advertised time); between October and December, this figure fell to 48 per cent. For London and South East operators, these figures were 88 per cent and 58 per cent respectively, and 87 per cent and 71 per cent for regional operators.

These problems contributed to a sharp increase in complaints made to the Train Operating Companies (TOCS) which run trains on Great Britain's rail system. Between the fourth quarter of 1999–00 and the fourth quarter of 2000–01, the rate of complaints received per 100,000 passenger journeys rose by 54 per cent. The largest increase was seen among the regional operators, where complaints almost doubled over the period. However, the nature of the complaints made in 2000-01 did not alter much from earlier periods (Chart 12.15). Complaints about train service performance, although the most common type of complaint, increased by only 2 per cent from 1998–99 to 2000–01.

Transport Safety

Despite improvements in road safety in recent years, other forms of transport such as rail, air and sea have much lower death rates from accidents, and it is also much safer to use public transport than private. Passenger death rates for travel by car, bicycle, on foot or especially motorcycle are all higher than death rates on public transport (Table 12.16). Death rates for motorcycling, cycling and walking are much higher, with that for motorcycling being over 46 times greater than that for the car. All major forms of transport, except motorcycling, are safer now than in 1981 – motorcycling has seen an increase in death rates in recent years, and rates are now higher than in 1981.

Although there are only about 30 per cent more male licence holders than female, male car drivers were involved in almost twice as many car accidents in 2000. However, those women who were involved in such accidents were at all ages more likely to be injured than their male counterparts. For example, over three-fifths of female drivers aged 20–24 who were involved in accidents in 2000 were injured, compared to over two fifths of male drivers. Accident and injury rates also vary with age, and those aged 40 to 70 are involved in fewer accidents than younger drivers. There were nearly 60,000 accidents involving male car drivers aged 40–70 in 2000, compared to over 100,000 involving male drivers aged 17–40.

In 2000, the Government announced a new road safety strategy, setting targets for reducing casualties by 2010. These targets included a 40 per cent reduction in the number of people killed or seriously injured in road accidents compared to the average in 1994–98; and a 50 per cent reduction in the number of children killed or seriously injured. In 2000, 13 per cent fewer people were killed or seriously injured compared to the 1994–98 average, while there was a fall of 24 per cent in the number of children killed or seriously injured.

Major contributors to road accidents are excessive speed and alcohol. Over the years there have been many campaigns to discourage drink-driving and the numbers of casualties from road accidents involving illegal alcohol levels in the United Kingdom fell sharply between the mid-1980s and mid-1990s, although with some increases in the numbers more recently (Chart 12.17). In 2000, over 560 people died from involvement in road accidents involving illegal alcohol levels, compared with over one thousand people in 1986. It is, however, an increase on 1999 when it was estimated that 5 per cent of all road casualties and 13 per cent of road deaths occurred when someone was driving over the legal limit for alcohol. There is also concern over the role illegal drug use may play in causing road accidents. For example, a

Table **12.16**

Passenger death rates[1]: by mode of transport

Great Britain					Rate per billion passenger kilometres
	1981	**1986**	**1991**	**1996**	**2000**
Motorcycle	115.8	100.3	94.4	97.9	129.7
Walk	76.9	77.6	74.6	54.3	47.5
Pedal cycle	56.9	49.6	46.8	47.7	30.5
Car	6.1	5.1	3.7	3.1	2.8
Van	3.7	3.6	2.1	1.0	1.0
Water[2]	0.4	0.5	0.0	0.8	0.8
Rail	1.0	0.9	0.8	0.4	0.4
Bus or coach	0.3	0.5	0.6	0.2	0.3
Air[2]	0.2	0.5	0.0	0.0	–

1 See Appendix, Part 12: Passenger death rates.
2 Data are for United Kingdom.
Source: Department for Transport, Local Government and the Regions

Chart **12.17**

Casualties from road accidents involving illegal alcohol levels, 1986–2000

United Kingdom

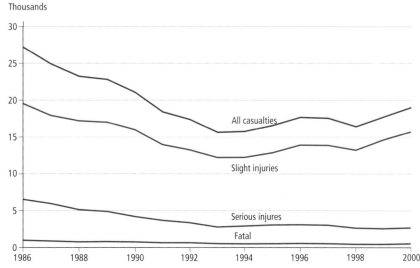

Thousands

Source: Department of the Environment, Local Government and the Regions; Royal Ulster Constabulary

Chart **12.18**

Road deaths: EU comparison, 1999

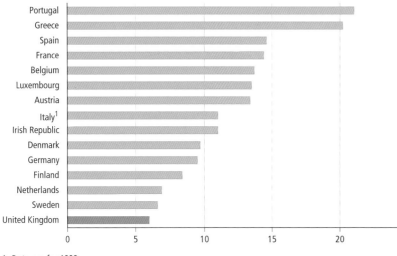

Rate per 100,000 population

1 Data are for 1998.

Source: Department for Transport, Local Government and the Regions

recent study which analysed blood and urine samples from fatally injured road accident victims found a six fold increase in the incidence of illicit drugs in the samples when compared to a similar survey conducted in 1985–87. Over 6 per cent of all fatalities had more than one illegal drug in their system.

The United Kingdom has a good record for road safety compared with most European Union (EU) countries. In 1999 the United Kingdom had the lowest road death rates per 100,000 population in the EU, at 6 per 100,000 of population (Table 12.18). This compares to figures of 9.3 per 100,000 population in Australia, 8.2 in Japan and 15.3 in the USA. Across the EU, the average road death rate for children was around 2.6 per 100,000 of population – again, the UK had the lowest rate at 1.9 per 100,000.

Travel to work and school

Trips to school account for around one-quarter of all trips for under 16 year olds. They usually take place at the same time each morning and evening, and as such can have an impact on levels of congestion in residential areas. For example, it is calculated that at the morning peak of ten minutes to nine, 16 per cent of all cars on the road are taking children to school. Table 12.19 shows that the majority of children aged 5–10 still walk to school, although the proportion fell from 67 per cent in 1985–1986 to 56 per cent in 1998–2000. However, only 43 per cent of young people aged 11–16 now travel to school on foot.

One factor involved in these trends is the distance children live from their school. The average journey distance to school for children in Great Britain is 3.6 kilometres. This falls to 2.5 kilometres in metropolitan built up areas, and rises to 8.1 kilometres for children in rural areas. The journey to school increased in length between 1985–1986 and 1998–2000, most markedly for those aged 11–16, whose average journey length increased by over a kilometre. Some of the reasons for these changes are thought to be the growth in the rural share of the population in the UK (rural dwellers travel further than their urban counterparts); the closure of rural schools; and changes in school admissions procedures which mean that parents can choose to send their children to non-local schools.

Table **12.19**

Trips to and from school per child per year: by main mode, 1985–1986 and 1998–2000

Great Britain				Percentages and kilometres
	Age 5–10		Age 11–16	
	1985–86	1998–00	1985–86	1998–00
Walk	67	56	52	43
Bicycle	1	–	6	2
Car/Van	22	36	10	19
Private bus	5	3	9	8
Local bus	4	4	20	24
Rail	–	–	1	2
Other	2	1	1	2
All modes	100	100	100	100
Average Length (kilometres)	1.8	2.4	3.7	4.9

Source: National Travel Survey, Department for Transport, Local Government and the Regions

The way in which children travel to school also varies with the type of area they live in. For example, in metropolitan areas, 58 per cent children of all ages walk to school, while in rural areas, 29 per cent do so. Children in rural areas are most likely to be driven to school, and over 30 per cent travel by car. However, even in Metropolitan areas, where the proportion who are driven to school is the lowest of all area types, almost 25 per cent arrive at school in this way. School buses are commonly used to take children to school in rural areas, and around 19 per cent of children use such services in those areas.

Adult workers also live further away from their place of employment than in the past. For example, the National Travel Survey found that the average distance between home and work increased from under 10 kilometres in 1985–1986 to over 13 kilometres in 1998–2000. The mode of transport used varies widely with the distances workers travel to their jobs. In 1998–2000, car commuting trips averaged 15.1 kilometres, local bus trips 8.2 kilometres, rail trips (including London Underground) 31.4 kilometres, bicycle trips 3.8 kilometres, and trips by foot 1.2 kilometres.

The Labour Force Survey (LFS) found that, on average, people in Great Britain took 25 minutes to travel to their place of work in Autumn 2000. People working in London took the longest, at 42 minutes, while people working in Wales and the East Midlands took the shortest time, only 20 minutes. The average time to travel to work has increased by 8 per cent since 1992. The LFS found that a large majority of trips to work are made by car – 70 per cent in Autumn 2000. The next most common way of travelling to work was walking, at 11 per cent in autumn 2000. Public transport (bus, train and underground combined) accounted for 14 per cent of journeys to work in the same period.

International Travel

The number of UK residents travelling abroad has increased enormously during the 1990s, up from 34.3 million in 1993 to 56.8 million in 2000, an increase of 66 per cent. Those aged 25–54 are the most frequent travellers, but international travel has increased in all ages, with the greatest increase in visits occurring in the 55–64 year old age group (Table 12.20). The most popular countries to visit do not vary much with age, with the top two being France and Spain. The USA and Eire are also popular amongst all ages.

Chart **12.20**

Total visits abroad: by age, 1993 and 2000

United Kingdom

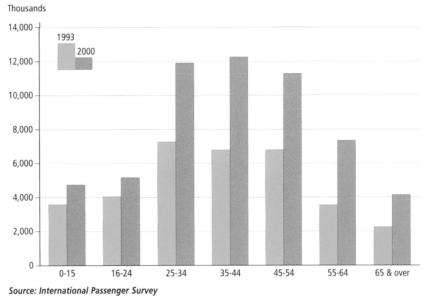

Source: International Passenger Survey

The UK is a net "exporter" of visitors – compared to the 56.8 million visits abroad made by UK residents visited abroad in 2000, 25.2 million overseas residents visited the UK (Table 12.21). Although this latter figure increased markedly since 1981, it levelled off at around 25 million visits a year from the mid 1990s. The numbers of UK citizens visiting abroad, however, continued to increase year on year. Air travel provided the major impetus for growth throughout the period. The number of visitors abroad carried by air increased by over 260 per cent from 1981 to 2000, and continued to increase rapidly in the late 1990s as sea and channel tunnel crossings started to decline in number.

Table **12.21**

International travel: by mode[1]

United Kingdom

Millions

	1981	1986	1991	1996	1998	1999	2000
Visits abroad by UK residents							
Air	11.4	16.4	20.4	27.9	34.3	37.5	41.4
Sea	7.7	8.6	10.4	10.7	10.5	10.4	9.6
Channel Tunnel	.	.	.	3.5	6.1	5.9	5.8
All visits abroad	19.0	24.9	30.8	42.1	50.9	53.9	56.8
Visits to the United Kingdom by overseas residents							
Air	6.9	8.9	11.6	16.3	17.5	17.3	17.8
Sea	4.6	5.0	5.5	6.2	5.1	5.0	4.3
Channel Tunnel	.	.	.	2.7	3.2	3.1	3.1
All visits to the United Kingdom	11.5	13.9	17.1	25.2	25.7	25.4	25.2

1 Mode of travel from, and into, the United Kingdom.
Source: International Passenger Survey, Office for National Statistics

Two-thirds of UK residents travelling abroad in 2000 were on holiday, a figure similar to that seen 20 years ago. However, from 1981 to 2000, the proportion of overseas visitors to the UK on holiday fell from 44 per cent to 37 per cent. At the same time there was an 8 per cent increase in the proportion of those visiting for business reasons. In 2000, around 9 million UK residents (over a sixth of those travelling) visited abroad for business reasons, compared to over 7 million overseas residents who visited the UK for business (nearly one-third of the total visitors).

Attitudes to Transport Issues

There is evidence that people in the UK perceive transport to be an important, and problematic, issue affecting their lives. A recent study by the UK Commission for Integrated Transport in Spring 2001 found that almost two in five people interviewed (in England) spontaneously cited at least one transport related issue, such as traffic congestion, frequency of public transport, shortage of car parking facilities or traffic noise, as being one of the main problems affecting their local area.

Table **12.22**

Impact of different transport policies on own car use, 2000

Great Britain

Percentages

	Might use car even more	Might use car a little less	Might use car quite a bit less	Might give up using car	No difference	All respondents[1]
Gradually doubling the cost of petrol over the next ten years	–	27	25	9	39	100
Greatly improving the reliability of local public transport	–	27	32	6	35	100
Greatly improving long distance rail and coach services	1	29	23	4	43	100
Charging all motorists around £2 each time they enter or drive through a city or town centre at peak times	–	25	26	9	39	100
Charging £1 for every 50 miles motorists travel on motorways	–	20	16	6	58	100

1 All respondents excludes people who do not have a car, and includes 'don't know' and not answered categories.
Source: British Social Attitudes Survey, National Centre for Social Research

There is also a widespread view that reliance on the car should be reduced and public transport should be improved. The British Social Attitudes Survey (BSA) found in 2000 that 75 per cent of those questioned thought it was very or fairly important to cut down on the number of cars on Britain's roads. Over 90 per cent of those questioned thought it very or fairly important to improve public transport. The BSA also asked what impact different transport policies might have on their own car use (Table 12.22). When asked what the impact of "greatly improving" the reliability of local public transport would have on their own car use, 65 per cent of respondents said they would use their cars a little or quite a bit less or might give up using it. Over 60 per cent thought that pricing, either through petrol costs or charging to enter cities or towns, would reduce their car usage.

There is little agreement, however, as to how improvements in public transport should be funded. The BSA gave a number of suggestions for methods of raising money to spend on public transport (Table 12.23). The only measure which did not attract the opposition of more than half of those questioned was cutting in half the spending on new roads. The suggestion attracting the least support was gradually doubling the cost of petrol over the next ten years, which was opposed or strongly opposed by over 80 per cent of those questioned.

Table 12.23

Attitudes towards methods of increasing the funding of public transport[1], 2000

Great Britain
Percentages

	Strongly support	Support	Neither support nor oppose	Oppose	Strongly oppose	Can't choose
Gradually doubling the cost of petrol over the next ten years	1	5	8	41	40	3
Charging all motorists around £2 each time they enter or drive through a city or town centre at peak times	4	24	14	31	22	3
Cutting in half spending on new roads	3	16	25	31	17	5
Cutting in half spending on maintenance of the roads we have already	1	4	13	46	29	4
Charging £1 for every 50 miles motorists travel on motorways	3	22	16	33	21	3
Increasing taxes like VAT that we all pay on goods and services	1	6	14	43	30	3
Increasing road tax for all vehicles	2	13	11	39	30	3
Taxing employers for each car parking space they provide for their employees	4	20	17	32	21	4

1 Respondents who didn't answer are not included.
Source: British Social Attitudes Survey, National Centre for Social Research

Websites

National Statistics	www.statistics.gov.uk
Department for Transport, Local Government and the Regions	www.transtat.dtlr.gov.uk
Police Service of Northern Ireland	www.psni.police.uk
Scottish Executive	www.scotland.gov.uk
Strategic Rail Authority	www.sra.gov.uk
National Centre for Social Research	www.natcen.ac.uk

Contacts

Office for National Statistics

Chapter author	020 7533 5701
Expenditure and Food Survey	020 7533 5756
Household expenditure	020 7533 5999
International Passenger Survey	020 7533 5765
Labour Force Survey	020 7533 5614
Retail Prices Index	020 7533 5874

Department of the Environment, Transport and the Regions

General Queries	020 7944 4847
National Travel Survey	020 7944 3097

Department of the Environment for Northern Ireland	01232 540807
Driving Standards Agency	0115 901 2852
Police Service of Northen Ireland	028 90650222 x 24135
National Centre for Social Research	020 7250 1866
Scottish Executive	0131 244 7255/7256
Strategic Rail Authority	020 7654 6072

Chapter 13

Lifestyles and Social Participation

Home-based activities

- Almost 4.5 million households were paying subscriptions to satellite and 3.3 million to cable television in 2000–01. (Chart 13.2)

Activities outside the home

- The number of cinema admissions in Great Britain more than doubled between 1984 and 2000, to 137 million. (Page 214)

- In 2000, the most popular European holiday destination for UK residents was Spain; the USA was the most popular destination outside Europe. (Table 13.13)

Gambling

- In 1999, 72 per cent of the adult population in Great Britain took part in some gambling activity, mostly on the National Lottery. (Table 13.14)

Communication and technology

- The proportion of households who own a mobile telephone has almost tripled since 1996–97, to reach 47 per cent in 2000–01. (Page 218)

- Forty four per cent of all households in the United Kingdom owned a personal computer in 2000–01. (Page 218)

Citizenship and social participation

- In 2000, 60 per cent of the adult population in Great Britain regarded themselves as belonging to a religion. (Table 13.19)

- The turnout in the June 2001 general election was the lowest since the election in 1918. Only 59 per cent of those registered turned out to vote. (Page 220)

The ways in which people spend their time outside of work have altered significantly over the past few decades. Changes in working patterns as well as technological advances have influenced the amount of time people spend on different activities. These activities are classified into home-based and outside the home activities.

Home-based activities

People spend on average 3 hours a day doing household chores. Advances in technology and the affordability of labour saving devices have led to an increase in ownership of consumer durables and in turn affects the amount of time people spend doing household tasks. In 2000–01, 93 per cent of households in the United Kingdom had a washing machine compared with around 65 per cent in 1970. Over the past 10 years, goods such as microwaves and tumble-dryers have also become more common.

Nowadays almost all households own a television and telephone (98 and 96 per cent of households, respectively). Ownership of media through which people can be entertained at home such as video recorders and compact disc players has also grown rapidly over the last decade. Watching television, visiting or entertaining friends at home and listening to the radio are popular activities for men and women of all ages (Table 13.1). However, gender and age differences exist in participation in other home-based leisure activities. For example, listening to records and tapes declines while gardening increases with age.

The type of television programme people prefer to watch does not vary with age. Drama and light entertainment are the most preferred types of programme in all age groups. Since the early 1990s, the choice of television channels has grown considerably with the introduction of satellite and cable channels. Some of these channels such as *Sky Sports* and *National Geographic* show only specific

Table **13.1**

Participation[1] in home-based leisure activities: by gender and age, 1996–97

United Kingdom   Percentages

	16–19	20–24	25–34	35–44	45–54	55–64	65 and over	All aged 16 and over
Males								
Watching TV	99	99	99	99	99	100	98	99
Visiting/entertaining friends or relations	97	97	97	96	94	94	92	95
Listening to radio	93	92	94	93	92	86	79	89
Listening to records/tapes	97	96	92	86	78	69	54	78
Reading books	51	59	58	61	57	59	58	58
Gardening	20	21	42	55	58	63	62	52
DIY	33	40	66	67	63	61	46	57
Dressmaking/needlework/knitting	4	4	4	3	3	3	3	3
Females								
Watching TV	99	98	99	98	99	99	99	99
Visiting/entertaining friends or relations	98	99	99	97	97	96	94	97
Listening to radio	97	95	92	89	86	83	77	87
Listening to records/tapes	99	96	92	89	79	65	47	77
Reading books	74	71	69	72	73	71	68	71
Gardening	10	21	40	52	58	56	43	45
DIY	16	28	40	38	36	25	13	29
Dressmaking/needlework/knitting	15	23	29	37	44	48	39	36

1 Percentage in each age group participating in each activity in the four weeks before interview.
Sources: General Household Survey, Office for National Statistics; Continuous Household Survey, Northern Ireland Statistics and Research Agency

types of programme. Subscriptions to cable television increased by 94 per cent and subscriptions to satellite by 51 per cent from 1996–97 to 2000–01. In 2000–01, 45 per cent of households had access to non-terrestrial television (by whatever platform) compared with 21 per cent in 1995–96. In 1996–97, social-class differences existed in subscription to satellite and cable television (Chart 13.2). Although these differences remained in 2000–01, subscription rates had increased in all social classes with a particularly large rise among professionals and the unskilled. In 2000–01, rates were highest among managerial and skilled manual, and lower among partly skilled and unskilled manual households.

The increase in ownership of video players over the last two decades has been accompanied by an increase in the number of videocassettes purchased, from around 6 million in 1986 to 114 million in 2000 (Chart 13. 3). Sales value increased from £55 million in 1986 to £1,104 million in 2000. Rentals on the other hand reached a peak in 1989 and then fell until the mid-1990s. However, the value of the rented sector increased from £284 million in 1986 to £444 million in the same period. The best selling video for 2000 was *Toy Story 2* and the most popular rented video was *The Sixth Sense*.

Nine per cent of VCR owners rented at least one video every week, and fewer than half have never rented a video. On average, videocassette recorder (VCR) owners rented ten videos in 2000, although if the non-renters are excluded this rises to over 18. Over half of all viewing of rented videos took place at the weekend (Friday evening, Saturday or Sunday). Saturday was the most common day for viewing with the majority of videos watched between 8pm and 10.30pm. Men are more likely than women to watch videos, particularly during the week. Also, younger people are more likely than older people to watch videos.

Digital Versatile Disc (DVD), which can play music, video and games, was launched in the United Kingdom in April 1998. Since then, both hardware and software sales have increased rapidly. Over 800 thousand DVD players and 17 million discs were sold in 2000 compared with under a quarter of a million players and 4 million disks in the previous year. According to the British Video Association (BVA), the DVD is the fastest growing consumer electronics format of all time, selling faster than the video and audio compact disc (CD) players did at the same stage of their launch. One-fifth of the participants in the 2001 BVA Consumer Research survey said that they were interested in buying a DVD player within the next two years. In 2000, the most popular DVD was *Gladiator*. It sold half a million copies in the first six weeks it was available.

Chart **13.2**

Subscription to satellite and cable television: by social class[1] of head of household, 1996–97 and 2000–01

United Kingdom

Thousands

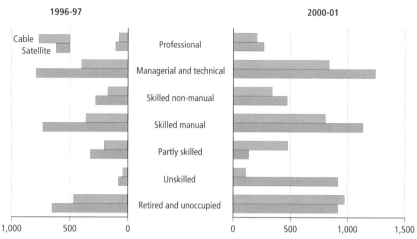

1 See Appendix, Part 13: Social Class.

Source: Family Expenditure Survey, Office for National Statistics

Chart **13.3**

Video rentals and purchases

United Kingdom

Millions

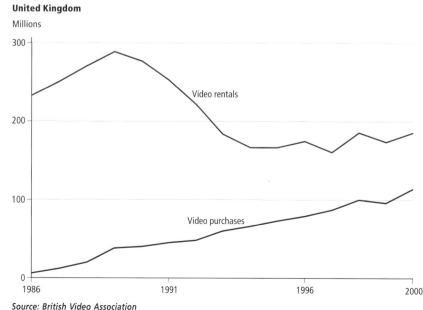

Source: British Video Association

Chart **13.4**

Sales[1] of CDs, LPs, cassettes, and singles[2]

United Kingdom

Millions

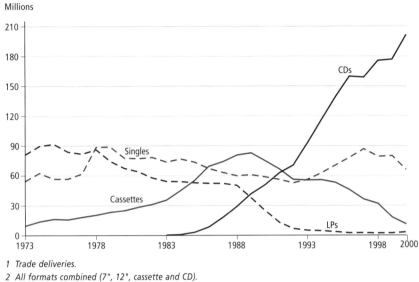

1 Trade deliveries.
2 All formats combined (7", 12", cassette and CD).
Source: British Phonographic Industry

Record company sales rose by 3 per cent in 2000. While CD sales continue to increase, sales of music cassettes continue to fall (Chart 13.4). Technological advances led to the introduction of the MiniDisc in 1996 but sales of pre-recorded MiniDiscs plateaued at 0.3 millions by the end of 2000. Sales of singles (all formats) decreased by 17 per cent between 1999 and 2000 while CD album sales increased by 9 per cent. The decline in singles sales is attributed to a combination of fewer singles retailing at £1.99 in their week of release and to a reduction in the number of individual big sellers. In the albums market, however, there was a proliferation of big sellers headed by the Beatles compilation, *1*.

Radio listening is a popular leisure activity. In 2000, the majority of listening to radio was done at home (70 per cent), 17 per cent at the workplace and 12 per cent in the car. Preference for radio stations varied with age. Young people (15–34 years) tended to prefer listening to BBC Radio 1 and independent local radio, while older listeners (over 55 years old) were more likely to listen to Radio 2 and 4, along with local and regional networks (Table 13.5).

Table **13.5**

Radio listening: by age, 2000

United Kingdom

Percentages[1]

	Under 15	15–24	25–34	35–44	45–54	55–64	65 and over	All
Radio 1	16	27	21	11	5	2	1	11
Radio 2	3	2	5	10	17	21	22	12
Radio 3	–	–	–	1	1	2	3	1
Radio 4	2	1	4	9	14	17	19	10
Radio 5 Live	2	2	4	5	5	4	4	4
BBC Local/National[2]	3	2	3	6	10	18	26	11
Other National[3]	6	6	8	8	8	9	10	8
Any ILR station[4]	67	57	53	50	38	25	14	41
Any Other	2	2	2	2	2	2	2	2
Total hours of listening per week (=100%)	9:41	19:17	20:28	21:15	22:53	23:32	22:26	19:50

1 Percentage of listeners in age group listening to each station.
2 Includes Radios Scotland, Wales, Cymru and Ulster.
3 Includes Classic FM, Virgin 1215, Talk Radio UK, Atlantic 252.
4 Independent local and regional radio network.
Source: RAJAR/IPSOS-RSL

Many people enjoy reading during their free time. The General Household and Continuous Household surveys found that in 1996–1997, 71 per cent of women and 58 per cent of men aged 16 and over had read a book in the four weeks prior to being interviewed. Nevertheless, there has been a general decline in the number of books issued by libraries in the United Kingdom. This number has fallen from 643 million in 1984–85 to 480 million in 1999–00 with the greatest fall being for adult fiction books. However, over the same period the number of junior issues has stayed reasonably constant. The number of books issued per head of population has also decreased considerably over the last 14 years (Chart 13.6). The average number of fiction books issued to adults has declined from around 7 in 1981–82 to around 4 in 1999–00. However, the number of junior books issued per head has remained relatively stable over the last 20 years.

The number of library service points (i.e. any library, static or mobile, through which the public library authority provides a service to the general public) has fallen between 1990 and 2000 with the majority of these cuts being in institutions not covered by agency agreements (e.g. old people's homes). In the last ten years, for the UK as a whole, there has been a fall of 3 per cent in the number of service points open for 10 hours per week or more, and a substantial fall, from 67 to 18, in the number open for 60 hours per week or more. Despite that, the proportion of adults who hold a public library ticket has remained stable, at an estimated 58 per cent, over recent years, although only 32 per cent of the total population are currently recorded as active borrowers. The Public Library User Survey 2000–01 found that, on average, 44 per cent of adult borrowers take home one or two books, while 24 per cent take home five or more. The same survey showed that, on average, 30 per cent of adult public library users were aged 65 and over.

The proportion of people reading a national daily newspaper in Great Britain has fallen since the early 1980s (Table 13.7). The most popular national newspaper among adults is *The Sun*. This newspaper is particularly popular among young people (15 to 24 years old). *The Daily Telegraph* and *The Times* are the most popular broadsheet newspapers with *The Daily Telegraph* more popular among older people. Men are more likely than women to read a newspaper while women are more likely than men to read a magazine.

Chart **13.6**

Library books issued per person: by type of book

United Kingdom

Number of books per person

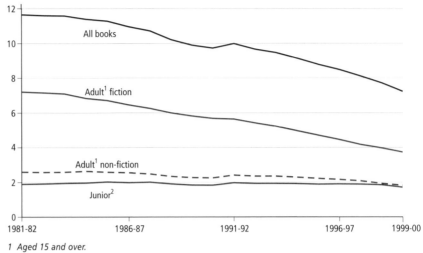

1 Aged 15 and over.
2 Aged under 15.

Source: Library & Information Statistics Unit, Loughborough University

Table **13.7**

Reading of national daily newspapers

Great Britain
Percentages[1]

	1993/94	1995/96	1997/98	1998/99	1999/00	2000/01
The Sun	22	22	21	21	21	20
Daily Mirror	16	14	13	14	13	12
Daily Mail	10	10	11	12	12	12
Daily Express	8	7	6	5	5	4
Daily Star	5	4	4	5	3	3
The Daily Telegraph	6	6	5	4	5	5
The Times	3	4	4	4	4	3
The Guardian	3	3	3	2	2	2
The Independent	2	2	2	1	1	1
Financial Times	2	2	1	1	1	1
Any national daily newspaper[2]	60	60	56	55	54	53

1 From July to June each year.
2 Includes the above newspapers plus The Daily Record, The Sporting Life and Racing Post.
Source: National Readership Surveys Ltd

Table **13.8**

Attendance[1] at selected events[2]: by socio-economic group, 2000–01

Great Britain   Percentages

	Managerial/ professional	Other non-manual	Skilled manual	Semi-skilled manual	Unskilled manual
Sporting events	24	20	18	15	7
Plays	29	17	8	6	5
Opera	9	3	2	1	1
Ballet	7	3	1	1	1
Contemporary dance	4	2	1	1	1
Classical Music	17	8	4	2	2
Concerts	19	17	13	9	5
Art Galleries/Exhibitions	30	18	8	6	7

1 Percentage of resident population aged 15 and over attending 'these days'.
2 See Appendix, Part 13: Cultural events.
Source: Target Group Index, BMRB International

Chart **13.9**

Cinema attendance[1]: by age

Great Britain

Percentages

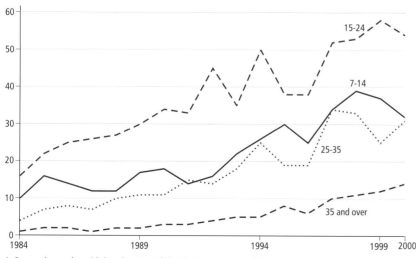

1 Respondents who said that they attend the cinema once a month or more.
Source: CAA/CAVIAR

Activities outside the home

A survey carried out in the UK in 2000–01 found that 15 per cent of the adult UK population said that these days they attended plays or art galleries/exhibitions while 8 per cent went to classical music concerts. The type of events people attended varied according to gender and socio-economic status. For example, a higher proportion of women than men attended ballet. Also, more people in the managerial and professional socio-economic group attended any of the types of event shown in Table 13.8 than did those belonging to other socio-economic groups.

Apart from cinema attendance, the proportion of adults going to particular cultural events has remained relatively constant over the last decade or so. The number of cinema admissions in Great Britain reached 137 million in 2000, more than double the total in 1984. This increase may be related to the development and expansion of multiplex cinemas across the country. There has also been a growth in the number of PG films available making cinema-going more available. Nevertheless, the present cinema attendance figures are lower than those in the early 1950s, which topped the 1 billion mark.

In 2000, the top box office film in the United Kingdom was *Toy Story 2* followed by *Gladiator* and *Chicken Run*. Cinema attendance varies with age and gender. Men tend to go to the cinema more frequently than women. Also, cinema-going is most popular among younger people (15–24 years). Although there has been a considerable increase in cinema-going across all age groups since 1984, this increase was greatest for the 15–24 years age group (Chart 13.9). However, there has also been a substantial rise in cinema attendance among older people (aged 45 and over) – the numbers going once a month or more increased by almost 500 per cent between 1990 and 2000.

The 1998 UK Day Visits Survey collected information about round domestic trips made for leisure purposes by GB residents. The majority of those trips were to towns/cities (72 per cent) while 22 per cent were to the countryside and 6 per cent to the coast. The most common activities on a day trip were: eating out, shopping, visiting friends and relatives and entertainment. The popularity of each of these activities varied according to the type of place visited. For example, 21 per cent of those who visited a city/town did some shopping during their trip. However, only 5 per cent of those who visited the countryside or the seaside did some shopping. Twelve per cent of visits to the countryside and 13 per cent of those to the seaside involved walking/rambling, while only 1 per cent of those who visited a city/town did.

Leisure activities which people do occasionally or while on holiday are considered as touristic activities. In the UK in 1999, there were 6,215 tourist attractions, and 84 per cent of visitors were UK residents. The popularity of certain museums in Great Britain has increased considerably over the past two decades. In 1999, the British Museum, Tate Gallery and National Gallery had approximately twice as many visitors as in 1981. In contrast, the Natural History Museum and Science Museum, which both introduced admissions charges in the late 1980s have seen a decrease in the number of their visitors since 1981. However, both museums now make no admission charge. In April 2000, the Tate Gallery was renamed Tate Britain and a new gallery was opened in London called the Tate Modern. The Millennium Experience at Greenwich attracted over 6.5 million people through 2000, making it the most popular pay-to-visit attraction in the UK.

Participation in sport activities remains a popular way of spending leisure time. The proportion of young people taking part in regular physical activity has remained unchanged between 1994 and 1999. In 1994, 87 per cent of young people took part in at least one sports activity at least ten times in the 12 months prior to the survey. This figure remained the same in 1999. The survey also found that 55 per cent of those aged 6 to 16 had been cycling and 50 per cent swimming in their free time. Football was the most popular activity for boys and swimming for girls (Chart 13.10).

Chart **13.10**

Top ten sports participated in by young people outside lessons[1]: by gender, 1999

England

Percentages

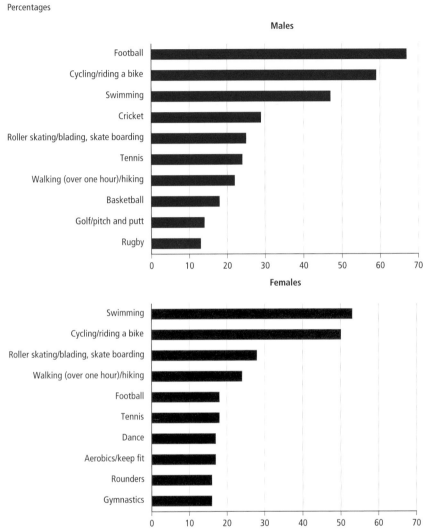

1 Those participating at least 10 times in the 12 months leading up to the survey.

Source: Sport England-Young People and Sports in England, 1999 (MORI Social Research)

Table **13.11**

Participation in the top ten sports, games and physical activities: by socio-economic group[1], 1996–97

United Kingdom   Percentages

	Professional	Employers and managers	Intermediate and junior non-manual	Skilled manual and own account non-professional	Semi-skilled manual and personal service	Unskilled manual	All aged 16 and over[2]
Walking	56	48	46	44	39	33	44
Swimming	23	19	17	11	11	6	15
Keep fit/Yoga	14	12	17	7	9	5	12
Cue sports	10	10	8	15	9	7	11
Cycling	19	12	9	11	10	7	11
Weight training	10	5	6	5	3	2	5
Football	5	4	3	6	3	3	5
Golf	11	9	4	5	3	1	5
Running	9	6	4	4	2	2	5
Tenpin bowls/skittles	4	3	4	3	2	1	3
At least one activity[3]	63	52	48	45	37	24	46

1 Socio-economic group is based on the person's current or most recent job.

2 Includes full-time students, members of the Armed Forces, those who have never worked, and those whose job was inadequately described.

3 Includes those activities not separately listed.

Source: General Household Survey, Office for National Statistics; Continuous Household Survey, Northern Ireland Statistics and Research Agency

Chart **13.12**

Domestic tourism: by year

United Kingdom

Millions

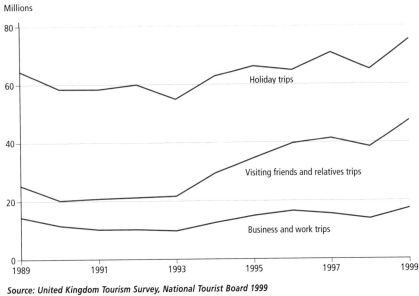

Source: United Kingdom Tourism Survey, National Tourist Board 1999

In 1996–97, the most common physical or sport activity in the United Kingdom was walking. Around 44 per cent of the population said they had been walking or rambling in the four weeks prior to interview. There are socio-economic differences in sport participation. Over three-fifths of professional people carried out some physical activity during their leisure time compared with under a quarter of unskilled manual workers (Table 13.11).

Domestic tourism grew substantially in the 1990s. From 1995 to 1999, domestic tourism trips increased from 121 to 146 millions (Chart 13.12). The biggest increase (88 per cent) was in visiting friends and relatives while holiday trips increased by 17 per cent. Trips for the purposes of business and work increased by 8 per cent.

For holidays abroad, Spain was the most popular holiday destination for UK residents in 2000. Although France was the second most popular destination, its share of all holiday visits abroad has declined from 27 per cent in 1981 to 18 per cent in 2000 (Table 13.13). The most popular destination outside Europe was the United States which accounted for 7 per cent of all holiday visits in 2000. Other long haul destinations such as the Caribbean and North Africa have become more popular in recent years. Younger people (aged 25 to 34 years) are most likely to travel furthest, with almost a quarter of all holidays taken by this group being to destinations outside western Europe.

The accommodation used while on holiday has changed over the past 20 years. This is partly due to the greater variety of choice. In 1971, a hotel or motel made up more than three-fifths of all accommodation used by UK tourists abroad but by the mid-1990s this had declined to under a half. Rented villas/flats became much more popular over the same period.

Gambling

The 1999 British Gambling Prevalence Survey (BGPS) showed that almost three-quarters of the population (about 33 million adults) took part in some gambling activity and over half had gambled in the week prior to the interview.

There has been a change in the nature of gambling mainly due to the introduction of the National Lottery and to the increasing availability of other forms of gambling such as spread betting and gambling on the Internet.

By far the most popular gambling activity is the National Lottery Draw. The BGPS found that two-thirds of the population had bought a National Lottery ticket in the last year and nearly half the population had played in the week before being interviewed. In addition to the National Lottery, the more frequent gambling activities were: buying scratch cards, playing on fruit machines, betting on horses and making a private bet with a friend.

Men are more likely than women both to gamble and to participate in a greater number of gambling activities. Bingo is the only gambling activity in which women are more likely than men to participate. Gambling is most popular with people aged 25 to 54 (Table 13.14).

Table **13.13**

Holidays[1] abroad: by destination

United Kingdom				Percentages
	1971	1981	1991	2000
Spain[2]	34	22	21	28
France	16	27	26	18
United States	1	6	7	7
Greece	5	7	8	7
Italy	9	6	4	4
Portugal	3	3	5	4
Irish Republic	..	4	3	5
Turkey	..	–	1	2
Netherlands	4	2	4	2
Cyprus	1	1	2	3
Belgium	..	2	2	2
Germany	3	3	3	2
Malta	..	3	2	1
Austria	6	3	2	1
Other countries	19	14	12	14
All destinations (=100%)				
(millions)	4.2	13.1	20.8	36.7

1 A visit made for holiday purposes. Business trips and visits to friends or relatives are excluded.

2 Excludes the Canary Islands prior to 1981.

Source: International Passenger Survey, Office for National Statistics

Table **13.14**

Participation[1] in gambling activities: by age, 1999

Great Britain								Percentages
	16–24	25–34	35–44	45–54	55–64	65–74	75 and over	All[2]
National Lottery Draw	52	71	72	72	69	61	45	65
Scratchcards	36	32	23	17	16	11	6	22
Fruit machines	32	22	15	8	6	3	1	14
Horse races	12	19	15	14	11	9	5	13
Private bets	21	18	11	10	6	5	3	11
Football pools	4	9	8	11	13	10	6	9
Another lottery	8	9	8	9	9	8	6	8
Bingo	7	7	7	6	7	9	10	7
Dog races	6	7	4	4	2	1	1	4
Other Betting with a Bookmaker[3]	5	5	3	2	2	1	..	3
Table games in a casino	4	5	3	2	1	..	..	3
Any gambling	66	78	77	78	74	66	52	72

1 Respondents aged 16 and over who said that they had participated in gambling in the past year.

2 Includes those for whom age could not be determined.

3 Betting other than on horse or dog racing.

Source: British Gambling Prevalence Survey, National Centre for Social Research

Chart **13.15**

Ownership of mobile phones: by income quintile group, 1996–97 and 2000–01

United Kingdom

Percentages

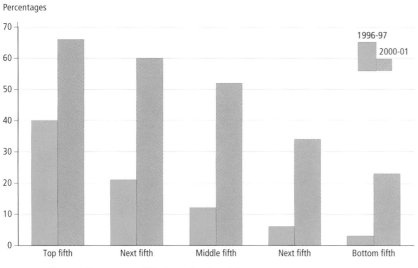

Source: Family Expenditure Survey, Office for National Statistics

Chart **13.16**

Use of the Internet[1]: by age and gender, July 2001

Great Britain

Percentages

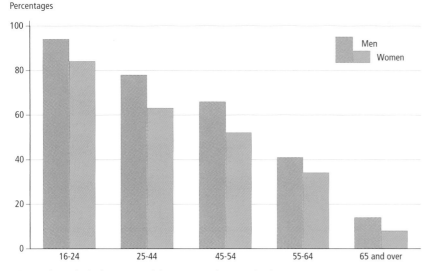

1 Respondents who had ever accessed the Internet at home or elsewhere.

Source: Omnibus Survey, Office for National Statistics

Communication and technology

The rapid developments in communication and technology have dramatically changed people's living and work patterns. The number of communication tools available have increased as mobile telephones, email and the Internet have become more affordable. Technological advances have not however affected the use of more traditional methods of communication such as letter writing. The number of letters posted has increased year on year since 1981 and almost 20 billion were posted in 2000.

Home telephones have become commonplace over the last two decades. In 1970, around 35 per cent of all households in the United Kingdom had a home telephone while around 95 per cent now do so. Mobile telephones have more recently become popular. They are not only used to talk to other people but also to send and receive text messages or to access the Internet.

The proportion of households with at least one mobile telephone (either *pay as you go* or subscription) has almost tripled from 17 per cent in 1996–97, to 47 per cent in 2000–01. Mobile phone ownership is related to income. In 2000–01, over two thirds of people in the top income group had a mobile phone compared with under a quarter of those in the bottom group. However, while ownership has grown in all groups, the rate of increase has been highest in the lowest income group (Chart 13.15).

More than two-fifths of all households in the United Kingdom owned a personal computer (PC) in 2000–01. This represents a substantial rise in computer ownership from 1985 when only 13 per cent of the population owned a PC. Households in the South East, South West and London. Those belonging to the professional socio-economic class are the most likely to own a PC. In 2000–01, 70 per cent of households whose head belonged to the managerial/technical class owned a PC, whilst only 39 per cent of households headed by someone with a partly skilled occupation were in the same position.

According to the National Statistics July 2001 Omnibus Survey, 40 per cent of adults had accessed the Internet in the month prior to the Survey. Women are still less likely to have ever accessed the Internet than men – 47 per cent of women have used the Internet at least once, compared to 56 per cent of men – but age is the main determinant (Chart 13.16). For example, over nine out of ten men aged 16–24 have ever used the Internet, whereas less than one in seven of those aged 65 and over have done so.

Seventy one per cent of those who had used the Internet for private use had used it as a tool for sending and receiving email and 74 per cent used it to gather information on goods and services. The main reason for not using the Internet is a general lack of interest rather than concerns about the connection cost or its content (Table 13.17).

Citizenship and social participation

Serving the community through volunteering is a long-established tradition in the United Kingdom. This is also recognised internationally and to highlight the value and role of volunteering, the UN established 2001 as the International Year of the Volunteer.

The British Social Attitudes Survey has researched participation in voluntary activities by Great Britain residents. Voluntary work was defined as an unpaid activity of benefit or service to the community or people other than friends or family. The survey found that in 1998 33 per cent of the adult population (over 18 years old) reported that they had done unpaid voluntary work at least once in the last year. The least supported voluntary activities were the political ones. While many adults participated in voluntary activities only a small proportion of the population had done voluntary work on more than six occasions in the previous 12 months. The BSA also found that, in general, people believe that it is a good thing to do some voluntary work. However, they also believe that society relies too much on volunteers (Table 13.18).

Table **13.17**

Reasons for not using the Internet

Great Britain		Percentages
	2000[1]	2001[2]
Lack of interest	32	42
No need	22	16
Lack of confidence/skills	21	16
No computer or access	16	26
Cannot afford it	8	7
Feels too old	8	9
No time	5	4
Do not want to use it	4	11
Have not got round to it yet	3	6
Poor opinion of the Internet	2	3
Health problems make it difficult	1	1
Other reasons	3	2

1 At October 2000

2 At July 2001

Note: Percentages do not add up to 100 per cent as respondents may give more than one answer

Source: Omnibus Survey, Office for National Statistics

Table **13.18**

Attitudes towards voluntary work and charities[1]: by age, 1996

Great Britain							Percentages
	18–24	25–34	35–44	45–54	55–64	65–74	75 and over
Doing voluntary work is a good thing for volunteers because it makes them feel they are contributing to society	81	66	75	79	84	84	84
As a society we rely too much on volunteers	48	54	57	64	58	62	52
Everyone has a duty to do voluntary work at some time in their lives	36	19	27	26	32	43	42
I would rather donate money to a charity than give up my time for it	29	24	23	26	16	29	31
Nowadays charities can only do their job properly if they are run by paid professionals, not volunteers	17	19	15	24	17	27	35

1 Those who said they 'agree strongly' or 'agree' with each statement.

Source: British Social Attitudes Survey, National Centre for Social Research

Religion is an important part of many people's lives. It involves contact with other individuals and participation in the local community. In 2000, 60 per cent of the population claimed to belong to a specific religion with 55 per cent being Christian (Table 13.19). However, half of all adults aged 18 and over who belonged to a religion have never attended a religious service.

The majority of people in the United Kingdom use their right to vote at general elections. However, the last three decades have witnessed significant fluctuations in the percentage of people who voted in general elections. The turnout in the June 2001 election was the lowest since the election in 1918 (with none of the unusual post-war circumstances). Only 59 per cent of those registered turned out to vote in 2001 compared to 76 per cent in 1979. In the last election, 41 per cent of all votes went to the Labour Party.

Age differences in turnout were evident in the last election. In general people who were under 34 were less likely to vote than those in older age groups (Table 13.20). This voting behaviour may be linked to young people's attitudes. In 1998 the British Social Attitudes Survey, found that a third of those aged 18 to 24 said everyone has an obligation to vote, compared with four-fifths of the 65 and over age group. The results from the same survey suggest that this attitude to voting held by young people may not change as they get older. According to the Young People's Social Attitudes Survey, political interest among young people was low in 1994 and even lower in 1998 when only one in three teenagers aged 12 to 19 years old expressed an interest in politics. Although interest in politics has also decreased among adults, they reported more interest in politics than their younger counterparts. However, people in education were more likely to be interested in politics. Teenagers were also less likely than older adults to have formed an attachment to a particular political party. This attachment was crucially influenced by the political affiliation of their parents.

Table 13.19

Belonging to a religion[1]

Great Britain

Percentages

	1996	2000
Church of England/Anglican	29.3	29.8
Roman Catholic	8.9	9.2
Christian – no denomination	4.7	6.3
Presbyterian/Free-Presbyterian/Church of Scotland	3.8	3.5
Baptist or Methodist	3.0	3.4
Other Protestant/other Christian	2.2	2.5
United Reform Church	0.8	0.5
Brethren	0.1	–
Islam/Muslim	1.8	2.0
Hindu	0.6	1.0
Jewish	0.3	0.8
Sikh	0.2	0.4
Other non-Christian	0.4	0.4
Buddhist	0.5	0.1
Refusal/not answered/didn't know	0.8	0.6
None	42.6	39.5

1 Respondents were asked 'Do you regard yourself as belonging to any particular religion?'.
Source: British Social Attitudes Survey, National Centre for Social Research

Table 13.20

Voting[1] turnout: by age and gender

Great Britain

Percentages

	1970		1983		1997		2001	
	Males	**Females**	**Males**	**Females**	**Males**	**Females**	**Males**	**Females**
18–24	67	66	74	73	56	64	60	46
25–34	74	77	76	79	67	70	59	56
35–44	81	84	87	88	77	78	66	74
45–54	86	85	88	90	83	86	76	81
55–59	88	86	89	93	90	87	79	82
60–64	79	84	82	90	87	88	80	80
65 and over	93	84	86	82	87	85	87	87

1 See Appendix, Part 13: Parliamentary elections.
Source: British Election Study, National Centre for Social Research; University of Essex

Websites

National Statistics	www.statistics.gov.uk
Department for Culture, Media and Sport	www.culture.gov.uk
National Centre for Social Research	www.natcen.ac.uk
British Election Study	www.essex.ac.uk/bes
Northern Ireland Statistics and Research Agency	www.nisra.gov.uk
British Video Association	www.bva.org.uk
British Broadcasting Corporation	www.bbc.co.uk
British Film Industry	www.bfi.org.uk
British Phonographic Industry	www.bpi.co.uk
Library & Information Statistics Unit	www.lboro.ac.uk/departments/dils/lisu
Cinema Advertising Association	www.carlton.screen.com
Centre for Research into Elections and Social Trends	www.crest.ox.ac.uk
Sports England	www.sportengland.org
English Tourism Council	www.staruk.org.uk
The Electoral Commission	www.electoralcommission.gov.uk

Contacts

Office for National Statistics

Chapter author	020 7533 5781
Family Expenditure Survey	020 7533 5756
General Household Survey	020 7533 5444
International Passenger Survey	020 7533 5765
Omnibus Survey	020 7533 5321
Omnibus Survey (Internet access)	020 7533 5878
British Broadcasting Corporation	020 7765 1064
British Election Study	01206 687 3567
British Phonographic Industry	020 7851 4000
English Tourism Council	020 8563 3011
British Video Association	020 7436 0041
Cinema Advertising Association	020 7534 6363
Department for Culture, Media and Sport	020 7211 6409
Library & Information Statistics Unit	01509 223 071
National Readership Surveys	020 7632 2915
National Centre for Social Research	020 7250 1866
Northern Ireland Statistics and Research Agency	028 9034 8246
Sport England	020 7273 1500

References and further reading

Those published by The Stationery Office are available from the addresses shown on the back cover of *Social Trends*.

General

Regional Trends, The Stationery Office

Social Focus on Families, The Stationery Office

Social Focus on Older People, The Stationery Office

Social Focus on Men, The Stationery Office

Social Focus on Women and Men, The Stationery Office

1: Population

Annual Report of the Registrar General for Northern Ireland, The Stationery Office

Annual Report of the Registrar General for Scotland, General Register Office for Scotland

Asylum Statistics – United Kingdom, Home Office

Birth statistics (Series FM1), The Stationery Office

Control of Immigration: Statistics, United Kingdom, The Stationery Office

Demographic Statistics, Eurostat

Demographic Yearbook, United Nations

Health Statistics Quarterly, The Stationery Office

International Migration Statistics (Series MN), The Stationery Office

Key Population and Vital Statistics (Series VS/PP1), The Stationery Office

Mid-year Population Estimates, England and Wales (Series PP1), The Stationery Office

Mid-year Population Estimates, Northern Ireland, Northern Ireland Statistics and Research Agency

Mid-year Population Estimates, Scotland, General Register Office for Scotland

Migration Statistics, Eurostat

Mortality Statistics for England and Wales (Series DH1, 2, 3, 4), The Stationery Office

National Population Projections, UK (Series PP2), The Stationery Office

Patterns and Trends in International Migration in Western Europe, Eurostat

Persons Granted British Citizenship – United Kingdom, Home Office

Population and Projections for areas within Northern Ireland, Northern Ireland Statistics and Research Agency

Population Projections for Wales (sub-national), National Assembly for Wales/ Welsh Office

Population Projections, Scotland (for Administrative Areas), General Register Office for Scotland

Population Trends, The Stationery Office

Regional Trends, The Stationery Office

Social Focus on Ethnic Minorities, The Stationery Office

Social Focus on Older People, The Stationery Office

Social Focus on Women and Men, The Stationery Office

Social Focus on Young People, The Stationery Office

The State of World Population, UNFPA

World Population Prospects: The 2000 Revision, United Nations

World Statistics Pocketbook, United Nations

Regional Trends, The Stationery Office

Social Focus on Families, The Stationery Office

Social Focus on Older People, The Stationery Office

Social Focus on Men, The Stationery Office

Social Focus on Women and Men, The Stationery Office

2: Households & Families.

Abortion Statistics (Series AB), The Stationery Office

Annual Report of the Registrar General for Northern Ireland, The Stationery Office

Annual Report of the Registrar General for Scotland, General Register Office for Scotland

Birth statistics (Series FM1), The Stationery Office

Birth statistics: historical series, 1837–1983 (Series FM1), The Stationery Office

British Social Attitudes, Ashgate Publishing

Housing in England 1999/00: Survey of English Housing, The Stationery Office

Human Fertilisation and Embryology Authority Annual Report, Human Fertilisation and Embryology Authority

Key Population and Vital Statistics (Series VS/PP1), The Stationery Office

Living in Britain: Results from the General Household Survey, The Stationery Office

Marriage, divorce and adoption statistics (Series FM2), The Stationery Office

Marriage and divorce statistics 1837–1983 (Series FM2), The Stationery Office

Population Trends, The Stationery Office

Personal Relationships and Marriage Expectations: Evidence from the 1998 British Household Panel Study, Institute for Social and Economic Research, University of Essex

Projections of Households in England to 2021, Department for Transport, Local Government and the Regions

Social Focus on Children, The Stationery Office

Social Focus on Ethnic Minorities, The Stationery Office

Social Focus on Families, The Stationery Office

Social Focus on Older People, The Stationery Office

Social Focus on Women and Men, The Stationery Office

Social Focus on Young People, The Stationery Office

Teenage Pregnancy, Report by the Social Exclusion Unit, The Stationery Office

The British Population, Oxford University Press

The Divorced and Who Divorces? ESRC Research Centre for Analysis of Social Exclusion

The Fragmenting Family: Does it matter?, The Institute for Economic Affairs

The Legacy of Parental Divorce, ESRC Research Centre for Analysis of Social Exclusion

3: Education and Training

Adult Literacy in Britain, The Stationery Office

Annual Survey of Trends in Education (Spring 2001), National Foundation for Educational Research, Digest No.10

Family Learning: a survey of current practice, OfSTED

Homework Learning from practice, OfSTED

Fourth Survey of parents of three and four year old children and their use of early years services (Summer 1999 to Summer 2001), National Centre for Social Research for Department for Education and Skills

Research Briefing: The effects of the selective system of secondary education in Northern Ireland, Department of Education, Northern Ireland, RB 4/2000

Statistical First Release: Youth Cohort Study: The Activities and Experiences of 16 year olds: England and Wales. SFR 02/2001, The Stationery Office

4: Labour Market

How Exactly is Unemployment Measured?, Office for National Statistics

Labour Force Survey Historical Supplement, Office for National Statistics

Labour Force Survey Quarterly Bulletin, Office for National Statistics

Labour Market Quarterly Report, Office for National Statistics

Labour Market Trends, The Stationery Office

Northern Ireland Labour Force Survey, Department of Enterprise, Trade and Investment, Northern Ireland

Northern Ireland Labour Force Survey Historical Supplement, Department of Enterprise, Trade and Investment, Northern Ireland

Social Focus on Older People, The Stationery Office

Social Focus on Women and Men, The Stationery Office

The Determinants of Promotion in Britain: evidence from panel data. Working paper 99–6, ESRC Research Centre on Micro-Social Change, Essex

The Search for Success: Do the Unemployed Find Stable Employment? Institute for Social and Economic Research, University of Essex

The State of Working Britain, Paul Cregg and Jonathan Wadsworth. Manchester University Press. 1999

5: Income and Wealth

British Social Attitudes, Ashgate Publishing

Changing Households: The British Household Panel Survey, Institute for Social and Economic Research

Economic Trends, The Stationery Office

Eurostat National Accounts ESA, Eurostat

Family Resources Survey, Corporate Document Services

Fiscal Studies, Institute for Fiscal Studies

For Richer, For Poorer, Institute for Fiscal Studies

Households Below Average Income, 1994/5 – 1999/00, Corporate Document Services

Income and Wealth. The latest evidence, Joseph Rowntree Foundation

Inland Revenue Statistics, The Stationery Office

Labour Market Trends (incorporating Employment Gazette), The Stationery Office

Monitoring Poverty and Social Exclusion, Joseph Rowntree Foundation

National Accounts, Main Aggregates, OECD

New Earnings Survey, The Stationery Office

Poverty and Social Exclusion in Britain, 2000, Joseph Rowntree Foundation, York

Regional Trends, The Stationery Office

Social Security, Departmental Report, The Stationery Office

Social Security Statistics, The Stationery Office

Tax/Benefit Model Tables, Department of Social Security

The Community Budget: the facts in figures, Commission of the European Communities

The Distribution of Wealth in the UK, Institute for Fiscal Studies

The Income of Ethnic Minorities, Institute for Social and Economic Research

The Pensioners' Incomes Series, Department for work and Pensions

United Kingdom National Accounts (The ONS Blue Book), The Stationery Office

6: Expenditure

Changing student finances: income, expenditure and the take-up of student loans among full-time higher education students in 1998/99, DfES Research Report 213, The Stationery Office

Consumer Trends, The Stationery Office

Economic Trends, The Stationery Office

Family Spending, The Stationery Office

Financial Statistics, The Stationery Office

Focus on Consumer Price Indices (formerly known as Business Monitor MM23) www.statistics.gov.uk/products/p867.asp

In Brief: Payment Markets Brief, Association for Payment Clearing Services

Plastic Card Review, Association for Payment Clearing Services

Statistical Yearbook, Credit Card Research Group

United Kingdom National Accounts (The ONS Blue Book), The Stationery Office

7: Health

The Annual Report of the Registrar General for Northern Ireland, Northern Ireland Statistics and Research Agency

Annual Report of the Registrar General for Scotland, General Register Office for Scotland

Smoking, Drinking and Drug Use among Young People in 2000, Department of Health press release, www.doh.gov/public/statpntables.htm

Cancer Trends in England and Wales 1950–1999, The Stationery Office

Community Statistics, Department of Health, Social Services and Public Safety, Northern Ireland

Health in Scotland. The Annual Report of the Chief Medical Officer on the State of Scotland's Health, Scottish Executive

Health Statistics Quarterly, The Stationery Office

Health Statistics Wales, National Assembly for Wales

Health Survey for England, The Stationery Office

Infant Feeding Survey 2000, The Stationery Office

Key Health Statistics from General Practice 1998, Office for National Statistics

Living in Britain: results from the 1998 General Household Survey, The Stationery Office

National Food Survey 2000, The Stationery Office

On the State of the Public Health. The Annual Report of the Chief Medical Officer of the Department of Health, The Stationery Office

Population Trends, The Stationery Office

Psychiatric morbidity survey among adults living in private households 2000, The Stationery Office

Report of the Chief Medical Officer, Department of Health, Social Services, and Public Safety

Social Focus on Men, The Stationery Office

Scottish Health Statistics, Information and Statistics Division, NHS Scotland

Statistical Publications on Aspects of Health and Personal Social Services Activity in England (various), Department of Health

Trends in life expectancy by social class – an update, Health Statistics Quarterly 2, Hattersley L, Office for National Statistics, The Stationery Office

Welsh Health: Annual Report of the Chief Medical Officer, National Assembly for Wales

World Health Statistics, World Health Organisation

8: Social Protection

Annual News Releases (various), Scottish Executive

Community Statistics for Northern Ireland, Department of Health, Social Services and Public Safety, Northern Ireland

Department of Health Departmental Report, The Stationery Office

Dimensions of the Voluntary Sector, Charities Aid Foundation

ESSPROS manual 1996, Eurostat

Family Resources Survey, 1999–2000, Corporate Document Services

Health and Personal Social Services Statistics for England, The Stationery Office

Hospital Episode Statistics for England, Department of Health

Hospital Statistics for Northern Ireland, Department of Health, Social Services and Public Safety, Northern Ireland

Health Statistics Wales, National Assembly for Wales

Laing's Healthcare Market Review 2001–2002, Laing & Buisson Publications Ltd.

Scottish Community Care Statistics, Scottish Executive

Scottish Health Statistics, National Health Service in Scotland, Common Services Agency

Social Protection Expenditure and Receipts, Eurostat

Social Security Departmental Report, The Stationery Office

Social Security Statistics, The Stationery Office

Social Services Statistics Wales, National Assembly for Wales

Statistical Publications on aspects of Health and Personal Social Services Activity in England (various), Department of Health

9: Crime and Justice

A Commentary on Northern Ireland Crime Statistics, The Stationery Office

British Crime Survey, Home Office

Chief Constable's Annual Report, Royal Ulster Constabulary

Civil Judicial Statistics, Scotland, The Stationery Office

Costs, Sentencing Profiles and the Scottish Criminal Justice System, Scottish Executive

Crime and the quality of life: public perceptions and experiences of crime in Scotland, Scottish Executive

Criminal Statistics, England and Wales, The Stationery Office

Crown Prosecution Service, Annual Report, The Stationery Office

Digest 4: Information on the Criminal Justice System in England and Wales, Home Office

Digest of Information on the Northern Ireland Criminal Justice System 3, The Stationery Office

Home Office Annual Report and Accounts, The Stationery Office

Home Office Research Findings, Home Office

Home Office Statistical Bulletins, Home Office

Judicial Statistics, England and Wales, The Stationery Office

Local Authority Performance Indicators, Volume 3, Audit Commission

Northern Ireland Judicial Statistics, Northern Ireland Court Service

Police Statistics, England and Wales, CIPFA

Prison Service Annual Report and Accounts, The Stationery Office

Prison Statistics, England and Wales, The Stationery Office

Prison Statistics Scotland, Scottish Executive

Prisons in Scotland Report, The Stationery Office

Race and the Criminal Justice System, Home Office

Regional Trends, The Stationery Office

Report of the Parole Board for England and Wales, The Stationery Office

Report on the work of the Northern Ireland Prison Service, The Stationery Office

Scottish Crime Survey, Scottish Executive

Statistics on the Race and Criminal Justice System, Home Office

The Criminal Justice System in England and Wales, Home Office

Scottish Executive Statistical Bulletins: Criminal Justice Series, Scottish Executive

The Work of the Prison Service, The Stationery Office

Young People and Crime, Home Office

Review of police forces' crime recording practices, Home Office

Review of crime statistics: a discussion document, Home Office

10: Housing

Becoming a home-owner in Britain in the 1990s. The British Household Panel Survey, ESRC Institute for Social and Economic Research

Bringing Britain Together: A National Strategy for Neighbourhood Renewal, Social Exclusion Unit, Cabinet Office

Changing Households: The British Household Panel Survey, Institute for Social and Economic Research

Department of the Environment, Transport and the Regions Annual Report, The Stationery Office

Divorce, Remarriage and Housing: The Effects of Divorce, Remarriage, Separation and the Formation of New Couple Households on the Number of Separate Households and Housing Demand Conditions, Department of the Environment, Transport and the Regions

English House Condition Survey, The Stationery Office

Housing Finance, Council of Mortgage Lenders

Housing in England: Survey of English Housing, The Stationery Office

Housing Statistics, The Stationery Office

Living conditions in Europe - statistical pocketbook, Eurostat

Local Housing Statistics, The Stationery Office

My home was my castle: evictions and repossessions in Britain, ESRC Institute of Social and Economic Research and Institute of Local Research

Northern Ireland House Condition Survey, Northern Ireland Housing Executive

Northern Ireland Housing Statistics, 2000–01, Department for Social Development, Northern Ireland

On the move: The housing consequences of migration, YPS

Private Renting in England, The Stationery Office

Private Renting in Five Localities, The Stationery Office

Projections of Households in England to 2021, The Stationery Office

Scotland's people: results from the 1999 Scottish Household Survey, The Stationery Office

Scottish House Condition Survey 1996, Scottish Homes

Social Portrait of Europe, Eurostat

Statistical Bulletins on Housing, Scottish Executive

Statistics on Housing in the European Community, Commission of the European Communities

The social situation in the European Union, European Commission

Welsh House Condition Survey, National Assembly for Wales

Welsh Housing Statistics, National Assembly for Wales

11: Environment.

A better quality of life, The Stationery Office

A Living Environment for Wales, Countryside Commission for Wales and the Forestry Commission

A Working Environment for Wales, Environment Agency, Wales

Accounting for Nature: Assessing Habitats in the UK Countryside, Department for Environment, Food and Rural Affairs

Air Quality Strategy for England, Scotland, Wales and Northern Ireland, The Stationery Office

Bathing Water Quality in England and Wales, The Stationery Office

Biodiversity: The UK Action Plan, The Stationery Office

British Social Attitudes, the 16th report, National Centre for Social Research

Britain. The Official Yearbook of the United Kingdom, The Stationery Office

Development of the Oil and Gas Resources of the United Kingdom, The Stationery Office

Digest of Environmental Statistics, The Stationery Office

Digest of United Kingdom Energy Statistics, The Stationery Office

Forestry Commission Facts and Figures 2000–2001, Forestry Commission

Forestry Statistics, Forestry Commission

General Quality Assessment, The Environment Agency

Hydrological summaries for the United Kingdom, Centre for Hydrology and British Geological Survey

Municipal Waste Management Survey, Department for Environment, Food and Rural Affairs

National Waste Strategy: Scotland, Scottish Environment Protection Agency

OECD Environmental Data Compendium, OECD

Organic Farming, Department for Environment, Food and Rural Affairs

Planning Public Water Supplies, The Environment Agency

Progress in Water Supply Planning, The Environment Agency

Quality of life counts, The Stationery Office

Scottish Environmental Statistics, Scottish Executive

Sustainable Scotland: Priorities and Progress, Scottish Executive

The Environment in your Pocket, Department for Environment, Food and Rural Affairs

The State of the countryside 2001, The Countryside Agency

The State of the Environment of England and Wales: The Atmosphere, The Stationery Office

The State of the Environment of England and Wales: The Land, The Stationery Office

The State of the Environment of England and Wales: Fresh Waters, The Stationery Office

The State of the Environment of England and Wales: Coasts, The Stationery Office

Waste management strategy for Northern Ireland, The Stationery Office

Waste Strategy 2000, England and Wales, Department of the Environment, Transport and the Regions

Water Pollution Incidents in England and Wales, The Stationery Office

Waterfacts, Water Services Association

12: Transport

A New Deal for Transport: Better for Everyone, The Stationery Office

A Strategy for Sustainable Development for the United Kingdom, The Stationery Office

Annual Report, Central Rail Users Consultative Committee

British Social Attitudes, Ashgate Publishing

Busdata, Department of the Environment, Transport and the Regions

Driving Standards Agency Annual Report and Accounts, The Stationery Office

Focus on Personal Travel: 1998 Edition, The Stationery Office

Focus on Public Transport, The Stationery Office

Focus on Roads, The Stationery Office

International Passenger Transport, The Stationery Office

Rail Complaints, Office of the Rail Regulator

Regional Trends, The Stationery Office

Road Accidents Great Britain – The Casualty Report, The Stationery Office

Road Accidents, Scotland, Scottish Executive

Road Accidents Statistics English Regions, The Stationery Office

Road Accidents: Wales, National Assembly for Wales

Road Traffic Accident Statistics Annual Report, The Royal Ulster Constabulary

Road Traffic Statistics Great Britain, The Stationery Office

Scottish Transport Statistics, Scottish Executive

Transport Statistics Bulletins and Reports, Department of the Environment, Transport and the Regions

Transport Statistical Bulletins, Scottish Executive

Transport Statistics Great Britain, The Stationery Office

Transport Trends, The Stationery Office

Travel Trends, The Stationery Office

Vehicle Licensing Statistics, Department of the Environment, Transport and the Regions

Vehicle Speeds in Great Britain, Department of the Environment, Transport and the Regions

Welsh Transport Statistics, National Assembly for Wales

13: Lifestyles and Social Participation

Annual Report of Department for Culture, Media and Sport, The Stationery Office

BBC Annual Reports and Accounts, BBC

BPI Statistical Handbook, British Phonographic Industry

British Social Attitudes, Sage Publishing

BVA Yearbook, British Video Association

Cinema and Video Industry Audience Research, CAA

Cultural Trends in Scotland, Policy Studies Institute

Cultural Trends, Policy Studies Institute

Digest of Tourist Statistics, British Tourist Authority

Family Spending, The Stationery Office

Film and Television Handbook, British Film Institute

LISU Annual Library Statistics, LISU, Loughborough University

Living in Britain. Results from the 1996 General Household Survey, The Stationery Office

Living in Britain. Results from the 1996 General Household Survey, The Stationery Office

Social Focus on Families, The Stationery Office

Social Focus on Women and Men, The Stationery Office

Social Focus on Men, The Stationery Office

Social Focus on Young People, The Stationery Office

The UK Tourist, Tourist Boards of England, Northern Ireland, Scotland and Wales

Travel Trends, The Stationery Office

UK Day Visits Survey, Countryside Recreation Network, University of Wales Cardiff

Young People and Sport in England, Sport England

Geographical areas of the United Kingdom

Standard Statistical Regions

SCOTLAND

—— SSR boundary

NORTHERN IRELAND

NORTH

YORKSHIRE AND HUMBERSIDE

NORTH WEST

EAST MIDLANDS

WEST MIDLANDS

EAST ANGLIA

WALES

SOUTH EAST

SOUTH WEST

Environment Agency regions

ENGLAND and WALES

—— Environment Agency region boundary

NORTH WEST

NORTH EAST

MIDLANDS

ANGLIAN

WELSH

THAMES

SOUTH WESTERN

SOUTHERN

NHS Regional Office areas
(from April 1996)

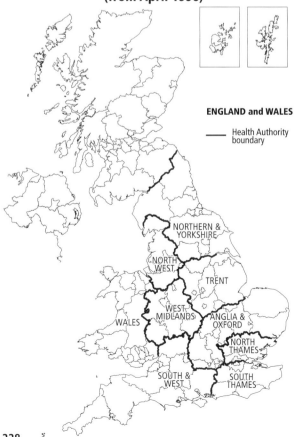

ENGLAND and WALES

—— Health Authority boundary

NORTHERN & YORKSHIRE

NORTH WEST

TRENT

WEST MIDLANDS

ANGLIA & OXFORD

WALES

NORTH THAMES

SOUTH & WEST

SOUTH THAMES

Government Office Regions

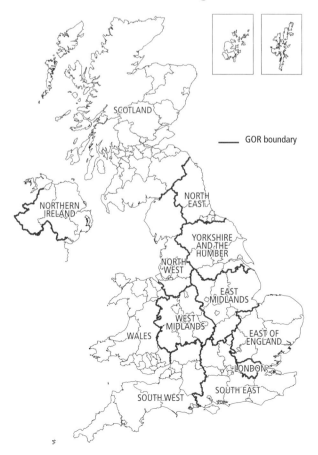

—— GOR boundary

SCOTLAND

NORTHERN IRELAND

NORTH EAST

YORKSHIRE AND THE HUMBER

NORTH WEST

EAST MIDLANDS

WEST MIDLANDS

WALES

EAST OF ENGLAND

LONDON

SOUTH EAST

SOUTH WEST

Police Force areas

GREAT BRITAIN

—— Police Force area boundary

Tourist Board regions

UNITED KINGDOM

—— Tourist Board region boundary

Appendix

Major Surveys

	Frequency	Sampling frame	Type of respondent	Coverage	Effective sample size[1] (most recent survey included in Social Trends)	Response rate (percentages)
Adult Dental Health Survey	Decennial	Postcode Address File in GB, Rating and Valuation lists in NI	All adults in household	UK	4,984 households	74
Agricultural and Horticultural Census	Annual	Farms	Farmers	UK	238,000 farms	80
British Crime Survey	Biennial	Postcode Address File	Adult in household	EW	26,291 addresses	74
British Household Panel Survey	Annual	Postal Addresses in 1991, members of initial wave households followed in subsequent waves	All adults in households	GB	5,160 households	97[2]
British Election Survey	With each election	Postcode Address File	One adult per household	UK	4,659 households	65
British Social Attitudes Survey	Annual	Postcode Address File	One adult per household	GB	5,523 addresses	62[3]
Census of Population	Decennial	Detailed local	Adult in household	UK	Full count	98
Continuous Household Survey	Continuous	Valuation and Lands Agency Property	All adults in household	NI	4,147 addresses	70
Employers Skills Survey	Annual	BT Database	Employers	E	26,952 interviews achieved	59
English House Condition Survey	Quinquennial	Postcode Address File	Any one householder	E	27,200 addresses	49[4]
European Community Household Panel Survey	Annual	Various	All household members aged 16 and over	EU	60,000 households	90[5]
Family Expenditure Survey	Continuous	Postcode Address File	Household in GB, Rating and Valuation lists in NI	UK	11,424 addresses[6]	60[7]
Family Resources Survey	Continuous	Postcode Address File	All adults in household	GB	34,636 households	66
General Household Survey	Continuous	Postcode Address File	All adults in household	GB	11,845 households	76
Health Education Monitoring Survey	Ad hoc	Postcode Address File	One adult aged 16 and over in household	E	8,168 households	71
Health Survey for England	Continuous	Postcode Address File	Adults, children over 2	E	12,250 addresses	74[8]
International Passenger Survey	Continuous	International passengers	Individual traveller	UK	261,000 individuals	82
Labour Force Survey	Continuous	Postcode Address File	All adults in household	UK	59,000 addresses	76[9]
National Food Survey	Continuous	Postcode Address File in GB, Valuation and Lands Agency Property in NI	Person responsible for domestic food arrangements	UK	9,311 addresses	64
National Readership Survey	Continuous	Postcode Address File	Adults aged 15 and over	GB	54,074 individuals	60
National Travel Survey	Continuous	Postcode Address File	All household members	GB	5,040 households per year	67[10]
New Earnings Survey	Annual	Inland Revenue PAYE records	Employee	GB	[11]	[11]
Omnibus Survey	Continuous	Postcode Address File	One adult per household	GB	3,519 individuals[11]	65[12]
Survey of English Housing	Continuous	Postcode Address File	Household	E	26,277 households	71
Survey of Personal Incomes	Annual	Inland Revenue	Individuals administrative data	UK	125,000	95
Youth Cohort Study	Biennial	School records	Young people (Aged 16 to 19)	EW	22,500 individuals	65

1 Effective sample size includes non-respondents but excludes ineligible households.

2 Wave on wave response rate at wave eight. Around 76 per cent of eligible wave one sample members were respondent in wave eight.

3 Response rate refers to 2000 survey.

4 The 1996 EHCS response combines successful outcomes from two linked surveys where information is separately gathered about the household and the dwelling for each address.

5 Response rates vary between EU countries.

6 Basic sample only.

7 Response rate refers to Great Britain.

8 Response rate for fully and partially responding households.

9 Response rate to first wave interviews quoted. Response rate to second to fifth wave interviews 91 per cent of those previously accepting.

10 Response rate for the period January 1997 to January 1999.

11 In the New Earnings Survey employers supply data on a 1 per cent sample of employees who are members of PAYE schemes. For the 2000 sample approximately 233 thousand were selected and there was an 87.4 per cent response, but some 53 thousand returned questionnaires were not taken onto the results file for various reasons.

12 The Omnibus Survey changes from month to month. The sample size and response rate are combined for January and March 2000.

Definitions and Terms

Symbols and conventions

Reference years. Where, because of space constraints, a choice of years has to be made, the most recent year or a run of recent years is shown together with the past population census years (1991, 1981, 1971, etc) and sometimes the mid-points between census years (1986, etc). Other years may be added if they represent a peak or trough in the series.

Rounding of figures. In tables where figures have been rounded to the nearest final digit, there may be an apparent discrepancy between the sum of the constituent items and the total as shown.

Billion. This term is used to represent a thousand million.

Provisional and estimated data. Some data for the latest year (and occasionally for earlier years) are provisional or estimated. To keep footnotes to a minimum, these have not been indicated; source departments will be able to advise if revised data are available.

Seasonal adjustment. Unless otherwise stated unadjusted data have been used.

Non-calendar years.
Financial year – eg 1 April 2000 to 31 March 2001 would be shown as 2000–01
Academic year – eg September 1999/July 2000 would be shown as 1999/00
Data covering more than one year – eg 1998, 1999 and 2000 would be shown as 1998–2000

Units on tables. Where one unit predominates it is shown at the top of the table. All other units are shown against the relevant row or column. Figures are shown in italics when they represent percentages.

Dependent children. Those aged under 16, or single people aged 16 to 18 and in full-time education.

Germany. Unless otherwise stated data relate to Germany as constituted since 3 October 1990.

Symbols. The following symbols have been used throughout Social Trends:
  ..   *not available*
  .   *not applicable*
  -    *negligible (less than half the final digit shown)*
  0   *nil*

Part 1: Population

Population estimates and projections

The estimated and projected populations are of the resident population of an area, i.e. all those usually resident there, whatever their nationality. Members of HM forces stationed outside the United Kingdom are excluded; members of foreign forces stationed in the United Kingdom are included. Students are taken to be resident at their term-time addresses. Figures for the United Kingdom do not include the population of the Channel Islands or the Isle of Man.

The population estimates for mid-1991 were based on results from the 1991 Census of Population and incorporate an allowance for census under-enumeration. Allowances were also made for definitional differences between Census and mid-year estimates. Mid-year estimates also allow for subsequent births, deaths and migration since Census Day. The estimates for 1982–90 have been revised to give a smooth series consistent with both 1981 and 1991 Census results. Due to definitional changes, there are minor discontinuities for Scotland between the figures for 1971 and earlier years and for Northern Ireland between the figures for 1981 and earlier years. At the United Kingdom level these discontinuities are negligible.

The most recent set of national population projections published for the United Kingdom are based on the populations of England, Wales, Scotland and Northern Ireland at mid-2000. Further details of these can be found on the Governments Actuary's Department's website (www.gad.gov.uk).

Boundaries

Map boundaries show government office regions, counties/unitary authorities and, where available, local authority districts in England; unitary authorities in Wales; the council areas in Scotland; health and social service boards/education and library boards/districts as available in Northern Ireland.

International migration estimates

Detailed estimates of migration between the United Kingdom and other countries are derived from the International Passenger Survey (IPS).

The IPS provides information on all migrants into the United Kingdom who have resided abroad for a year or more and stated on arrival the intention to stay in the United Kingdom for a year or more and vice versa. Migrants to and from the Irish Republic, diplomats and military personnel are excluded, as are nearly all persons who apply for asylum on entering the country. IPS migration figures exclude persons who enter the country as short term visitors but remain for 12 months or longer after being granted an extension of stay, for example as students, on the basis of marriage or because they applied for asylum after entering the country. Home Office estimates of asylum seekers and 'visitor switches' are added to the IPS figures. Estimates of migrants between the United Kingdom and the Irish Republic are produced using information from the Irish Labour Force Survey and the National Health Service Central Register. They are agreed between the Irish Central Statistics Office and the Office for National Statistics and are also added to the IPS figures.

Asylum

The basis for recognition as a refugee and hence the granting of asylum is the 1951 United Nations Convention relating to the Status of Refugees, extending in its application by the 1967 Protocol relating to the Status of Refugees. The United Kingdom is party to both. The Convention defines a refugee as a person who 'owning to a well-founded fear of being persecuted for reasons of race, religion, nationality, membership of a particular social group or political opinion, is outside the country of his nationality and unable, or owing to such fear, is unwilling to avail himself of the protection of that country'. In addition, the United Kingdom is prepared to grant, to applicants who do not meet the requirements of the Convention, exceptional leave to stay here for an appropriate period, if it would be unreasonable, or impracticable, in all circumstances, to seek to enforce their return to their country of origin.

The primary purpose rule of July 1997, stated that people could only be accepted for settlement in the United Kingdom if they were coming here to work, thereby excluding families of workers from joining them.

Part 2: Households and Families

Although definitions differ slightly across surveys and the census, they are broadly similar.

Households

A household: is a person living alone or a group of people who have the address as their only or main residence and who either share one meal a day or share the living accommodation.

Students: living in halls of residence are recorded under their parents household and included in the parents family type in the Labour Force Survey (LFS), although some surveys/projections include such students in the institutional population.

Families

Children: are never-married people of any age who live with one or both parent(s). They also include stepchildren and adopted children (but not foster children) and also grandchildren (where the parents are absent).

Dependent children: in the 1961 Census, were defined as children under 15 years of age, and persons of any age in full-time education. In the 1971 Census, dependent children were defined as never-married children in families who were either under 15 years of age, or aged 15 to 24 and in full-time education. However, for direct comparison with the Labour Force Survey (LFS) data, the definition of dependent children used for 1971 in Table 2.3 has been changed to include only never-married children in families who were either under 15 years of age, or aged 15 to 18 and in full-time education. In the 1991 Census, the LFS and the GHS, dependent children are childless never-married children in families who are aged under 16, or aged 16 to 18 and in full-time education.

A family: is a married or cohabiting couple, either with or without their never-married child or children (of any age), including couples with no children or a lone parent together with his or her never-married child or children. A family could also consist of grandparent or grandparents with grandchild or grandchildren if there are no apparent parents of the grandchild or grandchildren usually resident in the household. In the LFS, a family unit can also comprise a single person. LFS family units include non-dependent 'children' (who can in fact be adult) provided they are never married and have no children of their own in the household.

A lone parent family (in the Census) is a father or mother together with his or her never-married child or children.

A lone parent family (in the General Household Survey) consists of a lone parent, living with his or her never-married dependent children, provided these children have no children of their own. Married lone mothers whose husbands are not defined as resident in the household are not classified as lone parents because evidence suggests the majority are separated from their husband either because he usually works away from home or for some other reason that does not imply the breakdown of the marriage (see ONS's GHS Monitor 82/1).

A lone parent family (in the Labour Force Survey) consists of a lone parent, living with his or her never-married children, provided these children have no children of their own living with them.

Conceptions

Conception statistics used in Tables 2.10 and 2.13, include pregnancies that result in one or more live or still births, or a legal abortion under the 1967 Act. Conception statistics do not include miscarriages or illegal abortions. Dates of conception are estimated using recorded gestation for abortions and still births, and assuming 38 weeks gestation for live births.

Average teenage fertility rate

Teenage fertility rates are calculated for each age, summed and then divided by five to obtain the average rate for women aged 15 to 19. In previous editions of Social Trends, the overall teenage rate was calculated as the number of births to women under 20 per 1,000 women aged 15 to 19. This year's methodology is consistent with the Council of Europe publication.

Part 3: Education and Training

Main categories of educational establishments

Educational establishments in the United Kingdom are administered and financed in several ways. Most schools are controlled by local education authorities (LEAs), which are part of the structure of local government, but some are 'assisted', receiving grants direct from central government sources and being controlled by governing bodies which have a substantial degree of autonomy. In recent years under the Local Management of Schools initiative all LEA and assisted schools have been given delegated responsibility for managing their own budgets and staff numbers. From 1988 to 1999 it has possible for LEA schools in England and Wales to apply for grant maintained status, under which they receive direct

funding from the Department for Education and Employment or the Welsh Office. The governing bodies of such schools were responsible for all aspects of their management, including use of funds, employment of staff and provision of most educational support services.

Outside the public sector completely are non-maintained schools run by individuals, companies or charitable institutions.

From 1 September 1999, all previous categories of school, including grant-maintained, were replaced by four new categories, all maintained (or funded) by the LEA:

Community – schools formerly known as 'county' plus some former GM schools. The LEA is the legal employer of the school's staff, the land owner and the admissions authority.

Foundation – most former GM schools. The governing body is the legal employer and admissions authority, as well as landowner unless that is a charitable foundation.

Voluntary Aided – schools formerly known as 'aided' and some former GM schools. The governing body is the legal employer and admissions authority, but the landowner is usually a charitable foundation. The governing body contribute towards the capital costs of running the school.

Voluntary Controlled – schools formerly known as 'controlled'. The LEA is the legal employer and admissions authority, but the landowner is usually a charitable foundation.

Further Education (FE) courses in FE sector colleges are largely funded through grants from the Further Education Funding Councils in England and Wales. The FEFC in England is responsible for funding provision for FE and some non-prescribed higher education in FE sector colleges; it also funds some FE provided by LEA maintained and other institutions referred to as 'external institutions'. In Wales, the National Council for Education and Training for Wales (known as FEFCW prior to 1 April 2001) also funds FE provision made by FE institutions via a third party or sponsored arrangements. FE colleges in Scotland are funded by the Scottish FEFC (SFEFC) and FE colleges in Northern Ireland are funded by the Department for Employment and Learning.

Higher education courses in higher education establishments are largely publicly funded through block grants from the HE funding councils in England, the National Assembly for Wales, the Scottish Executive and the Department for Employment and Learning in Northern Ireland. In addition, some designated HE (mainly HND/HNC Diplomas and Certificates of HE) is also funded by the HE funding councils. The remainder is funded by FE funding councils.

Stages of education

Education takes place in several stages: primary, secondary, further and higher, and is compulsory for all children between the ages of 5 (4 in Northern Ireland) and 16. The primary stage covers three age ranges: nursery (under 5), infant (5 to 7 or 8) and junior (up to 11 or 12) but in Scotland and Northern Ireland there is generally no distinction between infant and junior schools. Nursery education can be provided either in separate nursery schools or in nursery classes within primary schools. Most public sector primary schools take both boys and girls in mixed classes. It is usual to transfer straight to secondary school at age 11 (in England, Wales and Northern Ireland) or 12 (in Scotland), but in England some children make the transition via middle schools catering for various age ranges between 8 and 14. Depending on their individual age ranges middle schools are classified as either primary or secondary.

Public provision of secondary education in an area may consist of a combination of different types of school, the pattern reflecting historical circumstance and the policy adopted by the LEA. Comprehensive schools normally admit pupils without reference to ability or aptitude and cater for all the children in a neighbourhood, but in some areas they co-exist with grammar, secondary modern or technical schools. In Northern Ireland, post primary education is provided by secondary and grammar schools.

Special schools (day or boarding) provide education for children who require specialist support to complete their education, for example because they have physical or other difficulties. Many pupils with special educational needs are educated in mainstream schools.

The term further education may be used in a general sense to cover all non-advanced courses taken after the period of compulsory education, but more commonly it excludes those staying on at secondary school and those in higher education, ie courses in universities and colleges leading to qualifications above GCE A Level, SCE H Grade, GNVQ/NVQ level 3, and their equivalents.

Higher education is defined as courses that are of a standard that is higher than GCE A level, the Higher Grade of the Scottish Certificate of Education, GNVQ/ NVQ level 3 or the Edexcel (formerly BTEC) or SQA National Certificate/Diploma. There are three main levels of HE course: (i) postgraduate courses are those leading to higher degrees, diplomas and certificates (including postgraduate certificates of education and professional qualifications) which usually require a

first degree as entry qualification; (ii) first degrees which includes first degrees, first degrees with qualified teacher status, enhanced first degrees, first degrees obtained concurrently with a diploma, and intercalated first degrees; (iii) other undergraduate courses which includes all other higher education courses, for example HNDs and Diplomas in HE.

Figures previously shown in this publication for England related to classes taught by one teacher. In 1999/00, the average Key Stage 1 class, taught by one teacher, had 25.8 pupils, with 8.8 per cent of classes having 31 or more pupils. Further information, including one-teacher class size data for Key Stage 2, primary and secondary schools can be found in DfEE Statistical First Release 15/2000.

The National Curriculum: assessments and tests

Under the *Education Reform Act (1988)* a National Curriculum has been progressively introduced into primary and secondary schools in England and Wales. This consists of mathematics, English and science (and Welsh in Welsh speaking schools in Wales) as core subjects with history, geography, information technology and design and technology, music, art, physical education and (in secondary schools) a modern foreign language (and Welsh in non-Welsh speaking schools in Wales) as foundation subjects. For all subjects measurable targets have been defined for four key stages, corresponding to ages 7, 11, 14 and 16. Pupils are assessed formally at the ages of 7, 11 and 14 by their teachers and by national tests in the core subjects of English, mathematics and science (and in Welsh speaking schools in Wales, Welsh). Sixteen year olds are assessed by means of the GCSE examination. Statutory authorities have been set up for England and for Wales to advise government on the National Curriculum and promote curriculum development generally. Northern Ireland has its own common curriculum which is similar but not identical to the National Curriculum in England and Wales. Assessment arrangements in Northern Ireland became statutory from September 1996. In Scotland, though school curricula are the responsibility of education authorities and individual head teachers, in practice almost all 14 to 16 year olds study mathematics, English, science, a modern foreign language, a social subject, physical education, religious and moral education, technology and a creative and aesthetic subject.

Qualifications

In England, Wales and Northern Ireland the main examination for school pupils at the minimum school leaving age is the General Certificate of Secondary Education (GCSE) which can be taken in a wide range of subjects. This replaced the GCE O Level and CSE examinations in 1987 (1988 in Northern Ireland). In

England, Wales and Northern Ireland the GCSE is awarded in eight grades, A* to G, the highest four (A* to C) being regarded as equivalent to O level grades A to C or CSE grade 1.

GCE A Level is usually taken after a further two years of study in a sixth form or equivalent, passes being graded from A (the highest) to E (the lowest).

In Scotland pupils study for the Scottish Certificate of Education (SCE) S (Standard) Grade, approximately equivalent to GCSE, in their third and fourth years of secondary schooling (roughly ages 14 and 15). Each subject has several elements, some of which are internally assessed in school, and an award is only made (on a scale of 1 to 7) if the whole course has been completed and examined. The SCE H (Higher) Grade requires one further year of study and for the more able candidates the range of subjects taken may be as wide as at S Grade with as many as five or six subjects spanning both arts and science. Three or more SCE Highers are regarded as being approximately the equivalent of two or more GCE A levels.

After leaving school, people can study towards higher academic qualifications such as degrees. However, a large number of people choose to study towards qualifications aimed at a particular occupation or group of occupations – these qualifications are called vocational qualifications.

Vocational qualifications can be split into three groups, namely National Vocational Qualifications (NVQs), General National Qualifications (GNVQs) and other vocational qualifications.

NVQs are based on an explicit statement of competence derived from an analysis of employment requirements. They are awarded at five levels. Scottish Vocational Qualifications (SVQs) are the Scottish equivalent.

GNVQs are a vocational alternative to GCSEs and GCE A levels . They are awarded at three levels: Foundation, Intermediate and Advanced. General Scottish Vocational Qualifications (GSVQs) are the Scottish equivalent.

There are also a large number of other vocational qualifications which are not NVQs, SVQs, GNVQs or GSVQs , for example, a BTEC Higher National Diploma or a City and Guilds Craft award.

Other qualifications (including academic qualifications) are often expressed as being equivalent to a particular NVQ level so that comparisons can be made more easily.

An NVQ level 5 is equivalent to a Higher Degree.

An NVQ level 4 is equivalent to a First Degree, a HND or HNC, a BTEC Higher Diploma, an RSA Higher Diploma a nursing qualification or other Higher Education.

An NVQ level 3 is equivalent to 2 A levels, an Advanced GNVQ, an RSA advanced diploma, a City & Guilds advanced craft, an OND or ONC or a BTEC National Diploma.

An NVQ level 2 is equivalent to 5 GCSEs at grades A* to C, an Intermediate GNVQ, an RSA diploma, a City and Guilds craft or a BTEC first or general diploma.

Literacy levels

Level	Prose	Document	Quantitative
Level 1	Locate one piece of information in a text that is identical or synonymous to the information in the question. Any plausible incorrect answer present in the text is not near the correct information.	Locate one piece of information in a text that is identical to the information in the question. Distracting information is usually located away from the correct answer. Some tasks may require entering given personal information on a form.	Perform a single simple operation such as addition for which the problem is already clearly stated or the numbers are provided.
Level 2	Locate one or more pieces of information in a text but several plausible distractors may be present or low level inferences may be required. The reader may also be required to integrate two or more pieces of information or to compare and contrast information.	Tasks at this level are more varied. Where a single match is required more distracting information may be present or a low level inference may be required. Some tasks may require information to be entered on a form or to cycle through information in a document.	Single arithmetic operation (addition or subtraction) using numbers that are easily located in the text. The operation to be performed may be easily inferred from the wording of the question or the format of the material.
Level 3	Readers are required to match information that requires low-level inferences or that meet specific conditions. There may be several pieces of information to be identified located in different parts of the text. Readers may also be required to integrate or to compare and contrast information across paragraphs or sections of text.	Literal or synonymous matches in a wide variety of tasks requiring the reader to take conditional information into account or to match on multiple features of information. The reader must integrate information from one or more displays of information or cycle through a document to provide multiple answers.	At this level the operations become more varied – multiplication and division. Sometimes two or more numbers are needed to solve the problem and the numbers are often embedded in more complex texts or documents. Some tasks require higher order inferences to define the task.

Literacy levels (continued)

Level	Prose	Document	Quantitative
Level 4	Match multiple features or provide several responses where the requested information must be identified through text based inferences. Reader may be required to contrast or integrate pieces of information sometimes from lengthy texts. Texts usually contain more distracting information and the information requested is more abstract.	Match on multiple features of information, cycle through documents and integrate information. Tasks often require higher order inferences to get correct answer. Sometimes, conditional information in the document must be taken into account in arriving at the correct answer.	A single arithmetic operation where thestatement of the task is not easily defined. The directive does not provide a semantic relation term to help the reader define the task.
Level 5	Locate information in dense text that contain a number of plausible answers Sometimes high-level inferences are required and some text may use specialised language.	Readers are required to search through complex displays of information that contain multiple distractors, to make high level inferences, process conditional information or use specialised language.	Readers must perform multiple operations sequentially and must state the problem from the material provided or use background knowledge to workout the problem or operations needed.

National Learning Targets – England

In October 1998, following consultation, the National Learning Targets were announced. They replaced the former National Targets for Education and Training. The Targets state that by 2002:

80% of 11 year olds will reach at least level 4 in the Key Stage 2 English test;

75% of 11 year olds will reach at least level 4 in the Key Stage 2 Mathematics test;

50% of 16 year olds will achieve 5 GCSEs at grades A*– C, or equivalent;

95% of 16 year olds will achieve at least one GCSE grade A*– G, or equivalent;

85% of 19-year-olds will be qualified to at least NVQ level 2 or equivalent;

60% of 21-year-olds will be qualified to at least NVQ level 3 or equivalent;

28% of economically active adults will be qualified to at least NVQ level 4 or equivalent;

50% of economically active adults will be qualified to at least NVQ level 3 or equivalent;

A learning participation Target is under development;

45% of organisations with 50 or more employees will be recognised as Investors in People; and

10,000 organisations with 10–49 employees will be recognised as Investors in People.

Learning and Training at Work

Learning and Training at Work 1999 (LATW 1999) is a new multi-purpose survey of employers that investigates the provision of learning and training at work. This information was previously collected in the annual Skill Needs in Britain (SNIB) surveys, along with information on recruitment difficulties, skill shortages and skill gaps.

Due to increasing focus on skills issues on the one hand and employer training on the other, and coupled with the increasing complexity and length of the SNIB questionnaire, the DfEE study decided to replace the single SNIB study with two separate surveys, one covering skills issues and another training. The Learning and Training at Work 1999 report relates to the latter study and includes information about; key indicators of employers' commitment to training, including the volume of off-the-job training provided, awareness of, and participation in, a number of initiatives relevant to training.

The LATW1999 survey consisted of 4,008 telephone interviews with emplyers having 1 or more employees at the specific location sampled and covered public and private business and all industry sectors. The main stage of interviewing was carried out between 3 November and 21 December 1999. The overall response rate from employers was 63 per cent, acceptable for a study of this nature. Sample design involved setting separate sample targets for each cell on a Government Office region by industry sector by establishment size matrix. In contrast the SNIB survey covered employers with 25 or more employees in all business sectors, except agriculture, hunting, forestry and fishing, in Great Britain.

Part 4: Labour Market

Estimates of employment rates

The employment rate series shown in Chart 4.1 uses estimates produced by the Department for Education and Employment for the period 1959 to 1991. Full details of the methodology for these estimates may be found in Labour Market Trends, January 2000 edition. They are provisional and will be replaced by modelled estimates produced by the Office for National Statistics during 2002. Data for 1992 onwards are from the Labour Force Survey.

ILO unemployment

The ILO definition of unemployment refers to people without a job who were available to start work within two weeks and had either looked for work in the previous four weeks or were waiting to start a job they had already obtained. Estimates on this basis are not available before 1984, as the Labour Force Survey did not then collect information on job search over a four week period. The former GB/UK Labour Force definition of unemployment, the only one available for estimates up to 1984, counted people not in employment and seeking work in a reference week (or prevented from seeking work by a temporary sickness or holiday, or waiting for the results of a job application, or waiting to start a job they had already obtained), whether or not they were available to start (except students not able to start because they had to complete their education).

Labour force

Since autumn 1993, the Labour Force had been grossed up using population projections based on 1992 mid-year population estimates. Data from Autumn 1993 to Autumn 1999 have been revised to take account of more up-to-date information on changes in the population (1998-based projections and more up-to-date population estimates). The revised data have led to an increase in the size of the growth between 1993 and 1999 in the number of people in employment (from about 1.6 million to about 2 million), and a very small fall in the size of the decrease in the numbers of ILO unemployed people. Data from Winter 1999–2000 have been grossed using the latest population data.

Standard Occupation Classification

The new Standard Occupation Classification (SOC) 2000 replaces SOC 90 in analyses of the Labour Force Survey from Spring 2001. The main features of the revision include a tighter definition of managerial occupations and an overhaul of new occupations introduced as a result of new technology (for example areas such as computing; the environment and conservation; and customer service occupations).

There is no exact correspondence between SOC90 and SOC2000 at any level. Most of the major groups have been renamed and all have a different composition in SOC2000 compared with SOC90. More details may be found in an article in Labour Market Trends, July 2001 (pp357-364).

Part 5: Income and Wealth

Household sector

Due to fundamental changes introduced in 1998 to the way that the national accounts are compiled, some of the data in Chapter 5 in this and the last three editions differ from those previously shown in Social Trends. These changes, needed to make better international comparisons, have affected the classification of people and institutions as well as transactions and assets.

The household sector is defined here to include non-profit institutions and individuals living in institutions as well as those living in households. The most obvious example of a non-profit institution is a charity: this sector also includes many other organisations of which universities, trade unions and clubs and societies are the most important. The household sector differs from the personal sector, as previously defined in the national accounts, in that it excludes unincorporated private businesses apart from sole traders. More information is given in United Kingdom National Accounts Concepts, Sources and Methods published by The Stationery Office.

Individual income

Gross individual income refers to the weekly personal income of women and men before deduction of income tax and National Insurance contributions as reported in the Family Resources Survey. Gross income includes: earnings, income from self-employment, investments and occupational pensions/annuities, benefit income, and income from miscellaneous other sources. It excludes income which accrues at household level, such as council tax benefit. Income from couples' joint investment accounts is assumed to be received equally. Benefit income paid in respect of dependants such as Child Benefit is included in the individual income of the person nominated for the receipt of payments, except for married pensioner couples, where state retirement pension payments are separated and assigned to the man and woman according to their entitlements. Full details of the concepts and definitions used may be found in Individual Income 1996/97 to 1999/00, available on the Women and Equality Unit website or from the Analytical Services Division, Department for Work and Pensions.

Equivalisation scales

The Department for Work and Pensions (DWP), the Office for National Statistics (ONS), the Institute for Fiscal Studies (IFS) and the Institute for Social and Economic Research (ISER) all use McClements equivalence scales in their analysis of the income distribution, to take into account variations in the size and composition of households. This reflects the common sense notion that a household of five adults will need a higher income than will a single person living alone to enjoy a comparable standard of living. An overall equivalence value is calculated for each household by summing the appropriate scale values for each household member. Equivalised household income is then calculated by dividing household income by the household's equivalence value. The scales conventionally take a married couple as the reference point with an equivalence value of 1; equivalisation therefore tends to increase relatively the incomes of single person households (since their incomes are divided by a value of less than 1) and to reduce incomes of households with three or more persons. For further information see Households Below Average Income, Corporate Document Services, Department of Social Security.

The DWP and IFS use both before and after housing costs scales, although only before housing costs scales have been used in this chapter.

McClements equivalence scales:

Household member	Before housing costs	After housing costs
First adult (head)	0.61	0.55
Spouse of head	0.39	0.45
Other second adult	0.46	0.45
Third adult	0.42	0.45
Subsequent adults	0.36	0.40
Each dependent aged:		
0-1	0.09	0.07
2-4	0.18	0.18
5-7	0.21	0.21
8-10	0.23	0.23
11-12	0.25	0.26
13-15	0.27	0.28
16 or over	0.36	0.38

Redistribution of income (ROI)

Estimates of the incidence of taxes and benefits on household income, based on the Family Expenditure Survey (FES), are published by the ONS in *Economic Trends*. The article covering 1999–00 appeared in the April 2001 issue, and contains details of the definitions and methods used.

Households Below Average Income (HBAI)

Information on the distribution of income based on the Family Resources Survey is provided in the DSS publication *Households Below Average Income: 1994/95 –1999/00*. This publication provides estimates of patterns of personal disposable income in Great Britain, and of changes in income over time in the United Kingdom. It attempts to measure people's potential living standards as determined by disposable income. As the title would suggest, HBAI concentrates on the lower part of the income distribution, but provides comparisons with the upper part where appropriate.

Disposable household income includes all flows of income into the household, principally earnings, benefits, occupational and private pensions, investments. It is net of tax, National Insurance contributions, Council Tax, contributions to occupational pension schemes (including additional voluntary contributions), maintenance and child support payments, and parental contributions to students living away from home.

Two different measures of disposable income are used in HBAI: before and after housing costs are deducted. Housing costs consist of rent, water rates, community charges, mortgage interest payments, structural insurance, ground rent and service charges.

Difference between Households Below Average Income and Redistribution of Income series

These are two separate and distinct income series produced by two different government departments. Each series has been developed to serve the specific needs of that department. The DWP series, HBAI, provides estimates of patterns of disposable income and of changes over time and shows disposable income before and after housing costs (where disposable income is as defined in the section on HBAI above). The ONS series, ROI, shows how Government intervention through the tax and benefit system affects the income of households; it covers the whole income distribution and includes the effects of indirect taxes like VAT and duty on beer, as well as estimating the cash value of benefits in kind (e.g. from state spending on education and health care). The ROI results are designed to show the position in a particular year rather than trends in income levels over time, although trends in the distribution of income are given. An important difference between the two series is that HBAI counts individuals and ROI counts households. Also, whereas ROI provides estimates for the United Kingdom, from 1994/95 onwards HBAI provides estimates for Great Britain only.

Disability

Disability is defined as having a long term illness, disability or infirmity that limits the activity of the individual in some way. No adjustment is made to disposable household income to take into account any additional costs that may be incurred due to the illness or disability in question.

Net wealth of the household sector

Revised balance sheet estimates of the net wealth of the household (and non-profit institutions) sector were published in an article *Economic Trends*, November 1999. These figures are based on the new international system of national accounting and incorporate data from new sources. Quarterly estimates of net financial wealth (excluding tangible and intangible assets) are published in *Financial Statistics*.

Distribution of personal wealth

The estimates of the distribution of the marketable wealth of individuals relate to all adults in the United Kingdom. They are produced by combining Inland Revenue (IR) estimates of the distribution of wealth identified by the estate multiplier method with independent estimates of total personal wealth derived from the ONS national accounts balance sheets. Estimates for 1995 onwards have been compiled on the basis of the new System of National Accounts, but estimates for earlier years are on the old basis. The methods used were described in an article in *Economic Trends* (October 1990) entitled "Estimates of the Distribution of Personal Wealth". Net wealth of the personal sector differs from marketable wealth for the following reasons:

Difference in coverage: the ONS balance sheet of the personal sector includes the wealth of non-profit making bodies and unincorporated businesses, while the IR estimates exclude non-profit making bodies and treat the bank deposits and debts of unincorporated businesses differently from ONS;

Differences in timing: the ONS balance sheet gives values at the end of the year, whereas IR figures are adjusted to mid-year;

IR figures: exclude the wealth of those under 18.

Funded pensions: are included in the ONS figures but not in the IR marketable wealth. Also the ONS balance sheet excludes consumer durables and includes non-marketable tenancy rights, whereas the IR figures include consumer durables and exclude non-marketable tenancy rights.

European Union expenditure

The figures in Table 5.33 come from *The Community Budget: The Facts in Figures* and have been converted to sterling at the following exchange rates:

1981	–	£1 = 1.8096 ECU
1986	–	£1 = 1.4897
1991	–	£1 = 1.4284
1996	–	£1 = 1.2467
1999	–	£1 = 1.5192

Part 6: Expenditure

Household expenditure

The national accounts definition of household expenditure, within household final consumption expenditure, consists of: personal expenditure on goods (durable and non-durable) and services, including the value of income in kind; imputed rent for owner-occupied dwellings; and the purchase of second-hand goods less the proceeds of sales of used goods. Excluded are interest and other transfer payments; all business expenditure; and the purchase of land and buildings (and associated costs). This national accounts definition is also used for regional analysis of household income.

In principle, expenditure is measured at the time of acquisition rather than actual disbursement of cash. The categories of expenditure include that of non-resident as well as resident households and individuals in the United Kingdom.

The methods used for estimating expenditure at constant prices often depend on the methods used for the current price estimates. Where the current price estimate is in value terms only, it is deflated by an appropriate price index. The indices most widely used for this purpose are components of the retail prices index. The index does not, however, cover the whole range of household final consumer expenditure, and other indices have to be used or estimated where necessary. If no other appropriate price index is available the general consumer price index implied by the estimates of consumers' expenditure at current and constant prices on all other goods and services is used. Where the estimate at current prices is one of quantity multiplied by current average value, the estimate at constant prices is in most cases the same quantity multiplied by the average value in the base year. All these revaluations are carried out in as great detail as practicable.

For further details see the article entitled 'Consumers' expenditure' in *Economic Trends*, September 1983.

The Family Expenditure Survey definition of household expenditure represents current expenditure on goods and services. This excludes those recorded payments that are partly savings or investments (for example life assurance premiums). Similarly, income tax payments, National Insurance contributions, mortgage capital repayments and other payments for major additions to dwellings are excluded. For purchases financed by hire purchase or loans, the amounts paid under the finance agreement are recorded as expenditure as they occur; the full cost of the item is not recorded at the time of the initial transaction. For further details see *Family Spending*.

From April 2001 the Family Expenditure Survey was replaced by the Expenditure and Food Survey (EFS). This was formed by merging the FES with the National Food Survey (NFS). It will continue to provide the information previously provided by the FES.

Retired households

Retired households are those where the head of the household is retired. All male heads of household are 65 years of age or more; all female heads of household are 60 years of age or more. For analysis purposes two categories are used in this report:

(a) "A retired household mainly dependent upon state pensions", also known as a pensioner household, is one in which at least three quarters of the total income of the household is derived from National Insurance retirement and similar pensions, including housing and other benefits paid in supplement to or instead of such pensions. The term "National Insurance retirement and similar pensions" includes National Insurance disablement and war disability pensions, and income support in conjunction with these disability payments.

(b) "Other retired households" are households that do not fulfil the income conditions of "pensioner" households because more than a quarter of the household's income derives from occupational retirement pensions and/or income from investments, annuities etc.

Retail prices index

The general index of retail prices (RPI) is the main domestic measure of inflation in the UK. It measures the average change from month to month in the prices of good and services purchased by most households in the United Kingdom. The spending pattern on which the index is based is revised each

year, mainly using information from the Family Expenditure Survey. The expenditure of certain higher income households, and of pensioner households mainly dependent on state pensions, is excluded. These households are:

(a) the 4 per cent (approximately) where the total household recorded gross income exceeds a certain amount (£1,340 a week in 1999/2000).

(b) 'pensioner' households consisting of retired people who derive at least three quarters of their income from state benefits.

Expenditure patterns of one-person and two-person pensioner households differ from those of the households upon which the general index is based. Separate indices have been compiled for such pensioner households since 1969, and quarterly averages are published on the National Statistics website, *Focus on Consumer Price Indices (formerly known as the Consumer Price Indices (CPI) Business Monitor MM23)*. They are chain indices constructed in the same way as the general index of retail prices. It should, however, be noted that the pensioner indices exclude housing costs.

A brief introduction to the RPI is given on the National Statistics website. Also additional information on data, articles and publication can be obtain from the RPI page on the National Statistics website, www.statistics.gov.uk/rpi

Part 7: Health

Expectation of life

The expectation of life, shown in Chart 7.1, is the average total number of years which a person of that age could be expected to live, if the rates of mortality at each age were those experienced in that year. The mortality rates that underlie the expectation of life figures are based, up to 2000, on total deaths occurring in each year for England and Wales and the total deaths registered in each year in Scotland and Northern Ireland.

Self-reported sickness

The General Household Survey and the Continuous Household Survey include two measures of self-reported sickness:

■ Chronic sickness. Respondents aged 16 and over are asked whether they have any longstanding illness or disability which has troubled them for some time. Information about children is collected from a responsible adult, usually the mother. Those who report a longstanding condition, either on their own behalf or that of their children, are asked whether it limits their activities in any way (this is shown in Table 7.2 as 'limiting longstanding illness').

- Acute sickness. Respondents are asked whether they had to cut down on their normal activities in the two weeks before interview as a result of illness or injury (this is shown in Table 7.2 as 'restricted activity').

Poor general health (as shown in Table 7.2). This refers to those respondents who, when asked whether their general health over the last 12 months was "good", "fairly good" or "not good", reported that their health had been "not good". For children, under the age of 16, this question was answered by an adult in the household.

Standardised rates

Directly age-standardised incidence rates enable comparisons to be made over time and between the genders, which are independent of changes in the age structure of the population. In each year, the crude rates in each five-year age group are multiplied by the European standard population for that age group. These are then summed and divided by the total standard population to give an overall standardised rate.

The rates on suicides in Chart 7.15 have been age-standardised within the given age groups. This process is the same as described above, except that it is applied to each age group separately, using appropriate total standard populations, rather than to the whole standard population.

General Practice Research Database (GPRD)

The GPRD is a large data collection system of continuous data on patients registered with participating general practices in the United Kingdom. The practices follow an agreed protocol for the recording of clinical data and submit anonymised, patient based clinical records on a regular basis to the database. Practices are recruited to GPRD on a volunteer basis rather than as a statistically representative sample. Data from 211 practices in England and Wales are included in the analysis presented here. These practices cover on average 2.6% of the population of England and Wales in 1998. Patients are allocated to regions according to the location of the practice at which they are registered.

The Medicines Control Agency (MCA) has been responsible for the overall management and financial control of the GPRD since April 1999, and its operation since October 1999.

The deprivation categories in Table 7.4 are derived using the Townsend Material Deprivation Score. This is a composite score calculated using information on unemployment, overcrowding, car availability and home ownership from 1991 Census data to categorise areas according to the level of deprivation.

Alcohol consumption

A unit of alcohol is 8 grams by weight or 1 cl (10 ml) by volume of pure alcohol. This is the amount contained in half a pint of ordinary strength beer or lager, a single pub measure of spirits (25 ml), a small glass of ordinary strength wine (9% alcohol by volume), or a small pub measure of sherry or fortified wine.

Sensible Drinking, the 1995 report of an inter-departmental review of the scientific and medical evidence of the effects of drinking alcohol, concluded that the daily benchmarks were more appropriate than previously recommended weekly levels since they could help individuals decide how much to drink on single occasions and to avoid episodes of intoxication with their attendant health and social risks. The report concluded that regular consumption of between three and four units a day for men and two to three units for women does not carry a significant health risk. However, consistently drinking more than four units a day for men, or more than three for women, is not advised as a sensible drinking level because of the progressive health risk it carries. The government's advice on sensible drinking is now based on these daily benchmarks.

Standardised death rates

To enable comparisons to be made over time which are independent of changes in the age structure of the population, directly standardised death rates have been calculated in Chart 7.11.

For each year, the age-specific death rates are multiplied by the European standard population for each age group. These are then summed and divided by the total standard population to give an overall standardised rate. Since the European population is the same for both males and females it is possible to directly compare male and female standardised death rates.

International Classification of Diseases

The International Classification of Diseases (ICD) is a coding scheme for diseases and causes of death. England, Wales and Northern Ireland are currently using the Ninth Revision of the ICD (ICD9), and Scotland is using the Tenth Revision. The rest of the United Kingdom began using the Tenth Revision in 2001.

The causes of death included in Chart 7.11 correspond to the following ICD9 codes: circulatory diseases 390–459: cancer 140–208: respiratory diseases 460–519 and infectious diseases 001–139.

Accidental deaths

The data in Table 7.14 exclude deaths where it was not known whether the cause was accidentally or purposely inflicted, misadventure during medical care, abnormal reactions and late complications.

Body mass index

The body mass index (BMI) shown in Chart 7.20, is the most widely used index of obesity which standardises weight for height and is calculated as weight (kg)/height (m)^2. Underweight is defined as a BMI of 20 or less, desirable over 20 to 25, overweight over 25 to 30 and obese over 30.

Immunisation

Data shown in Table 7.22 for 1991–92 onwards for England, Wales and Northern Ireland relate to children reaching their second birthday during the year and immunised by their second birthday. Data for 1981 in England, Wales and Northern Ireland relate to children born two years earlier and immunised by the end of the second year. For Scotland, rates prior to 1995–96 have been calculated by dividing the cumulative number of immunisations for children born in year X and vaccinated by year X+2, by the number of live births (less neonatal deaths) during year X.

Part 8: Social Protection

Benefits to groups of recipients

Elderly people

Retirement pension

Non-contributory retirement pension

Christmas bonus paid with retirement pension and other non-disability benefits

Principal income-related benefits and social fund payments to people over 60[1]

Sick and disabled people

Incapacity benefit

Attendance allowance

Disability living allowance

Disability working allowance/Disabled person's tax Credit

Industrial disablement benefit

Other industrial injuries benefits

Severe disablement allowance

Invalid care allowance

War pensions

Independent living fund

Motability

Christmas bonus paid with disability benefits

Principal income-related benefits and social fund payments to disabled people[1]

Statutory sick pay

Unemployed people

Jobseeker's allowance

Principal income-related benefits and payments from the social fund to unemployed and their families[1]

Families, widows and others

Child benefit

One parent benefit

Family credit/Working families tax credit

Income support

Statutory maternity pay

Maternity allowance

Social fund maternity payments

Principal income-related benefits and social fund payments to lone-parent families[1]

Widow's benefits

War widow's pensions

Guardian's allowance and child's special allowance

Industrial death benefit

Social fund funeral payments

Income support paid to people who do not fall within the other client groups

Benefit units

A benefit unit is a single adult or couple living as married and any dependent children. A pensioner benefit unit is where the head is over state pension age.

Health and personal social services staff

Nursing, midwifery and health visitors comprises qualified and unqualified staff, and excludes nurse teachers, nurses in training and students on '1992' courses.

Other non-medical staff comprises Scientific & Professional and Technical staff. A new classification of the non-medical workforce was introduced in 1995. Information based on this classification is not directly compatible with earlier years.

General medical practitioners includes Unrestricted Principals, PMS contracted GPs, PMS salaried GPs, Restricted Principals, Assistants, GP Registrars and PMS others. It excludes GP Retainers.

General dental practitioners is a headcount of General Dental Service (GDS) at 30 September. It includes principals on a Health Authority / Family Health list, assistants and vocational dental practitioners.

1 Principal income-related benefits are income-support, housing benefit and council tax benefits.

Personal social services staff includes staff employed only at local authority social work departments (whole time equivalent). The figures for Scotland relate to the first Monday in October.

In-patient activity

In-patient data for England and later years for Northern Ireland are based on Finished Consultant Episodes (FCEs). Data for Wales and Scotland, and data for Northern Ireland except acute after 1986, are based on Deaths and Discharges and transfers between specialities (between hospitals in Northern Ireland). An FCE is a completed period of care of a patient using a bed, under one consultant, in a particular NHS Trust or directly managed unit. If a patient is transferred from one consultant to another within the same hospital, this counts as an FCE but not a hospital discharge. Conversely if a patient is transferred from one hospital to another provider, this counts as a hospital discharge and as a finished consultant episode.

Waiting lists

Figures for Scotland exclude all patients awaiting deferred or planned repeat admission. In Scotland, once a person is classed as deferred they remain as deferred and these patients are excluded from the waiting list figures. In England and Wales patients who have been classed as deferred but who are now available for treatment will be included in the waiting list figures. This means that figures for Scotland are not directly comparable with those for other areas of the United Kingdom.

Recipients of benefits

The incapacity benefit and severe disablement figures are as at the end of February for Working Age client group analysis and as at the end of November for the Pension Age client group analysis. Incapacity benefit was introduced in April 1995 to replace sickness and invalidity benefits.

Income-based Jobseeker's Allowance (JSA) replaced income support for the unemployed from October 1996. Income support includes some income-based JSA claimants.

Disability working allowance was replaced by the disabled person's tax credit from October 1999. The disability living allowance includes attendance allowance and, before 1992, mobility allowance.

Family credit replaced the Family Income Supplement in April 1988. Family credit was replaced by the Working Families Tax Credit from October 1999.

Part 9: Crime and Justice

Types of offences in England and Wales

The figures are compiled from police returns to the Home Office or directly from court computer systems.

Recorded crime statistics broadly cover the more serious offences. Up to March 1998 most indictable and triable-either-way offences were included, as well as some summary ones; from April 1998, all indictable and triable-either-way offences were included, plus a few closely related summary ones. Recorded offences are the most readily available measures of the incidence of crime, but do not necessarily indicate the true level of crime. Many less serious offences are not reported to the police and cannot, therefore, be recorded while some offences are not recorded due to lack of evidence. Moreover, the propensity of the public to report offences to the police is influenced by a number of factors and may change over time.

In England and Wales, indictable offences cover those offences which must or may be tried by jury in the Crown Court and include the more serious offences. Summary offences are those for which a defendant would normally be tried at a magistrates' court and are generally less serious – the majority of motoring offences fall into this category. Triable either way offences are triable either on indictment or summarily.

Types of offences in Northern Ireland

In recording crime, the Royal Ulster Constabulary broadly follow the Home Office rules for counting crime. As from 1st April 1998 notifiable offences are recorded on the same basis as those in England and Wales (i.e. under the revised Home Office rules – see above). Prior to the revision of the rules, criminal damage offences in Northern Ireland excluded those where the value of the property damaged was less than £200.

Notifiable offences: are broadly the more serious offences. They include most indictable offences and triable either way offences and certain summary offences (for example, unauthorised taking of a motor vehicle). As from 1 April 1998, notifiable offences recorded in Northern Ireland are on the same basis as those in England and Wales.

Indictable only offences: are those for which an adult must be tried at the Crown Court, for example robbery, arson and rape. Figures for indictable offences given in this chapter include those for offences which are triable either way (see below).

Triable either way offences: are offences triable either on indictment or summarily. They may be tried in a magistrates' court unless either the defendant or the magistrate requests a Crown Court hearing. Most thefts, drug offences and less serious violence against the person offences fall into this category.

Summary offences: are those offences which are normally tried at a magistrates' court.

Offences and crimes

There are a number of reasons why recorded crime statistics in England and Wales, Northern Ireland and Scotland cannot be directly compared:

Different legal systems: The legal system operating in Scotland differs from that in England and Wales and Northern Ireland. For example, in Scotland children aged under 16 are normally dealt with for offending by the Children's Hearings system rather than the courts.

Differences in classification: There are significant differences in the offences included within the recorded crime categories used in Scotland and the categories of notifiable offences used in England, Wales and Northern Ireland. Scottish figures of 'crime' have therefore been grouped in an attempt to approximate to the classification of notifiable offences in England, Wales and Northern Ireland.

Counting rules: In Scotland each individual offence occurring within an incident is recorded whereas in England, Wales and Northern Ireland only the main offence is counted.

Burglary: This term is not applicable to Scotland where the term used is 'housebreaking'.

Theft from vehicles: In Scotland data have only been separately identified from January 1992. The figures include theft by opening lockfast places from a motor vehicle and other theft from a motor vehicle.

Offenders cautioned for burglary

In England and Wales offenders cautioned for going equipped for stealing, etc were counted against Burglary offences until 1986 and against Other offences from 1987. Historical data provided in Table 9.12 have been amended to take account of this change. Drug offences were included under Other offences for 1971.

Sentences and orders

The following are the main sentences and orders which can be imposed upon those persons found guilty. Some types of sentence or order can only be given to offenders in England and Wales in certain age groups. Under the framework for sentencing contained in the Criminal Justice Acts 1991 and 1993, the sentence must reflect the seriousness of the

offence. The following sentences are available for adults (a similar range of sentences is available to juveniles aged 10 to 17):

Absolute and conditional discharge: A court may make an order discharging a person absolutely or (except in Scotland) conditionally where it is inexpedient to inflict punishment and, before 1 October 1992, where a probation order was not appropriate. An order for conditional discharge runs for such period of not more than three years as the court specifies, the condition being that the offender does not commit another offence within the period so specified. In Scotland a court may also discharge a person with an admonition.

Attendance centre order: Available in England, Wales and Northern Ireland for offenders under the age of 21 and involves deprivation of free time.

Probation/supervision: An offender sentenced to a probation order is under the supervision of a probation officer (social worker in Scotland), whose duty it is (in England and Wales and Northern Ireland) to advise, assist and befriend him or her but the court has the power to include any other requirement it considers appropriate. A cardinal feature of the order is that it relies on the co-operation of the offender. Probation orders may be given for any period between six months and three years inclusive.

Community service: An offender who is convicted of an offence punishable with imprisonment may be sentenced to perform unpaid work for not more than 240 hours (300 hours in Scotland), and not less than 40 hours. Twenty hours minimum community service are given for persistent petty offending or fine default. In Scotland the Law Reform (Miscellaneous Provisions) (Scotland) Act 1990 requires that community service can only be ordered where the court would otherwise have imposed imprisonment or detention. Probation and community service may be combined in a single order in Scotland.

Combination order: The Criminal Justice Act 1991 introduced the combination order in England and Wales only, which combines elements of both probation supervision and community service. Meanwhile, Article 15 of the Criminal Justice (NI) Order 1996 introduced the combination order to Northern Ireland.

Imprisonment: is the custodial sentence for adult offenders. In the case of mentally disordered offenders, hospital orders, which may include a restriction order may be considered appropriate. Home Office or Scottish Executive consent is needed for release or transfer. A new disposal, the 'hospital direction', was introduced in 1997. The court, when imposing a period of imprisonment, can direct that the offender be sent directly to hospital. On recovering from the mental disorder, the offender is returned to prison to serve the balance of their sentence. The Criminal Justice Act 1991 abolished remission and substantially changed the parole scheme in England and Wales. Those serving sentences of under four years, imposed on or after 1 October 1992, are subject to Automatic Conditional Release and are released, subject to certain criteria, halfway through their sentence. Home Detention Curfews result in selected prisoners being released up to 2 months early with a tag that monitors their presence during curfew hours. Those serving sentences of four years or longer are considered for Discretionary Conditional Release after having served half their sentence, but are automatically released at the two-thirds point of sentence. The Crime (Sentences) Act 1997, implemented on 1 October 1997, included, for persons aged 18 or over, an automatic life sentence for a second serious violent or sexual offence unless there are exceptional circumstances. All offenders serving a sentence of 12 months or more are supervised in the community until the three quarter point of sentence. A life sentence prisoner may be released on licence subject to supervision and is always liable to recall. In Scotland the Prisoners and Criminal Proceedings (Scotland) Act 1993 changed the system of remission and parole for prisoners sentenced on or after 1 October 1993. Those serving sentences of less than four years are released unconditionally after having served half of their sentence, unless the court specifically imposes a Supervised Release Order which subjects them to social work supervision after release. Those serving sentences of four years or more are eligible for parole at half sentence. If parole is not granted then they will automatically be released on licence at two thirds of sentence subject to days added for breaches of prison rules. All such prisoners are liable to be 'recalled on conviction' or for breach of conditions of licence i.e. if between the date of release and the date on which the full sentence ends, a person commits another offence which is punishable by imprisonment or breaches his/her licence conditions, then the offender may be returned to prison for the remainder of that sentence whether or not a sentence of imprisonment is also imposed for the new offence.

Fully suspended sentences: may only be passed in exceptional circumstances. In England, Wales and Northern Ireland, sentences of imprisonment of two years or less may be fully suspended. A court should not pass a suspended sentence unless a sentence of imprisonment would be appropriate in the absence of a power to suspend. The result of suspending a sentence is that it will not take effect unless during the period specified the offender is convicted of another offence punishable with imprisonment. Suspended sentences are not available in Scotland.

Fines: The Criminal Justice Act 1993 introduced new arrangements on 20 September 1993 whereby courts are now required to fit an amount for the fine which reflects the seriousness of the offence, but which also takes account of an offender's means. This system replaced the more formal unit fines scheme included in the Criminal Justice Act 1991. The Act also introduced the power for courts to arrange deduction of fines from income benefit for those offenders receiving such benefits. The Law Reform (Miscellaneous Provision) (Scotland) Act 1990 as amended by the Criminal Procedure (Scotland) Act 1995 provides for the use of supervised attendance orders by selected courts in Scotland. The Criminal Procedure (Scotland) Act 1995 also makes it easier for courts to impose a supervised attendance order in the event of a default and enables the court to impose a supervised attendance order in the first instance for 16 and 17 year olds.

Custody Probation Order: an order unique to Northern Ireland reflecting the different regime there which applies in respect of remission and the general absence of release on licence. The custodial sentence is followed by a period of supervision for a period of between 12 months and three years.

Young offender institutions

The Criminal Justice Act 1991 made a number of changes to the custodial sentencing arrangements for young offenders in England and Wales. A common minimum age of 15 for boys and girls was set for the imposition of a sentence of detention in a young offender institution thus removing boys aged 14 from the scope of this sentence.

Civil courts

England and Wales: The main civil courts are the High Court and the county courts. Magistrates' courts also have some civil jurisdiction, mainly in family proceedings. Most appeals in civil cases go to the Court of Appeal (Civil Division) and may go from there to the House of Lords. Since July 1991, county courts have been able to deal with all contract and tort cases and actions for recovery of land, regardless of value. Cases are presided over by a judge who almost always sits without a jury. Jury trials are limited to specified cases, for example, actions for libel.

Scotland: The Court of Session is the supreme civil court. Any cause, apart from causes excluded by statute, may be initiated in, and any judgement of an inferior court may be appealed to, the Court of Session. The Sheriff Court is the principal local court of civil jurisdiction in Scotland. It also has jurisdiction in criminal proceedings. Apart from certain actions the civil jurisdiction of the Sheriff Court is generally similar to that of the Court of Session.

Publicly Funded Legal Services

In England and Wales, the Legal Services Commission operates two funding schemes: the Community Legal Service (CLS), which funds civil legal and advice services and civil representation; and the Criminal Defence Service (CDS) of which the Commission principally funds duty solicitor work and advice, and representation at the magistrates' court. The Commission was launched in April 2000, replacing the Legal Aid Board, and funds services through contracts agreed with quality assured service providers.

Community Legal Service

For clients whose capital and income are within certain financial limits, the Commission funds a range of legal and advice services in civil matters, either on a contributory or a free basis. The services include:

- *Legal Help* – this provides for initial advice and assistance with legal problems. This work was previously carried out under the advice and assistance, or 'green form', scheme

- *Help at Court* – this allows for somebody (a solicitor or adviser) to speak on a client's behalf at certain court hearings

- *Approved Family Help* – this provides for help in relation to a family dispute, including assistance in resolving that dispute through negotiation or otherwise. It can be in the form of either:

     (i) *Help with Mediation* – this is legal advice and assistance if the client is attending family mediation, or

     (ii) *General Family Help* – this is legal advice and assistance on family matters where no family mediation is involved

- *Family Mediation* – this covers mediation for a family dispute

- *Controlled Legal Representation* – for cases heard by the Mental Health Review Tribunal, the Immigration Appeal Tribunal and immigration adjudicators

- *Legal Representation* – previously known as civil legal aid, this provides for representation if the client is taking or defending court proceedings. It is available in two forms: Investigative Help and Full Representation

- *Support Funding* – this is partial funding of very expensive cases which are otherwise funded privately under conditional fee agreements. It is available in two forms: Investigative Support and Litigation Support

Criminal Defence Service

During 2000/01, the Commission provided criminal legal aid within the meaning of the Legal Aid Act 1988 and prepared for the launch of the Criminal Defence Service from April 2001. The services provided during the period covered legal advice and assistance (the 'green form' scheme) and representation in criminal cases. A similar range of services are now available through the CDS network of contracted suppliers.

The Commission also provides two duty solicitor schemes. One makes advice and representation available for certain criminal hearings in the magistrates' court. The second, known as the 24 hour duty solicitor scheme, provides for legal advice and assistance to people arrested or helping with enquiries at police stations.

The Commission is concerned only with funding proceedings in the magistrates' courts; funding of criminal legal aid in the higher courts is the responsibility of the Lord Chancellor's Department. In the criminal courts in England and Wales a representation order may be made if this appears desirable in the interest of justice. No limit of income or capital above which a person is ineligible for public funding is specified. However, since April 2001, the higher criminal courts have been able to order costs against defendants at the end of a case, usually following conviction.

Civil Legal Aid in Scotland operates on a similar basis to that operating prior to April 2000 in England and Wales. Advice and assistance has similar scope in Scotland but is available to those who are financially eligible either for free or on payment of a contribution. Assistance by way of representation (ABWOR) is granted mainly for summary criminal cases where a plea of guilty is made, though it also covers proceedings in mental health review cases, designated life prisoners before the parole board and disciplinary hearings before a prison governor, and other specified civil or criminal proceedings. Criminal Legal Aid, which is granted by the Scottish Legal Aid Board for summary cases and for all appeals, and by the courts for solemn cases, is not subject to a contribution.

Drugs seizures

The figures in this table, which are compiled from returns to the Home Office, relate to seizures made by the police and officials of HM Customs and Excise, and to drugs controlled under the Misuse of Drugs Act 1971. The Act divides drugs into three main categories according to their harmfulness. A full list of drugs in each category is given in Schedule 2 to the Misuse of Drugs Act 1971, as amended by Orders in Council.

Part 10: Housing

Dwelling stock

The definition of dwelling follows that adopted by the 1991 Census in which it was defined as "structurally separate accommodation". It is meant to refer to a building, or part of a building which forms a separate, or reasonably separate and self-contained, set of premises designed to be occupied by a single household.

In all stock figures, permanent and non-permanent dwellings as well as vacant dwellings are included. For housebuilding statistics e.g. completions, only data on permanent dwellings are collected.

Estimates of the total dwelling stock, stock changes and the tenure distribution for each country are made by the Department of Transport, Local Government and the Regions (DTLR), the Scottish Executive, the National Assembly for Wales, and NI Department for Social Development. These are primarily based on census output data for the number of dwellings (or households converted to dwellings) from the Censuses of Population for GB. Adjustments were carried out if there were specific reasons to do so. Census years' figures are based on outputs from the censuses. For in between census years, the total figures are obtained by projecting the base census year's figure forward yearly. The increment is based on the annual total number of completions plus the annual total net gain due to other housing flows statistics i.e. conversions, demolitions and change of use.

Estimates of dwelling stock by tenure category are primarily based on the census except in the situation where it is considered that for some specific tenure information, there are other more accurate sources. In this situation, it is assumed that the other data sources contain vacant dwellings also but it is not certain and it is not expected that these data are very precise. Thus the allocation of vacant dwellings to tenure categories may not be completely accurate. This means that the margin of error for tenure categories are wider than for estimates of total stock.

For the 1991 census, a comparison with other available sources indicated that for local authorities' stock, figures supplied by local authorities are more reliable. Similarly, it was found that Housing Corporation's own data is more accurate than those from the census for the Registered Social Landlord's (RSL's) stock. Hence only the rented privately or with a job or business tenure data directly from the census was used. The owner-occupied data was taken as the residual of the total from the census. For non census year, the same approach was adopted except for the privately rented or with a job or business for which Labour Force Survey results were considered to be appropriated for use.

For further information on the methodology used to calculate stock by tenure and tenure definitions, see Appendix B Notes and Definitions in DTLR publication *Housing Statistics* annual volume.

Dwellings completed

In principle, a dwelling is regarded as completed when it becomes ready for occupation whether it is in fact occupied or not. In practice, there are instances where the timing could be delayed and some completions are missed for example because no completion certificates were requested by the owner.

Tenure definition for housebuilding is only slightly different from that used for stock figures. For details see *Housing Statistics*.

Household Reference Person

As of April 2000 the *General Household Survey* adopted the term 'household reference person' in place of 'head of household'.

The Household Reference Person will be either:

- the sole householder (ie the person in whose name the accommodation is owned or rented); or
- if there are two or more householders, the one with the highest personal income from all sources; or
- if two or more householders have the same income, the eldest.

The householder must be a member of the household and is the person who owns or rents the accommodation or the person who is 'responsible' for household affairs.

Homeless households

England and Wales: Households for whom local authorities accepted responsibility to secure accommodation under the *Housing Act 1985*, and subsequently the *Housing Act 1996*. Data for Wales include some households given advice and assistance only. Figures for the period 1986–1996 are not strictly comparable with information provided for 1997 due to a change in legislation.

Scotland: Households assessed as being homeless or potentially homeless (likely to become homeless within 28 days) by local authorities.

Northern Ireland: Households for whom the Northern Ireland Housing Executive has accepted responsibility to secure permanent accommodation, not necessarily those for whom permanent accommodation has been found.

Bedroom standard

The concept is used to estimate occupation density by allocating a standard number of bedrooms to each household in accordance with its age/sex/marital status composition and the relationship of the members to one another. A separate bedroom is allocated to each married or cohabiting couple, any other person aged 21 or over, each pair of adolescents aged 10–20 of the same sex, and each pair of children under 10. Any unpaired person aged 10–20 is paired if possible with a child under 10 of the same sex, or, if that is not possible, is given a separate bedroom, as is any unpaired child under 10. This standard is then compared with the actual number of bedrooms (including bedsitters) available for the sole use of the household, and deficiencies or excesses are tabulated. Bedrooms converted to other uses are not counted as available unless they have been denoted as bedrooms by the informants; bedrooms not actually in use are counted unless uninhabitable.

The fitness standard

The fitness standard in England and Wales was set out in section 604 of the *Local Government and Housing Act 1989* with guidance in DoE circulars 5/90 and 6/90. It came into operation from 1 April 1990. A property is fit for human habitation unless it fails to meet any of the following requirements in the opinion of the local authority:

a) It is structurally stable.

b) It is free from serious disrepair

c) It is free from dampness prejudicial to the health of any occupants.

d) It has adequate provision for lighting, heating and ventilation.

e) It has adequate supply of wholesome, piped water.

f) It has satisfactory facilities for preparing and cooking food including a sink with supplies of hot and cold water.

g) It has a suitably located WC.

h) It has a bath or shower and basin, each with supplies of hot and cold water.

i) It has an effective system for draining foul, waste and surface water.

There is also a separate fitness standard for HMOs, apart from the general standard described above, that compares the available facilities with the number of occupants, and that also ensures that there are adequate means of escape from fire and other fire precautions. When a property has been surveyed by the local authority and the condition assessed, the authority has then to decide on the most satisfactory course of action. If a property is identified as unfit, then the authority is obliged by statute to take action. This action can include serving a notice, making a closing order or a demolition order, or including the property in a clearance area. The authority can also consider if the property could be dealt with by including it in a group repair scheme. Lastly there is a direct link between the standard of fitness and eligibility for mandatory renovation grants. Thus applications for renovation grants must be approved where the work is to bring a property up to the fitness standard, and the applicant meets the various conditions and undergoes the test of resources.

Acorn Classification

The ACORN classification is a means of classifying areas according to various Census characteristics devised by CACI limited. An ACORN code is assigned to each Census Enumeration District (ED) which is then copied to all postcodes within the ED.

The list below shows the 6 ACORN major categories and the 17 groups. Each ACORN group is further divided in a number of area types (not shown here). The descriptions are CACI's

Category A: Affluent suburban and rural areas
1. Wealthy achiever, Suburban Areas
2. Affluent Greys, Rural Communities
3. Prosperous Pensioners, Retirement Areas

Category B: Affluent family areas
4. Affluent Executives, Family Areas
5. Well-Off Workers, Family Areas

Category C: Affluent urban areas
6. Affluent Urbanites, Town and City Areas
7. Prosperous Professionals, Metropolitan Areas
8. Better-Off Executives, Inner City Areas

Category D: Mature home owning areas
9. Comfortable Middle Agers, Mature Home Owning Areas
10. Skilled Workers, Home Owning Areas

Category E: New home owning areas
11. New Home Owners, Mature Communities
12. White Collar Workers, Better-Off Multi-Ethnic Areas

Category F: Council estates and low income areas
13. Older People, Less Prosperous Areas
14. Council Estate Residents, Better-Off Homes
15. Council Estate Residents, High Unemployment
16. Council Estate Residents, Greatest Hardship
17. People in Multi-Ethnic, Low-Income Areas

Property transactions

The figures are based on the number of particular delivered (PD) forms processed by the Stamp Office or District Land Registry. They relate to the transfer of sale of any freehold interest in land or property, or the grant or transfer or a lease of at least 21 years and one day, and therefore include some non-residential transactions. In practice there is an average lag of about one month between the transaction and the date on which the PD form is processed.

Over the period from 20 December 1991 to 19 August 1992, the stamp duty threshold was temporarily increased from £30,000 to £250,000.

Sales and transfers of local authority dwellings

Right to buy was established by the *Housing Act 1980* and was introduced across Great Britain in October 1980.

In England, Large Scale Voluntary Transfers (LSVTs) of stock have been principally to housing associations/ registered social landlords; figures include transfers supported by Estate Renewal Challenge Funding (ERCF). The figures for 1993 includes 949 dwellings transferred under Tenants' Choice.

Scotland includes large scale voluntary transfers to registered social landlords and trickle transfers to Housing Associations.

Part 11: Environment

Greenhouse Gas Emissions

All six Kyoto gases are included, but fluorinated gas emissions are indicative. The base year is assumed to be 1990 for all gases (except for fluorinated gases, where it is 1995). Emissions for Denmark are not adjusted for electricity trade. Emissions and removals (sinks) due to land use change and forestry (LUCF) are excluded due to uncertainty in their estimates and because no decisions have yet been taken as to which LUCF activities can be included to meet the Kyoto Protocol targets.

Land Use

Agricultural grass and rough grazing: Includes sole right and common rough grazing.

Agricultural other: Set aside and other land on agricultural holdings, e.g. farm roads, yards, buildings, gardens, ponds. Excludes woodland on agricultural holdings which is included in 'Forest and Woodland'.

Forest and Woodland: Data for Great Britain are compiled by the Forestry Commission and cover both private and state-owned land. Estimates are based on the 1980 Census of Woodland and extrapolated forward using information about new planting and other changes. Data for Northern Ireland are compiled separately by Department of Agriculture for Northern Ireland and also cover both private and state-owned land.

Urban land and land not elsewhere specified: Data are derived by subtracting land used for agricultural and forestry purposes from the land area. Figures include land used for urban and other purposes, e.g. transport and recreation, and non-agricultural, semi-natural environments e.g. sand dunes, grouse moors and non-agricultural grasslands, and inland waters.

Landscape Features

Hedge: A more or less continuous line of woody vegetation that has been subject to a regime of cutting in order to maintain a regular shape. This category includes both recently managed and other hedges, including hedges with walls or fences.

Remnant Hedge: A woody field boundary feature with a residual hedge structure but without evidence of recent hedge management, with or without a fence

Wall: A built structure of natural stone or manufactured blocks, mostly of traditional dry stone wall construction but including mortared walls. Includes walls with fences and lines of trees or shrubs.

Bank/grass strip: An earth or stone-faced bank with or without a fence. A grass strip without a fence.

Fence: A permanent post and wire or rail structure, including wooden, concrete or metal posts without any associated feature other than a grass strip, ditch or stream.

Critical load of Acidity of soils

The exceedance map is based on the acidity critical loads data as revised in February 2001 and the national deposition data (non-marine sulphur and oxidised nitrogen only) for 1995–97. The units are given as kiloequivalents of hydrogen ions per hectare per year. The darkest areas on the map are therefore those where the critical loads are most highly exceeded by the deposition data used. Further information on the derivation and methods used to calculate critical loads in the UK can be found on the UK National Focus Centre web site: 'http://critloads.ceh.ac.uk'.

Rivers and canals

The chemical quality of rivers and canal waters in the United Kingdom are monitored in a series of separate national surveys in England and Wales, Scotland and Northern Ireland. In England, Wales and Northern Ireland the General Quality Assessment (GQA) Scheme provides a rigorous and objective method for assessing the basic chemical quality of rivers and canals based on three determinands: dissolved oxygen, biochemical oxygen demand (BOD) and ammoniacal nitrogen). The GQA grades river stretches into six categories (A-F) of chemical quality and these in turn have been grouped into two broader groups - good/fair (classes A, B C and D) and poor/bad (classes E and F. Classification of biological quality is based on the River Invertebrate and Classification System (RIVPACS).

In Scotland, water quality is based upon the Scottish River Classification Scheme of 20 June 1997 which combines chemical, biological, nutrient and aesthetic quality using the following classes: excellent (A1), good (A2) fair (B), poor (C) and seriously polluted (D). The chemical and biological components are shown separately for 2000 and are based on the new digitised network which is much smaller than that used for 1990.

Bathing waters

Directive 76/160/EEC concerning the quality of bathing water sets the following mandatory values for the coliform parameters:

for total coliform 10,000 per 100 ml; and

for faecal coliforms 2,000 per 100 ml.

The Directive requires that at least 95 per cent of samples taken for each of these parameters over the bathing season must meet the mandatory values. In practice this has been interpreted in the following manner: where 20 samples are taken a maximum of only one sample for each parameter may exceed the mandatory values for the water to pass the coliform standards; where less than 20 samples are taken none may exceed the mandatory values for the water to pass the coliform standards.

The bathing season is from mid-May to end-September in England and Wales, but is shorter in Scotland and Northern Ireland. Bathing waters which are closed for a season are excluded for that year.

The boundaries of the Environment Agency Regions are based on river catchment areas and not county borders. In particular, the figures shown for Wales are for the Environment Agency Welsh Region, the boundary of which does not coincide with the boundary of Wales.

Figures for 1991 include Almouth, which was undesignated in 1999.

In 1997 West Kirby was reclassified from the Welsh region to the North West region. West Kirby data are presented in the North West region for all years for consistency.

Electricity produced by renewable sources

For both *hydro power* and *onshore wind*, actual generation figures are given where available, but otherwise are estimated using a typical load factor or the design load factor, where known. Figures for *Municipal waste* include combustion of refuse derived fuel pellets. The *'other'* category includes the use of farm waste digestion, sewage sludge digestion, waste tyre combustion, poultry litter, combustion and solar photovoltaics.

Part 12: Transport

The National Travel Survey

The NTS has been conducted on a small scale continuous basis since July 1988. The last of the previous ad hoc surveys was carried out in 1985–1986.

Information is collected from about 3,000 households in Great Britain each year. Each member of the houeshold provides personal information (for example, age, sex, working status, driving licence, season ticket) and details of trips carried out in a sample week, including the purpose of the trip, method of travel, time of day, length, duration, and cost of any tickets bought.

Travel included in the NTS covers all trips by Great Britain residents within Great Britain for personal reasons, including travel in the course of work.

A trip is defined as a one-way course of travel having a single main purpose. It is the basic unit of personal travel defined in the survey. A round trip is split into two trips, with the first ending at a convenient point about half-way round as a notional stopping point for the outward destination and return origin.

A stage is that portion of a trip defined by the use of a specific method of transport or of a specific ticket (a new stage being defined if either the mode or ticket changes).

The purpose of a trip is normally taken to be the activity at the destination, unless that destination is 'home' in which case the purpose is defined by the origin of the trip. The classification of trips to 'work' is also dependent on the origin of the trip.

Cars are regarded as household cars if they are either owned by a member of the household, or available for the private use of household members. Company cars provided by an employer for the use of a particular employee (or director) are included, but cars borrowed temporarily from a company pool are not.

The main driver of a household car is the household member that drives the furthest in that car in the course of a year.

The purpose of a trip is normally taken to be the activity at the destination, unless that destination is 'home' in which case the purpose is defined by the origin of the trip. The classification of trips to 'work' are also dependent on the origin of the trip. The following purposes are distinguished:

Commuting: trips to a usual place of work from home, or from work to home.

Business: personal trips in the course of work, including a trip in the course of work back to work. This includes all work trips by people with no usual place of work (e.g. site workers) and those who work at or from home.

Education: trips to school or college, etc by full time students, students on day-release and part-time students following vocational courses.

Escort: used when the traveller has no purpose of his or her own, other than to escort or accompany another person; for example, taking a child to school. For example escort commuting is escorting or accompanying someone from home to work or from work to home.

Shopping: all trips to shops or from shops to home, even if there was no intention to buy.

Personal business: visits to services eg hairdressers, launderettes, dry-cleaners, betting shops, solicitors, banks, estate agents, libraries, churches; or for medical consultations or treatment, or for eating and drinking unless the main purpose was entertainment or social.

Social or entertainment: visits to meet friends, relatives, or acquaintances, both at someone's home or at a pub, restaurant, etc; all types of entertainment or sport, clubs, and voluntary work, non-vocational evening classes, political meetings, etc.

Holidays or day trips: trips (within Great Britain) to or from any holiday (including stays of four nights or more with friends or relatives) or trips for pleasure (not otherwise classified as social or entertainment) within a single day.

Just walk: walking pleasure trips along public highways including taking the dog for a walk and jogging.

Car ownership

Car: the figures for household ownership include four wheeled and three wheeled cars, off-road vehicles, minibuses, motorcaravans dormobiles, and light vans. Company cars normally available for household use are also included.

Type of area

London borough – the 33 London boroughs;

Metropolitan built-up area – the built-up area within the administrative areas of the former metropolitan counties of Greater Manchester, Merseyside, the West Midlands, West Yorkshire, Tyne & Wear and Strathclyde;

Large urban – self-contained urban areas of more than 250,000 population in 1991;

Medium urban – self-contained urban areas of not more than 250,000 population in 1991, but more than 25,000;

Small urban – self-contained urban areas of not more than 25,000 population in 1991 but more than 3,000;

Rural – other areas are designated 'rural', including 'urban areas' under 3,000 population in 1991.

Road Traffic

Figures for 1999 and 2000 have been produced on a new basis and are not directly comparable with earlier figures. In 2000/01, steps were taken to improve the quality of DTLR's major road network database. The net result of these improvements has been little change to the estimates of total motor vehicle traffic for Great Britain for 1999 and 2000, but some changes to the composition of the overall figure. In general, the new motorway traffic estimates are now higher than before, whilst those for other major roads are lower than before.

Passenger death rates

Table 12.16 provides passenger death rates for passenger travel by air, road, rail and water. Wherever possible, travel by drivers and other crew in the course of their work has been excluded from the calculated rates for public transport modes. A casualty rate can be interpreted as the risk a traveller runs of being injured, per kilometre travelled. The coverage varies for each mode of travel and the definitions of deaths and accidents are different. Thus, care should be exercised in drawing comparisons between the rates for different modes.

The air travel data refer to passenger carrying services of United Kingdom airlines for fixed and rotary wing aircraft of over 2,300kg. The accidents therefore cover flights throughout the world, not just within the United Kingdom. The average number of fatal accidents is less than 1 per year, and may not necessarily occur within the United Kingdom.

The rail casualty data refer to passengers in train accidents and train movement accidents. They exclude non-movement accidents such as falling over packages on platforms, confirmed suicides and trespassers. The figures for air and water, similarly, exclude accidents on the land side of air terminals and seaports.

The data for travel by water cover both domestic and international passenger carrying services of United Kingdom registered vessels. Data are not available for non-fatal accidents to passengers prior to 1983. Casualties exclude deaths from disease and confirmed suicides. Injuries are those which incapacitate the person for more than 3 days.

The road data which refer to Great Britain, are for drivers/riders and passengers of vans, cars, two wheeled motor vehicles and pedal cycles. The data for buses and coaches refer to passengers only. They illustrate the risk to passengers of travel on the road system using both public and private transport. The casualty rates per billion kilometres for those on foot are based on estimates of distance walked obtained from National Travel Surveys.

The article Comparative Accident Rates for Passengers by Modes of Transport , which provides additional information on the coverage and definitions used by the various modes was published in Transport Statistics Great Britain 1994 edition. These statistics of accidents and casualties are compiled from the reports submitted by the police to the Department of Environment, Transport and the Regions. More detailed information and analyses about road accidents and casualties is available in Road Accidents Great Britain – the Casualty Report 2000, published by the Stationery Office.

Transport expenditure

The Family Expenditure Survey data in Table 12.5 use unweighted adult only data. Other Family Expenditure Survey data referred to in the transport text use weighted data including children's expenditure.

Part 13: Lifestyles and Social Participation

Social Class

Social class is based on occupation and is a classification system that has grown out of the original Registrar-General's social class classification. These are defined in the *Classification of Occupations (1990)* prepared by the Office for National Statistics. The five categories are:

I. Professional, etc. occupations
II. Managerial and technical occupations
III. Skilled occupations
    (N) non-manual
    (M) manual
IV. Partly skilled occupations
V. Unskilled occupations

For the FES, social class of a household refers to the social class based on the occupation of the head of household. It is coded where the head is currently in paid work, or is economically inactive and has worked in the last 12 months, or is unemployed and has ever worked.

Socio-economic group

The basic occupational classification used is the Registrar General's socio-economic grouping in Standard Occupational Classification 1990, Volume 3 OPCS (HMSO, London 1991), pp13–14. Table 13.11 uses a collapsed version of this classification, which is as follows:

Descriptive definition	SEG numbers
Professional	3,4
Employers and managers	1,2,13
Intermediate and junior non-manual	5,6
Skilled manual	8,9,12,14
Semi-skilled manual and personal services	7,10,15
Unskilled manual	11

Cultural events

Data from the Target Group Index 1987–1988 and 1991–1992, BMRB International, and the Target Group Index 1997–1998 Doublebase, BMRB International were used in Table 13.8.

Parliamentary elections

A general election must be held at least every five years or sooner, if the Prime Minister of the day so decides. The United Kingdom is currently divided into 659 constituencies, each of which returns one member to the House of Commons. To ensure equitable representation, four permanent Boundary Commissions (for England, Wales, Scotland, and Northern Ireland) make periodic reviews of constituencies and recommend any change in the number or redistribution of seats that may seem necessary in the light of population movements or for some other reason.

Articles published in previous editions

No. 1 1970
Some general developments in social statistics Professor C A Moser, CSO

Public expenditure on the social services Professor B Abel-Smith, London School of Economics and Political Science

The growth of the population to the end of the century Jean Thompson, OPCS

A forecast of effective demand for housing in Great Britain in the 1970s A E Holmans, MHLG

No. 2 1971
Social services manpower Dr S Rosenbaum, CSO

Trends in certificated sickness absence F E Whitehead, DHSS

Some aspects of model building in the social and environmental fields B Benjamin, CSC

Social indicators – health A J Culyer, R J Lavers and A Williams, University of York

No. 3 1972
Social commentary: change in social conditions CSO

Statistics about immigrants: objectives, methods, sources and problems Professor C A Moser, CSO

Central manpower planning in Scottish secondary education A W Brodie, SED

Social malaise research: a study in Liverpool M Flynn, P Flynn and N Mellor, Liverpool City Planning Department

Crimes of violence against the person in England and Wales S Klein, HO

No. 4 1973
Social commentary: certain aspects of the life cycle CSO

The elderly D C L Wroe, CSO

Subjective social indicators M Abrams, SSRC

Mental illness and the psychiatric services E R Bransby, DHSS

Cultural accounting A Peacock and C Godfrey, University of York

Road accidents and casualties in Great Britain J A Rushbrook, DOE

No. 5 1974
Social commentary: men and women CSO

Social security: the European experiment E James and A Laurent, EC Commission

Time budgets B M Hedges, SCPR

Time budgets and models of urban activity patterns N Bullock, P Dickens, M Shapcott and P Steadman, Cambridge University of Architecture

Road traffic and the environment F D Sando and V Batty, DOE

No. 6 1975
Social commentary: social class CSO

Areas of urban deprivation in Great Britain: an analysis of 1971 Census data S Holtermann, DOE

Note: Subjective social indicators Mark Abrams, SSRC

No. 7 1976
Social commentary: social change in Britain 1970–1975 CSO

Crime in England and Wales Dr C Glennie, HO

Crime in Scotland Dr Bruce, SHHD

Subjective measures of quality of life in Britain: 1971 to 1975 J Hall, SSRC

No. 8 1977
Social commentary: fifteen to twenty-five: a decade of transition CSO

The characteristics of low income households R Van Slooten and A G Coverdale, DHSS

No. 9 1979
Housing tenure in England and Wales: the present situation and recent trends A E Holmans, DOE

Social forecasting in Lucas B R Jones, Lucas Industries

No. 10 1980
Social commentary: changes in living standards since the 1950s CSO

Inner cities in England D Allnutt and A Gelardi, DOE

Scotland's schools D Wishart, SED

No. 14 1984
Changes in the Life-styles of the Elderly 1959–1982 M Abrams

No. 15 1985
British Social Attitudes R Jowell and C Airey, SCPR

No. 16 1986
Income after retirement G C Fiegehen, DHSS

No. 17 1987
Social Trends since World War II Professor A H Halsey, University of Oxford

Household Formation and Dissolution and Housing Tenure: a Longitudinal Perspective A E Holmans and S Nandy, DOE; A C Brown, OPCS

No. 18 1988
Major Epidemics of the 20th Century: from Coronary Thrombosis to AIDS Sir Richard Doll, University of Oxford

No. 19 1989
Recent Trends in Social Attitudes L Brook, R Jowell and S Witherspoon, SCPR

No. 20 1990
Social Trends, the next 20 years T Griffin, CSO

No. 21 1991
The 1991 Census of Great Britain: Plans for Content and Output B Mahon and D Pearce, OPCS

No. 22 1992
Crime statistics: their use and misuse C Lewis, HO

No. 24 1994
Characteristics of the bottom 20 per cent of the income distribution N Adkin, DSS

No. 26 1996
The OPCS Longitudinal Study J Smith, OPCS

British Household Panel Survey J Gershuny, N Buck, O Coker, S Dex, J Ermish, S Jenkins and A McCulloch, ESRC Research Centre on Micro-social Change

No. 27 1997
Projections: a look into the future T Harris, ONS

No. 28 1998
French and British Societies: a comparison P Lee and P Midy, INSEE and A Smith and C Summerfield, ONS

No. 29 1999
Drugs in the United Kingdom – a jigsaw with missing pieces A Bradley and O Baker, Institute for the Study of Drug Dependence

No. 30 200
A Hundred Years of Social Change A H Halsey, Emeritus Fellow, Nuffield College, Oxford

No. 31 1999
200 Hundred Years of the Census of Population M Nissel

Index

The references in this index refer to table and chart numbers, or entries in the Appendix.